Praise for
Miriam Hopkins: Life and Films of a Hollywood Rebel

"Screen and stage star Miriam Hopkins has long deserved a full-length biography covering her extensive career. This meticulously researched book does the actress complete justice. The author presents a vivid study of a high-strung talent who, professionally and romantically, was often her own worst enemy. A great read!"

—James Robert Parish, author of *Hollywood Divas:*
The Good, The Bad, and The Fabulous

"Allan Ellenberger's thorough, empathetic biography captures the passionate, full-blooded story of celebrated actress Miriam Hopkins, revealing the remarkable life of one of Hollywood's most intelligent women."

—Mary Mallory, coauthor of *Hollywood at Play:*
The Lives of the Stars between Takes

"Tennessee Williams called her a 'magnificent bitch.' There's probably no better label to sum up the force of nature known as Miriam Hopkins, whose professional achievements both on Broadway and in Hollywood were as notable as her feuds with Bette Davis, Edward G. Robinson, Samuel Goldwyn, Warner Bros. head Jack Warner, and other luminaries of the studio era. Allan Ellenberger's *Miriam Hopkins* is a must-read for those interested in getting to know this complex, contradictory, and immensely talented twentieth-century personage who dared to rebel against conventional 'women's roles' both on- and offscreen."

—André Soares, author of *Beyond Paradise:*
The Life of Ramon Novarro

MIRIAM HOPKINS

MIRIAM HOPKINS

LIFE AND FILMS OF A HOLLYWOOD REBEL

ALLAN R. ELLENBERGER

UNIVERSITY PRESS OF KENTUCKY

Scholarly publisher for the Commonwealth,
serving Bellarmine University, Berea College, Centre College of Kentucky,
Eastern Kentucky University, The Filson Historical Society, Georgetown
College, Kentucky Historical Society, Kentucky State University, Morehead
State University, Murray State University, Northern Kentucky University,
Transylvania University, University of Kentucky, University of Louisville,
and Western Kentucky University.

Editorial and Sales Offices: The University Press of Kentucky
663 South Limestone Street, Lexington, Kentucky 40508-4008
www.kentuckypress.com

Unless otherwise noted, photographs are from the author's collection.

Library of Congress Cataloging-in-Publication Data

Names: Ellenberger, Allan R., 1956– author.
Title: Miriam Hopkins : life and films of a Hollywood rebel / Allan R.
  Ellenberger.
Description: Lexington : The University Press of Kentucky, [2018] | Series:
  Screen classics | Includes bibliographical references and index.
Identifiers: LCCN 2017042898| ISBN 9780813174310 (hardcover : acid-free
  paper) | ISBN 9780813174327 (pdf) | ISBN 9780813174334 (epub)
Subjects: LCSH: Hopkins, Miriam, 1902–1972. | Motion picture actors and
  actresses—United States—Biography.
Classification: LCC PN2287.D315 E45 2018 | DDC 791.4302/8092 [B] — dc23
LC record available at https://lccn.loc.gov/2017042898

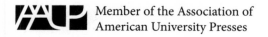

To
Michael Hopkins (1932–2010)
Christiane Carreno Hopkins (1931–2016)

Contents

Illustrations follow page 174

Prologue

One fall afternoon in 1940, stage and screen actress Miriam Hopkins opened the door to her suite at New York's Ambassador Hotel. Standing before her was a short young man wearing thick glasses, a threadbare corduroy jacket, and muddy riding boots.

A southerner like herself, they had met once at the opening of her recent play *The Guardsman,* in Upstate New York. The prestigious Theatre Guild was producing the young man's first play, and he was here to give Hopkins his script, hoping she would portray the play's central character: a lonely, disillusioned Mississippi Delta housewife trapped in an unfortunate marriage.

The fledgling playwright was Tennessee Williams, and the play was *Battle of Angels.* Another southern actress, Tallulah Bankhead, had turned it down, claiming sex and religion didn't mix onstage—or so she said.

Hopkins read the script and thought it needed work, but she agreed to do it and willingly invested her own money.

Now, in that second, more intimate, setting, Williams was nervous. After a champagne dinner, Hopkins "raised the roof" about her part. She construed Williams's anxious behavior as indifference, and that annoyed her. Then, her tone became more heated, and Williams, having had enough, prefaced his response with, "As far as I can gather from all this hysteria." Hopkins was speechless. Such conduct from a gentleman was— un-southern. But what appeared as conceit and arrogance on Williams' part was sheer panic.[1]

Their sparring continued through rehearsals on *Battle of Angels,* right up to its opening in Boston, where the critics and the city council called the play, among other things, "dirty."

Hopkins jumped to Williams's defense. She called a press conference and told reporters that their reviews were "an insult to the fine young man who wrote it." The play was "not dirty," she insisted. The "dirt" was in the minds of the beholders. After all, she wasn't at a place in her career where she had "to appear in dirty plays."[2]

Hopkins endeared herself to the playwright, and they became close allies for the rest of her life. Throughout their long friendship, Tennessee Williams accepted Hopkins's contradictory extremes, describing her sometimes as "morning mail and morning coffee" and at others as "like a hat-pin jabbed in your stomach. The quintessence of the female, a really magnificent bitch."[3]

Hopkins was smart. A woman ahead of her time, she never let anyone find out how smart she was until it was too late. After years of research, I was amazed by her intellect and temperament, which flared up unexpectedly and disappearing as quickly. Sometimes her demanding mother would trigger it, but usually she was fighting for her career—or so she thought.

Throughout the 1930s, the freewheeling Hopkins was a unique case, remaining a top Hollywood star at no less than four studios: Paramount, RKO, Goldwyn, and Warner Bros. And no matter where she worked, in her quest for better opportunities, Hopkins fearlessly tackled the studios' powers-that-be, from the venerated Samuel Goldwyn to the irascible Jack Warner.

Whatever drove her—ambition, insecurity, or something altogether different—she created conflict with her costars. She was either loved or hated; rarely was there an in-between.

Having said that, whenever she trusted her director and costars, she was an ideal team player; but if she did not, life for them wasn't worth living. If rewriting screenplays, directing her fellow actors and her directors, and fighting with producers and the studio's front office were necessary, so be it.

Yet, in Hopkins's mind, she was not difficult, not temperamental. "Proof of that is that I made four pictures with Willie Wyler, who is a very demanding director," she once insisted. "I made two with Rouben Mamoulian, who is the same. Three with Ernst Lubitsch, such a dear man. When you are asked to work again with such directors, you cannot be temperamental."[4]

But Tennessee Williams thought differently: "Difficult? I guess so. But not with me. She was every Southern divinity you could imagine. Smart and funny and elegant, and I kept looking for her in Joanne [Woodward], and Carrie Nye and Diane Ladd, but there was no one like her. No one. I will hear nothing bad of Miriam Hopkins."[5]

Ironically, I started Miriam Hopkins's life story because of Bette

Davis, who was always a favorite of mine. I enjoyed watching Hopkins clash with the indomitable Warner Bros. star in their two films together: *The Old Maid* and *Old Acquaintance.*

There were stories about their dynamic real-life feud and, later, the image of a gaunt, poststroke Davis ranting on television about how difficult her former costar could be. Hopkins denied the bad blood between them. That intrigued me. She would say, "Yes, I know the legend is that Bette Davis and I were supposed to have had a feud. Utter rubbish. Bette and I got along fine. I'd love to make another picture with her."[6]

Even more rubbish!

I watched Hopkins's films on which she collaborated with Lubitsch, Mamoulian, and Wyler and her lesser-known Paramount fare. I discovered a Miriam Hopkins in command of her sexuality. Whether as a dance-hall prostitute in *Dr. Jekyll and Mr. Hyde,* a participant in a ménage à trois in *Design for Living,* or a rape victim in the scandalous *The Story of Temple Drake,* she proved sex was more than a three-letter word: At times, it could be raw and terrifying; at others, it could be sensual, sophisticated fun.

She received her Best Actress Academy Award nomination for *Becky Sharp,* the first Technicolor feature film. She was Thackeray's Becky in the flesh. Hopkins had featured roles in thirty-five films and forty stage plays and made guest appearances in the early days of television, not to mention on countless radio shows. In these media, she worked with Carole Lombard, Gary Cooper, Jane Fonda, Edgar Bergen, Bing Crosby, William Powell, Sally Field, Henry Fonda, Loretta Young, Orson Welles, Olivia de Havilland, Peter Lorre, Merle Oberon, Claudette Colbert, Ray Milland, Elizabeth Montgomery, Coleen Dewhurst, Robert Redford, and dozens more.

Her friendships were as celebrated, but instead of actors, she hung around with writers and intellectuals such as Theodore Dreiser, Dorothy Parker, Gertrude Stein, and, of course, Tennessee Williams.

In her love life, she was independent-minded and discriminating. She had four husbands and dozens of lovers. Most were writers, such as Bennett Cerf, William Saroyan, and John Gunther.

She was an avid reader, a writer herself, a lover of poetry, and a patron of the arts. Over the years, her political beliefs vacillated from the far right to the far left, and she held positions in political organizations that had the FBI tracking her for three decades.

Hopkins was one of Hollywood's brainiest women, yet she was absurdly superstitious. A believer in the occult, she would not accept roles, move to a new home, or take long trips without consulting a psychic.

Despite her faults and idiosyncrasies, Hopkins proved she was a capable performer who happened to have both her own set of rules and her own personal demons. Although she was aware that she was a part of film history—how could Margaret Mitchell's choice to play Scarlett O'Hara not have been?—she was not sentimental about her existence or her career. She kept no scrapbooks, clippings, or photographs; it was irrelevant to document or discuss her past.

But no matter. Once you read about the complex, ambiguous, larger-than-life character that was Miriam Hopkins, you may agree with Tennessee Williams that she truly was a "magnificent bitch."

1

"From a Fine Old Family"

Miriam Hopkins's elitist ancestral legacy wasn't as important to her as it was to her self-admitted southern belle mother, Ellen Dickinson Cutter Hopkins. Mrs. Hopkins spent years of arduous work in the Bainbridge, Georgia, and New York chapters of the United Daughters of the Confederacy. Also, she was a member of the Dixie Club and the Society of Virginia Women. But try as she might, no amount of persuasion could get Miriam to those meetings. Miriam never argued; she just didn't show up.

Mrs. Hopkins admitted that aside from her genuine love for these organizations, she had another motive for wanting Miriam to attend: to establish the southern background of her daughter-the-actress and to show her to the public as a *real* person, with a heritage she could feel the greatest pride in. But none of that mattered to Miriam.

So, Mrs. Hopkins took it upon herself to enhance Miriam's publicity, or at least try to. Going to the mogul himself, Mrs. Hopkins enlightened Paramount's Adolph Zukor about her family's southern heritage—she, for example, was a trained singer and pianist—and added that she was from a "fine old family" and, as Miriam recalled, other "such rubbish!"

At last, Miriam had had enough. She told her mother that if she ever darkened Paramount's door again—on either coast—she would stop paying her monthly stipend. But it was of no consequence. Mrs. Hopkins called Miriam "an unnatural daughter," asserting "God would take care" of her.

"I wish to Christ he would," Miriam muttered.[1]

Truthfully, Miriam—between shouting matches with reporters and being a no-show for interviews—cared little about her publicity. According to whether she selected her most picturesque past residence, she would say her birthplace was either Bainbridge or the actual city of her birth, Savannah. But even then, the facts would get muddled.

She once claimed that she was "born in Savannah in a brick house on Gordon Street"—the same type of house as those "charming old brownstone fronts" in New York—facing a park. Miriam did indeed live in a brick house on Gordon Street—221 East Gordon Street overlooking Calhoun Square—but she was not born there. The Gordon Street house was the last of several in Savannah that her relatives occupied before she moved to the town of Bainbridge in southern Georgia in 1912, with her mother, sister, and grandmother.[2]

Miriam was born at 307 East Jones Street, four short blocks away from the Gordon Street house. On that eventful day, October 18, 1902, Savannah's tree-lined streets of hanging moss shook as a moderate earthquake, centered along the east side of Rocky Face Mountain in North Carolina, rumbled across the Southeast. The sharp jolt rattled a few nerves, much as Miriam Hopkins would during her lifetime.

As a young girl, her parents divorced, and in her father's absence, her dominant mother and grandmother raised her and her older sister, Ruby. Despite that, or maybe because of it, family duty—and not love of family—ruled her life, be it out of responsibility, pride, or some unfathomable instinct.

Decades later, in a moment of insight, Miriam would admit her true feelings. Author George Eells recalled that as she looked back on her life, it seemed that all her "nonstop talking, all her achievements as an actress, all the houses she had bought and furnished" had been unconscious attempts to "show Daddy what a marvel she was" and to bring the family together again. However, by then it was too late. The damage was done.[3]

Miriam Hopkins's maternal lineage goes back to Londoner Charles Dickinson and his three sons, Walter, Henry, and John. The three brothers immigrated to America in 1653, settling in Carolina County, Virginia, and Talbot County, Maryland. Miriam is descended from Walter, whose great-grandson was John Dickinson, a distinguished figure in the American Revolution, a signer of the Constitution, and the writer of the petition to King George III urging redress of grievances for the colonies (for those who remember their high school history).

James Edward Dickinson, Miriam's great-grandfather, was born at Berry Plain, Virginia, in 1822. His wife, Ellen Carmichael Middleton, of Fredericksburg, Virginia, was a descendant of Arthur Middleton, a signer of the Declaration of Independence. While serving in the Civil War as a Confederate major, Dickinson fell in love with the Georgia countryside.

Once the war ended, he left his home, "Moon Mount," on Virginia's Rappahannock River, and built a large house in Bainbridge, the county seat of Georgia's Decatur County. In 1867, he was elected as the city's fourth mayor, and he held that office for two terms.[4]

Five Dickinson children survived to adulthood. Miriam's grandmother, Mildred Middleton Dickinson, was the eldest. Born in Fredericksburg in 1847, she was twenty years old when she married George Wilmer Hines, a prominent Bainbridge lawyer. Their son, future writer and drama critic, George Jr., was born in 1872 and grew up with the nickname Dixie. Seven weeks after his birth, his father was killed in a freak accident, leaving Mildred a widow. Six years later, she married Yale-educated attorney Ralph Hastings Cutter.[5]

The family of the Kentucky-born Cutter, Miriam's maternal grandfather, made their fortune distilling J. H. Cutter Old Bourbon, an incredibly popular brand of whiskey. At age fourteen, Cutter returned with his family to their New England roots at Hollis, New Hampshire. There, bouts of depression and anxiety plagued Cutter throughout his teenage years, landing him in asylums.

In adulthood, Cutter graduated from Yale and passed the bar. He spent several months in Boston before moving to Bainbridge, where he opened a law practice. Not long after, he met the widow Mildred Hines, and they married on February 21, 1878, at St. John's Episcopal Church.

That autumn, Cutter accepted a law partnership in Barnesville, Georgia, a town two hundred miles north of Bainbridge. There, on November 29, 1878, Mildred gave birth to twins: John Hastings Cutter and Ellen Dickinson Cutter, Miriam's mother. Five months later, the Cutters returned to Bainbridge, where Ralph resumed his law practice.

To pass the time during Cutter's repeated absences, Mildred wrote and had published several books of poetry and edited a poetry page for the nation's first mass-market magazine, *Munsey's Weekly*. While Cutter's visits to Bainbridge were infrequent, the couple found time to conceive daughters Raymonde and Ruby Hollis. Ruby Hollis died at the age of two, in 1886. Deeply affected by her death, Cutter committed himself to a hospital in Pepperell, Massachusetts.[6]

Between his bouts of depression and melancholia, Cutter functioned normally, practicing law at locations in the South and New England, while Mildred and the children lived quietly in Bainbridge. She continued her writing endeavors, as their son John engaged in mercantile work and

Ellen grew into a lovely young woman. Gifted with a beautiful voice, Ellen attended Boston's New England Conservatory of Music for one semester.[7]

Before returning to Bainbridge, Ellen visited her half-brother Dixie in Savannah, where he was a partner in an insurance agency with Homer Ayres Hopkins, a young man he had met on a train some time earlier. A Pennsylvania-born Yankee, Homer was the son of Isaac Hopkins, a foundry worker from Clearfield County and a former Union Army soldier, and Mary Ann Glenn, a young woman of French descent.[8]

Homer was fond of this attractive, blue-eyed, southern belle. After a short engagement, the couple married on December 28, 1898, in Savannah's historic Christ Church. Several months after the April 1, 1900, birth of their first daughter, Ruby, named after Ellen's deceased youngest sister, Homer sold his share of the agency back to Dixie and was employed by an insurance company in Jacksonville, Florida.[9]

That city was not what Homer expected. Also, Ellen was both pregnant and homesick. After a brief stay in Jacksonville, the Hopkins returned to Savannah and moved in with Mildred at 212 East Gaston Street. Within days, Homer was working as a clerk for the local office of the New York Life Insurance Company.

Once they were financially stable, they rented the house on East Jones Street, sharing it with Ellen's twin brother, John, and their younger sister, Raymonde. It was here that Ellen Miriam Hopkins was born. She was baptized at Savannah's St. John's Church.

By all outward appearances, the Hopkins were a happy, loving family, but Ellen's domineering nature was chipping away at their marriage. Many believed the arrival of the new baby would bring them closer. Their arguments centered on money: the lack of it and the necessity of living in a crowded brownstone with Ellen's siblings. After each fight, Ellen, her mother, and sometimes her sister would sweep the girls off to Bainbridge. After a cooling off period, they would return to Savannah.

As for Ralph Cutter, he didn't attend his daughter's wedding, nor was he there for the births of his two granddaughters. By 1898, Cutter was a patient at the Foxboro State Hospital in Massachusetts, where they treated psychiatric disorders. There, doctors diagnosed him with "nervous dyspepsia and involution melancholia," which today would be the same as advanced anxiety and depression. By then, Mildred and the children had abandoned him. When questioned for the 1900 census, Mildred gave her marital status as "widowed"; to her, Ralph was dead. In the late nineteenth century, the stigma of an institutionalized relative was tremendous, and most traditional southern families did not acknowledge them.[10]

As the new century began, Cutter's doctor transferred him to Massachusetts's infamous Taunton Lunatic Hospital, where Cutter died from complications of a stroke on February 20, 1904. They sent his body not to the Dickinson plot in Bainbridge but to Hollis, where his brothers buried Ralph next to his parents.[11]

As a child, Miriam, whom they called Mims, was like a miniature version of her mother: petite, with curly, platinum blonde hair, blue eyes, and a peaches-and-cream complexion. To her older sister, Ruby, she was her "private doll . . . so cunning-looking the other kids would pull her curls and things," and if another child touched her, Ruby would knock them down. Because of these brawls, the other parents no longer allowed their children to play with Ruby and insisted she go to reform school. Ellen, nonetheless, blamed everything on Miriam. Ruby maintained that her mother was at fault for dressing "Mims in all those dainty dresses with sashes and bows like that."[12]

Savannah, Georgia's oldest city, held many childhood memories. Some were pleasant, such as sitting on the banks of the yellow Savannah River, gazing at the ships coming in and at the workers sitting on bales of cotton on their decks. Others were less so.

When she was six years old, Miriam developed a cold and sore throat during an unusually bitter winter. Ellen thought little of it at the time, attributing it to common childhood afflictions. The sickness came on abruptly and soon worsened. Miriam developed chills and swollen joints; within thirty-six hours, she was rushed to the hospital and diagnosed with rheumatic fever. Recuperation took several months, but her health had been severely affected. Doctors told her parents the disease had weakened the young girl's heart and could have an impact on her well-being for the rest of her life.

As Miriam healed, life at the Hopkins's household returned to normal—at least what was normal to them. However, by the time Miriam was seven, Homer and Ellen's arguing had reached its limit. Homer received a job offer from an insurance company in Dallas, but Ellen refused to leave Georgia for that "God-forsaken wasteland." She filed for divorce.[13]

Unable to provide for his family in Savannah, Homer had to go on his own. Once he was settled in Dallas, he sent for the girls to visit, but their stays were short-lived. On their last time with their father, Ellen insisted that Miriam and Ruby be sent home early. In a moment of desperation, Homer fled with his daughters across the border to Mexico, where he planned to raise them. Realizing it would be impossible, he returned to Dallas and put them on the train to Savannah.

Over the months, he wrote to them daily, but Ellen intercepted and destroyed his letters. When he telephoned, she would say the girls were napping or playing outside. Finally discouraged, Homer stopped writing and had no further communication with Miriam for a quarter of a century.

With Homer gone, Mildred moved Ellen and the girls from a wooden row house on the southwest corner of Whitaker and Thirty-Third Streets to the house on Gordon Street, because of the education they would get at nearby Massie School (227 East Gordon Street), where Miriam made the honor roll.

Bitter from the divorce and inspired by her mother's actions a decade earlier, Ellen told the 1910 census taker that she was "widowed." She would never see, communicate with, or talk about her former husband again. Even so, her strict Episcopalian beliefs would keep her from remarrying.[14]

In September 1912, Ellen left Savannah and returned to her childhood home on the northwest corner of Shotwell and Scott Streets at what was then the edge of Bainbridge—in Miriam's words, "one of those Georgia towns where old-fashioned houses, often white, sit back in gardens, where magnolias and Japonicas and azaleas and honeysuckle seem always to be in bloom."[15]

Ellen found a job as a milliner at Haddon's department store. Ruby, who was twelve, and Miriam, almost ten, spent their after-school hours in the woods behind their grandmother's home, whether reading on the grass, playing with friends, or taunting some unfortunate child with cries of "Oh Yankee, Yankee, Yankee."[16]

On Sunday afternoons, Miriam would climb one of the low-sweeping evergreen trees bordering each side of the Flint River, the waterway flowing through Bainbridge. Perched there on branches draped with wisteria and Spanish moss, she would sneak a peek as members of the local black church baptized new converts.

Of more lasting impact than hopscotch and children's games were Miriam's psychological battles with her mother. When Miriam was eleven years old, she developed a crush on a handsome boy who had recently moved to Bainbridge. His father was a tradesman, a job Ellen felt was beneath them.

On her birthday, Miriam had a party and wanted to invite the boy, but, as Miriam recalled, her mother explained that "he wasn't the sort of child she wanted me to play with." Miriam felt terrible. She thought how "cruel it was to be separated from the one you love." To work through her grief, Miriam wrote two poems on the spitefulness of separating lovers that the local newspaper published. One day she overheard her mother and grandmother, herself a writer, laughing and poking fun at her writing. Miriam was mortified. "That's the most terrible thing of all to children—ridicule."[17]

When it came to Miriam's future, Ellen had lofty plans, envisioning her daughter as a singer or a pianist. Obediently, Miriam learned to play, but she firmly rejected music as a career.

She recalled singing in the boys' choir at St. John's Episcopal Church. "You see, there weren't enough boys, so they took in a few little girls, and we wore our white vestments and sang with all our might to prove we were as good at it as the regular choristers." While it was enjoyable, she didn't inherit her mother's singing voice, nor did she make an impression. "I was born, and I grew up without any fixed objective at all," she admitted. "I had to find one."

Throughout her childhood, she had no burning desire to be an actress. She never posed in front of mirrors as other girls did at her age, nor did she dress up in her mother's cast-off clothes. There were school plays and the occasional shows she performed in with her friends in the backwoods of Bainbridge, but these were part of childhood, like playing hopscotch or studying grammar.

Teaching geography and nursing ("It appeared that all nurses married stunning doctors") were brief considerations, but she dreamed of being a dancer. Except for some ballet, she wasn't allowed lessons; a stage career wasn't respectable unless it involved singing or playing the piano.[18]

While Ellen raised her two daughters, her twin brother, John Hastings Cutter, moved to Charlotte, North Carolina, and started a successful cotton brokerage that he later expanded. Also, he was active in local commercial real estate development. By 1916, John Cutter had accumulated more than one million dollars, and he assumed support of Ellen and the girls.

When Ruby graduated from high school, Ellen insisted she attend

Syracuse University, where Homer's brother, Thomas, headed the geology department. The Hopkins were a sensitive topic, but Ruby's education was important, and despite her ex-husband, Ellen liked Thomas. She thus packed up the girls and set out for Syracuse.

Thomas Cramer Hopkins was educated at Stanford and received his PhD from the University of Chicago. At Syracuse University, he was well liked and respected by his students. His second wife, Bess, was not pleased when Ellen, Ruby, and Miriam appeared on their doorstep. Thomas, however, could not turn them away.

Ruby and Miriam adored Thomas, but their youthful enthusiasm annoyed Bess. She found fault in everything they did. During the day, they audited high school–level classes at the university. Later in the evenings, Thomas played the fiddle while Bess hid in her room. Thomas suggested that Ellen and the girls stay longer. Ellen considered it a "lovely idea," but Bess was against it and made that clear.[19]

Because of her less-than-cozy living arrangement, Ellen took the girls to New York, where her brother Dixie now lived, having left Savannah's insurance business a decade earlier. By then, he had found success as a Broadway press agent and as a writer of a syndicated show business column.

In 1917, New York was the country's largest city. Its population continued to swell thanks to a surge of immigrants from southern Europe. New zoning laws that year prompted new types of architecture, changing the city's skyline.

The city's breathless haste thrilled Miriam, as did the lavish and eye-catching fashions adopted by the New York women she saw on the streets. She would never return to the comfortable lifestyle of a small Georgian town.

Ruby found work, while Ellen enrolled Miriam as a junior in public school. But New York life had its complications. In the spring, Miriam had an attack of appendicitis and underwent surgery. Returning to school, she fainted twice while climbing the stairs. Concerned about Miriam's heart, Ellen asked that she ride the elevator but was denied by the principal. A loud argument ensued. Ellen and Miriam both stormed out, promising never to return.

As Miriam was approaching her senior year of high school, a friend, who was attending Goddard Seminary, a private theological preparatory school in Barre, Vermont, asked Miriam to go back with her. Ellen consented, and with her brother's financial help, she packed up her daughter and sent her north.

Miriam's first day at Goddard didn't go well. At roll call, her foreign-sounding southern accent brought smiles to her New England–born classmates. "You better speak like the rest of us," whispered a voice beside her. Defiantly, Miriam stood and declared, "Ah thank you all, but ah'll speak as ah please." Although later in life her southern accent would trouble her, throughout her Goddard school days the ever-rebellious southerner strove never to lose it. "Miriam stood out," a former schoolmate recalled. "She was a little spoiled, a little vain but very attractive."[20]

Sizzling with suppressed creative energy, Miriam plunged headlong into the study of art, music, and literature. Showing herself to be a woman ahead of her time, she shocked her more conservative fellow students when she became one of three girls at the seminary to bob her hair. Besides that, she found the most popular student and made him her boyfriend.[21]

She considered becoming one of the "greatest writers" in the country, writing "wastebaskets full of poetry." The seminary's weekly journal printed some after New York magazines rejected them. Admittedly, her "faith was colossal."[22]

Most notably, Goddard offered Miriam her first real taste of stage acting. She played the Girl Graduate in Goddard's Fifty Year Pageant and played Dorothy Dudley, the female lead in her senior class two-act play, Helen Bragg's *The Fascinating Fanny Brown.*

Although she didn't break a leg on opening night, April 29, 1919, she did fracture an ankle falling on a cement stairway between the first and second acts. Once again proving her determination to persevere, she continued with the performance, wearing one slipper. Her first review, published in the *Barre Daily Times,* made it seem worthwhile, saying the role "could not have been better portrayed than by E. Miriam Hopkins. . . . She was a creditable actress and disclosed much talent."[23]

At the graduation ceremony, she hobbled to the podium on crutches to accept her diploma. Despite her success in the school play, her career choices were clear: She would be a writer or a painter—and to overcome the weakness in her ankle, her doctor advised some dancing on the side.

Upon her return to New York, Miriam found Ellen sharing a small apartment with a friend from Bainbridge. At first, she wasted her time lounging around, playing music on an out-of-tune piano and pressing wrinkles from a blue organdie dress. Whether because of her looks, her accent, her manner, or her dewrinkled dress, before long, the neighborhood men took notice. But her uncle Dixie was there to ward off unwanted suitors.

From his cluttered, dust-covered office in the old Knickerbocker Theatre Building, Dixie Hines ran the International Press Bureau. A tall, lanky man, Dixie was recognized on Broadway by his trademark bow ties and horn-rimmed glasses. As a press agent, his clients were some of the most prominent in the world of entertainment, while his weekly syndicated column, "The Seamy Side of Broadway," was a favorite source of theater gossip across the country.[24]

Dixie's apartment at 68 West Thirty-Eighth Street was a showplace for celebrities. Autographed pictures hung on the walls, and his library shelves were bursting with the latest best sellers.

Besides his devotion to both his job and his books, Dixie was also devoted to his nieces. "We thought Uncle Dixie was a very grand person," Miriam recalled. "He went everywhere, knew everybody."[25]

He included them in his professional circles, introducing them to many famous people. The exposure awakened Miriam's childhood dream to be a dancer. "What a beauty," they often remarked and asked why Miriam was not on the stage. Whether he answered them honestly, we cannot know, but Dixie was against the idea of either of his nieces pursuing a theatrical career. The stage—the lifeblood of his work—was unsuitable for young, refined southern women.

As Miriam seemed professionally adrift, Ellen suggested she become a private secretary, so she signed up for a twenty-lesson correspondence course. After she had completed it, Dixie hired her to work in his office, where she was efficient, except when she fell asleep. He told her to find a job somewhere else.

While Ruby worked at Macy's department store demonstrating toys, Miriam went from one job to another. She had a lively, pleasant personality, but she failed to keep working because of what appeared to be incompetence. The few times she did show promise, boredom set in. She would then amaze her employers by quitting, applying for another job that same day.

Between jobs, Miriam posed for both well-known and struggling artists. Dixie introduced her to artist and sculptor Harry Stoner, for whom she modeled for one dollar an hour. Stoner maintained an old studio with a skylight on West Thirty-Seventh Street. While she posed, they would talk about her dancing aspirations.

Stoner also noticed her dramatic talents. He encouraged her, loaning her plays to study. Later, when she started getting small parts, he critiqued her work as she practiced her lines in his studio.

Miriam wanted independence and a place of her own, but it had to be the right atmosphere. She moved into a boarding house at 46 West Thirty-Sixth Street, a small dark cell on the fourth floor that delighted her because it was utterly shabby. Struggling artists and authors lived there, including future playwright Marc Connelly, who occupied the room below hers. They often met on the walk up, but at the time, he didn't impress her any more than the others in the building. Later, when both were successful, their paths would cross again.

Dixie represented many successful clients in vaudeville and on Broadway. Some were not so successful and considered him a soft touch. He complained that they could not, or forgot, to reimburse him for his services. Miriam suggested that he take what his clients owed "out in trade" with lessons or services that she and Ruby would use. Dixie thought about it and agreed.

A professional designer clothed them, and Shakespearean actress Roselle Knot gave them acting and diction lessons. They attended the Vestoff-Serova Dancing School, leading to Miriam's first professional stage appearance, accompanying school founder Sonya Serova and Japanese dancer Michio Ito at the Selwyn Theatre.

Soon, she had her first job in vaudeville, but her poor professional luck continued. She was fired at the end of three days because she "could not be heard beyond the third row."[26]

Another time, with the Vestoff-Serova dancers, she performed in a fund-raiser sponsored by the Bankers Club. Dressed as Armenian refugees in tattered clothing, she applied "dirt streaks" to the other dancers' faces. As they waited in the hallway outside the banquet room, a stocky, dignified gentleman spouted last-minute instructions. In the excitement, Miriam had forgotten to apply her makeup. The dignitary called her out, took the grease paint from her, and applied streaks to her face. He entered the hall to a burst of applause. The other girls stared wide-eyed. "Aren't you thrilled?" one of them said.

"Who was he?" Miriam asked.[27]

As it turned out, the dignitary was Herbert Hoover, the food commissioner and the man in charge of the fund-raiser. Years later, Miriam would brag that she was the only performer who had had her makeup applied by a future president of the United States.

2

Broadway Bound

As far as Dixie knew, Miriam's only theater exposure was her dance school. He was unaware of her vaudeville stint and that both she and Ruby auditioned for roles on Broadway. To ensure that they followed his wishes, he spread the news along the Great White Way that he would shoot any casting agent who hired either of his nieces. "I don't want them on the stage!" he demanded, adding that he preferred they were "dead and buried" than in show business.

When he discovered they were auditioning behind his back, he regretted approving those free lessons. Dixie's reaction amused Ruby: "In Uncle Dixie's mind, there was no thought that we'd use this training. To him, it was just nice for gentle-born Southern girls to develop their—their little assets."[1]

Despite Dixie's threats, the girls auditioned for countless shows, but because he was a respected agent and columnist, no legitimate producer would hire them. Miriam took a different approach.

At one of Dixie's parties, she overheard a conversation about the opening of The Music Box, Irving Berlin's new theater on West Forty-Fifth Street. Berlin had written a revue for the premiere, and Hassard Short, a well-known stage director, was holding auditions the following morning. Miriam would be there.

Arriving at the unfinished theater dressed in her finest clothes, she told the guard that Hassard Short, a person she had never met, was expecting her. Inside, she walked among construction workers and chorus girls until she saw a white-haired man instructing several dancers. Believing he was the choreographer, she told him Hassard Short asked her to audition that morning. Miriam recalled that the man "grinned from ear to ear" and said, "Young lady, *I* am Hassard Short, and I have never seen you before in my life."

Miriam mischievously smiled while fingering the lace trim on her collar. "Well, I'm sorry about that, Mr. Short, but since I'm here wouldn't you like to see what I can do?" Without waiting for a reply, she introduced herself. Then, assuming Dixie had warned him, she made light of his threats, explaining how unfair her uncle was to believe that a real lady should not go on the stage.

Short hesitated, but he was enchanted, so he allowed her to audition. For several minutes, she "talked" a song and performed a few ballet and tap steps. "Lord knows how long I'd have gone on if Mr. Short hadn't stopped me," Miriam would recall, adding without modesty, "He was charmed." He hired her on the spot as one of Irving Berlin's "Eight Little Notes," at forty dollars a week—more money than she had made her entire life.[2]

Even at the start of her career, Miriam—who was clueless about what she wanted, who was lazy, who got fired from jobs she wasn't suited to— became a fearless go-getter once she made up her mind to dance onstage. She determined that nothing would stop her: not producers, directors, or her mother; not even Uncle Dixie.

Dixie was furious when he heard, and he called his sister right away. At first, Ellen "stood on her hind legs," but when the *Music Box Revue* turned out to be "the most beautiful show in New York," she felt differently.[3]

An army of workers rushed to complete the finishing touches for The Music Box's debut, but the curtain rose twenty-five minutes late. At the end of the show, Berlin was interviewed by eight chorus girls; one was Miriam. The girls dressed as twinkly musical notes, "sweet as barley sugar," and appeared "dancing from a large music box."[4]

"The most beautiful show," however, had its share of glitches. On opening night, Miriam was "paralyzed with excitement" while dancing onstage when she spotted Norma Talmadge, Lillian Gish, and other movie stars in the front row. As the story goes, at another performance she "nearly died of alarm and mortification" when both the (hawk-eyed) audience and dance partner Chester Hale laughed at her—as Miriam, the "ethereal adagio dancer in her petal-like costume," was sporting a "broad rim of chocolate ice cream soda all around her mouth."[5]

In any case, the opening reviews for the *Music Box Revue* were flawless. In the words of the *New York Times*'s irascible Alexander Woollcott, it "proved to be a treasure chest out of which the conjurers pulled all manner of gay tunes and brilliant trappings and funny clowns and nimble dancers." The first of four *Music Box Revues* was a solid hit for more than a year.[6]

Yet, Miriam was not as "nimble" a dancer as her fellow chorines. Because of rookie mistakes, they suggested she look for a new career. She was the type, they told her, that should "find a rich boyfriend."[7]

Fate almost provided one when F. Scott Fitzgerald, without his new bride, the former Zelda Sayre, attended a *Music Box* performance. From his seat, he singled out Miriam from the chorus. Fitzgerald, who was enjoying the success of his recent novel *This Side of Paradise,* had returned from spending the summer in Westport, Connecticut.[8]

After the show, Fitzgerald worked his way backstage to the dancers' dressing room. Miriam was removing her makeup when she felt a tap on her shoulder. Looking up, a tall, handsome stranger was smiling at her. The other girls stared as Fitzgerald introduced himself. Miriam recognized the name, as did the others. Soon, they were "talking over dinner at a small, romantic restaurant in the Village."[9]

Miriam, however, was not the lone "other woman" in Fitzgerald's life, as he reportedly was seeing Tallulah Bankhead's older sister, Eugenia. In time, Zelda became suspicious when she heard rumors about her husband's interest in Miriam. A few weeks later, Fitzgerald ended their affair.

Years later in Hollywood, Miriam and Fitzgerald, now a disillusioned Hollywood screenwriter, crossed paths again. Fitzgerald, somewhat cryptically, wrote: "From now on I go nowhere and see no one because the work is hard as hell, at least for me and I've lost ten pounds. So farewell Miriam Hopkins who leans so close when she talks. . . . You will never know me. Except Miriam who promised to call up but hasn't."[10]

The breakup upset her, but her brief time with Fitzgerald—likely her first serious adult romance—instilled a maturity she lacked. The other girls noticed it, too. They stopped teasing her and calling her "Miss Priss," since their risqué jokes and coarse language no longer shocked her.

They had further proof when a rival chorus girl had an abortion before a show and was experiencing pain. Miriam stepped up, sent the girl home, and told the stage manager she had pulled a ligament. In the same breath, she offered to take the girl's place in the front line, stage right, instead of her usual back-row spot. Miriam was the first to admit her deed "wasn't entirely altruistic." She was learning.[11]

Miriam had been with the *Music Box Revue* for four months when the Désirée Lubovska National Ballet invited her on a South American dance tour. She had no passport, so with artist Harry Stoner as a witness, and a permission letter from her mother, she filled out an application at the custom house.[12]

Two days before the troupe's departure, as rain and severe winds breezed through New York City, Miriam picked up her passport. Walking down the icy steps, she slipped and fell, spraining her ankle—the same ankle she had injured at Goddard. Her hopes of dancing with the tour ended.

Later, one of the dancers explained that they were stranded penniless in Rio de Janeiro; some had to work their way back to the United States as stewardesses. Miriam then expressed regret about cursing her ankle and theorized that had it not been for that broken ankle, she would never have become a "motion picture star."[13]

Once again Miriam was unemployed; she was broke and about to be thrown out on the streets. Looking to make extra cash, she wrote two short stories and sent them to Elisabeth Marbury, the best-known literary agent in New York. Marbury read the stories, liked them, and invited Miriam to lunch at her Sutton Place home on the city's Upper East Side.

Marbury asked what else she had written and what her plans were. Miriam said she hoped she would be an actress but was "out of a job and needed money." Could Marbury sell the stories? Possibly, was the reply, and Marbury would also see about employment in the theater. As they lunched in the paneled dining room with its view of the East River and the Queensboro Bridge, Miriam announced, "Miss Marbury, someday I shall own this house." Marbury laughed.[14]

Regrettably, her stories never sold, but when her ankle healed, she danced for the remainder of 1922 in vaudeville, and later in stock for George M. Cohan.

It was the playwright and vaudeville performer May Tully who recognized Miriam's dramatic possibilities. Tully mentioned a vaudeville sketch she had written, adding there was a part in it for Miriam. She auditioned and won the role. The skit, "Sister Wives," played on the United, Keith, Shubert, and Pantages circuits for more than six months. After that, Miriam returned to vaudeville in *The Garrick Gaieties* and later played with a Shubert musical comedy unit, appearing with Dan Healy in the cabaret act "One Night in June."

As 1923 began, Miriam had several stage gigs, among them *Give and Take,* starring the roly-poly vaudevillian George Sidney, and "The Man

Hunt," with which she spent several months on the Pantages circuit with writer Harlan Thompson. Miriam's friendship with Thompson opened the door for her first stage success. Thompson wrote the book and lyrics for a musical play, *Little Jessie James*, convincing former sports promoter-turned-theater manager L. Lawrence Weber to produce it. It was Miriam's brief exposure in "The Man Hunt" and an earlier appearance in Helen Holmes Hinchley's *The Clam Digger* that convinced Weber to gamble on her. Miriam came to Broadway for $250 a week.

Little Jessie James opened at West Forty-Eighth Street's Longacre Theatre on August 15, 1923. Miriam played a lively flapper, performing with actor-singer Allen Kearns in the opening duet, "Quiet Afternoon." Russian actress Nan Halperin had the title role, but it was Miriam who walked away with the lion's share of the reviews. The *New York Times* reported, "The most refreshing member of the cast is a young woman named Miriam Hopkins . . . a tremendous head of yellow hair and two nimble legs." The equally delighted *New York American* added, "She is entirely delicious."[15]

Even though Miriam saw herself as a "scrawny kid with a mop of yellow hair," she had succeeded in landing a lead in the biggest Broadway hit of the season. *Little Jessie James* ran for a year, allowing her to buy her first expensive fur coat and move from the dark room on West Thirty-Sixth Street into a nicer West Village apartment.[16]

The experience led to a marked inner change as well. Miriam established herself as a person with a definite niche in the world. Her own apartment gave her assurance and stature. She became a "conscious human being," opening her eyes and mind to New York and what it offered and selecting what she wanted: "concerts, art exhibits, odd restaurants, friends" who shared her tastes.[17]

Based on the impression she had made on New York audiences when *Little Jessie James* closed, the prestigious Chamberlain Brown Agency signed her. Operated by brothers Chamberlain and Lyman Brown, the agency's clients included Clark Gable, Helen Hayes, Alfred Lunt, Rudolph Valentino, Ruth Chatterton, and Spencer Tracy.

Lyman Brown introduced the relative newcomer to the influential newspaper columnist Ward Morehouse, a short and slightly overweight man who also hailed from Savannah and who would become a lifelong friend and confidant. Part of the theater world since 1920, Morehouse was on intimate terms with most of Broadway royalty. He wrote about drama for the *New York Tribune* and later for the *Herald-Tribune,* the *Brooklyn Times*, and the *New York Sun.*

The morning of their meeting, Miriam, wearing a full-length squirrel coat, threw herself into Brown's office. Morehouse claimed that "here was one of the most attractive human beings" he had ever seen. Miriam had returned from Stamford, where she appeared in a tryout of a musical. She wanted out of it and asked Brown to tear up her contract.

Morehouse recalled: "She talked breathlessly and entertainingly. Her charm and personality were overpowering. Lyman Brown, who had placed her in that Stamford musical piece, was helpless. Certainly, she had a contract. Certainly she was obligated to stay with the play, but certainly, he would get her out of it. And so he did."[18]

Now, Miriam wanted to play straight drama, despite her success in musical comedy. Theater managers wouldn't take her seriously, even with Brown's help. After two shows, she was "typed" as a Broadway musical showgirl. Miriam couldn't blame them. She was the musical-comedy type—little and blonde—and producers had no way of knowing what she was inside. "But I was convinced that I had the makings of a dramatic actress," she insisted, "so I set out to prove it."[19]

Producers tried giving her a chance, without much luck. Her problem was not a lack of talent but an excess of temperament. She accepted a role in the stage skit "The Two Mrs. Smiths" on Staten Island, but when she disagreed about her part, the director fired her.

By now, Dixie had given up trying to keep her out of show business. She had proven she had talent, so he promoted her upcoming role in the new Broadway show *My Man*: "Miriam Hopkins, the skillful ingénue of *Little Jessie James,* has been chosen by L. Lawrence Weber for elevation to the leading role in *My Man* which is to be produced in the fall."[20]

But despite her uncle's budding support, Miriam's big break as a dramatic star in *My Man* turned out to be a big bust. After rehearsals began, producers pulled the financial backing and canceled the play.

In time, it was not her convincing personality that won her a chance at stage acting but her physique. Lyman Brown sent his twenty-two-year-old client on an audition for the Broadway-bound *High Tide,* a three-act melodrama by Eleanor Holmes Hinkley. The diminutive Miriam won the part of Marielle, the love interest of costar and matinee idol Louis Calhern because he refused to carry a heavier leading lady up a long flight of stairs.

Miriam received mixed reviews at its opening on December 16, 1924, at the Shubert-Belasco Theater in Washington, DC. "Miriam Hopkins, as Marielle, struggled desperately with a difficult role," opined the *Washington Post* reviewer, "but her mass of golden bobbed hair seemed more appropriate for the Klieg lights of a cinema than the melodramatic part in which she was cast." The more confident *Washington Star* remarked, "Hers is no simple part. She handled it capably and will handle it better."[21]

But the theater fates were against her. The following week, *High Tide* moved to Atlantic City's Apollo Theater, where it died over the Christmas holiday, never making it to Broadway.

With two flops under her belt and low on funds, Miriam returned to New York, homeless. Ward Morehouse introduced her to Marion Tanner, who within a few decades would gain fame as the inspiration for *Auntie Mame*. Miriam rented a room at Tanner's West Village home, which even then was a haven for artists and bohemians alike, Miriam among them. She lived at 72 Bank Street for a year and had pleasant memories of her landlady: "Marion was a doll, and when I knew her she was 'madcap,' but that was years before her nephew [Patrick Dennis] wrote the book. I understand they're estranged now. What a pity."[22]

Equally pitiful was Miriam's financial state. Desperately in need of work, Lyman Brown sent her on several auditions. Despite that, she considered herself lucky. She lived alone and was independent, free to plan and direct her life as she wished. The space between jobs was seldom long enough to distress her. There were times, as now, when she fell into debt and was anxious about the future, but before despair set in, there would be another job.

She decided to hold out for the serious roles. She could go into another musical comedy or gamble on getting a dramatic show. She decided to gamble. Long and stubbornly, she sat in every casting agent's office in town. If she didn't, she believed producers would type her as a song-and-dance girl for the rest of her theater life. Even if the play flopped, or she was a personal flop, it would be drama from then on.

Her stubbornness paid off. Within a month, she was cast in the Frances Lightner play *Puppets,* replacing her future *The Smiling Lieutenant* costar Claudette Colbert to appear opposite her *Dr. Jekyll and Mr. Hyde* leading man Fredric March. Several years later, March recalled, "Little did she know I would one day choke her to death in front of the camera."[23]

No one gets strangled in *Puppets,* the story of a Mulberry Street marionette theater owner (C. Henry Gordon) and his cousin Bruno (March); both are in love with cute, Georgia-born drugstore employee Angela Smith (Hopkins).

The role gave Miriam a chance to show off her abilities and to realize how much she wanted to be a dramatic stage actress. With few exceptions, the New York critics panned the play, but Miriam gained a few new fans.

"A slim little girl with a head of thick blond hair, thin legs and a beautiful voice—whose previous experience on Broadway had been confined to musical shows—came on stage at the Selwyn Theatre last night and ran away with the show," wrote the *New York Telegram*'s Bernard Simon. "The girl was Miriam Hopkins." The *Times* reviewer was less impressed: "Miriam Hopkins carried her role of Angela into no little sweetness, too much for some in the audience and not enough for others perhaps."[24]

Despite the lukewarm notices, *Puppets* did the trick and established Miriam as a dramatic actress. *Puppets* lasted fifty-four performances before getting a new location, the Frolic Theatre, and a new title, *The Knife in the Wall.*

Next, playwright Channing Pollock cast Miriam in his new play *The Enemy,* taking place in Vienna during World War I. *The Enemy* had its tryout at the Shubert Theater in New Haven, Connecticut, where many plays had their first exposure before opening on Broadway. Its reception was tremendous; critics praised Pollock for presenting his subject with unflinching honesty. The star of the show, future Oscar winner Fay Bainter, was a last-minute replacement and received the highest praise.[25]

"Miriam Hopkins," the *New Haven Journal-Courier* began, "of whom we said glorious things in the ill-fated play [*Puppets*], cause us to retract none of them by her splendid performance." Miriam was thrilled when she read the reviews—and shocked when Pollock fired her before the play opened on Broadway, giving no other reason than the petite, girlish-looking actress was unsuitable to play the mother of a six-year-old.[26]

Undaunted, Miriam landed in rehearsals for *Lovely Lady*, a new play in three acts by Jesse Lynch Williams. Once again the pre-Broadway tryouts were at the Shubert, where the play received lukewarm praise from the local papers. Yet Miriam captivated at least one reviewer, who rhapsodized, "The door opened, and Miriam Hopkins walked in, and I dreamed I was in heaven, face to face with the pattern from which the angels were made."[27]

Broadway audiences apparently had a less spiritual experience, as

Lovely Lady, opening on Broadway at the West Forty-Eighth Street Belmont Theatre on October 14, 1925, ran for just twenty-one performances. Once again Miriam was without a job.

Within a few weeks, Miriam reluctantly signed to appear in another musical comedy, *The Matinee Girl.* She needed the money, but she believed that if the play was a success her efforts as a dramatic actress would be for naught. The pre-Broadway tryouts were held on Christmas Day, 1925, at the Irving Theatre in Wilkes-Barre, Pennsylvania. She knew it was a mistake and asked to cancel her commitment.

After four years of highs and lows, Miriam's career reached an unsatisfying professional plateau. Her luck seemed to change at the beginning of 1926, when she won the lead role of Lorelei Lee in Anita Loos's new Broadway play, *Gentlemen Prefer Blondes.* This role, Miriam felt, would be her big break. But her hopes for stage success didn't last. During rehearsals, Loos and her producer husband, John Emerson, claimed she conveyed too much intellect for the wide-eyed, whimsical Lorelei. She was, once again, fired. June Walker was her replacement.

Staying idle until May, Miriam joined a pre-Broadway tryout of George M. Cohan's *The Home Towners* at his renovated Four Cohan's Theatre in Chicago. She would later refer to it as "one of the pleasantest engagements" of her stage career. With plenty of free time, she took sketch classes at the Chicago Art Institute. Even though she claimed to have "no talent," Miriam found "great personal satisfaction" expressing her "surplus enthusiasm and energies" on a sketch pad. Along with other urges, she caught the writing bug again and wrote six short stories. Despite several attempts, none of them sold.[28]

While appearing in *The Home Towners,* Miriam was introduced to actor Brandon Peters at supper one evening after the show. She was infatuated with the handsome young Troy, New York, native who had toured with several Shakespearean companies before his first Broadway appearance in the short-lived *The Cave Girl.*

Like other young men in Miriam's life, Peters was fascinated by her bubbly vivacity. As a plus, he discovered beneath this allure and machine-gun-like chatter, a woman of depth who was capable of coping with the mind of any man. At twenty-three years old, Miriam married Brandon Peters in a brief ceremony at Chicago city hall on May 11, 1926. Mysteriously, they wouldn't discuss the reasons for their quick union and what occurred during their short marriage.

While Miriam was in *The Home Towners,* her photographs found their way to Louis Cline, a representative of Boni & Liveright book publisher Horace Liveright, who was preparing Theodore Dreiser's best seller *An American Tragedy* for the stage. One of the showiest book publishers of the 1920s, Liveright began producing plays with his partner, Albert Boni. Their first project was an adaptation of Dreiser's novel.[29]

An American Tragedy was based on an infamous 1906 criminal case in which authorities found an overturned boat and a woman's body in a lake at an Upstate New York resort. Factory worker Chester Gillette (Clyde Griffiths in the book and play) was put on trial and convicted of killing the young woman, though he claimed her death was an accident. Gillette was executed in the electric chair two years later.

Louis Cline caught Miriam's performance in *The Home Towners* and returned to New York convinced she was perfect for the role of Sondra, the real love of Clyde Griffiths. After a barrage of telegrams from Liveright, George M. Cohan agreed to release her if he could find a replacement. After several days, he hired a girl. "She was Peg Entwistle," Miriam remembered, "the girl who committed suicide by jumping off the Hollywoodland sign. Such a tragic thing."[30]

In August, Miriam was selected from among two hundred hopefuls, ending a frenzied search for the most sought after role that year. Rehearsals for *An American Tragedy* began on September 8, with Morgan Farley as Clyde Griffiths and Katherine Wilson as the unfortunate woman he is accused of killing. Patrick Kearney, who had one play produced, wrote the adaptation.

After a tryout at the New Haven Shubert, *An American Tragedy* opened on October 11, 1926, at the Longacre Theatre. Under Edward T. Goodman's direction, the play was as trendy as the novel—and it was among five shows the New York district attorney regarded as "morally undesirable." Opening night showers didn't hinder the plays audience: From the first curtain to the last, the occasion was, in the words of reviewers, "absorbing" and "intensely interesting."[31]

Because of opposition from the district attorney, Louis Cline was concerned about a lukewarm response from the critics. To compensate, he reportedly hired seventy-five people to applaud and shout, "Bravo, Dreiser!" If true, the scheme worked. As the curtain fell, the audience reacted with unbridled cheers and ovations.[32]

Newspaper columnist Walter Winchell, who would later gain fame as a feared radio gossip commentator, was in attendance that evening. He reported: "Not in the young life of this play observer, has there ever been so wild a demonstration as one that acclaimed *An American Tragedy*. . . . They went mad! They yelled! Their applause was as deafening as the rat-a-tat-tat of a score of machine guns, and they remained in their chairs, too, for ten minutes after the play ended, to cheer the players."[33]

An American Tragedy made stage history, grossing, on average, $30,000 per week. Critics spared no adjectives praising Miriam's performance; raves like "inspired," "dynamically emotional," and "arresting personality" liberally peppered their reviews.[34]

Miriam's future looked bright.

On the downside, her marriage was in the doldrums, and before *An American Tragedy* opened, the couple was facing financial difficulties. Peters had a supporting role in the comedy *Potash and Perlmutter, Detectives*, but it closed on October 9, two days before Miriam's *An American Tragedy* debut. Right away, Peters was cast in the touring company of *The Jest*, opening in Worcester, Massachusetts.

Before leaving, he came home with a large box of American Beauty roses for Miriam's twenty-fourth birthday. She asked where he had gotten them. "Well, dear, I got them at the florist's." Then she asked if he had charged them—he did. Since the account was in her name, she reminded him that they were broke and that she couldn't afford to have American Beauties sent to her, "so take them right back."[35]

Peters returned the flowers and walked out on their marriage. The problem was not the cost or the roses. Thanks to *An American Tragedy*, Miriam had a decent paycheck and could afford the wayward roses. Unknown problems were gnawing at the marriage. Neither Miriam nor Peters would speak about their brief time together or the reasons for their separation.

Not until 1956—after Peters's death on February 27—did a reporter ask Miriam about him. She stopped, paused for a moment, and mumbled, "My husband once removed," and she continued. That was it. To her death, she refused to comment further about her puzzling time with Peters.[36]

Remarkably, Miriam's son, Michael, was oblivious of Brandon Peters's existence: "Maybe she didn't think it was important, or it was none of my business." He was unaware of his mother's first marriage until he read about it in her obituaries.[37]

But, as one door closes, another opens. For Miriam, that door opened for Bennett Cerf, an investor in Horace Liveright's publishing company. Within the year, he would establish his own publishing company, Random House. Cerf might be better known for his syndicated newspaper column and for his role as a panelist on the 1950s game show *What's My Line?* Tall, brown-eyed, bespectacled, and flawlessly tailored, Cerf had inherited a fortune from his French-Jewish maternal grandmother. To recoup his $50,000 investment, Cerf spent time at Liveright's office honing his personal publishing skills.

One autumn morning, Miriam was at Liveright's office to pick up her paycheck. Cerf saw her enter. He invited her to go to New Haven the following day for a Yale-Princeton game. She accepted. Soon, Cerf learned she had "no great gift for silence—she never stopped talking."[38]

In the morning, instead of taking the trolley, they walked the short trek from the train station to the Yale Bowl. Passing a pet store, Miriam noticed a puppy in the window and asked Cerf to buy it for her. Cerf pointed out they were going to a football game, and she wasn't going to "sit there with a puppy" in her arms. He would buy it on their walk back to the station.

Miriam's presence in the football stands created a sensation. Before the first quarter was seven minutes over, ten young men were explaining football to her: "five guys in front of us and five guys behind us." She was the center of attention, not because they knew who she was, but "because she was so attractive." Men were crazy for her. She had allure, charm, and a great amount of sex appeal.

After the game, they returned to the train station. Along the way, Miriam looked for the pet shop, until it dawned on her that Cerf had brought her back another way. They had "quite a battle," but despite that, Cerf was smitten. "Now, I fell—oh, did I fall—for Miriam."[39]

During *An American Tragedy*'s run, Miriam relished her friendship with Theodore Dreiser and how the play influenced her career. "It was a distinguished play," she acknowledged, "and through Theodore Dreiser, the author, I came to know several vitally interesting people."[40]

Every Thursday evening, the subway took her to Dreiser's St. Luke's Place apartment to socialize with these "interesting people." There, she met world-famous figures of letters, arts, and national events. A typical night would include such noted writers and critics as Sherwood Anderson; British novelist John Cowper Powys; the banker-producer

Otto Kahn; author Elinor Wylie; and the multifaceted intellectual Max Eastman.[41]

She also befriended writer Dorothy Parker. The satirist's wit and wise-cracks amused Miriam, and through Parker, she met many well-regarded authors. Between Dreiser's parties and Dorothy Parker's literary world, Miriam developed an appreciation for writers that remained for life.

Occasionally, Miriam joined Parker at the Algonquin Hotel's Rose Room, where, for seven years, Parker met with satirist Robert Benchley, playwright Robert E. Sherwood, and journalist Heywood Broun, among others. Here at the Algonquin Round Table Miriam made friends with columnist Franklin Pierce Adams, actor Harpo Marx, and critic Alexander Woollcott and picked up her friendship with Marc Connelly, the playwright who once lived below her in the West Thirty-Sixth Street rooming house.

The *American Tragedy* playwright, Patrick Kearney, further influenced Miriam's literary education. During the play's run, they had a brief affair. Miriam found Kearney captivating. A magazine contributor, his first success was writing one-act plays produced by the Washington Square Players. His first Broadway play, *A Man's Man*, from the year before, had been a moderate success.

No longer with his second wife, his latest romance fascinated him, and he shared with Miriam his love of "poetry, theater and high drama in private life." Encouraged to start a library, Miriam's first book was a signed edition of Lewis Carroll's *Alice's Adventures in Wonderland* that she purchased for $300—a week's salary at the time. Kearney became her passion, while she, in her words, was "his spiritual echo."[42]

Whenever they discussed the theater with playwright Eugene O'Neill or the Irish Renaissance with novelist Ernest Boyd, prohibition liquor flowed freely. Miriam admittedly, and without her mother's knowledge, enjoyed an occasional drink. For Kearney, drinking was a habit, often leading to a "hectic literary life."

When *An American Tragedy* closed in the spring of 1927, Miriam stepped into rehearsals for *Thou Desperate Pilot*, a play by Zoë Akins. Despite Akins's popularity, the play was a resounding flop. The *New York Times* reported, "Miriam Hopkins, lately the Sondra of *An American Tragedy,* did as well as possible with a-none-too-believable part." However, she did well during contract negotiations, getting a guarantee of six weeks of pay. When *Thou Desperate Pilot* closed after six performances, Miriam sailed to Bermuda for as long as her salary lasted.[43]

There, she reflected on Patrick Kearney and their relationship, which had run its course. Kearney wanted marriage even though she was still with Brandon Peters. Also, Kearney's drinking was uncontrollable. He had introduced her to a world of culture, but marriage would sever her ties to Peters, a husband she liked pointing to whenever a liaison became threatening.

Before facing Kearney, she accepted George M. Cohan's invitation to Chicago for a revival of Aaron Hoffman's *Give and Take*. When it closed that spring, she returned to New York to end the affair.

According to reliable sources, an intoxicated Kearney was angry. He grabbed a knife and declared that if she didn't reconsider, he would slash her throat and take his own life. Between Kearney's shouting and Miriam's cries for help, the neighbors notified police. But Miriam escaped as the knife-wielding Kearney chased her through the streets of Greenwich Village until she reached Ward Morehouse's office. Oddly, he hid her in a Harlem maternity hospital. She was contracted for a series of summer plays with a Rochester stock company and opted to hide out in Harlem until Kearney sobered up.

After their split, Patrick Kearney tried putting his life back together. He was married for a third time, to an artist's model, and fathered a daughter. Then, Kearney wrote screenplays for Universal and invested that money in two plays that failed, forcing him into bankruptcy. Separated from his third wife and living in the same apartment he had shared with Miriam, on March 28, 1933, Patrick Kearney was found dead on the kitchen floor, fully clothed, with a hose leading from the gas outlet still in his mouth. He left no note.

George Cukor gained international fame as a favorite Hollywood director, but in the summer of 1927, he was in a professional partnership with Rochester native George Kondolf. His summers were devoted to the town's two-thousand-seat Lyceum Theatre, where, from 1922 to 1928 (the year they were forced to move to the Temple Theatre), he directed such contemporary and future stars as Louis Calhern, Frank Morgan, Robert Montgomery, Billie Burke, Dorothy Gish, Bette Davis, and a score of others destined to find fame in pictures.

"That's when I began directing plays," Cukor told writer and film historian Gavin Lambert. "If I do say so, I worked goddamned hard and managed the whole thing brilliantly. I did everything. I chose the plays and the scenery; I tried out new plays with only one week's rehearsal. Nothing daunted me. We'd do musical comedy one week, then an all-colored play, and so on. I think it was the most exciting stock company in the United States and damned good preparation for Hollywood. The leading man was Louis Calhern and the leading lady Miriam Hopkins."[44]

Cukor had a blanket option of more than fifty plays for the summer productions, including the successes of the current and past few Broadway seasons. Alternating leading roles with stage actress Helen Menken, Miriam appeared in six plays over two months opposite her leading man, Minor Watson. Her first work was the "super-sophisticated lady" in *The Last of Mrs. Cheyney*. Following that, she played "an eleven-year-old child" in *The Family Upstairs*.[45]

In Rochester, Miriam shared an apartment and a bed with fellow castmate Robert Montgomery, a stock player in Cukor's company.

One weekend in May, Miriam was returning to Rochester by train after visiting New York. While eating a chicken salad in the Pullman diner's car, a bone became lodged in her throat. The conductor wired ahead to have a physician and ambulance waiting to take them to Highland Hospital, where they operated. Although traumatic, the ordeal was excellent publicity for the theater. The Pullman Company paid her hospital bill and gave her a $500 check for pain and suffering.

Ever the rebel, while recuperating in the hospital, Miriam entertained patients and secretly supplied them with gin, courtesy of the Seneca Hotel's bellhops. Her actions worried the hospital staff, but not like Robert Montgomery did—a frequent visitor who hid under her hospital bed until all hours of the morning.

After a three-week recovery, she returned to the Lyceum for the final two plays, *Applesauce* and *The Ghost Train*. Broadway producer and theater owner Sam H. Harris caught a performance of the latter and signed Miriam and Minor Watson for his Broadway production, *The Medicine Man*. During rehearsals, Miriam argued with Harris over the writing. In frustration, she walked out before the tryouts in Washington, DC. Future wife of Humphrey Bogart Mayo Methot replaced her, but the play failed to make it to Broadway.

Unemployed and low on finances, Miriam considered borrowing money from investment banker and patron of the arts Otto Kahn. He had backed *An American Tragedy* and was a frequent guest at Theodore Dreiser's parties. Miriam called Kahn from Ward Morehouse's office in the *New York Sun* building. Kahn agreed to see her. She hoped to return with a $5,000 check.[46]

Nervous, she entered Kahn's office. When he turned around in his huge chair, she was startled and blurted out, "I've come for cash." Businesslike, Kahn made a list of her outstanding debts and told her what she could borrow. A half-hour later, back in Morehouse's office, she had her check, not what she hoped for, but $1,250—all he would give her. "Mr. Kahn is a very conservative man," she told Morehouse. "He thought this was all I'd need to pay my bills. And he said he wants to keep a friend; he wants me to pay him back." She paid him back.[47]

The next week her luck improved. Following Tallulah Bankhead's success in the London production of Avery Hopwood's *The Garden of Eden,* stage producer Archibald Selwyn spent one season searching for an actress to re-create the role of Toni Lebrun in the United States. After rejecting many of the country's finest actresses, Selwyn chose Miriam.

She started rehearsals opposite her former Cukor cast and bedmate, Robert Montgomery. With this role, he believed "the tide began to turn" for him. However, after the Washington, DC, tryouts, Montgomery was replaced by Douglas Montgomery (no relation) for the New York opening on September 27, 1927, at the Selwyn Theatre.[48]

In London, *The Garden of Eden* owed much of its success to a mix of comedy and drama, lesbian overtones, and Tallulah Bankhead baring herself to her underwear. In contrast, Broadway's version was diluted and played as broad comedy. Even so, Miriam's role was considered risqué. In the climactic scene, the young lady's fiancé refuses to marry her when he learns of her past as a dancer in cheap cabarets. In a gesture of defiance, she tears off her wedding dress and stands before him in her teddy and girlish innocence.

When Miriam's mother read the reviews, she boarded the train from Bainbridge to New York to pull her daughter from the play. At times, she and Mildred were embarrassed by Miriam's career, listening to their Bainbridge neighbors "whispering about having a daughter on the stage." That was bad enough, but appearing nearly nude before the population of New York City was unacceptable.[49]

Ellen may have considered it scandalous, but to New York theatergoers it was all a letdown. Compared to Bankhead's London introduction, in New York, there were more yawns than gasps at the unveiling of a skinny, tousle-headed Miriam Hopkins with undeveloped shoulders and arms, no chest, and thin legs. One reviewer noted she "did nobly with the material afforded" to her, but that wasn't enough. Whether in response to the critics or in answer to Ellen's outraged prayers, *The Garden of Eden* closed after twenty-three performances.[50]

But surprisingly, Miriam wasn't the only Hopkins bringing embarrassment to the family. In the mid-1920s, the Black Bottom dance was wildly popular in New York. Ruby, the soft-spoken, somewhat withdrawn eldest daughter, had returned to Bainbridge and, using her "New York education," offered dancing lessons to the town's younger generation. One of the dances was the Black Bottom.

The town's elder residents were shocked. One Sunday, a local minister devoted his entire sermon to "that shameless young hussy from New York who is leading Bainbridge youth down the road to sin." The next day, an editorial in the *Bainbridge Post-Searchlight* sided with the minister. Ellen was mortified, and even her mother, the liberal and independent-minded Mildred Dickinson Cutter, "took to her bed."[51]

Since childhood, Miriam and Ruby had had dissimilar personalities. "Ruby had like features, but she was the opposite of Miriam," recalled Tom, Miriam's grandson. Whereas Miriam was "dominant," Ruby was "very quiet." Becky Morehouse, the fourth wife of Ward Morehouse, was dismissive of the latter, asserting "Ruby was not very interesting. Not into one thing or another. They weren't anything alike."[52]

Miriam's son, Michael, recalled that the sisters were close when growing up, but added: "Once they became adults, they went their own way." As Miriam gained success on the stage, Ruby found it difficult to find her niche, leading her to resent her younger sister.[53]

Ruby had occasional dancing gigs in Broadway choruses and vaudeville, and if nothing was available, she worked for Macy's or Gimbels department stores. When New York bored her, she returned to Bainbridge. Miriam was not around, but later, when she earned a decent income, she helped Ruby financially; Miriam's career took precedence over family.

But now, a genuinely impressive man entered Miriam's life, someone who would challenge her priorities as she reached a new level of stardom.

3

Billy

Known to his friends as Billy, Austin Parker was a tall, well-built man with blue eyes, a strong face, and graying hair. A magazine writer and the author of several books, Parker had filed for a Paris divorce from his first wife, Phyllis Duganne, a short-story writer and novelist. The Great Falls, Montana, native was educated at Columbia University and worked as a reporter on the *Helena Daily Independent* during the summer.[1]

In World War I, Parker was a correspondent in France for the *New York Tribune*. He was certain the fighting would be over quickly, and he could return to his newspaper job. Instead, he became involved with the cause, resigning his position at the *Tribune* to join the Lafayette Escadrilles. When the war finally ended, he tried his hand at dropping bombs on the Riffs for the Sultan of Morocco.[2]

Later, Parker moved to the French town of Barbizon, where he freelanced until 1927. When the *Saturday Evening Post* published a serial he had submitted, he ended four years of self-exile in France, sailing to New York for a short visit. Not in his plans was meeting Miriam Hopkins.

At the time, Miriam was rehearsing her upcoming play *Excess Baggage*, a comedy by John McGowan opening at the Ritz Theatre (now the Walter Kerr Theatre). One evening, a girlfriend took her to a party where she saw a bored Austin Parker sitting alone in a corner. They talked until the party broke up. Afterward, they continued at Childs Restaurant, where they stayed into the early morning hours.

Parker, or Billy as she called him, was unlike the men she knew. No subject was off limits to the intellectually daring, broad-minded journalist. By chance, they both lived near Washington Square, but to be sure she would see him again, she invited him to the opening of her play.

Excess Baggage premiered on December 26, 1927, allegedly the busiest night in Broadway history. In the story, vaudevillian Eddie Kane (Eric

Dressler) juggles while his wife Elsa McCoy (Hopkins) stands by to assist, claiming to be "excess baggage." Hoping to find her own success, Elsa auditions for a film and becomes a big star. Eddie quits and lives off Elsa until shame forces him back to the stage. One evening, his act appears to fail, but Elsa, who is in the audience, rescues him.[3]

One member of the cast, Doris Eaton, was already a stage veteran at age twenty-two, having first appeared in vaudeville with her sisters at seven years old. "I had one of my best roles in the 1927–28 season in a play called *Excess Baggage*," Eaton recalled many years later.[4] "I didn't have a close relationship with Miss Hopkins which isn't a reflection on her; I was the ingénue. It was a friendly relationship, but a distant one, nor did I do anything about it. I was polite like my mother taught me to be. . . . Miss Hopkins seemed to have a bright personality—when she came into the room, you knew she was there. I thought she was an excellent actress."[5]

Broadway critics concurred. Miriam's reviews for *Excess Baggage* were exceptional. According to one critic, she "would, of course, be irresistible in any part." The *New York Times* gushed that Miriam was "always beautiful, and her acting at all times showed finesse."[6]

Miriam was at an excellent time in her life, a period of high emotions. She was in a successful Broadway play and in love with a man she deemed to be intellectually and emotionally her equal. She was comfortable. But life has a way of shattering one's comfort zone.

One evening, on her way to the theater, Miriam and *Excess Baggage* costar Frances Goodrich were walking east from the subway on West Forty-Ninth Street. As they passed the Forrest Theatre (now the Eugene O'Neill Theatre) and were approaching the entrance to the connecting Forrest Hotel, they heard a rustling above them. Looking up, they saw a man hurtling toward them from the third floor. Charles Falke, the fifty-five-year-old manager of a New Jersey burlesque show, landed a few feet in front of them, narrowly missing crushing them.[7]

The women were taken to their dressing rooms at the Ritz and treated for shock. Upon reflection, Miriam saw this as an omen. It inspired her to make what many believed were two irrational life decisions: never to pass the Forrest Hotel (a promise she kept) and always to consult a psychic when making important decisions.

This near tragedy brought out her feelings for Billy. Could she be in love after a few months? The subject of marriage had come up, but there was a concern it would ruin their friendship. More importantly, both were still married to their estranged spouses. Billy would know about his French divorce in August. Miriam had yet to file.

When her *Excess Baggage* contract ended, Miriam boarded a train for Chicago to divorce Brandon Peters. On Friday, June 1, 1928, she appeared with attorney Milton Smith before Circuit Court Judge Thomas Lynch and cited three occasions of cruelty by Peters, who was in Australia performing in a play. The judge would announce his decision in a few days.

Smith knew his client was eager to remarry and counseled her against any precipitate steps. Whether Miriam didn't understand or didn't care is not clear, but she cabled Billy from the Chicago train station to meet her in Newark the following day. At the courthouse that morning, a magistrate secretly married them. They returned to New York and hid out at the Fifth Avenue Hotel, where Billy was living.[8]

The following Tuesday, a story appeared in the *Newark Star Eagle* revealing the couple's marriage. Billy faced the press alone to confirm the story, adding that Miriam had divorced Brandon Peters in Chicago (his pending French divorce was unknown to the American press).

On Wednesday, the couple sailed on the SS *De Grasse* for an extended European honeymoon. They would return in the fall, when, hopefully, Miriam would have a play.

In Chicago, the news of Miriam's overnight nuptials caught Milton Smith off guard. Aggravating the situation was her apparent impertinence, which infuriated Judge Lynch, who threatened to withhold his final judgment. Smith intervened, asking the court to sign the decree in a day or two when a transcript of the evidence was available.

Miriam believed she was free to marry Billy. Was she lying or just naive? In any event, the press put the story to good use. The Hearst papers took a lighthearted approach, running a cartoon showing Miriam torn from her bridegroom when they docked in France. Less spirited journalists and gossip columnists speculated that authorities would annul the marriage or file bigamy charges.

Billy's Paris attorney, Pierre Massie, was baffled, averring that he hadn't notified his client of the court's decision. Since it would be another two months until his divorce, his marriage to Phyllis Duganne was still valid. The Newark marriage was null.[9]

The so-called newlyweds were not concerned. They were having a great summer in Europe, reveling in discoveries that took them off the tourist lanes. Billy brought his typewriter and sent stories from pictur-esque old country gardens to the *Saturday Evening Post* while Miriam sketched scenes in pencil and pastel.

Miriam was discovering a new world that offered new views and experiences and broadened her mind. Patrick Kearney had exposed her to writers, poets, and intellects. According to Ruby, Billy "opened the world to her," teaching her to appreciate good paintings and excellent wines, among other things.[10]

One day in Monte Carlo, when Miriam was lounging in the crowded hotel lobby, gazing through the high bay windows at the blue waters of the Mediterranean, her thoughts were interrupted by a buzz of conversa-tion. People jumped to their feet and rushed to the door and windows. Miriam looked up and saw a chic Frenchwoman staring in the direction of the commotion with a bright, expectant face. "Why—what is it?" Mir-iam asked her in French.

"It's Constance Bennett—the famous American movie actress," the woman replied. "She's just now arriving. She's—" Her awed voice broke off as the crowd at the doorway parted to admit the famous actress and her entourage.

Miriam glanced about anxiously. Everyone was standing out of respect, or to get a better view. Not wanting to be conspicuous, Miriam stood as Bennett sashayed to the reverberation of enthusiastic applause. The "height of fame" was passing in front of her, the recognition she desired.

In New York, Miriam had some celebrity, but she wasn't in Bennett's league. Maybe in the lobby of the Waldorf, Miriam would be recognized, but not outside Manhattan. Nevertheless, she was a realist. She knew fame was fleeting. According to her worldview, lasting fame was for those who made a difference. "Fame?" Miriam contemplated in the early 1930s. "An actress is rarely famous. . . . And of all the actors and actresses in Hollywood today, how many will be remembered? Only Charlie Chaplin, Garbo, and Mary Pickford stand any chance of enduring fame. The rest of us are merely people who flit across the screen and then, often while we are still young, merge into living shadows."[11]

Was fame desirable while it lasted? It wasn't enjoyable unless one earned it, and actors sometimes took their successes too seriously. "No one ever became famous without sacrifice, struggles, and much effort," she naively believed. "Life would be much easier if one just ambled through. Success is worth being proud of it."[12]

To have success, she would have to be single-minded. She confided to Billy that in addition to her career, she wanted a baby. However, several doctors warned that pregnancy would be dangerous because of her childhood bout of rheumatic fever. Billy, who also wanted children, knew they could adopt. When he asked, "Well, why don't we?" she replied: "My career." He countered with, "Hang the career," but Miriam cautioned that she couldn't ignore "contracts and obligations."

Neither could she ignore her professional ambition. According to the newspapers, producers were casting plays in New York—and without her vying for them. Career oblivion awaited unless they returned at once. "Billy and the others urged me to relax," she would later say. "But I couldn't. And I was really very uncivil about it."[13]

Billy thought he had an excellent reason for lingering in Europe: He was broke. One night in Antibes, as he was about to cable his agent for an advance, Miriam placed her last few francs at the baccarat table of a local casino. "I watched as long as I could," Billy recalled, "and finally I couldn't bear it any longer." The miracle that happens in movies happened for them; Miriam won enough to pay their passage back to the States. The honeymoon was over. On September 20, 1928, the couple rushed to Marseilles, where they boarded the SS *President Harrison* for their return trip.[14]

It was fortunate they did. The day before arriving in New York harbor, Miriam received word that Dixie, age fifty-six, had died from complications of a hip infection. Miriam was inconsolable. Dixie had been a father figure, and despite his initial reluctance to help her, he was supportive of her success. Attended by two hundred mourners, the funeral was held the following day at Campbell's on Broadway and West Sixty-Sixth Street. Mildred took Dixie's body to Bainbridge and laid her son near his father at Oak City Cemetery.

While Billy searched for an apartment, Miriam accepted an invitation from George Cukor to return to Rochester for his winter season at the Temple Theatre. Their premiere play was *Excess Baggage*, her Broadway success from earlier that spring. The cast included a talented young ingenue who had impressed Cukor in the previous summer's production of *Broadway*. Cukor tried finding Bette Davis other parts, but the schedule was full, so he invited her for the winter season. Rochester would be Davis's first encounter with Miriam.

"Miriam Hopkins had the prettiest blond hair I'd ever seen," Davis recalled in her autobiography, "and she'd drive us all crazy with envy when she'd emerge from a shower and simply toss her golden curls dry. She seemed oblivious, but she knew what she was doing. I was to learn later she always knew what she was doing. It sort of kept all of us who didn't have golden curls in our places."[15]

The players knew Davis had talent, but she often resisted Cukor's direction. "She had her own ideas," Cukor said about Davis, "and though she only did bits and ingénue roles, she didn't hesitate to express them." When Cukor disapproved of some move or action, Davis argued, never admitting fault. Miriam and fellow actor Louis Calhern resented Davis's stubbornness and complained to Cukor.[16]

Davis had complaints of her own. She claimed Miriam's scene-stealing—monopolizing the spotlight, cutting short another's lines and seizing the center stage—was a compulsion.

Excess Baggage opened on October 15, 1928, to good reviews. "Of course, one was hardly surprised that the performance and production, having been supervised by George Cukor, were, in general, high grade," reported a local newspaper. Another singled out Davis as "a blonde slip of a miss." Miriam was praised for her "youthful charm and beauty" in a "role that allowed her to display the varied resources of her acting ability."[17]

When *Excess Baggage* completed its run, Miriam returned to New York. Davis remained in Rochester with Cukor and the Temple Players for several plays, including the audience favorite *The Squall* and *The Man Who Came Back*.

In her last production for Cukor, *Yellow*, Davis played Louis Calhern's girlfriend. Calhern, who was much taller and was thirteen years older, complained that his leading lady looked "more like my kid than my mistress." Davis agreed and repeated Calhern's remarks to Cukor. According to Davis, a stage manager informed her during final rehearsals that *Yellow* would be her last play.[18]

"Why?" she asked.

"Cukor says you won't be needed anymore," he replied curtly.

Although Davis's dismissal came several weeks after Miriam had left Rochester, several Bette Davis biographers have blamed the *Excess Baggage* leading lady for Davis's firing from Cukor's company. The assumption came from undocumented sources claiming that Miriam was bisexual and was attracted to Davis.

According to one story, Miriam allegedly patted Davis's backside and made an offhand remark about her "beautiful neck." When Davis resisted her advances, Miriam was outraged. Days later during a rehearsal, Miriam stopped the play mid-scene and accused Davis of stepping on her lines. "That bitch doesn't know her place!" Miriam screamed at Cukor. "I'm the star of this show—not that little nobody." A dramatic response, even for Miriam.[19]

The origin of this nonsense may have been a 1970s *Playboy* interview in which Bette Davis alluded that her dismissal came when she refused to sleep with the right people: "I didn't live up to what was expected in those days of a stock company ingénue, who had other duties; you know what I'm talking about. Socializing. Socializing very seriously, let us say, with people in the company. That was just not my cup of tea."[20]

Whether Davis's interpretation was right we'll never know; she never named the person (or persons) she was pressured to "socialize" with or why Cukor would go along with it.

In truth, it was Cukor's business partner George Kondolf—not Miriam Hopkins—who made unwanted advances toward Davis. "Kondolf felt that every ingénue who came into the company had to go to bed with him," explained Benny Baker, who played Frank in *Excess Baggage*. "It was part of his routine." According to Baker, Davis's rejection bruised Kondolf's ego when he saw how she partied with cast members and had her suitors.[21]

Over the years, Davis's story changed, and she claimed George Cukor fired her. Cukor later affirmed, "I did not fire Bette. She insists I did, and says I had a low opinion of her then. Somehow she got it into her head that I sacked her on the spot."[22]

Davis, however, would remain adamant that Cukor was responsible for her first professional setback. As for her future with Miriam, it was unrelated to whatever took place in Rochester.[23]

When Miriam returned to New York, she learned that her divorce from Brandon Peters and her marriage to Billy remained in limbo. "Thank heavens we are not lawyers," Billy told reporters. "Thank heavens we have nothing to do with the law—that is, any more than necessary. Our marriage is quite all right so far as we are concerned. We are satisfied. Who should care?"[24]

They might have cared had authorities arrested them for bigamy. But the Chicago judge ultimately granted Miriam's divorce from Brandon Peters. There's no evidence that Billy and Miriam had another wedding to replace the bogus ceremony in New Jersey. They never resolved the issue.

By the time she returned to New York, Billy had found an apartment in a quaint three-story stone building at 108 Waverly Place, in their old neighborhood near Washington Square. In her third-floor studio, Miriam scattered Persian rugs and black-and-silver floor cushions to complement the deep-cushioned divan and armchairs.[25]

It was here at a loud and lavish party that she first met Ernst Lubitsch. With his lit cigar clenched firmly in his jaw, the German import who had directed box office hits starring Pola Negri and Mary Pickford would play Chopin on a grand piano for hours.

Many of Miriam's lifelong friendships were born or nurtured at these parties, including her friendship with Dorothy Parker, screenwriter and playwright Anita Loos, who had fired her from *Gentlemen Prefer Blondes*, and future fellow Paramount contract-player Kay Francis. Guests mingled for hours as they discussed politics, acting, writing, art, and the juicy gossip of the season. Waverly Place became Miriam's university. In these surroundings, her interests expanded and matured.

While her social life thrived, her career was at a standstill. Compounding matters, the European honeymoon had gobbled much of her savings, forcing them to live off Billy's meager earnings as a short-story writer. An opportunity arose when producer Bela Blau showed an interest in *Week-End*, a three-act comedy play Billy had written. As for Miriam, she appeared in a short talking film based on an Edna Ferber story, *The Home Girl*, at Paramount's East Coast Astoria Studios. Her costar was the future minor Hollywood leading man Otto Kruger, and the popular Vincent Lopez Orchestra. Miriam had resisted doing "the movies," thinking they were "beneath" her, but it paid well for a few day's work.[26]

When *The Home Girl* was released, producer Mack Sennett, best known for his hundreds of comedy shorts, saw it and remembered Miriam's stage shows. Impressed with how well she photographed, he offered to sign her as one of his "Bathing Beauties," which was nearing the end of its popularity. Miriam had good experiences on *The Home Girl*, but it wasn't enough to convince her to leave the theater, even though films were beginning to talk. She considered "Sennett's nonsense," but realizing only a handful of Bathing Beauties moved on to successful film careers (e.g., Gloria Swanson, Phyllis Haver), she declined his offer.

Not to matter. Within days, Miriam's agent, Lyman Brown, found her a part in *Cane Crop*, a play by Bates Hunter. "Here is an opportunity to see and hear one of New York's favorite young leading women," the *Hart-*

ford Courant announced. But within a week, she had a counter-offer for the lead in a new play, *Flight*, and gave notice to *Cane Crop*'s producers.[27]

Flight, about a modern flapper who falls for an old-fashioned young aviator, opened at Broadway's Longacre Theatre on February 18, 1929. Critics hated the play, but the trustworthy *Time* magazine expounded on its few merits, which were "thanks to a brilliant performance by actress Miriam Hopkins, who seems to become a better actress with every new play while growing not one whit less personable." *Flight* closed after forty performances.[28]

On April 15, Miriam appeared in the Czech playwright František Langer's three-act play *The Camel through the Needle's Eye* at the Martin Beck Theatre (now the Al Hirschfeld Theatre). Philip Moeller directed the Theatre Guild production with an excellent cast, including future big-screen names Claude Rains, Henry Travers, and Helen Westley, who received the highest tribute playing Miriam's crabby, disreputable mother. This time, Miriam received halfhearted praise. The *New York Times*, for one, opined that although she lacked in variety, "she gives, on the whole, an understanding, easy performance."[29]

Proving popular, *The Camel through the Needle's Eye* ran for 195 performances, but Miriam left the play in August when she accepted the female lead in the London production of *The Bachelor Father*. The Edmund Childs Carpenter comedy would open at the West End's Globe Theatre (now the Gielgud Theatre) on September 29, 1929. It was a success on Broadway, with June Walker and husband Geoffrey Kerr in the starring roles. Except for Walker and Kerr, the original members of the New York cast, including character actor C. Aubrey Smith, were appearing in the London production.

While Miriam prepared, Billy remained in New York polishing the final draft of his play, *Week-End,* scheduled to open in October. Billy would cross the Atlantic in time to be with his wife for her London stage debut.

On September 20, several days before the premiere of *The Bachelor Father*, London's stock market crashed when British authorities jailed several investors for fraud and forgery. A few weeks earlier, in New York, the stock exchange had reached a "permanently high plateau" according to economist Irving Fisher. But then, two days before the London crash, New York stock prices fell. The market was volatile, but economists on both sides of the Atlantic hoped for a recovery.

The restlessness of the London market didn't keep audiences away from *The Bachelor Father*'s premiere, yet many critics had reservations about the play—"an example of the worst taste," wrote one reviewer. Nevertheless, Miriam's performance impressed one London critic, who called her "a discovery." The *Daily Mail* enthused, "She is a most accomplished actress, bubbling over with fun and natural charm. I hope she may be persuaded to stay with us in London." Despite the overall lukewarm reviews, *The Bachelor Father* ran for more than three months.[30]

In the meantime, back in New York, weeks of uneven investing in the Stock Market came to a climax on October 29, 1929, when investors traded millions of shares of stocks. Panic set in. When it was over two days later, the market had lost over $30 billion. Miriam read about the crisis in the London papers. Both she and Billy were living job-to-job, as most Americans were, so they had little invested in the market and little to lose. However, Miriam worried about the Broadway investors and their ability to bounce back. How would the "crash" affect the financing of new shows, and what opportunities would there be for actors?

When Miriam's contract on *The Bachelor Father* ended, the play was still attracting audiences, but she was anxious to return to the States. The Parkers sailed to New York from Le Havre on November 20. Although the look of the city greeting them five days later was the same, the spirit was different. Moreover, surprises awaited them. The owner of their Waverly Place apartment had lost the building in the crash, and the new owners canceled their lease. They found a place around the corner at 46 Washington Square South.[31]

While they were in London, Billy's play, *Week-End*, with Vivienne Osborne and Warren William, opened. The reviews were lukewarm. "If Mr. Parker were more temperate in his marshalling of tribulations," wrote the *New York Times,* "if he were brisker about his story and clearer in establishing the motives, *Week-End* might not seem to be rather muddled and artificial in the last scenes. But Mr. Parker, who is a short story writer, spins amusing dialogue whenever he lets himself go."[32] *Week-End* closed after eleven performances.

For Miriam, it would be three months before Broadway beckoned again, this time in L. Lawrence Weber's *Ritzy* at the Longacre Theatre. A comedy in three acts by Viva Tattersall and Sidney Toler, who would gain fame as the screen's Charlie Chan, *Ritzy* was not well received. Although hindered by what critics called "artificially contrived," the principals were singled out for praise. "Ernest Truex and Miriam Hopkins," wrote one critic, "are such excellent actors that they have taken a perfectly worthless play and made of it good entertainment."[33] But "good entertainment" wasn't good enough. *Ritzy* ran for a mere thirty-two performances.

Miriam was in dire need of a solid Broadway hit. Then, her agent Lyman Brown worked out a deal with the Philadelphia Theater Association for her to appear in Aristophanes's Greek comedy, *Lysistrata*. Author and critic Gilbert Seldes, who was also the father of future Broadway actress Marian Seldes, put his touch on this ribald classic, giving it a 1930s flavor.

Norman Bel Geddes, the play's theatrical designer, and its director molded the play about a group of women banding together to withhold sex from their warrior husbands and lovers until they agree to give up fighting. The fun begins when some less abstinence-inclined maidens arrange secret trysts.

Fay Bainter, who some thirty years later would costar with Miriam in *The Children's Hour*, was cast as Lysistrata. Behind her was an impressive supporting cast, including Miriam's *Ritzy* co-star Ernest Truex as the comic servant Kinesias, and the rotund Sydney Greenstreet, later of *The Maltese Falcon* fame, as the president of the Senate.

Miriam was ignorant about classical Greek drama ("you might say it was Greek to me") and had no interest in the play. She told Bel Geddes it would run less than a week in Philadelphia, so she'd rather not do it. Bel Geddes, who was impressed by her brief but memorable performance in *Cane Crop*, offered her an incredible $700 a week (nearly $10,000 a week today), but the part was small, providing but a few lines. The pay was tempting, but she felt guilty when so many people were standing in bread lines because they didn't have enough to eat. Besides, the high salary for such a small role made no sense. She suggested that the leader of the chorus take her lines, and they could cut her part. Bel Geddes admired her civic responsibility but believed she was perfect for the role. He assured her the oversexed Kalonika was an extraordinary character and persuaded her to stay.

This change forced Gilbert Seldes to rearrange Aristophanes's two-thousand-year-old play to satisfy the whims of twenty-six-year-old Miriam Hopkins. He enlarged her part, taking extra bits of comedy and stealing lines from a handful of characters until Miriam was confident the role was worthy of her talents. "It's a lot of fun playing the part," Miriam acknowledged, adding she made "no attempt to be ultra-classical in it. I try simply to be natural; for I figure she [Kalonika] is a very real girl, with strong impulses."[34]

The city's cultural elite and social leaders attended the sold-out premiere at Philadelphia's historic Walnut Street Theatre. The following day, J. Brooks Atkinson wrote in the *New York Times*, "To judge by the robust performance of *Lysistrata* . . . Aristophanes deserves his classroom reputation as a comic writer."

In New York, *Lysistrata* opened at the 44th Street Theatre on June 5, 1930, running for 252 performances. "Well, that should have been a lesson to me," the naysayer earning $700 each week said. "*Lysistrata* ran a year, and I bought a fur coat and furnished a flat."[35]

For the Broadway production, Fay Bainter left because of prior obligations. Violet Kemble Cooper took over the title role and earned excellent notices. The bawdy nonsense of the play tickled the public's funny bone. "Cries of 'Bravo' were to be heard frequently in applause of some of the comedy's more unrestrained freedoms," wrote one reviewer, "and the occasion may be described as a jolly riot."[36]

To Miriam's surprise, the part she wanted to discard because it was too small was a critical success. Critic Robert Garland sang her praises, calling Miriam "a joy," and noted she brought "an air of honesty to an age which, in spite of our what-the-hell-do-we-careness, is in need of."[37]

Besides a fur coat and a furnished flat, *Lysistrata* opened doors for the next phase of Miriam Hopkins's career. Thanks to an ancient Greek play, she would achieve the international acclaim she desired.

4

Of Paramount Importance

Appearing in *Lysistrata* exposed Miriam to many famous show business people. Broadway producer Lee Shubert offered her the lead in the stage production *The King's Forty-Horsepower Motor*. Rehearsals would begin in late August, so Miriam continued in *Lysistrata* until then.

Following the release of Warner Bros.'s blockbuster *The Jazz Singer*, which had scenes of synchronized dialogue, motion pictures learned to talk. Hollywood urgently needed trained stage actors to replace (costly) silent film stars whose voices didn't match their screen personas.

Walter Wanger, the head of Paramount Pictures's East Coast Astoria Studios, was raiding the Broadway stages. By 1928, he had signed Fredric March, Tallulah Bankhead, Claudette Colbert, Ginger Rogers, Herbert Marshall, Jeanne Eagels, Helen Morgan, Kay Francis, and several others.

After seeing a performance of *Lysistrata*, Wanger was pleased with Miriam's risqué performance, as were most of New York's audiences. He offered her a Paramount contract, but she refused. "I wasn't a bit crazy about going into pictures," she told a fan magazine some years later. "When studios first asked me to take tests in New York, I said, 'I am making more money on the stage than I can spend. So what is the inducement?'" Besides, Miriam believed the stage was superior to films. Her popularity was at its highest, and job offers were coming in for important Broadway shows.[1]

Wanger returned with an offer of $1,000 a week for four weeks. To sweeten the deal, they would film her scenes during the day so she could be in *Lysistrata* at night. Wanger had her attention. Although it would be demanding work, she could stay in the theater. With nothing to lose, except some sleep, and an extra $1,000 a week to gain, she accepted Wanger's offer, and the offer from Shubert.

On June 21, 1930, Miriam signed a contract to appear in *The King's*

Forty-Horsepower Motor for $700 a week. Rehearsals would start on August 23, and then they would go on the road for three weeks before opening at Broadway's Bijou Theatre in November.

Four days later, she signed a one-picture deal with Paramount for $1,000 a week and $500 for "rehearsals and/or tests of vocal recordings and photography." Filming was guaranteed to be completed on schedule so she could start *Motor* rehearsals.[2]

Miriam's first feature film was a remake of the 1925 silent film *The Best People,* starring Warner Baxter and Ester Ralston, now renamed *Fast and Loose.* Part of her contractual agreement included Billy contributing to the dialogue, though he received no credit.

In the story, two thoroughly spoiled siblings (Hopkins and Henry Wadsworth) have been prize scandal-sheet stories for some time. Hopkins is engaged to a British peer but falls in love with an automobile mechanic (Charles Starrett). Wadsworth, for his part, horrifies his parents when he announces his intention to marry a chorus girl (up-and-coming Paramount leading lady Carole Lombard). In the end, police raid the nightclub, but all ends happily.

Filming began on the Astoria lot on July 21, 1930. Knowing how, in her words, "well-heeled" film actors were, she was ashamed to drive through the front gate in Billy's old, beat-up car, so she hired a taxi driver to "do this thing in style." They drove to the studio, but the "dear boob didn't even know enough to hop out and open the car door." Miriam had to tell him, with the gateman listening.[3]

For four weeks, Miriam's schedule was rigorous. Arising at six o'clock in the morning, she was on the Astoria lot by nine o'clock until filming ended at six o'clock that evening. Then, she would rush back to Manhattan dressed and in full makeup for an eight o'clock curtain call for *Lysistrata* at the 44th Street Theatre. If everything went well, she would be in bed by midnight to begin the routine again the next morning.

On the first day of filming, Miriam and her co-star, Charles Starrett, were trucked out to Long Island Sound for a swimming scene. Miriam wasn't the best swimmer, and when she had to make love underwater, she was so nervous she "didn't sleep for days after it was over."[4]

Nervousness was a part of the insomnia problem, but that evening she developed an ear infection that left her bedridden for three days. The *Fast and Loose* schedule was rearranged to cover for her, while her understudy went on in her place in the play.[5]

Also, she was overwhelmed with insecurities. She told everyone, including Paramount president Adolph Zukor, that she was uncertain whether films were the right career path for her. Zukor smiled and listened patiently before suggesting she should wait to see how well the public responded to her.

Much of her insecurity was about her looks. She had flyaway, silver-blonde, thistle-down hair, and her eyebrows and lashes were so light they disappeared under the bright lights. She needed help.

At the time, Paramount's red-headed Nancy Carroll was about to receive a Best Actress Academy Award nomination for *The Devil's Holiday*. Miriam felt simpatico with Carroll and asked how she could be photogenic. Miriam had experience on the stage, but films were not her forte.

Nancy Carroll, who had been in a dozen films the prior two years, became her mentor. Besides makeup, she taught Miriam about lighting, camera angles, and how to use them to her advantage. Moreover, they had similar character traits. Carroll had a reputation for being short-tempered and difficult to please, refusing roles she found unworthy of her talents. She taught Miriam the importance of using the best the studio had to offer—whether it was the best properties, roles, or directors.

Miriam never forgot Carroll's kindness. She would repay it going forward, helping future actors break into the business. Ironically, by mid-1932 Carroll was gone from Paramount and was no longer considered a star.

When it premiered, *Fast and Loose* charmed some critics. The *New York Times'* Mordaunt Hall, for one, called Miriam's performance "most pleasing as the impudent and charming Marion," while the *Los Angeles Times* raved, "Miss Hopkins, who is not yet a past mistress of the art of acting, reveals such definite promise and such a slim, golden, Jeanne Eagels-like fascination that in no time at all her name should be a household necessity."[6]

Laurence Reid, a *Motion Picture News* critic, gave the film a negative review but said it proved Miriam's "beauty is filmable and that her stage technique may be well adapted to the screen if she persists and is provided with better, far better vehicles."[7]

Hours after finishing *Fast and Loose*, Miriam gave her final performance in *Lysistrata*. Rehearsals on *The King's Forty-Horsepower Motor* started the following day, but in two weeks she developed an ear abscess and was admitted to the Alice Fuller LeRoy Sanitarium on East Sixty-

First Street. According to Billy, the doctors said her sickness was due to a weakened immune system from "working before the camera by day and playing in a show by night."[8]

Shubert approved a Bermuda vacation before opening the play he retitled *Everybody's Secret*. It would go on the road to Baltimore the following week and Miriam's understudy, Jane Bramley, would stand in for her until she returned. But Shubert wasn't pleased with Bramley's performance and wanted Miriam back to take over the role. "Understudy opened," cabled Lyman Brown. "Shubert wants *you* immediately."

Miriam wired that her ship would dock in New York on the following Sunday, October 9. Brown said the show would open two days later in Washington, with the New York premiere following. It sounded "impossible," Miriam responded, but she wanted "success both for show and myself." She urged Shubert to have Bramley continue in Washington while she would appear in Great Neck, New York, on October 18, her twenty-eighth birthday. The switch would allow time for rehearsals. The play opened at the Ethel Barrymore Theatre under the new title *His Majesty's Car*.[9]

His Majesty's Car was based on a Hungarian play about a female bank clerk (Hopkins) living in a small central European kingdom who gains fame and fortune on idle gossip that she is the monarch's mistress. Critics hated the play. The *New York American*'s Robert Garland, for one, called it "no great shakes as comedy." Even the leading lady felt their disdain. "Miss Miriam Hopkins, late of *Lysistrata,* is cute and little else as Lily Dornik, the one mistress of song or story who manages to eat her cake and have it, too."[10] After the reviews, the play continued for twelve performances—the run of the advance sales—and closed.

Lysistrata, however, was still popular with audiences, and the actress that inherited Kalonika was leaving, giving Miriam the opportunity to return. Within days, she rejoined the cast, but there was a new leading lady, the veteran actress Blanche Yurka. Miriam was unprepared for Miss Yurka and her unique method of acting.

In one scene, Lysistrata catches Kalonika feigning pregnancy using the helmet of the goddess Athena hidden under her robe. The script called for Yurka to chase Miriam back through the city gates. Once she catches her, she smacks her on the rear with the helmet.

As Miriam tried to flee, Yurka supplemented the scripted smack with two or more resonant ones on her backside. The audience reacted with loud chuckles. In each performance, the blows to her rear grew in both passion and number. José Limón, who played a guard, recalled that actors standing in the wings would "count, speculate, and lay bets on the next performance, and watch Yurka, a hefty woman, enjoying herself tremendously, and Hopkins's discomfiture and mounting indignation as she rubbed her burning posterior on her way to the dressing room."

One evening, Miriam had had enough. After the scene had played, she waited for Yurka backstage. "Miss Yurka, don't you dare do that again. I won't have it," she screamed at the expert actress. "But darling," Yurka responded, "it finishes the scene so beautifully."

Miriam remained unmoved. Her behind was black-and-blue from her "sadistic treatment," and she threatened to file a complaint with management. Limón recalled that Yurka was obliged to cease her nightly attacks. "Thereafter, there was to be only a light, anemic tap on Miss Hopkins's bottom during her flight back to the Acropolis, and the play was robbed of one of its most delightful moments."[11]

Miriam's return to *Lysistrata* was brief. Perhaps it was Blanche Yurka's beatings, but a month later she moved across town as Mimi in the Broadway revival of Arthur Schnitzler's 1893 play *The Affairs of Anatol*. Bela Blau, the Hungarian-born producer, impresario, and theater manager, shortened its title to *Anatol* for its opening at the Lyceum Theatre on January 16, 1931.

The talented cast included the expert stage actress Patricia Collinge and in the title role the Austrian-born eventual Academy Award winner Joseph Schildkraut. Critics singled out Collinge's performance, but Miriam's hilarious Mimi was a standout.

"An uproariously funny splash of animal life and color, brilliantly vulgar, disarmingly young, frank and greedy," wrote Robert Littell of the *New York World*. "This Mimi ought to be kept permanently in a cage, so we can all go when we are feeling depressed and watch her gobble up the oysters, or fall asleep heavily in the middle of the party, or dig into the soufflé with her eyes still streaming with tears."[12]

The unexpected death of Mildred Dickinson Cutter, who had passed her independent temperament to her granddaughter, came after the New Year, during rehearsals for *Anatol*. Miriam's absence at the funeral was evident to all; Ellen was embarrassed and furious. Miriam understood the concept of "family duty," but another concept, "the show must go on," took precedence. Still, with nothing to keep her mother in Bainbridge,

Miriam, now financially stable, moved Ellen to Queens—far enough away from Manhattan that she didn't have to see her daily.[13]

In February, Miriam left the cast of *Anatol* when Paramount offered her another one-picture deal with director Ernst Lubitsch, renowned for the sophisticated, "European" flair of his films. She jumped at the opportunity. "Lubitsch changed her whole attitude towards pictures," Billy would later say. "The first film had been work and grief; this became an enchanting adventure."[14]

Miriam first met Lubitsch when he entertained guests on a baby grand piano at her loud parties on Waverly Place. She was captivated by Lubitsch, a little man with a dark, cherubic face, a lank strand of black hair hanging over his right eye, and a big cigar rolling restlessly from one side of his mouth to the other.

The Smiling Lieutenant, based on the Oscar Straus operetta *A Waltz Dream*, was set in Vienna, where amorous Lieutenant Niki (Maurice Chevalier) falls in love with girls' orchestra leader Franzi (Claudette Colbert). Miriam played the prim daughter of a visiting Central European monarch, who mistakenly believes Niki's wink at Franzi is for *her.* Only marriage could rectify the ocular offense.

Lubitsch had a unique directorial style that publicists called "The Lubitsch Touch." The phrase suggests the delicacy he gave to scenes that became the showpieces of his work. First making sure he knew his actors thoroughly, their capacities and temperaments, Lubitsch would demonstrate to them what to do, but in their way. He would meticulously rehearse his actors, so each scene ran smoothly. "Rehearsals. Everyone quiet!" he would announce. "This is a take."

If something went wrong, he growled, "Cut!" Typically, everyone would laugh and begin the scene again. If Lubitsch saw an opportunity for improvement, he would do another take, sometimes shooting a scene eighteen or twenty times until he found the nuance he wanted.

It was no different on *The Smiling Lieutenant.* Lubitsch would say, "Now Miriam, try that line without the 'Oh.'" Finally, he would be satisfied. "Cut," he ordered. "This is okay for me." Then, Lubitsch repeated the scene for the French version. Hardly fluent in French (she had three years in high school), Miriam rehearsed her lines parrot-like, fearing she couldn't compete with the French-born Colbert and Chevalier. Instead of repeating the words slowly, she had to do it "rat-a-tat-tat just like the others." Paramount had a French coach on the set, but there were still mistakes. "But they [the French audiences] will think it charming," Chevalier told her.[15]

Miriam and Chevalier had a good rapport. Many believed they were *too* amiable off the set, perhaps enjoying a brief affair during the six-week shoot.

As for Lubitsch, he was attracted to blondes, so it was no surprise he favored Miriam over Colbert, a fact Miriam took full advantage of. Ever the southern belle, Miriam managed to charm Lubitsch while keeping him at arm's length. Around town, they frequented the director's favorite Second Avenue restaurant where they supped on calves' brains and wine.

But to those around them, Miriam appeared to use Lubitsch. John Engstead, a photographer who rarely said anything positive about anyone, told author John Kobal that "Lubitsch never saw through Miriam Hopkins."[16]

That is unlikely. While Miriam was an expert at getting what she wanted, Lubitsch was an intelligent man. Lubitsch liked her bubbly personality, but he also believed in her talent, a conviction that was justified. It's doubtful their relationship went further than harmless flirtations, but if Lubitsch enjoyed himself along the way, so be it.

The director used this flirtatious behavior to his advantage while playing referee for Miriam and Claudette Colbert. Six years earlier, Miriam had replaced Colbert in the Broadway play *Puppets*, so there may have been some bad feelings. In any event, Colbert knew that despite her top billing opposite Chevalier, Miriam was stealing the picture. She resented the intrusions and sensed she might end up a footnote in the finished film. As minor differences arose, an altercation seemed imminent.

On the day the "Jazz Up Your Lingerie" number was rehearsed, music arranger Johnny Green played on the sidelines while Colbert went through the motions on a dummy piano. Miriam sat beside her, listening attentively. Colbert's temper flared. "Jesus, Miriam! You're not doing much to help."

"I'm doing what I'm supposed to," Miriam calmly replied.

"Like hell you are!"[17]

Lubitsch interrupted the argument but tried not to discourage their dislike for each other because it suited their characters. The rehearsal ended with both women exchanging glaring looks and Colbert walking off the set.

Then, in the princess's bedroom, the two women prepare to have a slapping match before throwing themselves on the bed, sobbing. Lubitsch called for silence. As the scene begins, Miriam admires a piece of clothing Colbert is holding. In response, Colbert, fingering Miriam's dress, asks her:

"Who bought that for you?"

"Not Niki."

"I'm sure he didn't. Niki has taste."[18]

Miriam paused, and slapped Colbert hard, delivering the whack with such force that the sound booth technician lowered his receiver to record the blow that followed. Recovering, Colbert pulled a right and slapped Miriam twice as hard, almost knocking her on her rear end. Both women fell on the bed sobbing.

During rehearsals, rumors spread that after each had slapped the other, Miriam came back with a second smack that jarred Colbert, and she forgot to react. Coming to her senses, she evened the score with another crack to Miriam's face, leaving a bright handprint showing through her makeup. Stunned, both women burst into tears and flung themselves on the bed, per the script. Once Lubitsch yelled "Cut!" they noticed an audience had gathered on the catwalk above, watching the entire scene. Slowly, they walked off in opposite directions to their dressing rooms.

Both women tried to dispel the inevitable stories about how they couldn't get along. "Absurd," affirmed Colbert. When asked, Miriam coolly told a reporter she liked Colbert "very much" and enjoyed working with her.[19]

Nine years later, Colbert reminisced about the slapping session: "When Miriam Hopkins and I made *The Smiling Lieutenant*, there were scenes in which we slapped each other. The stories started. Not long ago Miriam told me that for years afterward, she had to explain that we *had* to fight [in] the picture."[20]

Billy's contributing dialogue on *Fast and Loose* earned him his first original screenplay credit for Paramount, *Honor Among Lovers*. Directed by Dorothy Arzner and starring Claudette Colbert and Fredric March, the film received mixed reviews. According to the *Los Angeles Times*, "up to a certain point, the piece appears to be one of the smartest of the season. Then comes the let-down. Cleverness gives way to triteness."[21]

The tepid reception of *Honor Among Lovers* and the failure of his play *Week-End* the year before were blows to Billy's pride. He doubted his talent, and he feared Miriam was committed neither to him nor their marriage. Her success in *Lysistrata* thrilled him, but he was bothered her focus lay strictly on *her* career.

Miriam, too, considered Billy unsupportive. "When I was reading for a new dramatic part in those beginning days," Miriam later recalled, "and being very upset or distraught if my lines were not good, Billy would say to me, 'Why worry? What if they are poor? The show is a dud, anyway.' Now what I needed and wanted was someone to say, 'The lines may be insignificant and stupid, but it's the way you read them that matters.'"[22]

By Miriam's admission, she loved Billy, but she suspected he was cheating on her. Paramount executive Walter Wanger saw *Honor Among Lovers* and believed Billy had promise, so he asked him to collaborate on a screenplay with *Vogue* and *The New Yorker* contributor Lois Long, the wife of cartoonist and sometime playwright Peter Arno.

"I thought she was a bitch," Long told author George Eells years later. "She went around saying, wasn't it nice Billy was having an affair with such a nice girl! Oh my God, I thought Arno would hear about it. He was trying out a play in Philadelphia. She kept repeating it."[23]

The script collaboration with Long never happened, but because of *Honor Among Lovers*, RKO offered Billy a contract. Accepting would mean moving to Hollywood. All these changes caused Miriam's marriage to fall apart. Several gossips claimed the affair with Chevalier was to blame, but others said the relationship had run its course. In any event, Billy needed a break, so he accepted RKO's offer.

They separated but kept it private, telling just a few friends. They met one last time before Billy left for the coast. Afterward, from the dining room of the Algonquin Hotel, a distraught Miriam called several friends, asking them to join her because she was "feeling blue," and they were drinking champagne.[24]

That evening, Billy hosted a party at Tony's restaurant. Lois Long was there, and as they were "getting all the credit" for having an affair, Billy asked her, "What about it?" Long explained she was faithful to Arno when she was in New York, but in a couple of months she would be in California, so maybe . . . He shook his head. He had someone there, but he wouldn't name names.[25]

The next day, Billy left for the West Coast on the Twentieth Century Limited. On his way, he sent a telegram to Long and playfully asked, "Meet me in St. Louis?"[26]

Meanwhile, *The Smiling Lieutenant* was receiving positive reviews.

"The Princess is Miriam Hopkins," wrote the *Dallas Morning News*, "a blonde from better-Broadway casts, who brings to the screen an interesting face, Constance Bennett's quizzical look, and a custom-built body. Her voice and diction are excellent, and there is nothing to keep her from a dominant position in the industry."[27]

Based on her success, Miriam signed a five-year contract with Paramount in May for $1,500 (nearly $24,000 today) a week. On the downside, persistent rumors spread that Astoria Studios were closing and all productions would transfer to the West Coast. Paramount representatives claimed the reports were "without foundation," while Adolph Zukor had "nothing to say" about it.[28]

The rumors worried her since she had signed her contract assuming she could appear in plays in-between film commitments. She had her answer a few days later; her next picture, *The Man I Killed*, would be made in Hollywood with Lubitsch. She wanted to work with the director again but wasn't pleased to be leaving New York, so she confronted Paramount executive and cofounder Jesse Lasky, who was visiting the corporate offices. Miriam warned that if she didn't like Hollywood, she would return to New York. Lasky, though affable, assured her she would *not* because she had a long-term contract. Miriam respected, and liked, Lasky, and she promised to honor her commitment but asked that they consider her Broadway ambitions. Lasky assured her that neither he nor Paramount would interfere with her stage aspirations so long as they didn't impede her film assignments.

She wasn't willing to abandon the theater. Her career was at a place where she could read the plays she wanted, and besides, she didn't get "the kick out of pictures" that the theater provided her. "But it's hardly fair to compare the two," she reasoned, saying that compared to "hearing phonograph music" the talkies were "sort of canned and second-hand emotion."[29]

Having no choice, "with the equipment, the cameras, the electrical light bulbs and so forth," she was shipped to California. She had to go.[30]

Until then, she hid in her Washington Square duplex with her maid, Cassie, and Jerry, a wire-haired terrier, a birthday gift from Billy, with whom she kept in touch through telephone calls, telegrams, and letters. The emotional wounds were healing, and a new friendship had formed between the exes that would result in a stronger bond. During their interactions, Billy told Miriam about the women he dated, and she spoke fondly of the men in her life.

When Billy learned Paramount was sending her to Hollywood, he proposed that they be roommates. He was leasing a quaint replica of a German cottage at the foot of fashionable Whitley Heights, but now he would search for a larger house in the Hollywood Hills.

Word spread among her New York friends that she was leaving. Bennett Cerf, who was now overseeing the book publisher Random House, planned a blowout going away party at their Fifth Avenue offices the evening before her departure. Miriam invited her friends and Cerf invited his, and these friends brought guests that were unknown to either of them.

Harry Stoner, Miriam's artist pal was there, as was photographer Carl Van Vechten and actresses Katherine Wilson (*An American Tragedy*) and Lily Cahill (*Lovely Lady*). An acquaintance of Cerf's from Havana brought a twelve-piece rumba band that played "as loudly and continuously as possible." The low ceilings of the office exaggerated the clamor, adding to the cocktail consumption. By midnight, the intoxicated party guests had moved several blocks away to the basement swimming pool of the then stylish Shelton Hotel.[31]

The next morning, exhausted, sleepless, and hungover, Cerf escorted Miriam to Grand Central Station, where she boarded the Twentieth Century Limited to a new life on the West Coast.

5

Hollywood

Miriam's train pulled into Pasadena's Santa Fe Station on Monday, June 8, 1931. On the same train were Paramount contract players: actress-singer Jeanette MacDonald and Peggy Shannon, a Clara Bow type who would have a minor career in the early 1930s. Both had been called to the West Coast to make pictures as well.

Miriam, who had been no farther west than Denver, marveled at how much brighter the sun was in Pasadena than in New York. A suntanned Billy greeted her as she stepped from the Chief dressed in black crepe with white organdy trimmings and a black hat to match. "Where's the Brown Derby?" she shouted as he helped her off the train. "I want to see it. That's all they ever write about to me in the east—the Brown Derby and the sirens." Embracing her estranged husband, she stepped back to admire him. "Darling. What a marvelous sunburn you have. Do you really get things like that out here?"

Interrupting their moment, a Paramount publicity agent with a photographer wanted her to pose in a bathing suit. She shook her head, telling him a woman can't do those things "when you're over 20." A reporter for a local paper asked how long she planned to be in California. "Until September," she told him, and then she would return to the East to do a play.[1]

Miriam settled into the Hollywood Hills apartment Billy had found and waited. After several weeks, she still hadn't heard from Paramount. "Nobody seems interested," she wrote to Ward Morehouse. "They called up and said greetings but, fortunately, I wasn't in, and I've forgotten to call back. The paychecks continue every week plus two hundred extra for California expenses."[2]

Paramount was keeping Miriam's name in the newspapers and fan magazines through speculation about projects they planned for her. The Lubitsch film, *The Man I Killed* (now titled *Broken Lullaby*), the reason she came to Hollywood, was now postponed. When it received the green light, Miriam was on *Dr. Jekyll and Mr. Hyde* and the part went to Nancy Carroll.

Until Paramount contacted her, Miriam went on photograph shoots on the Malibu beaches, which inspired in her a love of sun-worshipping, something she had avoided as a child in Savannah, when her parents made her wear big hats and stay out of the sun because southerners desired a milky white complexion. Stimulated by the California sunshine, she rented a beach house in Pacific Palisades and tanned herself to a golden brown, a practice she continued.[3]

After five weeks of sun tanning, the Russian-born former stage director Marion Gering wanted to audition her for the role of Rosie Dugan in the adaptation of Louis Bromfield's latest novel *24 Hours*. In preparation, she bought Bromfield's book and stayed up all night reading it, so she would "know exactly what it was about."[4]

Lacking sleep, Miriam reported to Paramount for hair and makeup in the morning. The hairdresser mentioned she was the fifth actress to test for the part. Priding herself on how Paramount perceived her, Miriam was taken aback. The studio spent large sums of money promoting her for spreads in national magazines. Also, she was getting rave reviews for *The Smiling Lieutenant*, but now Gering was tossing her into a typical cattle call.

While in wardrobe, she happened upon actress Vivienne Osborne wearing a "slinky black dress" like hers. "Are you being tested for the nightclub hostess in *24 Hours*?"[5] Miriam asked. She was. Miriam considered walking out and taking a train to New York, but she remembered Jesse Lasky's admonition about her contractual responsibilities. She decided to stay.

Waiting for her turn to audition, she roamed the halls of Paramount and met the head of the music department. She asked for a piano and someone to play so she could mimic the style of torch singer Helen Morgan, belting out songs on a piano top.

She chose familiar songs, including the traditional jazz standard "I Can't Give You Anything but Love." It went smoothly, but during the second number, "Don't Blame Me," she forgot the lyrics and burst into tears.

Gering was impressed by her raw emotion, which she later claimed was a nervous breakdown. In any case, Gering gave her the part.

The following day, director Rouben Mamoulian asked for a meeting. They had met in New York, where he had staged several plays and directed two films at the Astoria Studios: the well-received *Applause* and the Gary Cooper starrer, *City Streets*. Now in California, they had been reacquainted at a Malibu beach party on her first weekend in town.

Mamoulian was casting his first Hollywood film, a remake of Robert Louis Stevenson's horror classic, *The Strange Case of Dr. Jekyll and Mr. Hyde*. He wanted Miriam to play "Champagne Ivy," the cabaret singer-prostitute who catches the eye of Stevenson's protagonist. After reading the script, she preferred to play Muriel, Jekyll's fiancée. Since Ivy was like Rosie in *24 Hours*, the fiancée role would prove she could play a woman with class.

Mamoulian was disappointed. He told her she wouldn't make an impression as Muriel. But he knew that if she had no enthusiasm for the role, her performance would suffer. "Fine," he told her, "if you want to play Muriel, you have Muriel. But Ivy would have made you a star." He added he would "have no trouble finding an actress for Ivy. Any actress can make a big hit in it." Whether it was Mamoulian's psychological play or her insecurities, we'll never know, but she told him, with some trepidation, "I'll do it your way."[6]

Alan Brock, an agent for older stars in the 1950s, had an uncredited but pivotal bit part in *24 Hours* playing the thug who shoots and kills Rosie's estranged husband. According to film historian Joseph Yranski, who was friends with Brock later in life, Miriam impressed the one-time extra. She was delightful in a social context, but her behavior could be odd. Brock recalled that between scenes, "Hopkins would sit in her chair reading a book"; for whatever reason, she would "pick up the book and turn it upside-down on her lap" and glare at him.

Brock felt she was metaphorically setting up "a wall" to block people she didn't want to know. He told Yranski that if Miriam "were interested in you sexually, the wall came down," otherwise you didn't exist.[7]

But during the making of *24 Hours*, Miriam's "wall" fell for one man: assistant director Dudley Murphy, who lamented, "There is a myth that one can fall in love with a girl on the screen. I had seen a picture which Lubitsch had made in New York with a lovely blonde actress . . . and I had actually fallen for her on the screen."

Murphy charmed Miriam into a passionate affair. At the time, he was separated from his wife, Katherine, and not spending much time with her or their children. When Katherine heard of their liaison, she wanted to divorce him but was puzzled that her husband considered Miriam an "innocent ingénue."[8]

Billy, too, heard of their affair but was hardly the injured party. Since arriving in Hollywood, he had dated several up-and-coming actresses and a couple of veterans such as Billie Dove and Thelma Todd. Miriam was aware, but neither one had problems with the other's "indiscretions." The problem was that gossip columns reported Miriam's dalliance. Louella Parsons wrote that Murphy was at Miriam's beach house and was seen walking hand in hand with her along Hollywood Boulevard.

Continuing the appearance of a united front was useless. "We tried another go at matrimony, but it was the same thing over again," Billy admitted. "Matrimony between two persons in pictures is the most difficult thing to maintain you can imagine."[9] Mulling it over, they separated on July 27, 1931. It was a case of two lives that would not blend, so they decided to "call it quits" but remain good friends. There were no plans to divorce.[10]

For Murphy, their affair was fleeting. Even so, he considered it the most intense love affair of his life, and for a moment, he considered ending it all. He had an open cockpit Butler Blackhawk plane he kept at Santa Monica airport. One day, in a "suicidal frame of mind," he did tailspins, seeing how near the ground he could come before pulling out.[11]

Moving on, Miriam rented an apartment at Hollywood's Château Élysée on Franklin Avenue before leasing Greta Garbo's former Santa Monica house at 1717 San Vicente Boulevard. There, she found solitude behind the high walls, hedges, and tall cedars surrounding the property. From the shaded flagstone patio, she had an unobstructed view of the mountains, canyons, and the Pacific Ocean a mile away.

When movie actors arrived in Hollywood, the town became a mecca for spiritual and occult practices. From charms worn day and night to necromancy, clairvoyance, numerology, palmistry, astrology, and consultation with spirits, charlatans, and the like, Hollywood attracted them all.

The summer of 1931, the Irish-born psychic Cheiro, also known as Count Louis Hamon, was the hottest clairvoyant in the country. His prophecies were considered cheap at $100 an hour. Cheiro predicted that Lillian Gish's place was on the stage rather than in pictures and that

Norma Talmadge's interests would be in business with beneficial consequences. Both predictions ended up having some truth.

Miriam became a believer in the mystical arts after her brush with death by the suicide jumper in New York. The price was never too high nor the distance too far to meet a new seer with promise.

Miriam's family wasn't aware of the extent she believed. Her son, Michael, assumed it was an oddity, stating, "I don't think she would follow it to the letter. She was very interested in it, but it did not rule her life."[12] Tom Hopkins, her grandson, agreed, believing astrology was an "interest," and not a belief. "I don't know if she took it seriously because if anything about it came up, she referred to it as a philosophy. I don't think she looked at it as something she would follow strictly. She was an intelligent woman—she took everything with a philosophical view unless there was enough empirical evidence."[13]

One day, she met Cheiro. He prophesied she would have a terrible accident in her late thirties, but to sound less negative, he added, "You will recover from that and have several good years, after which you will be completely helpless as the result of illness or accident, thus terminating your career." The reading upset her, but she wasn't discouraged about her beliefs. Until the end of her days, she studied mysticism and consulted psychics before making important decisions.[14]

Miriam's superstitions didn't prevent her from taking the role of "Champagne Ivy" Pierson in the shocking *Dr. Jekyll and Mr. Hyde*. Based on the Robert Louis Stevenson novel, it wasn't the first time the 1866 horror classic was translated to film. In 1920, Paramount had produced a silent version starring John Barrymore, and the role had made him a star. Before that, a London play starring the matinee idol Richard Mansfield had influenced these and other film adaptations that followed.

Dr. Jekyll and Mr. Hyde is the story of a kindly doctor who creates a potion that turns him into a crude murderous lunatic. The film's scenarists, Percy Heath and Samuel Hoffenstein, changed Stevenson's Mr. Hyde from a child-beating murderer to one whose desire for two loves lend his character a complicated sexuality.

While casting the lead, producers invited Barrymore to reprise his role, but instead, the actor accepted an offer from MGM. Staying faithful to the original novel, middle-aged character actor-turned-director Irving Pichel was assigned the role since he physically resembled Stevenson's vision of Jekyll, a large, striking man of fifty. But director Rouben

Mamoulian wanted Fredric March, a younger, more handsome actor. The studio balked at casting March, who they claimed was a light comedian, even though he had appeared in several dramatic Broadway roles and films for their studio, such as *Jealousy* and *Sarah and Son*. Even so, Mamoulian insisted it was Fredric March or nothing: "So we got him, and he was superb."[15]

Production of *Dr. Jekyll and Mr. Hyde* began on Monday, August 24, 1931. Filming was at Ivy's flat, where Jekyll examines her after being brutalized by a client. "Look where he kicked me," she tells Jekyll, showing him her bare leg. "It's only a bruise," he says while eyeing the garter on her thigh. Ivy continues flirting, looking into the camera as she begins her strip, first her shoes and then her garter. She throws it to Jekyll's feet. Removing her stocking and the garter of her other leg, she tosses it to the doctor. He playfully, in a Freudian gesture, inserts his cane in the center and flings it back.

In the next shot, Ivy is naked as she pulls the bed covers over her. As Jekyll leans over Ivy, she embraces him, and they kiss. Ivy sits exposing her leg over the side of the bed, swinging it back and forth. "Come back soon, won't you," she coos to the doctor as he is leaving. The image of Miriam's slim white leg swinging along the bedside, accompanied by her voice entreating Jekyll to "Come back soon . . . come back . . . come back" lingers in a slow dissolve of image and sound.

Miriam's scenes with Fredric March have an undeniable chemistry. March's sexual violence as Mr. Hyde compliments her sadomasochistic, sexually insinuating performance.

Author and historian Gregory W. Mank agreed that Miriam was dedicated, throwing herself "into the role of Ivy with all the scene-stealing tricks in her soon to be legendary repertoire." Rose Hobart, a Universal contract player, was Jekyll's fiancée, Muriel, and said she "would have given anything to play the Miriam Hopkins part." Years later in an interview, Hobart was asked if working with Miriam could be difficult:[16]

"Difficult is an understatement! I had no scenes with her, but I used to go on the set and hear about her endlessly from Freddie March. She was always upstaging everyone, all the time. I don't even think she thought about it anymore because she was so used to doing it. She'd maneuver around until Freddie would have his back to the camera, practically."[17]

Moving about before the camera to force fellow actors out of a shot appears to have been Miriam's favorite tactic. She would do it in countless films, such as *Trouble in Paradise*, with Kay Francis; *Becky Sharp*, with Cedric Hardwicke; and most famously in both *The Old Maid* and *Old Acquaintance*, with Bette Davis. Each time she would feign innocence, promising not to do it again.

Miriam learned this, and other unpredictable ploys, on the stage. Actress Doris Eaton, who worked with her in the Broadway hit *Excess Baggage*, claimed Miriam could be "a little temperamental." She recalled: "Backstage, once or twice there was something that didn't appeal to her, and she had a few words with the stage manager and a couple of the actors. I didn't get close enough to know what it was about, but I could see they were a little disturbed and not very happy. I saw it happen two or three times."[18]

Miriam's overzealousness for perfection added to her insecurities, making her a force on any stage or film set, including the set of *Dr. Jekyll and Mr. Hyde*. For example, in the music hall scene, Mamoulian set up a hidden camera behind a curtain. As expected, Miriam finessed her way, pushing March out of the scene. Behind her, Mamoulian yelled, "Cut!" She swung around and said, "Is *that* where the camera was?"

"Yes," Mamoulian said, "*that's* where the camera was. Print!"

"And she didn't do it quite as often after that!" Rose Hobart said, adding, "She was an excellent actress, though."[19]

While Mamoulian had his moments, his memories of Miriam differ from those of the cast and crew. Early on he recognized her insecurities and planned for them, thus limiting her "difficult" times. "All the stories I hear about Miriam Hopkins, her temper tantrums, and her demonic ego were not in play at the time we were filming *Dr. Jekyll and Mr. Hyde*," he later recalled. "For me, as a director, Miriam was a very gifted and talented actress who could play comedy (as she did for Lubitsch) or a tragic figure such as Ivy."[20]

That doesn't mean she stopped wielding her influence over directors. While Miriam respected the director's job, as history tells us, she had disagreements with many of them. But Mamoulian's rapport with his actors made him different. "The director is the captain of the ship," Miriam once said. "The director can say: Do this, do that, and do the other! But Rouben Mamoulian has a feeling for molding his people and getting the quality and the scenes the way they should be." He made her feel safe.[21]

She made suggestions to *all* her directors, including Mamoulian, Lubitsch, and later William Wyler, about dialogue, the placement of the cameras, and lighting. At some point, many directors would throw up their hands and say, "Miriam darling, you should be directing this picture."[22]

In an interview with author John Kobal shortly before her death in 1972, she revealed how Mamoulian allowed her to direct herself in the scene in *Dr. Jekyll and Mr. Hyde* wherein Ivy begs Jekyll to rescue her from Hyde. Miriam nervously told Mamoulian, "I know it all very well, Rouben," and explained how she would "drop down and hold him [March] by the knees" and beg him to help. She asked if she could do the entire eight pages of dialogue in one shot, "like in the theater," instead of in little pieces. Mamoulian agreed.

Then, she stalled, having second thoughts. She asked for an audience, so Mamoulian brought in the crew, gathering them around the set as if it were a theater stage. Pointing to March's mark on the stage floor, Mamoulian asked her to set *her* mark. "Well, I've come through the door, halfway, and then I'll go right over to him, there," she told him. Next, he asked about the placement of the cameras. Since the scene began with quiet pleading and ended with broad hysterics, she wanted to catch every nuance: "Maybe if one's [a camera is] over near his knees there, and one here, [and] one there."

When all was ready, she started, but at the fifth or sixth line, she stumbled. Mamoulian gave her a second chance. She then went through the entire scene in one take and everyone applauded. Miriam was still sobbing on the floor, holding onto March's shoes at the end, but that was the scene printed.[23]

It was an emotionally exhausting experience, and while it turned out well, she never pushed Mamoulian again. Perhaps that was his reason for doing it. Yet, she continued being "pushy" with other directors. In one way or another, she continued to dominate a set.

On the home front, the press speculated whether Miriam and Billy would reconcile. Even separation didn't change their behavior. "We're both terribly fond of each other and spend a lot of time together," Miriam explained. "But there are no ties. I can go with whom I please, and Austin [Billy] does likewise. And right here I'd like to go on record as saying that there is no sizzling or ignited romance lurking in the background, regardless of who I'm with."[24]

Miriam visited Billy's home on Laguna Beach, and he dropped by her Santa Monica house. They lunched and sometimes had dinner but had no intentions of reuniting. "In fact," she added, "while we were having luncheon the other day we had a big laugh over one of our reconciliation stories that appeared. We're both very happy the way it is now and there is a great friendship between us."[25]

As friends, they attended the opening of the Dumas classic *Camille*, starring Jane Cowl and Gilbert Roland, at Hill Street's Belasco Theater. It was Miriam's first time at live theater in Los Angeles, and the experience left her yearning for Broadway and her New York City lifestyle. "Look at that divine East River, the city!" she would say, gazing from her library window. "It's glorious. And there are books. There is music. There are plays. Here are people, who are all creative, intelligent."[26]

On *Dr. Jekyll and Mr. Hyde*'s last day of filming, she was removing her makeup when her longing for New York overwhelmed her. She called Schulberg's office, but he was available for only a few minutes and would be busy the rest of the day. With cold cream smeared on her face, she dashed across the lot to Paramount's administration building. "I've got to go to New York," she blurted out to a stunned Schulberg, "even if it's only for a few days." Schulberg, so unnerved by her appearance, he couldn't say no. In a few hours, she was on an eastbound plane.[27]

Making the most of her brief stay, she visited friends, took in a few plays, and, out of curiosity, caught a showing of the French language version of *The Smiling Lieutenant* at the Little Carnegie Playhouse. While she stayed away from her films, she was curious how her French dialogue compared to Colbert and Chevalier. Evidently, she held her own, even though her accent "could have been better."

Friends asked the obvious question: "And how do you like Hollywood?"

"I've grown so sick of that question," she protested. "I have no idea how I like Hollywood. Give me a little time." In New York, she lived in the same neighborhood and shopped at the same delicatessen for years. "How can I say, 'Oh I think Hollywood's just too damn dandy' before I'm even vaguely familiar with any of it except the road between the studio and my house." Indeed, Miriam would never have affection for Los Angeles. New York was home and would be until her death.[28]

Before *Dr. Jekyll and Mr. Hyde* could be released, Paramount worked with censors, who restricted the offensive scenes; most were Miriam's. "Her scenes were considered very erotic for 1931," Mamoulian later recounted. "In fact, we filmed her bed sequence when she first encounters Dr. Jekyll with her removing her clothes under the sheets. Not much of that remained, I am told."[29] When *Dr. Jekyll and Mr. Hyde* previewed in December 1931, at the Westwood Village Theater, Colonel Jason S. Joy of the MPAA wrote to B. P. Schulberg that Miriam's undressing scene was too long and should not drag on "simply to titillate the audience." Joy opposed Jekyll watching her undress but agreed it should be "saved." The scene was intact upon the film's release, but once state censors started cutting, most, if not all, of the scene was gone.[30]

The same was true in England when Lillian Brind of Paramount's London office told her American bosses "we had to cut out the scenes of Miriam Hopkins undressing and some of the later censorable scenes in the bedroom, also the actual strangulation of the girl." A British friend of Mamoulian's, who saw the film in London, wrote the director that the censor's cuts were noticeable, stating "there were a few places in the film where the continuity didn't seem smooth to me, but I had no idea that as much as 1,000 ft. had been cut."[31]

A few years later, on the film's 1935 rerelease with the Code now in full-force, Miriam commented: "*Dr. Jekyll and Mr. Hyde* was cut before it could be shown." All prints deleted the undressing scene and the line where Jekyll tells Ivy he "wants her."[32]

The censors' intrusion didn't affect the audience's reception of *Dr. Jekyll and Mr. Hyde*, which premiered on New Year's Eve to enthusiastic reviews. Fredric March's performance was considered a triumph, winning him his first Academy Award. Miriam was another unanimous standout. "Miss Hopkins, until now identified with madcap comedy, emerges as a dramatic player of extraordinary facility in the role of the Soho lady," opined the *Los Angeles Times*. "Her abhorrence of her lord and master is too real to be studied; it is, in short, amazing. And by contrast, I can only indicate her tenderness in the later episode with good, kind Dr. Jekyll. It, too, is amazing."[33]

Miriam was exuberant about the success of *Dr. Jekyll and Mr. Hyde*, her previous three films, and the direction her career was taking. "Pictures are lots of fun, and the opportunities for intense interest are tremendous," she said at the time. "I mean the different roles one can play at the same time he would do one character in a play and lots of other fascinating things in pictures."

Those thoughts and those feelings were about to change.

6

"An Expensive Leading Woman"

Miriam returned to Hollywood to film the adaptation of Robert E. Sherwood's play *This Is New York*, now titled *Two Kinds of Women*. Directed by William C. de Mille, the brother of Cecil, it's the story of a country-bred daughter (Hopkins) of a North Dakota senator (Irving Pichel) who finds romance in the big city with a rich playboy (Phillips Holmes).

Two Kinds of Women was the third film released in 1931 that was based on the plays of future Pulitzer Prize–winner Robert E. Sherwood. Even though *This Is New York* had a short Broadway run of fifty-nine performances, Paramount hoped that audiences would remember Miriam's brilliant work on *Dr. Jekyll and Mr. Hyde* and that that would make up for the humorless screenplay and its plot.

That Thanksgiving, Miriam hosted a buffet dinner for a houseful of friends. Amid rumors that they were "getting serious," Billy invited actress Thelma Todd. Miriam's friends questioned why she welcomed the so-called other woman. She explained: "I don't see anything extraordinary in my being nice to the women that Bill is interested in! I like meeting and knowing all my other friends' friends. So why should I feel any different about knowing my dearest friend's friends—just because we happened to be married at one time?"[1]

Also "thankful" were the Donald Ogden Stewarts, the Basil Rathbones, and silent film heartthrob John Gilbert, who was involved passionately with Miriam. Gilbert's daughter, Leatrice Gilbert Fountain, didn't recall her father's affair with Miriam, but as she said, "It would have been impossible to have kept track of all of them."[2]

Gilbert, however, could be a jealous lover. His career was adjusting to the advent of sound, and the substandard films MGM cast him in depressed him. One night, according to author George Eells, Gilbert was suspicious of Miriam's intentions and accused her of unfaithfulness. Her nonchalance angered him, and he shot a bullet above her into the headboard of her bed. Miriam could be unflappable when being confronted. Slowly, she inched her way out of bed, speaking softly as she took away his gun.

Director King Vidor told Gilbert Fountain that her father kept a gun and threatened him once when he was drunk, "so it's possible, and apparently not out of character," she said. "Jack bought the gun to protect himself from Louis B. Mayer's henchmen, whom he was convinced were out to get him."[3]

For Miriam, Gilbert's attack recalled memories of the knife-wielding Patrick Kearney in the streets of Greenwich Village. If the Gilbert incident is accurate, evidently, Miriam could bring out the worst in men. The exception was Billy. Although they had differences, they remained supportive of one another. "Why Billy's the nicest friend I have," said Miriam. "We tried marriage and found it just didn't work. It wasn't right for us. But I've found a finer, sweeter, dearer Bill in his friendship, and I hope I shall never know what it is to be without that."[4]

Two Kinds of Women received decent reviews under de Mille's capable direction. *Life* magazine wrote, Miriam "proves worthy of everything enthusiastic reviewers have said of her. She handles every situation with finesse, with a subtle comedy touch, and it needs no far-seeing prophet to declare that she will soon be at the very top of the Hollywood roster and a star in her own right."[5]

Life magazine was kind, but in many critics' opinion, Miriam's career advancement was interrupted by *Two Kinds of Women*, implying she should have "meatier roles" or was "miscast as a sweet ingénue." Still, they recognized her potential, and one critic said, "She is coming, and her future greatness shows clearly in this picture."[6]

To make a path to "future greatness," Paramount moved her into rehearsals for *Dancers in the Dark*, a tale of a dance hall romance between a taxi dancer (Hopkins) and an innocent sax player based on James Ashmore Creelman's play *Jazz King*.[7]

William Collier Jr., a former child actor who would again share the screen with Miriam the following year in *The Story of Temple Drake*, is the sax player and boyhood friend of bandleader Jack Oakie. Oakie had a long Paramount career as a top-notch comedian and musical star. Oakie tries to break up the romance between Collier and Miriam with the help of a slick underworld character played by George Raft, who yearns for the taxi dancer himself. Raft would be a standout as the nickel-flipping gangster in the Paul Muni starrer, *Scarface*.

On the *Dancers in the Dark* set, Miriam played well with everyone except George Raft, her studio-assigned escort at film premieres. He considered her spoiled and unprofessional. She critiqued his acting, a habit that irritated him.

One day, their bickering led to a shouting match. Raft threatened to punch her in the nose; instead, as she stormed off, he grabbed her, giving her rear end a pinch. Miriam screamed, spun around, and took a swing at Raft, but he ducked as Jack Oakie wrapped his arm around her waist and held her back. Raft shook his head, chuckled, and walked off. Russian-born director David Burton tried to intercede, but he could not control her. Miriam's suggestions on how to "perk up" a scene overwhelmed him, and his rejections of her "ideas" infuriated her.[8]

Ruby was visiting from New York, so Miriam had her dance in the film's chorus, giving them more time together. According to Ruby's daughter, Margot, she "quickly found she didn't care for film work." The stopping, repeating, and starting again bored her, and she missed live audiences. When her part finished, she took the train to New York with "a plan" to explore all the fascinating scenery she had seen on the trip west.

Unbeknownst to Ruby, in true *A Star Is Born* fashion, a *Dancers in the Dark* bigwig saw her in the rushes and wanted to test her for the lead dancer in an upcoming film. "Miriam tried frantically to locate mom," Margot recalled, "who was happily getting on and off the train to explore the West and Nana (Ellen) combed New York but mom couldn't be found."

By the time Ruby arrived in New York, the producer had cast another dancer. She was met by Jack Welch, a young Irish actor she was dating, and "who later became my father," Margot said. Ellen had to tell her brother John (who had paid for Ruby's round-trip ticket) that instead of another movie star daughter she was getting "another actor son-in-law."[9]

Dancers in the Dark was not a critical or financial success. Critics blamed the dialogue-laden screenplay by Herman J. Mankiewicz (who would win an Oscar for *Citizen Kane*) and David Burton's spotty direction. The acting, however, was admirable. "Miriam Hopkins is such an excellent actress, and Jack Oakie is so spontaneously amusing, that a poor picture cannot faze them," wrote one reviewer.[10]

Irrespective of the film's reception, Paramount was grooming her to become one of their first-rank players. Columnist Cal York picked Miriam as the "best bet for stardom," ranking her above Joan Blondell, Jean Harlow, Carole Lombard, Sylvia Sidney, and Helen Hayes. The critics raved, and Paramount reported that her fan mail had increased.[11]

She wanted to make something of herself. Author H. G. Wells once told her that most people were "meanwhiling their lives away," just drifting along, "dreaming of a future which they won't take the trouble to achieve." Miriam wouldn't be that person. She would have a say in her career. Elated by the success of *The Smiling Lieutenant, 24 Hours,* and *Dr. Jekyll and Mr. Hyde,* she was disappointed with her last two films— average programmers that were not well received. Her next film was no different.[12]

The World and the Flesh was an adaptation of the European play *On the Black Sea* by Philip Zeska and Ernst Spitz, the tale of a sea captain (George Bancroft) who comes to the aid of a ballerina (Hopkins) during the Russian Revolution. Gorgeously mounted, with high production values (budget of $490,000), the film was enhanced by John Cromwell's splendid direction and the creative photography of Karl Struss. Critics, in general, praised the two leads but found the story lagged. One claimed the film's asset was the "fine acting of Bancroft and Miriam Hopkins. But the greatest actors in the world cannot make an impossible story seem real."[13]

Miriam's salary was $1,500 a week, yet Paramount made no effort to place her in quality projects. She questioned B. P. Schulberg's judgment on the roles he assigned to her. In one instance, she applied Nancy Carroll's standards and rejected one film, telling Schulberg it wasn't "a good story." When he argued that he bought it for Sylvia Sidney, Miriam snapped, "That doesn't make it a good story."[14]

Metro-Goldwyn-Mayer's Irving Thalberg wrote to producer Joseph Schenck that there was no difference in the box office value of Jean Harlow at his studio and Miriam at Paramount. Instead of capitalizing on Miriam's success, Jesse Lasky and Schulberg cast her in three or four ordinary films that didn't help her or Paramount.

"Can it honestly be said that they were saving money by using Hopkins?" Thalberg asked Schenck. "In my opinion, they cost themselves a great deal more. Had they been able by real effort to . . . make an intensely interesting Hopkins story, they might have had a real asset instead of just an expensive, leading woman."[15]

For the past year, Paramount had been experiencing financial problems, because of the Great Depression and Adolph Zukor's mismanagement. To save money, they gave Miriam and other stars inferior stories, but at what cost? After years of big-budget films with little profit, they were in receivership. Now, a shakeup was coming.

RKO had brought Billy out to the coast to pen two screenplays for Constance Bennett: *Dangerous for Love* and *Doubtful Lady.* Both projects were unproduced. Instead, his second screenplay, *The Rich Are Always with Us*, was waiting for a May release by Warner Bros. In a supporting role was George Cukor's stock company ingenue, Bette Davis. Since then, Davis had appeared in three Broadway plays before signing a contract with Universal in 1931. Still an ingenue, she moved to Warner Bros.; *The Rich Are Always with Us* was her third picture for the studio.

Billy contributed scenarios to various studios, including two additional ones for Warner's, both Kay Francis films: *The House on 56th Street* and *Mandalay.*

Billy was still dating Thelma Todd, and the rumor was they wanted to marry, but he was still married to Miriam. In March 1932, they agreed to a "mutual consent" Mexican divorce; it was granted one week later via air-mail from Juarez.

Then, Billy disappeared. Todd dated other men, including Pat DiCicco, the agent and alleged mobster whom she later married. It appeared the couple had split, but no one knew the reason. According to the gossip sheets, Billy had left on a freighter for Veracruz, Mexico, to clear his head.

Meanwhile, in New York, Ward Morehouse married publicist Jean Dalrymple at Essex House. When they boarded the Twentieth Century for Los Angeles, Morehouse had a Warner Bros. contract for two screenplays featuring Joan Blondell: *Central Park* and Mervyn LeRoy's *Big City Blues.* Their Hollywood sojourn doubled as a honeymoon.

Miriam met the newlyweds at Pasadena's train station. In her well-meaning but imposing manner, she had rented Carmel Myers' Santa Monica beach house as a trysting place for the honeymooners. When they arrived at dusk, the electricity wasn't on, so they "felt rather than saw" their way around. Miriam chatted as she pointed out the hidden beauties of the place and its many drawbacks such as no linens, no blankets, no silver, and no dishes or cooking utensils.

Luckily, Morehouse had reserved bungalow eight at the Garden of Allah. Morehouse friends James Cagney, Cary Grant, and Fred Astaire had filled the small apartment with flowers and several bottles of prohibition liquor.[16]

Now Miriam was free to begin a two-month leave that Schulberg had promised her. In Pasadena, she waited to board the Chief with her travel companion Dorothy Parker. Miriam revealed that for several months, she had been contemplating adopting a child. She discussed it with Billy during their marriage, but the timing was never right. Now that Billy was gone, she was lonely. The state of California didn't allow single men and women to adopt, so she was working with the Cradle Society, an orphanage in suburban Evanston, Illinois, on the outskirts of Chicago.

A few days earlier, she heard from Cradle Society founder Florence Dahl Walrath. There was a baby boy that was a good match; he was "healthy and cute." The following morning at the orphanage, Miriam met a blonde, blue-eyed infant called "Baby Boy Wilson."[17]

In court, Dorothy Parker appeared as Miriam's character witness. Miriam told presiding Judge Edmund Jarecki that she had divorced her husband and would raise the child alone; a trust fund was already set up for the baby.

Miriam meant to keep the adoption a secret, but the orphanage or someone at the judge's office leaked it. After signing the adoption papers, a mass of reporters awaited them outside the courthouse. Miriam was livid. At first, she ignored the questions shouted at her while they pushed through the crowd. Abruptly, a reporter grabbed her arm. She stopped and glared at him. "Why did you decide to adopt a baby?" he asked loudly, trying to be heard over the din. She screamed, "I hate all this publicity over a simple thing. I don't have to give any reasons!" She pulled her arm away, and they jumped into a waiting taxicab.[18]

The anxiety was overwhelming. The fourth estate frequently tested her. She valued her privacy in a profession that had no respect for anonymity. A journalist's meddling to get a scoop she could accept, but this was different. She was protecting a child and wouldn't tolerate their prying.

With legal matters still pending, the child couldn't leave the orphanage for several days. In the interim, Miriam and Dorothy Parker continued to New York. She would pick up the baby, who she named Michael Hopkins (no middle name), on her return trip to California.

Miriam's adoption of Michael was part of an epidemic of Hollywood adoptions. Earlier that year, actor Wallace Beery had adopted his daughter, as had Miriam's costars, Fredric March and Florence Eldridge. Over the years, the Cradle Society placed children in the homes of Gracie Allen and George Burns, Joe E. Brown, Pat O'Brien, and Al Jolson.

In 1938, Joan Crawford, a close friend, "wanted to adopt a baby" and discussed it with Miriam, who was by then a board member of Cradle. Yet, when Crawford adopted her daughter Christina the following year, it was not from Cradle but reportedly through a black-market baby ring.

Although adoption as a single mother was unusual, it was not without precedence in Hollywood. In 1923, silent film vamp Barbara La Marr, who was also single at the time, adopted a baby boy from a Texas orphanage. When the actress died three years later because of drug addiction, her son, Marvin Carville La Marr, was taken in by her closest friend, actress ZaSu Pitts. Decades later, the boy was revealed to be La Marr's birth son, allegedly fathered by MGM producer Paul Bern. Evidently, she went through the adoption ruse to avoid an impending scandal.

Likewise, in 1935, actress Loretta Young secretly gave birth to a daughter conceived with Clark Gable during production of *Call of the Wild*. For more than a year, Young placed the girl she named Judy (Lewis) in orphanages before "adopting" her. As the child grew, it became apparent that she resembled Young's sister Sally Blane and her father Clark Gable, big ears and all. Still unaware thirty years later, her future husband told her the "open secret" that Hollywood already knew. Stunned, Judy confronted her mother, who admitted the truth.

As Michael grew, gossips whispered that he was Miriam's biological son, but those rumors soon dimmed. Miriam's grandson Tom believes Miriam "probably gave birth" to his father, but it would have damaged her career if it were known.[19]

There may have been a "resemblance" between mother and son, but there are kinks in the theory of Miriam being Michael's birth mother. Michael was born near Chicago on March 29, 1932. Studio records show that Miriam was on the Paramount lot or in San Pedro filming *The World and the Flesh*. Also, there are newspaper accounts that she attended several public events. And finally, because of her childhood rheumatic fever, doctors advised her to avoid pregnancy; it could have been life-threatening, if it was even possible.[20]

To end the speculation, Tom and Ruby's daughter, Margot, would have to take DNA tests. For her own reasons, Margot has declined their request. Until then, there is only one conclusion: the Cradle, according to their guidelines, tried to match children with their adoptive parents based on their coloring, overall conformation, or racial origin. It seems they did their job well.[21]

As for Michael, he accepted Miriam as his adopted mother and wasn't "curious" about his real parents. "Miriam's my mother as far as I'm concerned," he insisted. But the truth about his birth was kept from him while growing up. Whatever Miriam's reasons, Michael wouldn't learn the truth about his adoption for two decades.[22]

Meanwhile, Billy had accepted his breakup with Thelma Todd and was sailing to New York on the SS *Morro Castle*, unaware of the headlines his ex-wife was creating in the States. When Miriam found out Billy was in town, she convinced him to join her at the Hotel Pierre. That evening over dinner, she explained Michael's adoption. "Bill, do you think I ought to?" she asked hesitantly. Billy was dumbfounded. He knew she wanted children, but could she handle the responsibilities of a single mother?

Billy asked a well-known psychologist they both knew if Miriam should adopt a baby. The psychiatrist told him it would be "good for her as a professional woman who could not have a baby of her own," adding, without any explanation, that an adopted child would be "even more of a blessing."[23]

Until she could take custody of Michael on May 29, she made public appearances for *The World and the Flesh*. She also met with her mother to talk about the baby. Ellen had opinions and expressed them. Why would she adopt a child without a husband? She reminded her daughter of her fatherless childhood and the problems she had had as a single mother.

Then, Ellen posed questions that created a wider gap between mother and daughter: "What do you intend to do about Michael if you die? Would you leave him your money or send him into a home? After all, he's no blood relation, and your money should go to your kin." An argument ensued. Furious, Miriam returned to Hollywood. It was several months before she spoke to her mother again.[24]

Fearing more publicity at the orphanage, Miriam bypassed Chicago and called writer Ben Wassan, a friend in Los Angeles, and asked him to take a train to pick up the baby.

A friend observed that Michael's arrival was a "turning point like A.D. and B.C."[25] Information about Michael's birth parents was private. By the same token, according to the Cradle Society's rules, if the birth parents were living, they wouldn't know who had adopted the child. Miriam's role in raising Michael was to "give him the environment and indirect guidance that will develop the best of his natural tendencies."[26]

Miriam's return to Paramount was just as dramatic as her personal life. With their debt increasing, the studio was nearing collapse. When Miriam signed with Paramount in 1930, the studio recorded a profit of $18 million (nearly $290 million today), but by the end of 1932, it was running a deficit of more than $15 million ($240 million today). The New York office, Paramount's actual headquarters, wanted to clean out the West Coast leadership. They blamed Jesse Lasky in part for the studio's difficulties, so in April 1932, he took a three-month leave of absence until he could renegotiate his contract. Instead, they ousted him from his position.

While B. P. Schulberg was away, Emanuel Cohen, the editor of Paramount News and director of the short subjects department, was appointed vice-president in charge of all productions for the studio. Cohen, a risk-taker of small stature, was an assistant to Lasky, whom he reportedly bad-mouthed to Adolph Zukor. Telling the mogul he could do a better job, Zukor instructed Cohen to tighten the budget.

When Miriam returned, the studio atmosphere had changed. The positive responses to her earlier films had spoiled her, but Schulberg's recent choice of projects left her doubtful. With new leadership, she adopted a hands-on approach. Nancy Carroll's schooling at Astoria had taught her to argue for better scripts, for without a good story, the director, stars, and production values didn't count for much.

Before her vacation, Schulberg wanted to star her in a remake of Hermann Sudermann's *The Song of Songs,* directed by Rouben Mamoulian. She trusted Mamoulian and liked the script, but producers postponed production. Cecil B. DeMille considered her for his religious epic *The Sign of the Cross* but cast Claudette Colbert instead.

Across town at Culver City, MGM was remaking Norma Talmadge's silent film *Smilin' Through* with their top actress, Norma Shearer. In a deal with Paramount, MGM would borrow Fredric March, and they would loan Clark Gable to be with Miriam in an adaptation of Val Lewton's best-selling pulp novel *No Bed of Her Own*. At the time, Gable was completing *Strange Interlude* with Shearer and would not be available until later in the fall.

Miriam wanted to work with Lubitsch again, but studio producers had shelved his current project *I Married an Angel*. But Emanuel Cohen granted her wish and assigned her to Lubitsch's replacement film, *Trouble in Paradise*. The film's budget was a trifle over $500,000—lower than that of his prior films—the result of Cohen's new cost-cutting measures.[27]

Samuel Raphaelson, who cowrote *The Smiling Lieutenant*, adapted Aladar Laszlo's play *The Honest Finder*, but Lubitsch insisted he not read it. "It's bad. We work with this material, you see." And did they work! As a rule, Lubitsch chose materials for what he could mold into his style or "touch."

For instance, they wrote a "brilliant opening shot," set in a Venice hotel. Herbert Marshall, an English actor in his second American film, is a master crook impersonating a baron. He meets Miriam, a lady thief pretending to be a countess. On their first encounter, she pick-pockets his watch, and he lifts her jeweled brooch and garter. Raphaelson called the gag "phony, incredible, and inconsistent with the image of Marshall as a supreme crook." Lubitsch loved it and "juggled it past all sanity." He also loved Raphaelson's wild doodle of Miriam handing Marshall his watch and remarking, "It was five minutes slow, but I regulated it for you."[28]

After their introduction, Marshall (Gaston) and Miriam (Lily) form an alliance, traveling about Europe pillaging the continent until they come upon a vulnerable heiress to a perfume fortune. To play the part, Paramount borrowed Kay Francis from Warner Bros., who had left the studio the year before.

This time, Francis was upset. Paramount billed her after Miriam, yet the year before on *24 Hours*, she was above her costar. She felt her new ranking was Paramount's punishment for jumping ship to a competing studio. Yet, in salary, Francis dominated her friend, pulling in $4,000 a week, more than double Miriam's newly contracted $1,750.

Herbert Marshall, earning a respectable $3,500 a week, kept busy behind the scenes according to Lubitsch biographer Scott Eyman, who wrote that the "much married, Marshall managed affairs with both Kay Francis and Miriam Hopkins." If correct, the bed-hopping didn't interfere with their friendship, though Miriam's scene-stealing could have. In one scene, Miriam was sitting in profile and slowly turned her chair until her full face was on camera. Francis was furious and complained to Lubitsch; he promised to take care of the matter. For the next take, Lubitsch had Miriam's chair nailed to the floor.[29]

Many called *Trouble in Paradise* Lubitsch's finest film. The reviews were positive, with one reviewer calling it "civilized, suave, enchanting and light-minded." Critics gave all three principals credit for the film's success. "There cannot be enough said about Miriam Hopkins, Kay Francis, Herbert Marshall . . . , in praise of their workmanship in this film," said the *Hollywood Citizen-News*. Miriam was singled out in what was called her best role. "The picture is a triumph too for Miriam Hopkins," noted the *Los Angeles Times*, adding that her "roguish humor and pervasive charms have never before been so evident."[30]

The film, however, lost money for Paramount, unlike *The Smiling Lieutenant*, the studio's biggest grosser of 1931. For the critics and the movie-going elite, *Trouble in Paradise* was a brilliant production, but it was too smart for the general public.

As *Trouble in Paradise* wrapped, the former vaudevillian and now producer Albert Lewis was finalizing *No Bed of Her Own*, set to be Miriam's follow-up film. The script, however, was going through significant changes to satisfy the censors. First, the title was considered too racy, so Lewis changed it to the less suggestive *No Man of Her Own*.

Billy Parker worked on the treatment and the original screenplay, but to satisfy the anticipated censorship problems, Lewis made further revisions. To dilute the original narrative further, Paramount purchased the rights to *Here Is My Heart*, along with a story idea by Benjamin Glazer and Edmund Goulding to mix in with the story.

More problems were imminent. James Flood, the original director, was replaced by Lowell Sherman. Miriam was unhappy with the latest script revisions and complained that her part was too weak, too saccharine. They rewrote the script again. A week later, Sherman walked off the set after a pay dispute, and Wesley Ruggles, whose *Cimarron* had been RKO's biggest box office hit the year before, stepped in.

Miriam was fed up with the delays. She sent Michael and his new nanny, Christiane Deveraux (whom everyone called Mademoiselle), to Palm Springs along with Ruby, who was visiting the West Coast again. The following day, she chartered record-breaking aviator Colonel Roscoe Turner's plane and flew to New York. That afternoon, the story broke in the newspapers that Miriam had walked off the Paramount lot and was holding up production on a big budget film.

Along her flight path, the plane stopped at Albuquerque, Kansas City, and Midway Airport in Chicago. As Miriam exited the plane, *Chicago Tribune* photographer Mike Rotunno asked for her side of the story. At first, Miriam was confused, as she hadn't seen the newspapers. "I should say not," she replied curtly and kept walking. Rotunno tagged after her, the whole time explaining how holding up production on an expensive film was important news. "Will you get the hell away from me?" Miriam yelled. Relentless, Rotunno ran ahead and set up his camera for a candid shot of her screaming at him. "You son of a bitch, get out of my way!"

In the morning, a quarter of a page on the back side of the *Chicago Tribune* showed a photo of an angry Miriam with the caption: "Miriam Hopkins, who walked off the Paramount set, arrives in Chicago and curses the photographer for taking her picture."[31]

A few months later, Rotunno photographed Carole Lombard at the airport. Afterward, they had coffee and talked about his face-off with Miriam. They laughed, and Lombard added, "Mike, I gotta tell you before I came here I was with Miriam, and she warned me, 'be careful when you get to Chicago because there's a gangster photographer at the airport.'"[32]

Miriam arrived in New York and checked into the Hotel Pierre. Ignoring the messages left by studio executives at the front desk, she called Palm Springs to check on Michael and, afterward, dined with Billy at Tony's restaurant. Later, she could go to a Connecticut farm with multimillionaire John "Jock" Hay Whitney and his wife or take a short trip to Cuba on the new Italian liner, *Rex*. Instead, she traveled to a friend's snow-hidden house in the Catskills.

On her return, she rushed to Bergdorf Goodman's for a dress fitting for a party for Noël Coward. Aside from her troubles with Paramount, she enjoyed herself. But the fun ended when Lewis and the studio insisted that she return to Hollywood.

On that first day back, she read the revised script for *No Man of Her Own*. She was still unhappy; Clark Gable now overshadowed her part. Frustrated, she went to lunch and didn't return. A prop boy, who overheard Wesley Ruggles asking for her, told the director she was "going home on account of how she thought her part was lousy."[33]

Someone else told Albert Lewis she went to Palm Springs to be with her son. Lewis telephoned her hotel in the desert. He telegraphed. He begged, pleaded, and threatened. At last, she returned on November 7. Although Emanuel Cohen, Paramount's new production head, had been in charge of the studio for several months, Miriam only now had her first face-to-face meeting with him. Miriam had little respect for Cohen, based solely on his reputation; she called him that "little man . . . from Chicago."

When she walked into his office, her first words were, "At least you could stand up and be a gentleman." Cohen was confused. He glanced about and replied, "I *am* standing." Miriam looked again and noticed the four-foot-eleven mogul was, indeed, on his feet.

"Oh, I beg your pardon." They both sat.

She called the picture "very cheap," blaming the poorly written script and the uneven characterizations. She persisted, as she later said, in a "phony-arty way," though, in her mind, she was not "getting to first base" with this "little cheap man." Frustrated, she yelled, "Listen, it stinks! It's lousy!" Now, speaking on his level, he asked, "Why didn't you say so?" and they came to a compromise. Cohen agreed to remove her from the cast of *No Man of Her Own* and another film they were planning. Instead, she would appear in an adaptation of William Faulkner's thrilling novel, *Sanctuary*.[34]

When Val Lewton, the author of *No Bed of Her Own* met Miriam a few years later, he asked why she declined the part. Lewton understood that while adapting his book for the screen, the studio had changed it so he "would never have recognized it" at the theater. Believing Miriam's refusal to play the part was not a reflection on his work, he was still anxious to know why she had thought the script, "as re-written by her ex-husband, Austin Parker," was not suitable.

She explained it was a bad script. "They only kept the title of your book, and then they hatched up an artificial story that didn't ring true to me. I couldn't see myself playing it."[35]

Also, casting Clark Gable as her leading man wasn't a selling point. Miriam recalled her first meeting with Gable at a portrait sitting during preproduction: "We were introduced to each other in the gallery. Two minutes later we were clinging to each other for dear life while the cameraman shot us from all sides. After nearly two hours of this, we said goodbye and went our separate ways. And do you know I've never seen Clark since!"[36]

In any case, gossips were aghast that an actress would decline a chance to play opposite Clark Gable, MGM's and the world's reigning heartthrob. Thus, she willingly stepped aside for Carole Lombard.

Miriam was free to proceed with *Sanctuary*. However, the Hays office rejected the latest script revision, the first of many, so they delayed filming until after the new year.

In the spring of 1931, Paramount had paid $6,000 for the screen rights to William Faulkner's best-selling novel, *Sanctuary*, the story of the brutal kidnapping and rape of a Mississippi debutante and her descent into a Memphis brothel. Faulkner based his tale on a story he heard from a woman in a New Orleans nightclub about her abduction by an impotent gangster. Calling it a "potboiler," Faulkner alleged he penned the novel "to make money" and, in a matter of weeks, invented the "most horrific tale" he could imagine. Upon reading it, his publisher exclaimed, "Good God, I can't publish this. We'd both be in jail." Although discouraged, Faulkner transformed the novel into a "haunting study of evil triumphant."[37]

When it was published, reviewers complimented Faulkner's writing but were appalled by the subject matter. The *New York Times* told its readers "the steps which *Sanctuary* follows to complete the horrifying ruin of a girl, daughter of a Mississippi judge, through no fault of her own, are too devious to be followed in a review." *Time* magazine advised censors to stay away from the novel, "because no one but a pathological reader will be sadistically aroused."[38]

Women's groups protested when Paramount bought the film rights. Lamarr Trotti, a journalist and newly arrived screenwriter at Fox studios, remarked it was "utterly unthinkable as a motion picture." James Wingate, the chief censor of the Motion Picture Producers and Distributors of America (MPPDA), claimed they were unaware, insisting, "If that has been bought, it was bought without any knowledge before the purchase by any of us."[39]

The MPPDA was formed more than a decade earlier in response to the Roscoe "Fatty" Arbuckle rape trial and director William Desmond Taylor's murder, both of whom worked for Paramount. In 1930, the so-called Hays Code (named after the organization's leader, Will Hays) was implemented, dictating what was and was not acceptable for a motion picture audience.

They demanded the book's title couldn't be used, nor could it show in the film's credits or publicity. Hoping to retain remnants of the novel, producer Benjamin Glazer, who won a Best Writing Oscar for *Seventh Heaven*, titled the script *The Shame of Temple Drake* before settling on *The Story of Temple Drake*. In the credits, it simply showed as based on "a novel by William Faulkner."

Former newspaper and magazine writer Oliver H. P. Garret had the arduous task of translating Faulkner's work into a screenplay that both Paramount and the Hays office would accept. For the director, Paramount selected Stephen Roberts, who made shorts and later directed *The Trumpet Blows* and *Star of Midnight*.

George Raft, who battled with Miriam on *Dancers in the Dark*, was cast as Popeye, the novel's antagonist, a brutal and impotent gangster who savagely rapes Temple with a corncob.

Raft, who made an impression as a gangster in *Scarface*, was hesitant about playing this type of outlaw. Claiming his screen image was at stake, Raft declared he would do the film if Adolph Zukor paid him $2 million, because "once this movie is out I'll be through as an actor."[40]

"Raft didn't want to do it," explained George Raft biographer Stone Wallace. "*Temple Drake* is no more than a gangster movie, but Raft didn't think that the character was very moral the way he was presented. Another reason he rejected *Temple Drake* was he didn't want to work with Hopkins again, which is odd because he made *All of Me* with her the following year, and he played a gangster in that film. Raft wasn't known for making great career moves."[41]

Ignoring Raft's reluctance, and his unreasonable demands, both Emanuel Cohen and Benjamin Glazer stayed firm.

In the meantime, Paramount filed a script with the Hays office. Days later, Adolph Zukor received a three-page letter from James Wingate listing the revisions to make. Will Hays pressured Paramount not to "allow the production of a picture which will offend every right-thinking person who sees it." Despite what Hays believed, Wingate credited Paramount with coming up with the best script possible despite the story matter, but he added, "even with the most expert treatment, it is still a sordid story."[42]

Nevertheless, *The Story of Temple Drake* went before the cameras the second week of February 1933, without George Raft. "Listen; do you know what I would have to do in that picture?" Raft told a reporter. "First I had to kill a feeble-minded boy and then I had to rape a girl—in a corn-crib, see. Then I take her to a sporting house [brothel]. That's the part they asked me to play. That's the part I refused to play."[43]

Paramount could wait no longer and suspended its opposing contract player. However, the MPPDA and P. S. Harrison, the founder of *Harrison's Reports* who believed "dirty" movies were bad for the business, praised Raft for standing his ground. According to Paramount executives, they suspended Raft because he demanded a sizable salary increase.

Raft's replacement was Jack La Rue, a minor actor who was often cast in bit parts but who had made an impression on Broadway as Mae West's Latin lover in *Diamond Lil* and as an Italian priest the year before in Paramount's *A Farewell to Arms*. Because of script changes, his character would no longer be called Popeye; he was now a city punk named Trigger, and he wouldn't be impotent.

James Wingate was anxious to see the rushes, especially the "dangerous sequences," that is, the rape in the corn crib and Miss Reba's whorehouse, but they hadn't filmed those scenes yet. To ease tensions, Emanuel Cohen assured Will Hays that if Dr. Wingate had problems with *Temple Drake* the studio would reshoot the offending scenes, adding that Wingate could "discuss it with me personally."[44]

To handle the rape sequence tastefully, Glazer used the talents of the newly hired thirty-one-year-old Romanian sketch artist and technical adviser Jean Negulesco. Negulesco's first job at Paramount was to provide the opening plans for the Frank Tuttle film *This Is the Night*, the film debut of Cary Grant. Pleased with Negulesco's work, Glazer assigned him to design the delicate rape sequence for *Temple Drake*.

On the day it was filmed, the stage was dark except for light streaming in through the slats of a rundown barn. Corn cobs covered the floor. Negulesco supervised the shooting, showing Miriam the positions she should take. "This better be good," mumbled an electrician behind him. "Rape with a foreign touch." The crew laughed.

Adding to Negulesco's discomfort, Miriam asked provocatively, "Jean, are my legs opened at the right angle? Shouldn't my dress be up higher? Do I scream? And are my eyes opened in terror of what I see? Or do I close my eyes and let things happen? Jean, do I enjoy it?"

Everyone laughed. Although Miriam felt guilty teasing him, she added to his embarrassment by grabbing him and kissing him "fiercely on the mouth." The crew yelled, applauded, and Miriam and Negulesco "were friends."[45]

The scene was shot in a style as close to Negulesco's black-and-white ink drawings as the censors would allow without showing the actual rape. At the end of the scene, as Trigger approaches Temple, the screen goes black. Years later, Miriam recalled, "There was just the scream. But [Negulesco] planned how it could be done. . . . If you can call a rape artistically done, it was."[46]

Irrespective of its artistic merits, Miriam's mother was offended that her daughter was playing a rape victim. In her opinion, "it was a bad book." But Miriam believed that *Temple Drake* wouldn't be offensive. "Certain situations will be handled with great delicacy," she tried to explain. "And if we can present characters who are 'misfits' according to our standards, and present them sympathetically, doesn't that help all of us to a better understanding of our fellow creatures?"[47]

Also, would Miriam's fans be alienated if it wasn't in good taste? Few actresses could believably play Temple, but Miriam brought "suggestiveness" to the role while being repulsed by Trigger's actions. Many held that it took courage to play the part. Miriam disagreed. "I don't think it took any courage at all. The story had truth—it was real." She loved Faulkner's book and was friends with the author. When the opportunity came to be in the film version, she jumped at it. "There was a real chance to do something fine and artistic on the screen. I don't call that courage."[48]

Not surprisingly, the atmosphere on the *Temple Drake* set was gloomy, so the cast played practical jokes to lighten the mood. One stunt ended up shaking the halls of Paramount all the way to the Hays office. It began when Miriam and Stephen Roberts wanted Jack La Rue to pick up a corncob, look at it, and smile into the camera. They knew it was in bad taste, but the brief scene wouldn't be in the film. Only those in the screening room would see it—including the intended victim, Emanuel Cohen. Miriam knew he watched the rushes every morning and she wanted to give that "little man a shock."[49]

At the end of the day's filming, when the cast and crew were gone, they completed the shot in a matter of minutes. The next morning, Cohen viewed the rushes. When the offending scene appeared, he jumped to his feet and shouted, "Has Roberts lost his mind?" After Cohen had calmed, his staff told him it was a gag. Miriam and Roberts watched from the projection booth and had a good laugh.[50]

Less humorous was an anonymous tip about the corncob gag sent over to James Wingate. When the MPPDA's top dog grasped what had happened, he dictated a letter to Adolph Zukor expressing his disgust at Paramount's distinct lack of respect for the Code: "I am not assuming, of course, that any part of the shot would be allowed to be in the picture, if this report is accurate it indicates an attitude that makes important a compliance with the spirit of the Code by those who are party to it."[51]

Both Zukor and Cohen denied Paramount's disrespect for the Code, reaffirming that the shot was for the rushes only.

That wasn't the end of it. Cohen gave a sharp reprimand to Miriam, Stephen Roberts, Jack La Rue, and cinematographer Karl Struss. To strengthen his point, he chose to slap their wrists on the day they screened *The Story of Temple Drake* for members of the Hays office. One by one, they were called into Cohen's office in view of Wingate and his staff, hopefully sending the message that Paramount took the Code seriously. Miriam recalled years later how they were "chewed out" for their stunt: "Stephen and I deserved it, but poor Jack and Karl were following our orders. They didn't speak to us for a week. But it was worth it 'cause we got Cohen—good."[52]

Hays's henchman, Joseph Breen, who judged the moral content of films, viewed *Temple Drake*; while he hadn't read the novel, he considered it "a sordid, base and thoroughly unpleasant picture that will add nothing to the advancement of the screen." Breen agreed that with modifications, it was possible for it to meet the Code's requirements.[53]

When *The Story of Temple Drake* premiered at the Times Square Paramount Theater on May 6, 1933, the *Motion Picture Daily* called it "a powerful picture." The *New York Times* hailed it as a "highly intelligent production. It is grim and sordid but at the same time a picture which is enormously helped by its definite dramatic value."[54]

Most reviews, however, were far from positive. The subject matter offended some critics, with the *Washington Times* complaining it couldn't "understand such trash on screen" and the *New York American* dismissing it as "shoddy, obnoxiously disagreeable . . . a trashy, sex-plugged piece." Despite the negative reviews, *The Story of Temple Drake* was a solid box-office hit for Paramount.[55]

Even though the Code had been in effect since 1930, James Wingate and his predecessor, Jason Joy, were ineffectual in terms of enforcing it with the studios. Even Joseph Breen was shocked at how Wingate did little to challenge the film's most offensive scenes.

The following year, a list of forbidden films issued by the Roman Catholic Church included, besides *The Story of Temple Drake*, *Baby Face* and the Mae West comedy *She Done Him Wrong*. In part because of the newly formed Catholic Legion of Decency, these films and others were the catalyst for the strict enforcement of the Motion Picture Production Code that would continue for twenty years.

Miriam believed the audience should trust producers more than censors or the self-appointed moral watchdog groups. In a *Movie Classic Magazine* interview later that year, Miriam said she thought that *Temple Drake* being "morally good or bad, clean or unclean, depended on the flip of a coin—obviously, the censors are to blame here; the producers have to do the stories that will *get* by the censors."[56]

Even so, years later, Miriam insisted it could have been worse. "Of course, the Hays Office stopped us from being too bad! *The Story of Temple Drake* is the best picture I ever made. There was talk of reissuing it, but it couldn't get by the censors." After its first run, the film was never exhibited in theaters again. Even then, it took several decades to be shown in museums and at film festivals.[57]

Miriam garnered enthusiastic reviews for her performance, and one critic reported that she "plays this part with brilliance." The *Dallas Morning News* commented that the character of Temple Drake, "made from the fumes of scenarist invention, is the chief reality of the picture, thanks to the careful and penetrating acting of Miriam Hopkins. False as Temple is, the actress limns her clearly, emphatically and with some effort at modeling."[58]

Stephen Roberts, who died from a heart attack three years after making *The Story of Temple Drake*, was praised for "exacting the last ounce of horror" out of a superb script written by Oliver H. P. Garrett. Unlike many of her directors, Roberts gained Miriam's respect. "He has courage, honesty and he knows character," she said, praising Roberts. "They didn't pay much attention to him in Hollywood—you know how they overlook their own best bets that are right there under their noses. But they'll pay attention to him now."[59]

As for Jack La Rue, he believed the role would mark a turnaround in his career, but instead he went back to supporting roles. When author Stone Wallace interviewed La Rue in the 1970s, he asked why his career never advanced after *Temple Drake*. "He kind of shrugged too," Wallace recalled, "and was uncertain as to why it never worked out. . . . I think the notoriety didn't bode well on La Rue, which is unfair because he plays the gangster great in *Temple Drake*, and it should have opened more doors for him, but it didn't."[60]

For many years, *The Story of Temple Drake* remained one of Miriam's favorite film roles. "That Temple Drake, now, there was a thing. Just give me a nice un-standardized wretch like Temple three times a year! Give me the complex ladies, and I'll interpret the daylights out of them."[61]

With less than a year remaining on Miriam's Paramount contract, Emanuel Cohen wanted his money's worth. He tried pairing her again with George Raft in *The Trumpet Blows*, but when that failed, she asked to be in Ernst Lubitsch's new project *Design for Living*. That was put on hold while they continued working on the script. Instead, Paramount loaned her to Metro-Goldwyn-Mayer, giving her another chance to work with Clark Gable in director King Vidor's film *Stranger's Return*, based on author Phil Stong's novel of life on a country farm.

But before the MGM cameras rolled, *Dancers in the Dark* scenarist Herman J. Mankiewicz had a project for her. When Miriam went to his house to discuss it, she fell on his newly polished floor in her high heeled shoes and sprained her ankle. Doctors confined her to bed for two weeks, delaying the start of the film. Whether it was because the film was held up or the role was too small, we cannot know, but Clark Gable was replaced by Franchot Tone.

The Stranger's Return (executives added *The* for the film) follows Grandpa Storr (Lionel Barrymore), a lovable old farmer whose relatives believe he has lived long enough and use every means to gain control of his valuable farm. Miriam plays his recently divorced, city-born granddaughter (Louise) who arrives in the countryside to bring him hope.

Vidor filmed on location in nearby Chino, the closest place to a farming community in the Los Angeles area. Looking for an architectural style inspired by Grant Wood paintings, he used an old fifty-acre farm that had a huge barn with a pigeon cote on top, a corn crib, and pigs rooting around.

At the time, a "real movie" fad was taking place in Hollywood with such films as *State Fair* (also authored by Phil Stong), *The Man Who Dared*, and now, following that trend, *The Stranger's Return*. Vidor's attempt at realism is why he chose the farmlands of Chino; it looked more like Iowa than the back lot at Metro-Goldwyn-Mayer. Because Chino was at least an hour's drive from the studio, Vidor arranged for the cast and crew to stay at an abandoned country club nearby. Miriam worried how she would spend her spare time while Barrymore refused to remain at all and commuted each day in an old coupe.

The *New York Times* called *The Stranger's Return* a "shrewd, delightful and altogether effective entertainment," praising Barrymore's performance as "hearty and brilliant" and calling Miriam "engagingly natural and intelligently appealing."[62]

Even with good reviews, the film did little to enhance Miriam's career. Since she was a Paramount commodity and with them for only one film, MGM did little to feature her in their publicity. But if *The Stranger's Return* did anything, it showed Miriam's versatility as an actress. With her performance sandwiched between *Temple Drake* and her role as Gilda in the upcoming *Design for Living*—three radically distinct roles—her prestige as an actress would continue to increase.

7

The Lubitsch Touch

Noël Coward's darkly witty comedy *Design for Living* opened on Broadway on January 24, 1933, at the Ethel Barrymore Theatre. The play, about "three people who love each other very much," explored risqué subjects such as infidelity and a ménage à trois with traces of homosexuality.

Within days of the play's opening, the Hays office worried that Hollywood would make a film adaptation. Coward excused the quirkiness of his characters, on the grounds that artists are responsible "to their own code of morals." The Hays office disagreed. In a memo, it stated, "It is somewhat doubtful whether a motion picture audience would take that viewpoint, and a motion picture treatment would be faced with that basic difficulty."[1]

Paramount bought the screen rights and sent Ernst Lubitsch to New York to see the play. Lubitsch told Coward that "motion pictures should not talk about events in the past," adding that he would replace much of the playwright's dialogue with action. Whereas the play's characters discuss where they met, what they did in the past, and how they loved, Lubitsch would *show* those plot points.[2]

Ben Hecht wrote the screenplay, keeping the title but little else. When Coward heard of the radical rewrite, he quipped: "I am told that there are three of my original lines left in the film—such original ones as 'Pass the mustard.'" Coward's sarcasm aside, only one of his original lines remained, and it had nothing to do with passing any mustard. The line in question was "For the good of our immortal souls"—a drinking toast.[3]

Lubitsch worked with Hecht, changing the "'how' but not the 'what.'" All through the writing, Lubitsch and Hecht were at odds. The director wasn't familiar with Hecht's routine, and Hecht insisted that not even Lubitsch would tell him how to write a script. Then, Hecht suggested that he show his completed scenes to Lubitsch: "If you don't like it, we fight it out." Lubitsch agreed.[4]

One Lubitsch "touch" was acting out the parts at the typewriter, including the love scenes. This annoyed Hecht. He told Miriam, "If he grabs me once more, to show me how Freddie March is supposed to embrace you, I'll turn pansy."[5]

Casting also had problems. Someone suggested Ronald Colman and Leslie Howard to play the painter and playwright. Colman wanted too much money, and Howard didn't want critics comparing him to Noël Coward. In their place, Fredric March was chosen for the writer Tom while Douglas Fairbanks Jr. would play George, the painter. At the last minute, Fairbanks came down with pneumonia and was replaced by leading man Gary Cooper.

From the beginning, Lubitsch wanted Miriam for Gilda, the commercial artist who gets involved platonically with the playwright and painter. He knew Paramount was uneasy about her sluggishness at the box office, but he believed that being opposite two sophisticated leading men would increase her audience attraction.

Lubitsch sent the completed *Design for Living* script to the set of *The Stranger's Return*. At the time, Miriam was in a clandestine relationship with the film's director, King Vidor, who was "infatuated with the soft Southern talk of this Georgia queen." Their liaison was a secret, or so they thought.

"One evening we had a dinner engagement which was known only to the two of us," Vidor recalled in his autobiography, *A Tree Is a Tree*. "Miss Hopkins told me she had been sent a new script by Ernst Lubitsch with the request that she gives an answer the following day. She asked if I would help her decide whether she should play the part. She read straight through, and we were both elated with Miriam's part and with the sharp humor of the story. As Miriam read the final lines on the last page of the manuscript, her eyes fell on a scribbled notation at the bottom of the page. It read: 'King—any little changes you would like, I will be happy to make them. Ernst.' The Lubitsch touch had exploded our secret world."[6]

Now, their not-so-hush-hush affair heated up the gossip columns. Their first outing was at the Oscar Hammerstein musical *Music in the Air* at the downtown Belasco Theater. Soon they were seen everywhere.

Meanwhile on *Design for Living*'s first day of filming, Lubitsch told the cast and crew "critics will not like our picture. They will say we have ruined Noël Coward's play, and it is true that our picture will be quite different. But the people who do not read reviews or care about them will love it, and Noël Coward means nothing to most of them."[7]

Production was off to a shaky start. A technicians' strike in July nearly brought filming to a halt. Paramount brought in "strike breakers," as did many of the studios, to take up the slack.

Then, Miriam developed an abscess on her tonsils requiring surgery. Lubitsch closed the set for a week. In the hospital, Vidor sent flowers to Miriam's crowded room, dwarfing the one-dozen roses sent by Lubitsch. The infatuated director did anything to please her, but when he rented the house beside her San Vicente Boulevard property, Miriam had had enough. In two weeks, she broke the lease on Garbo's former estate, claiming to have bought an avocado ranch in Bel Air. Instead, she moved into an apartment.

Miriam liked Vidor. She enjoyed his company, and the "sex was good," but his continuous courting was "overwhelming"; she couldn't reciprocate his feelings.[8]

The Sunday before their affair ended, they went to a gathering at screenwriter Salka Viertel's Santa Monica home. Her afternoon salons, known in Hollywood as Salka's Sundays, were hosted by Viertel and her husband, Berthold.[9]

Their son, fourteen-year-old Peter Viertel, who would be a successful novelist and the screenwriter of Hemingway's *The Sun Also Rises*, had a crush on Miriam: "She had come to my parents' house for tea, accompanied by King Vidor, one of the top directors of the first half of the century. Vidor was a big, handsome man with a pleasant baritone voice and, like Hopkins, a southerner. Accompanied on the guitar by his driver, Tony Guerrero, he sang 'Water Boy,' 'Nobody Knows the Trouble I've Seen' and 'Ol' Man River.' The moment Vidor began to sing, Hopkins began to talk. She was a voluble young woman, witty and intelligent, with a seductive voice she apparently liked the sound of. No doubt she'd heard Vidor's renditions before and did not enjoy sitting quietly to listen. Even to my less than worldly eyes, it was apparent that the relationship was not going to be a permanent one."[10]

Miriam had no hesitation showing her displeasure for Vidor. She was rude, even if Vidor was a bore. Not surprisingly, a week later, their affair ended. Distraught and heartbroken, Vidor suffered the breakup "with a terrible torch." Reacting dramatically and oddly, he consoled his heavy heart by sawing the legs off his couch.[11]

Despite the changes to Noël Coward's play, many critics loved the Lubitsch version. "What was a thoroughly delightful evening in the the-

ater now becomes an equally delicious almost two hours of screen entertainment," wrote the *Hollywood Reporter.* Yet, some recognized the
changes. Having seen the play and loved it, many New Yorkers missed
Coward's oft-quoted lines. "If you can look at it without prejudice," one
reviewer wrote, "as an original story, you will probably think it could not
have been better."[12]

Critics praised Miriam. The *Hollywood Reporter* wrote that she "never
looked as well or performed as invitingly as she does in this picture," and
another reported that she succeeded moralistically in "making her pro-
miscuity comprehensible and appealing."[13]

Miriam was Lubitsch's favorite actress, and Miriam credited her
career success to the director's influence. She once affirmed: "I consider
Lubitsch the greatest screen director because he has the qualities of exact-
ness, sureness, and authority. He knows just what he wants and gets it, not
by screaming or ranting, but with a Billiken-like grin. When you 'go up' in
your lines he just laughs. I asked him how he could be so even-tempered
with all that responsibility. He said it was because he has all the pain at
home—he works his problems out there, but once he has the solution he
can be patient on the set because he knows exactly what effect he's striv-
ing for."[14]

At any rate, Miriam was harmful to his health. A decade later, Lubitsch
had heart problems. Her visits to his hospital room raised his pulse to an
alarming rate. He blamed her rapid-fire conversation for forcing his heart
to a Hopkins-inspired 125 beats per minute (only the ever-placid Charles
Brackett could restore it to normal). Despite that, they remained close
friends, seeing one another at parties or on holidays. *Design for Living* was
their last film together.

Miriam relaxed before her next picture, *All of Me*, an adaptation of
Rose Albert Porter's play *Chrysalis*, which had a brief run on Broadway.
The casting wasn't complete, but her temperature rose when she learned
that George Raft was a costar. Once again, Fredric March played her love
interest. Sylvia Sidney initially had a supporting role, but Helen Mack
replaced her. Mack had stepped in for Fay Wray in *The Son of Kong*, the
much-anticipated sequel to *King Kong*.

Miriam's contract was about to expire, as were the contracts of fellow
Paramount stars Fredric March and Charles Laughton. All three hinted at
taking their talents elsewhere. Paramount intended to hang on to them,
but the studio was still in receivership and facing financial problems from

the record profit loss of $21 million (more than $375 million today) the year before. Giving up the salaries of three pricey stars would cut their losses.

Miriam personally asked Adolph Zukor not to renew her contract. She compared her tenure at the studio to incarceration: "You belong to the company, body, and soul; you might as well have been sold down the river. You may not like the director of your new picture. You may think the story is cheap and disgusting. You may think the leading man is inadequate. But you can't complain. The company, very politely, says you are getting your salary every week to do what is required of you. And that's all the argument there is. You go in and make the picture and look forward to the days when you can freelance."[15]

Was freelancing in Miriam's future? Other female stars were freelancing or were about to: Constance Bennett, Irene Dunne, and Barbara Stanwyck were finding success without the security of a studio.

In New York, Lyman Brown still represented Miriam's Hollywood interests. With a difference of nearly three thousand miles, Miriam believed his long-distance negotiating resulted in her studio headaches. She criticized Brown privately for "not earning his 10 percent," but then her complaints reached him. "I hear you are not saying things favorable to me," Lyman wrote after confirming that five mutual friends had heard Miriam "make certain very unkind statements." Brown was critical to her early career, but she had to move on. They went their separate ways.[16]

To prepare for independence, she hired Myron Selznick, one of Hollywood's leading agents. Selznick was a "competent and reputable thoroughfare for talent," and along with Leland Hayward in New York, he represented such stars as Katharine Hepburn, William Powell, and Ginger Rogers. Miriam signed with him, hoping he could do the same for her.[17]

Right or not, Emanuel Cohen doubted Miriam's box office clout, even though *Design for Living* was one of the top ten highest grossing films that year. When Miriam asked to let her contract lapse, it took Selznick's negotiating skills and several heated arguments to make it so. In the end, Cohen dropped her option.

Besides wanting control over her film career, Miriam was thinking again of Broadway, despite critics' accusations that she had deserted the stage. "I never did; I was just 'on location' in Hollywood," she said defensively. "But desert the theater? Never! I would never make a picture contract that didn't permit me to return to the stage occasionally."[18]

With the echoes of applause beckoning her, she listened when Broadway producer and director Guthrie McClintic called with an offer. His current project with business partner and wife Katherine Cornell, the First Lady of the Theatre, was an Owen Davis play entitled *Jezebel*.

McClintic had problems with the play's star, Tallulah Bankhead. She was ill and couldn't take the part, so McClintic offered it to Miriam. Hoping to resurrect her theater career, she told McClintic she would be in New York as soon as she completed *All of Me*.

To verify that *Jezebel* was the right decision, Miriam saw her astrologer, who confirmed the planets were favorable. Her numerologist evaluated the addresses of the Ethel Barrymore Theatre, where the play would have its run, and her suite number at the Hotel Pierre—all was in order. The fates were aligned for *Jezebel*'s success.

But first, Emanuel Cohen had to approve a six-month leave, thus extending her contract. At first, he hesitated. He wanted Miriam to be walking out of Paramount's iconic gate as soon as possible, but Selznick reminded him of the clause in her contract allowing for time off for the theater. Cohen approved the leave.

Miriam rushed through *All of Me* and on November 16, 1933, she flew to New York. Michael and his nanny, Mademoiselle, would join her later. Rehearsals for *Jezebel* would begin the following day.

According to its author, Owen Davis, the tragic drama *Jezebel* was a "rather wooden, old-fashioned Southern melodrama, but it had some strong meat in it, and the part of Jezebel had everything any actress could ask for." When Tallulah Bankhead read the play, she recognized it was a good part. However, two weeks into rehearsals, the actress was hospitalized with severe abdominal pains. Heavily medicated, she was released, and she returned to rehearsals. But the pain was too intense, and she asked McClintic to replace her.[19]

Following Bankhead's departure, relative newcomer Margaret Sullavan, who had been in the hit *Dinner at Eight* the year before, accepted the role of the willful southern belle Julie. But McClintic had a change of heart, hoping Bankhead would recover in time for the opening.

On October 16, Bankhead was released from the hospital, but she relapsed and had a hysterectomy two weeks later. Now that Sullavan was off to Hollywood to make her first film, McClintic had to find another actress and offered the role to Miriam.

"With Miriam Hopkins as Julie, he [McClintic] placed it in rehearsal again," said Tallulah Bankhead. "Miriam was an old Georgia gal, with accredited drawl. Guthrie felt Julie might be her mutton."[20]

Leland Hayward brokered a deal with *Jezebel*'s producers, giving Miriam a piece of the play, but an unexpected love affair bloomed. At the time, Hayward was seeing Katharine Hepburn, and when she learned of Miriam, she confronted Hayward. He denied the rumors, but Hepburn called him a liar. Hepburn's confrontation may have achieved the desired result. Miriam's liaison with the agent was short-lived, lasting only through the run of *Jezebel*.[21]

Jezebel's out-of-town tryout was on December 14, 1933, at New Haven's Shubert Theater, where Miriam had opened many of her former Broadway shows. The play received less-than-stellar reviews. Complaining about a lack of "vivacity and sparkle," *Variety* noted that "in her present vehicle, these assets register 'No sales,' partly due to the remoteness of the stage from the audience and partly due to the use of half lighting which had her reading lines in the shadows. Aside from this, Miss Hopkins does a first-rate job."[22]

With its staging issues corrected, *Jezebel* had a glitzy opening at the Ethel Barrymore Theatre on December 19. Miriam had confessed that seeing her name in lights made her nervous. It must have been doubly nerve-wracking to see her name simultaneously on two New York marquees: at the Barrymore for *Jezebel* and in Times Square at the Criterion, where *Design for Living* was showing.[23]

The opening night audience at the Barrymore was what society editors liked to call "smart." Dressed in coattails and ermine wraps, the star-studded celebrity guests included stage and silent film star Laurette Taylor, Conrad Nagel, Dorothy Parker, Irving Berlin, American socialite and actress Rosamond Pinchot, Kay Francis, and Paramount mogul Adolph Zukor. It surprised her that much of the New York audience consisted of motion-picture friends.

Miriam's popularity among her friends notwithstanding, the reviews were not enthusiastic. *Jezebel* benefitted from Donald Oenslager's scenery and McClintic's meticulous production but fell short due to Owen Davis's writing. "What still passes all understanding," opined the *New York Post* critic "is why Mr. McClintic should have thought that—with or without Miss Bankhead—this script could ever have been possessed of any quality."[24]

Owen Davis, however, placed the blame on the shoulders of his new leading lady. "The only thing we could do was to go ahead without Miss Bankhead. We had a lot of trouble and no time at all to get things right. I was forced to rip my poor play apart and change the character of Jezebel from a sort of female Dr. Jekyll and Mr. Hyde to a sweet little Southern belle, and the audiences hated the resultant mess almost as much as I did."[25]

Davis never explained why he had to rewrite his play for Miriam, but with few exceptions, her personal opening night reviews were kind. Robert Garland of the *New York World-Telegram* noted she did "her best. As you know, her best is excellent." The *New York Times's* Brooks Atkinson called her "rhapsodically beautiful" and added she was "lovely and glowing enough to console the most craven of theatergoers. When she cannot out dazzle an awkward line or scene, every honest votary of beauty is ready to lay the blame on Mr. Davis's worn door-step." Publically, the play's lackluster reception was not Miriam's burden.[26]

Also among her admirers was her boss, Adolph Zukor, who sent flowers and a telegram of congratulations. "How perfectly sweet," Miriam responded. "I can't tell you how happy you made me. The show isn't very hot but the critics I thought were very kind to me and with the notices."[27]

Before opening night, author and screenwriter Donald Ogden Stewart bet Leland Hayward a case of champagne that *Jezebel* would run less than a week. Surprisingly, Hayward told Miriam about the wager. After the opening night performance, Stewart and his wife, Beatrice, and a friend, writer George Oppenheimer, stopped by Miriam's dressing room to take her to dinner and wait for the reviews.

Instead of greeting them warmly, Miriam went into a "long, long tirade about their theatrical obtuseness," as author George Eells put it, and gave them hell—a tirade cut short by a knock at the door and Stewart's quip that that was "the man with the champagne."[28]

Miriam may have berated Stewart for his insensitive joke about *Jezebel's* lasting power, yet she had been in that position before and knew the play was bound to have a limited run. That meant Paramount would demand her return to Hollywood.

While appearing in *Jezebel*, she read several plays and decided on a one-act version of *The Affairs of Anatol*, which she had done on Broadway two years earlier. Since silent pictures, studios had used prologues as a gimmick to attract audiences, and now during the Depression, it treated fans to live stage shows featuring popular entertainers. Miriam convinced Emanuel Cohen to let her take a truncated version of *Anatol* on the road to several of Paramount's larger theaters as a prologue to one of their films. Hank Potter, the stage manager of the 1931 production of *Anatol*, agreed to direct.

While waiting for the death knell to ring for *Jezebel*, Miriam was a southern belle by night at the Barrymore and *Anatol*'s Mimi by day in rehearsals in her suite at the Hotel Pierre.

Jezebel folded after thirty-two performances—in McClintic's words, "a complete flop, one of the few real failures that I've ever had." Tallulah Bankhead later added the "jury brought in a verdict of guilty as charged. . . . I'm not trying to pin the rap on Miriam. Had I been in it *Jezebel* might have lasted five weeks."[29]

As a thank you to the cast, stagehands, and everyone associated with the play, Miriam hosted a farewell party on the Barrymore's stage after the last performance. Caterers set up long tables of food, along with plenty of champagne. "Not gin, nor cocktails, nor highballs. Champagne—that's what that farewell needed, and that's what it got," she later told friends.[30]

Two weeks later, audiences who paid to see Cecil B. DeMille's *Four Frightened People* at the Times Square Paramount Theatre saw Miriam, along with Rollo Peters and Austin Fairman, in a one-act version of *Anatol*. Hank Potter insisted they were reverent in their adaptation of Schnitzler's play but "broadened it" so fans who came to see "movie stars doing five a day" could appreciate it. Luckily it worked. Audiences loved Miriam. She was the "funniest thing since Jack Benny"; as excellent at the ten-thirty morning show as she was at the fifth show at night.[31]

After completing a week at the Paramount, the troupe moved to Chicago, and then it was off to Boston for several days at the Metropolitan Theatre.

After *Anatol*'s run, she returned to Hollywood, where Cecil B. DeMille wanted her for his epic *Samson and Delilah*, with Henry Wilcoxon. When that continued to be postponed (in 1949, Hedy Lamarr would costar as Delilah for DeMille), Cohen gave her a role opposite Bing Crosby in the musical film version of the Broadway stage comedy *She Loves Me Not*. But before that would happen, she had a decade-long dream to fulfill in New York.

8

Sutton Place

New York's Sutton Place is one of the city's most affluent streets, running six blocks along the East River, from East Fifty-Third Street to East Fifty-Ninth Street (where it becomes York Avenue), and offering a stunning view of the Queensboro Bridge.

The neighborhood's history goes back to Effington B. Sutton and James Stokes, who bought the land in 1875 and built a brownstone private dwelling complex that attracted several famous tenants. Around 1880, in recognition of Sutton's creation of an upscale development, the city renamed that section of the street Sutton Place.

At the turn of the century, when the brownstone era faded because of poverty and the invasion of street toughs known as the Dead End Kids, so did Sutton Place. Soon it degenerated into a slum lived in by slaughterhouse workers, coal passers, barge loaders, and other laborers.

In 1920, noted theatrical and literary agent Elisabeth Marbury bought 13 Sutton Place when it was nothing more than an uninhabited, bleak brownstone house with a chipped brown stoop and windows tacked up with newspaper. Between the house and the East River, there were high fences and a scrubby mound of earth, stones, and rusted cans.

Marbury hired famed architect Mott B. Schmidt and spent a fortune to restore the ramshackle townhouse. Not long afterward, she encouraged Anne Tracy Morgan, the daughter of financier J. P. Morgan, to buy 3 Sutton Place and convert it from a slum to a manor. Mrs. William K. Vanderbilt was the newest Fifth Avenue alumna to move in, when she took over 1 Sutton Place.

With Marbury ensconced at 13 Sutton Place, the red-lacquered door greeted scores of noted personalities of literature, the arts, politics, and society who came to partake of her hospitality. Marbury never married, living openly with the interior decorator Elsie de Wolfe in what everyone accepted as a lesbian relationship. However, in 1926, de Wolfe surprised everyone, including Marbury, when she married Sir Charles Mendl, a British diplomat—a liaison many considered no more than a "marriage of convenience." From then on, she was known as Lady Mendl, and on her frequent visits to New York, she stayed with her old friend.[1]

Miriam met Elizabeth Marbury in 1923. Broke at the time, and trying to sell a few short stories, Miriam admired the house. While soaking in the ambiance and the view of the Queensboro Bridge, she told Marbury that one day she would own it. A decade later, Marbury died from a heart attack in her bedroom. More than two thousand people attended her funeral, at St. Patrick's Cathedral, among them city, state, and national political leaders.

Not surprisingly, Marbury's beneficiary was Lady Mendl. When Miriam saw 13 Sutton Place on the market the following November, she was in rehearsals for *Jezebel*. She offered Lady Mendl $20,000, which she accepted.

When escrow closed in March, Miriam asked *Jezebel*'s set designer Donald Oenslager to redecorate the house. This was something he hadn't done before and wasn't interested in doing. Yet, Miriam was persuasive. She explained she would be on the coast in a film, and added: "You don't have to send me anything for approval. I don't want to see anything until I come back to New York, and then I want you to take me through the house." Oenslager was "fond of her and respected her"; he agreed to do it.[2]

With Sutton Place in Oenslager's hands, Miriam flew to Hollywood with Michael and her entourage for rehearsals of *She Loves Me Not*. She had planned to stay in New York until September, but when *She Loves Me Not* became available, she figured, "Well, it's a good part. If I don't go back until September, my contract won't end until November or December. The fall season in New York will be ruined for me." By returning now, she could complete both *She Loves Me Not* and the follow-up Paramount project before September. She would be free of any Hollywood commitments.[3]

She Loves Me Not was based on the Broadway hit by Howard Lindsay. Curley Flagg (Hopkins), a nightclub entertainer, witnesses a gangster's murder and leaves New York in fear of her life. With enough money to get as far as Princeton, she finds herself in the dorm room of college musical show writer Paul Lawton (Bing Crosby). Touched by Curley's story, Lawton and his roommate, Buzz (Eddie Nugent), decide to hide her from the mob by cutting her hair and dressing her up as "one of the boys."

Bing Crosby, the country's leading radio sensation, became famous in the medium while performing as a singer in local nightclubs. He impressed critics in Paramount's 1932 hit *The Big Broadcast*, where he played a carefree crooner at an unsuccessful radio station.

Miriam, who had appeared on Crosby's radio program, called him "another doll," adding she "liked working with Bing more than almost any other leading man she had ever faced a camera with." They got along well even though she couldn't convince him to rehearse more than once. His reputation for letter-perfect first takes frustrated her. Once during a radio show, they practiced a routine one time before having a cigarette in the parking lot. Miriam begged him to rehearse it again, but Crosby shook his head. "Sweetie, no! We'd get stale. Let's just do it, you know, we've got the line. I'll say something and [you] ad-lib back and forth with me."[4]

Several times illness and accidents interrupted filming, and threatened Miriam's New York fall schedule. First, Bing Crosby sprained his right wrist, and then singer Kitty Carlisle developed laryngitis. One day, Miriam and Crosby were chatting when director Elliott Nugent gave them a script change: She was to jump three feet from a window ledge onto a mattress. Miriam's mouth dropped open. A few months earlier, during *Anatol*, a Boston psychic had predicted that she would jump from a ledge and break her ankle.

"I just can't do it," she howled to a flabbergasted Nugent. "I've spent most of my life recovering from sprained, broken and twisted ankles. I know it sounds silly, but a fortune teller in Boston told me . . ." Nugent, Charles Lang, the cinematographer, and the electricians nearby burst out laughing. "It's only a three-foot jump," insisted Nugent, "and you jump on a mattress. Nothing can possibly happen."[5]

So, Miriam jumped, but a stabbing pain coursed through her ankle. Expecting to be ribbed, she worked until the pain was so intense that she almost fainted. At the hospital, X-rays revealed a torn ligament and two small broken bones. For three weeks, her left foot was braced in a steel cast, forcing the company to film around her. When she healed, her costars teased her unmercifully.

"Bing, Eddie Nugent and Warren Hymer [Mugg] used to kid me to death. They used to look at me, shake their heads and say, 'Hoppy, you're limping on the wrong foot. You'll give yourself away.' But I loved it."[6]

Crosby's love interest, Kitty Carlisle, was a relative newcomer to films. Miriam took a liking to the unseasoned actress, helping her whenever she could. Carlisle recalled that Miriam was "the most generous of colleagues, offering to rehearse before each scene," despite what Crosby wanted.

"She took care of me and decided I needed help because, I think it was my second picture, and I didn't know much about Hollywood. She made it her business to look after me, and I'm told that was very unusual for her because she was tough. But she protected me and gave me useful tips, and I loved her for that."[7]

Upon its release, *She Loves Me Not* received decent reviews. The *Chicago Daily Tribune* offered an assessment of the romantic comedy, calling the dialogue "fast and funny, [the] photography and direction expert" and calling Miriam "excellent as the rather crude little go-getter" and successful "in making you laugh at her antics."[8]

Miriam's Paramount contract was nearing its end. She owed them one picture, but no projects suited her. The press reported that the studio had cast her in *Wharf Angel* and *Peter Ibbetson*, but she had declined both parts. After discussions about loaning her to Warner Bros. for the Paul Muni film, *Bordertown*, fell through, RKO wanted her for Norman Krasna's *The Richest Girl in the World*, after their contract star Ann Harding refused. That let Paramount off the hook.

The Richest Girl in the World reportedly was patterned after the life of Barbara Hutton, the heiress to the Woolworth department store fortune and future wife of Cary Grant. Miriam plays Dorothy Hunter, who has more money than any other woman in the world. To find a man who will love her for herself, she switches places with her secretary, played by Fay Wray, who was basking in the success of *King Kong* from the year before.

Wray considered Miriam an exceptional actress. "I learned something working with her that I never did forget," Wray told film historian William Drew. "I think very often if an actor or actress is told they've done something wrong in a scene, they can kind of curl up. But I just loved the way she responded to Mr. Seiter when he brought something to her attention. She said, 'Oh, thank you, thank you.' And I wasn't aware that she even meant it—maybe she did—but I just thought that was wonderful. It opens up a different aspect of a relationship between a director and an actor that for me, anyway, was great."[9]

Miriam's love interest, actor Joel McCrea, who caused a controversy for his nude scenes with Dolores Del Rio in 1932's *Bird of Paradise*, had recently settled his much-publicized differences with the studio over refusing to be loaned to Universal. *The Richest Girl in the World* would be the first of five films they would make.

But first, Miriam flew to New York to tour her newly decorated Sutton Place home. Donald Oenslager nervously walked her through the house. "She was more astonished room after room and, I must say, very pleased," the designer said. In the entrance, he placed a piano with baroque accouterments on the wall. Ivory and cobalt blue was the theme throughout the living room, and in the kitchen, he used light spring green paint.

"She also had paintings," Oenslager explained, "first rate ones, including a Matisse and a Monet. But the paintings and the house she thought of as investments—unlike the first editions, which she would never part with." Two rooms were left untouched—one Elsie de Wolfe had designed and a paneled drawing room with a distinctive Oriental wallpaper.[10]

Miriam cut short her New York trip so she could begin on *The Richest Girl in the World*. Screenwriter Norman Krasna had a reputation for writing intelligent, amusing screenplays with social commentary. Overall, the Hays office liked the finished script but recommended changes so it could be more compliant with the Code. For one, they objected to a scene that shows Miriam and Joel McCrea having too much to drink and ends with a "fadeout of the two falling asleep" on the floor. Their protest was ignored by the studio.[11]

The Richest Girl in the World was a huge success for RKO, coming in with the sixth highest box office receipts that year. It was also a critical success for Miriam. Richard Watts Jr. of the *New York Herald-Tribune* called it, "Amusingly written by Norman Krasna, wisely directed by William A. Seiter and delightfully played by Miss Miriam Hopkins." *Picture Play* magazine wrote, "Miriam Hopkins, everybody knows, can be the perfect baby-doll type, but in this film, she achieved real distinction, and subdued the desire, if any, to wear curls, or to look like a French pincushion, or candy box." William Boehnel of the *World-Telegram* called Miriam "brisk, lovely and exciting" and said she "proves herself a truly clever comedienne in the part."[12]

RKO, still soaring from *The Richest Girl in the World*'s success, considered offering her a contract. Executives even instructed director William Seiter to find her more stories. But, she was on a short list for the Becky Sharp role in Jock Whitney's new Technicolor version of Thackeray's *Vanity Fair*.[13]

Whitney was in several ventures, including politics, horse racing, and Broadway shows. "Jock Whitney was terrific," according to Broadway musical historian Miles Krueger. "He loved the theater, and he backed shows on Broadway knowing perfectly well that they would lose money, but Whitney didn't care, he had enough."[14]

But filming in Technicolor was expensive—more so than the stage—and Whitney didn't want to waste more on the budget. When Whitney and Myron Selznick couldn't agree on Miriam's salary, he asked to borrow Myrna Loy from MGM.

Besides Whitney and RKO, Selznick was negotiating with independent producer Samuel Goldwyn about adding Miriam's talents to his studio roster. For the past year, Goldwyn had been building up Russian actress Anna Sten, who had successes in both Russian and German films. Hoping to rival Greta Garbo, Goldwyn cast Sten in an adaptation of Emile Zola's *Nana*, but the period drama was a disappointment, as were her two subsequent films for his studio.

Merle Oberon, a dark beauty with several popular British films to her credit, was also a so-called Goldwyn girl, but Miriam would be his first homegrown American actress since the silent days. Although he worried about her legendary temper, he recognized her star potential. Her audience appeal could increase were her talents matched with the right story rather than squandered in routine pictures, as Paramount had done.

On August 31, 1934, Miriam signed a four-year contract with Samuel Goldwyn. Her first project for him was in limbo, but F. Scott Fitzgerald hoped it could be an adaptation of his novel *Tender Is the Night,* whose rights Goldwyn had acquired.

"If you can honestly see her in that light," Fitzgerald wrote to Bennett Cerf, "for God's sake drop her a line telling her so, though I don't know whether she will have any say in the final choice. When I thought that the thing would be sold immediately, she was one of the three (the others were Hepburn and Ann Harding) that I could see in the role, which requires intelligent handling, but of all of them, she was my favorite."[15]

Miriam hadn't seen Fitzgerald since their affair nearly a decade earlier. She was "extremely anxious to do it," promising to let Cerf know when Goldwyn decided. But even so, it was unlikely the script would be in shape for Miriam's first picture.[16]

Besides, Goldwyn knew that Whitney would most likely choose Miriam for *Becky Sharp,* which gave him time to find a suitable script. It would probably be an adaptation of the bawdy novel *Barbary Coast.* So with nothing to keep her in Los Angeles, Miriam would return to New York to furnish her new house. Goldwyn, who preferred his stars to work and live in Hollywood, asked why she bought a house on the other side of the country. He insisted that she put it up for sale.

Not to be bullied, Miriam told him, "Sam, I'm going to die in that house." She walked out of his office. Miriam's first act of defiance gave Goldwyn a hint of his future with her.[17]

Instead of flying or taking the Chief to New York, she booked passage on the SS *California*, sailing through the Panama Canal. Two weeks later, at the Port of New York, she was greeted by her mother, who had recently returned with a friend from a summer in Europe, at Miriam's expense. Sending her mother to Europe "was not generosity" on her part, Miriam noted, "but bribery to keep her out of California, where she seems determined to land and run my life."[18]

While her battle with Ellen continued, her long-absent father was back in her life. She received a letter from an Oklahoma City minister explaining that Homer needed expensive dental care but couldn't afford the procedure. Despite her feelings of abandonment, she wrote out a check but "barely resisted writing across it, 'Daddy, here I come!'" They found each other but communicated only through letters and telephone calls. Over time, she would learn the truth about her father's absence of twenty-five years.[19]

After moving to Dallas, Homer had worked as an insurance salesperson. In November 1911, he married Katie Robinett, a schoolteacher from El Paso, Texas. In 1916, they moved to Oklahoma City and had a daughter, Katherine, who was now eighteen years old.

Homer knew that Miriam Hopkins, the stage and film actress, was his daughter, yet he never contacted her. His former life was a secret that he kept from his new wife and daughter. Charlotte Smith, Homer's granddaughter, said the fault was with his "first wife," calling her "a real bitch." Ellen held back Homer's letters, and when he "never heard from them, it hurt him."[20]

Ellen was furious when she learned that Miriam was in touch with her ex-husband. Miriam didn't care. "If I'm in New York for a month, I see her probably three times," Miriam recalled to her Aunt Minnie in Syracuse. "Trying to take her to a matinee and lunch to avoid as much as possible her vain talk about how important she is in all those stupid Southern clubs, and how clever she was to make over this or that dress.

That, I might add she doesn't have to do. Several times a year she is sent large boxes of summer and winter clothes, because being in a completely phony profession, it's difficult to repeat them the second season."[21]

Ruby was another story. The year before, she and her boyfriend, Jack Welch, had found themselves expecting a baby. Welch wasn't interested in marrying Ruby, and the feeling was mutual, but Ellen, worried about their reputations, forced them to wed. Five months later, when their daughter, Margot, was born, Welch left. Ruby's morale was low after being with the "moron she married, and never really wanted to," Miriam said. As Ruby's depression worsened, Miriam grew concerned.[22]

Ruby was like Miriam and their mother in appearance—petite, blonde, and pretty—but in terms of personality, she was different. Miriam and Ellen were extroverted and apt conversationalists. Ruby was quiet, shy, and, according to her daughter, Margot, "an excellent listener." Ruby was kind-hearted and an animal lover who would never say "'no' to any of the stray dogs and cats" Margot brought home.

According to Margot, the even-tempered Ruby was an avid reader, played the piano, and was a talented painter. "I never saw her angry or in a fight. She was her own person and despite her gentleness, couldn't be pushed into doing something that was wrong or prevented her from standing up for what she believed was right. Above all, she loved to dance and to explore, and she was a person of the present, not the past."[23]

Ruby's depression may have been a bipolar disorder like that of her grandfather Ralph Hastings Cutter, whose family had forced him into mental institutions, where he died. At times, Miriam worried that she had inherited her "grandfather's condition." At any rate, she knew her mother was "crazy." Rumors abounded on Broadway and in Hollywood that Miriam's mother and sister were both "mental cases," with the assumption that her "temperament" was the result. If Ralph Cutter's illness was genetic, Miriam and Ellen were stronger than Ruby, who, Michael said, had "had a nervous breakdown." Miriam took Ruby "under her wing."[24]

Ruby's failed attempts at fame had caused resentment and jealousy toward her sister. But no matter the source of Ruby's problems, Miriam blamed Ellen. For a time, Ruby worked at Macy's department store on West Thirty-Fourth Street, earning twenty dollars a week for selling records. Gradually, she revamped the music department. Her bosses were impressed and wanted to promote her to a buyer. But Ellen had no mercy. Every evening she would call Ruby, reminding her that she was disgracing the family by working as a "shop-girl." What if someone recognized her as Miriam Hopkins's sister, she questioned? It would be an "insult." Soon, because of her mother's nagging, Ruby found it impossible to work at Macy's and gave notice.

For years, Miriam sent her sister $150 a month. While Ellen insisted that Ruby should live on that, Miriam encouraged her to continue working if she wanted to. "I told Ruby I thought it was fine for her to do this, but her check would come just the same."[25]

Between her husband's desertion, Ellen's nagging, and her silent resentment toward Miriam, Ruby's self-esteem suffered. Alone with a baby, Ruby became reclusive. Having few friends, she moved to Flushing, Long Island, and rented a room to make extra money. She would go into the city for job interviews, but only if Miriam arranged them.

"Mother, long ago I gave up as hopeless," Miriam said, "but I'm trying to instill in Ruby, some sense of ambition and responsibility for the rearing of her child. It's difficult when she knows the check is coming. She sleeps late, lies around with the apathetic attitude of a person on relief. I don't care if she works, but I'd like her to want to. And I must try hard to make her make an effort for her sake. I love her deeply, and I have faith in her future. She seldom sees Mother, who drives her crazy by telling her she has made a failure of her life while I, her younger sister, am a success. That, I might add is no help."[26]

Family problems aside, Miriam was faced with an important choice. Desperate to find his Becky Sharp, Jock Whitney went back to Miriam after Myrna Loy and Claudette Colbert rejected the role. Her gamble to hold out for more money paid off. On September 25, 1934, Myron Selznick negotiated, and Miriam signed a lucrative, nonoption, one-picture contract. Besides director approval and star billing, it included a flat-rate salary of $60,000 and 10 percent of the film's gross receipts after RKO recovered the production's negative cost of $800,000. The additional percentage was warranted, according to Selznick, since Technicolor had to be proven, and Miriam was carrying the film; her career was at risk.[27]

Director Lowell Sherman would start filming in November. Until then, Miriam appeared on radio, including in an adaptation of *Seventh Heaven*, opposite John Boles, in the first episode of the *Lux Radio Theatre*.[28]

Later that month, author Gertrude Stein and her life partner, Alice B. Toklas, arrived in New York on a six-month book tour for Stein's *Portraits and Prayers*. Miriam enjoyed Stein's work and first met her at a dinner party hosted by Bennett Cerf and his business partner, Donald Klopfer. According to Cerf, "Miriam adored Gertrude, and Gertrude adored Miriam. She had Miriam running errands for her, day after day. This amused her—having a movie star calling for shoes for her and having her clothes dry-cleaned. Miriam thought she was the greatest thing that ever came down the pike."[29]

Miriam went with Stein and Toklas to Brentano's for a book signing. Then, she tagged along on a coast-to-coast radio interview on NBC. Now to the American public, Stein could explain her writings. Cerf was proud to be Stein's publisher despite admitting, "As I've always told you, I don't understand very much of what you're saying."

"Well, I've always told you, Bennett," Stein quickly responded, "you're a very nice boy, but you're rather stupid."

After the broadcast, Miriam raved about the interview and asked, "How much did you get for it?" Stein was shocked. No one had told her that she "should" be paid for a radio interview. Cerf jumped in, explaining it was customary *not* to pay authors; as such, these public forums were a way to market their books. Miriam admonished Cerf and advised Stein not to "ever go on radio again unless you get at least five hundred dollars for it." For the remainder of her book tour, Stein heeded her advice. Cerf begged her to reconsider, but she reminded him, "Miriam said I should get five hundred dollars. I won't do it for less." That ended Stein's radio career and limited her possible book sales.[30]

Miriam and Stein had mutual interests in art. Stein collected seminal modernist paintings, while Miriam purchased her art as a financial investment, displaying them at Sutton Place. Based on Stein's recommendations, Miriam added the works of Picasso, Matisse, and Rembrandt to her collection.

Miriam was an art patron, which was fitting for someone who herself was the subject of several paintings. As a struggling actress in New York, she posed for Harry Stoner for one dollar an hour, becoming his special subject. For years, her portrait hung over the fireplace in his studio. In 1928, he created a nude bronze statue of her, which is still owned by Stoner's family. She also was a model for artists John Carroll and her good friend Jean Negulesco.

When Miriam became acquainted with Japanese-American Isamu Noguchi, she solicited a gold-plated bronze sculpture of herself and a bust of Michael's head in Tennessee marble. At Miriam's insistence, Noguchi came to Hollywood to produce works for her friends, including actress and future politician Helen Gahagan Douglas. Douglas was impressed, calling Noguchi "a genius" and a "richly humane man with no sharp edges."[31]

But now, Miriam was needed on the *Becky Sharp* set. From the first day, the new color medium had problems, but in the end, the film would earn Miriam the recognition of her peers.

Technicolor, in some form, had been used sporadically in films since 1916. Jock Whitney, along with his cousin Cornelius Vanderbilt Whitney, founded Pioneer Films, producer of the Academy Award–winning full-color short, *La Cucaracha*. The Whitneys were also 15-percent shareholders in Technicolor. In 1934, Pioneer announced several adaptations, one of which would be their first full-length Technicolor film.

Many in the industry were confident that color film would dominate the screen and be popular. For example, the *New York Times* forecast that color would "become an integral motion picture element in the next few years." Rouben Mamoulian, who took over the direction of *Becky Sharp*, said, "All but a few pictures will be made in color within two years." Many believed color was a distraction; a fad, much like sound was seven years earlier.[32]

Miriam felt color shouldn't dominate a film, for the script, the cast, and the direction must still be good. Color should be realistic, not there to "broadcast to the world that this is a 'color' film, but simply to present—as the eye would see it—a picture of everyday life, with the everyday colors in life. Then color will be here, and to stay." Miriam's predictions were more accurate than many of the countless Technicolor clairvoyants and fortune-tellers.[33]

The filming of *Becky Sharp* began under Lowell Sherman's direction on December 11, 1934, at RKO's Pathé Studios in Culver City. Starting his career as an actor, Sherman was now earning a livelihood on both sides of the camera, interspersing his time between acting and directing and sometimes directing films he appeared in.

For some time, Sherman had been fighting a severe cold. He disregarded his doctor's orders and continued working, with a nurse on the set. Two weeks later his condition worsened, and he checked into the Cedars of Lebanon Hospital. Although he was diagnosed with pneumonia, doctors believed he would recover, but on December 28, with his mother and manager at his bedside, Lowell Sherman went into convulsions and died.

Jock Whitney flew to Los Angeles on Sunday. On Miriam's suggestion (she had director approval), Whitney asked Rouben Mamoulian, Miriam's director on *Dr. Jekyll and Mr. Hyde*, to take over the project. But Mamoulian hated both the script and the two weeks of film Sherman had already in the can. After much haggling, he agreed to take the helm if they rewrote the script and scrapped the existing footage, because it was "contrary" to how he would develop "color through the script. It needed as much dramatic importance as the dialogue or the movement."[34]

At a loss of $150,000, Whitney agreed to Mamoulian's demands, closing the deal within twenty-four hours.

Besides rewriting the script and supervising the film's color scheme, Mamoulian made changes to the cast. He stayed with most of Sherman's original actors, including British imports Sir Cedric Hardwicke, Alan Mowbray, and Nigel Bruce, but for the role of Mrs. Crowley, he replaced the legendary Broadway actress Mrs. Leslie Carter with the matronly Alison Skipworth.

A few years later, when Miriam portrayed Mrs. Carter in the Warner Bros. biopic *Lady with Red Hair*, she spoke about their meeting, calling the actress "unforgettable," with her hair "still tawny" and her eyes "emerald green, and flashing."[35]

During Lowell Sherman's time, Miriam upstaged her costars. In one scene, she maneuvered Alan Mowbray around the set forcing his face away from the camera until Sherman yelled "cut."

"May I see a little more of your face, Mr. Mowbray?" Sherman asked.

"Sure, if Miss Hopkins will let me," snapped Mowbray, adding, "Personally, I don't care if you photograph the lower part of my back or my elbow." Miriam joined in the laughter and agreed to be more charitable to Mr. Mowbray in the future. However, she wasn't as generous to Nigel Bruce, who she bullied and, in one scene, reportedly reduced to tears.[36]

When Mamoulian took over, everything changed. Stories persisted that he exercised "directorial discipline" to bring Miriam in line, but he disagreed. "Let me clarify that. She started out as a scene-stealer the first couple of days. She didn't give it up because I told her to but because she felt she didn't need to do that. She was one of the best troupers I ever worked with."[37]

In January, during the ballroom scene, Miriam collapsed with a mild case of bronchial pneumonia. She called Jock Whitney from her sick bed at Good Samaritan Hospital, begging him not to replace her. "I'm already feeling better," she sighed, hoping her acting was convincing. "Please do not get another blonde for the part."[38]

Miriam insisted that her illness was due to the drafty Pathé studios, and not, as some had hinted, to the Technicolor lights. In any event, she wore Whitney down until he agreed to wait for her recovery; but it put *Becky Sharp* at a standstill for ten days.

Miriam's illness was the start of several unprecedented mishaps on the set. When she returned, both Mamoulian and Frances Dee developed influenza. Later, while filming a scene, Miriam reached over a lit candle, igniting the imported lace on her sleeve. Property man Sid Vogel snatched the blazing lace from her dress and stamped it out. Her arm was singed but didn't require bandaging.

These misfortunes didn't affect Miriam's libido, especially when writer William Saroyan arrived on the set. Saroyan, who was born in Fresno, California, of Armenian parents, was a friend of fellow Armenian Mamoulian (who was born in the Caucasus republic of Georgia). His first book was *The Daring Young Man on the Flying Trapeze*, which Miriam had read.

Out of his experiences on the set, Saroyan wrote a short story, "Rouben Mamoulian Directing Miriam Hopkins in *Becky Sharp* for Me." "Even the people in the thing had this large improbable aura of other worldliness," he explained, "especially one little bit of a saucy thing named Miriam Hopkins, and all of a sudden there she was, apparently absolutely excited to be speaking to me, all about my first book, speaking in the breathless way that goes with a beautiful woman's excitement and secret language that says or seems to say, Well, now, I think I love you, I really believe I like you, and by that I don't mean talk-love, talk-like, I mean let's-get-into-bed-love."[39]

Miriam flirted with the writer, almost to his embarrassment, but not enough for him to discourage her. "I wanted to grab that little lovely thing right there," Saroyan admitted. Her body language—and every form of communication available—told him she wanted him. But then, Mamoulian intervened, ready for the next shot.

Dickran Kouymjian, a professor emeritus of Armenian studies at California State University and a friend of Saroyan's in his later years, recalled that the writer spoke about Miriam Hopkins "with great warmth and apparent affection." Referring to her as "his girl friend, 'my gal,' or something like that and they had a long and torrid affair."[40]

Things apparently weren't that sizzling hot, as two days after their meeting, Miriam told Saroyan over the telephone that soon, though not that night, she would have him over for dinner and talk. "After hanging up," Saroyan wrote, "I heard my old self say, *Talk,* did she say?"[41]

Saroyan returned to Fresno and filming on *Becky Sharp* ended. Two days later, on March 22, 1935, Miriam was in New York, relaxing in her Sutton Place townhouse. From the library, she gazed at the green lawn rolling into the East River. Growing nearby was a tree bearing a pale green bud. "I wanted to see trees budding," she told a reporter, remembering why she returned to New York. "Things never bud in California. It just rains, the sun shines and flowers burst out, full grown."

During her time in California, she yearned for New York, its familiar restaurants and fresh aroma of damp pavements. "And walking," she added. "You cannot walk any place out [there], the distances are so great. I love to walk across Fifty-Seventh Street and look in all the shop windows."[42]

Miriam relaxed at Sutton Place, waiting to return to Hollywood, where she would start filming *Barbary Coast,* her first film for Samuel Goldwyn. She was asked about *Becky Sharp* but wasn't concerned about Technicolor. Rather, she worried that audiences would forget that *Becky Sharp* was a thrilling romantic drama, adding "we have made a fine picture of it" and calling that colorful *Vanity Fair* character "one of the most imposing I've ever had to play."[43]

Miriam was annoyed when RKO executives insisted that she promote the film. She hated "selling herself" at Paramount, where she was contractually required to do so. Even now, when she stood to gain financially because her contract gave her a percentage of the profits, her feelings had not changed. Nevertheless, while her self-promotion benefited RKO, it would also help her in the long run.

Pioneer Film's Lowell Calvert explained to his bosses that Miriam's endorsement of the film was vital to making it a box office hit. Considering the lucrative percentage deal that Myron Selznick had negotiated for her, Calvert argued that Miriam "should be breaking her doggone little neck" to do everything possible to promote the film. However, her indifference to publicizing *Becky Sharp* lessened the movie's gross and her share of it.[44]

When *Becky Sharp* was released, critics applauded Miriam's performance *and* Technicolor, but the screenplay failed to excite them. The

New York Mirror declared, "Its pictorial beauty compensates for its lack of action, depth, and suspense," an opinion shared by many when *Becky Sharp* premiered on June 13, 1935, at Radio City Music Hall.[45]

Whatever misgivings the critics had about the film, they applauded Miriam's performance. One reviewer wrote that *Becky Sharp* was "the greatest work of her career as the almost entirely mercenary Becky, and rivals any scene any theatergoer wishes to select for the best of the year. Her portrayal is brilliantly done and is enhanced by her understanding, sincerity, [and] intelligence."[46]

The *Hollywood Reporter* agreed that there "couldn't have been a better choice than Miriam Hopkins for the role of Becky. The vitality of the girl, the sly humor, the complete understanding of the witch that was Becky Sharp are breath-taking as a series of vivid portraits."[47]

Ward Morehouse was delighted about his old friend's performance. He referred to Miriam, who graced the cover of *Time* magazine, as the embodiment of Thackeray's antiheroine. "She is Becky Sharp to the life. Just as Becky was feminine, so is Miriam; just as Becky was appealing, so is Miriam; just as Becky was a natural menace to the peace of mind of all men, so is Miriam."[48]

9

Goldwyn

In Hollywood, Goldwyn delayed the start of *Barbary Coast*. Goldwyn wanted to produce an authentic, sweeping panorama of San Francisco in the halcyon days of the 1849 gold rush. He had bought the rights to Herbert Asbury's novel, but *Harrison's Reports* called it "one of the filthiest, vilest, most degrading books that has ever been chosen for the screen." Fearing potential censorship issues—the Production Code was now in full force—Goldwyn rejected the story but kept the title. For two years, a dozen synopses, treatments, and completed scripts for *Barbary Coast* bounced around the Goldwyn lot, costing nearly $80,000.[1]

In late May 1934, with a script by Ben Hecht and Charles MacArthur, Goldwyn cast contract stars Anna Sten and Gary Cooper in the leads for director William Wyler. Goldwyn wasn't pleased with the results and halted filming several weeks later.

Hecht and MacArthur made revisions, and Goldwyn brought in Howard Hawks to replace Wyler. Miriam stepped into Sten's role as the gambling hall hostess Swan, and Edward G. Robinson was borrowed from Warner Bros. to play Chamalis, the controlling owner of the gambling house. Replacing Cooper was Goldwyn's new contract player Joel McCrea (who had signed a five-year contract) as the naive young prospector, James Carmichael.

The supporting line-up included future three-time Academy Award–winner Walter Brennan and, as a Cockney sailor, soon-to-be Goldwyn star David Niven in one of his first film roles. "I was thrown out of the window of a brothel in San Francisco and into the mud," Niven recalled about his one scene, "where Miriam Hopkins, Joel McCrea, Walter Brennan, thirty vigilantes and some donkeys walked over the top of me."[2]

Filming began on June 17, 1935, and continued for the next two months on a massive stage on the United Artists back lot. Sets included the entire Barbary Coast, the San Francisco waterfront, and a full-size sailing schooner.[3]

An intense heat wave had hit Los Angeles and was making it uncomfortable for the actors, but that was only part of their problems. Edward G. Robinson was not getting along with Howard Hawks and had a stronger dislike for Miriam. Referring to her as "a horror" in his autobiography, Robinson wrote: "I worked with her in Samuel Goldwyn's *Barbary Coast*. Well, you couldn't exactly say that. I *tried* to work with her. She made no effort whatever to work with me."[4]

Robinson added that discussions were highly politicized. Tempers flared as cast, director, and screenwriters took sides. Robinson, Hecht, and MacArthur were liberals and supported Franklin D. Roosevelt, who was in his first term as president. His New Deal was called un-American by right-wingers, and according to Robinson they included Hawks, McCrea, Brennan, and Miriam. There were "two warring camps," and as Robinson later remembered, during those times political disputes were "going on in every studio and every living room." Arguments ranged from "polite freezing" to "occasional outbursts of rage." Consequently, little socializing went on between Robinson and most of the cast.[5]

Robinson blamed Miriam's behavior on their political differences. He accused her of being "puerile and silly" but acknowledged they had things in common that could have made them friends. Robinson came from the theater, as did Miriam, and both believed films were beneath them. Their differences, however, were greater. Miriam did what she could to upstage Robinson. He knew the same tricks but discovered they didn't work in film because the editor could cut them. Also, Miriam wouldn't feed Robinson her offscreen lines in close-ups—a common courtesy.[6]

In several scenes, Miriam's period costumes and headdresses, by Goldwyn designer Omar Kiam, made her taller than the small-sized Robinson. She asked him to stand on a box, but Robinson considered it "undignified" and said he would be "self-conscious." He refused, suggesting she take off her shoes instead. After debating it for an hour, Hawks sided with Robinson, and Miriam played the scenes in her stocking feet.

Other issues were pitting Robinson against Miriam. For one, when she read the *Barbary Coast* script, she "almost had a fit," until Hecht and MacArthur made several improvements. Even then she "played it grudgingly." On the set, Hawks adjusted Miriam's dialogue to please her. If not, she would improvise. With so many rewrites, Hecht and MacArthur wanted their names removed from the credits, but Goldwyn refused since they were respected screenwriters.[7]

Miriam also had problems with Hawks, who, despite his reputation as a strict taskmaster, couldn't control his leading lady. Despite her poor relationship with Hawks and Robinson, she had a great rapport with Joel McCrea, and the feeling was mutual. "She was a fine actress, and I was a new unproven actor," McCrea recalled. "She was adorable to me (a former cowboy) trying to make good."[8]

According to McCrea, when Robinson saw how well they worked together, it frustrated him. "Eddie Robinson had a hard time with her, . . . and he complained to me a lot. He'd say, 'Oh, that son of a bitch, I'm doing something, and she's fixing her dress. Oh, how unprofessional. I'm going to kill her.'" McCrea was sympathetic, but since Miriam was "nice" to him, he knew no way to assuage Robinson's frustrations.

"Why is she nice to you and not to me?" Robinson asked. "I've spent my *life* doing this business. You've just started."

McCrea reasoned that Miriam liked him because of the differences in their height. At that angle, when she looked up at him, the "chins go away," he explained, eager to convince Robinson it was nothing personal. But whatever her reasons were, McCrea didn't intimidate her.[9]

While her difficulties with actors are known, several have enjoyed a good camaraderie with her, among them Maurice Chevalier, Kay Francis, Bing Crosby, and especially McCrea. Miriam's insecurities about her talents played into her interactions with costars. Robinson was an excellent actor, so she may have feared he would shine in their scenes. The obstacles she threw his way may have been her effort to prevent her performance from falling flat.

In any event, Robinson had his fill with her "tricks," calling them "chickenshit." Hawks claimed he had no influence, or maybe he had decided it wasn't worth his effort. Considering that Paramount's Emanuel Cohen had stopped giving her choice roles, Goldwyn could do the same.[10]

As filming progressed, Miriam's transgressions against Robinson mounted. She was always late, making everyone wait. Robinson, like Bette Davis a few years later, claimed that Miriam indulged "in every trick to delay, to confuse, to obstruct—and to prove that she and not I was the star."

One day, in the presence of cast and crew, Robinson spouted off a "litany of her mischief," including that her "temperament had gone out of fashion" and no longer had "any place on a movie set." She was selfish and was too aware of the camera, and it hurt her. Then he illustrated how, "in her attempts to upstage me, she would back up on her own lights." Everyone was silent. Miriam offered an "insincere apology" as Hawks called for an early lunch.[11]

Robinson was furious at both Miriam and Hawks. Once again, everyone took sides: Joel McCrea and Walter Brennan sided with Miriam, while Ben Hecht and Charles MacArthur congratulated Robinson and agreed she "was a pain."[12]

After lunch, both actors pretended that all was well. In the next scene, the script called for Robinson to slap Miriam. He wanted to rehearse the "fake" slap, but Miriam insisted he hit her for real. Maybe she assumed this would alleviate the actor's aggression toward her. She also believed she could take it, but apparently, she had underestimated the usually temperate actor.

Miriam said, "Smack me now so we won't have to do it over and over again. Do you hear me, Eddie? Smack me hard." Without hesitating, Robinson gave her a whack that knocked her to the floor. Hawks yelled "cut" as Robinson and Miriam glared at each other. After a brief awkward moment, the crew burst into applause.[13]

Even though she had asked Robinson to slap her, Miriam was humiliated. Robinson extended his hand as an apology and helped her up, and then she stormed off to brood in her dressing room. Known as a gentle man, Robinson would later claim he was ashamed and embarrassed, yet the crew congratulated him for "punching the bitch." For the remainder of the shoot, Miriam acted professionally, except for ignoring Robinson.[14]

Years later, when Miriam was at Warner Bros., Jack Warner tried to convince Robinson to accept a part, but Robinson didn't want to carry the picture alone. He wanted other stars to support him. Warner paused, and then grinned. "I can get you Miriam Hopkins."

"We both laughed," Robinson recalled. "Hollowly."[15]

Barbary Coast was well received. The *New York American* wrote, "The film blazes with action and romance through every sequence, is studded with color and bespangled with the scintillance of a half dozen stirring performances."[16]

Miriam's performance contributed to the film's success.

"As the Swan, Miss Hopkins has what it takes to make strong men forget their hard-won gold dust," reported the *New York Times*. The *Hol-*

lywood Reporter agreed that she gave "an unusually fine performance as the slightly soiled, intrinsically 'good' heroine. She lends great dignity and finesse to the role and makes it most sympathetic and believable."[17]

Howard Hawks's direction was called "first-rate," but he disagreed with the critics, saying he "didn't like the picture much." He thought it was a "contrived thing, more or less done to order, and a lot of trouble." As Ben Hecht added, "Miriam Hopkins came to the Barbary Coast and wandered around like a confused Goldwyn Girl."[18]

Goldwyn too was disappointed. "*Barbary Coast* was successful," Hank Potter recalled, "but it wasn't the greatest."[19]

Miriam's next film was *Hands Across the Table*, a light comedy-drama written for her by Viña Delmar. But Goldwyn ignored the success of her Paramount comedies. He had decided she was more suited for drama, and he allowed the option on the film to lapse. Instead, Carole Lombard, Miriam's lighthearted blonde successor at Paramount, landed the leading lady role in *Hands Across the Table*.[20]

On the day *Barbary Coast* wrapped, Goldwyn walked Miriam and Joel McCrea into a neighboring soundstage where sets were under construction for *Splendor*, their next film. "She had to do it because she was under contract," Potter said, "but she didn't like it. She was discouraged and uninterested."[21]

Assigned a budget of $494,600, *Splendor* was a typical Rachel Crothers story of a young southern girl (Hopkins) who marries into a once-wealthy family of snobs. They force her into a liaison with a wealthy and influential man (Paul Cavanagh) who makes it possible for them to recover their lost fortunes.

The part of Clarissa, an intrusive socialite, was played by veteran actress Billie Burke, the widow of famed Broadway impresario, Florenz Ziegfeld. In a few years, Burke would gain iconic popularity as Glinda the Good Witch in MGM's 1939 classic *The Wizard of Oz*.

While making *Splendor*, Burke was also acting as a technical consultant for MGM's biopic about her late husband, *The Great Ziegfeld*. She wanted to portray herself in the film, but studio executives claimed she wasn't a big draw, so Myrna Loy got the part.

Unhappy about the studio's choice, Burke later told actress Barbara Rush that Loy "was lovely, but she doesn't much look like me, does she?" Surprisingly, Burke's first choice to play herself in *The Great Ziegfeld* was Miriam, saying she "always felt that Miss Hopkins is much as I was years ago"; she insisted that Miriam's "spirit, fire, optimism, [and] love of life" was comparable to her own as a young actress.[22]

Because of Miriam's friendship with McCrea, there were few problems on the *Splendor* set. It was easy to get along with the dependable, even-tempered leading man who, in the years to come, would find his niche in westerns. Miriam liked McCrea but thought it was a mistake to be "coupled with him so often," believing the public would get "tired" of seeing them together. Goldwyn disagreed and would pair them in two more films.[23]

Despite her improved demeanor, Miriam's past behavior had turned Goldwyn's crew against her, and she knew it. After *Splendor*, their next assignment was Eddie Cantor's *Strike Me Pink*. However, if *Splendor* didn't complete filming on schedule, the crew would be replaced and lose several weeks work. To redeem herself, Miriam moved into her dressing room, working nonstop for forty-eight hours to finish the film on time so the crew wouldn't be laid off.

Miriam had doubts about *Splendor*, but the experience was pleasant. She later said, "As a matter of fact, the only picture I really enjoyed making [at Goldwyn] was *Splendor*, of all things."

The reviews for *Splendor* were mixed. "Here is a rare combination of a well-written story, interpreted in skilled and sympathetic action under able and understanding direction," *Variety* wrote. The *New York Times* was more critical, yet it was enthusiastic about Miriam. After dismissing *Splendor* as having a "too commonplace theme to hold an audience," the *Times* added, "No praise is withheld from Miriam Hopkins, however. She is credited with a brilliant performance that far exceeds in beauty and truth her more widely acclaimed contribution to *Becky Sharp*."

Still, Miriam was uncertain about her future at Goldwyn. After seeing *Splendor* with a preview audience, she had more doubts. Goldwyn didn't agree. Afterward, he telephoned her, obviously pleased with the film's reception, asking, "Wasn't it wonderful?"

"I don't know," she replied hesitantly. "You see, Sam, they coughed so during the first part, I'm afraid they didn't like it."

"But they stopped coughing toward the end, didn't they? I guess they liked it better then, maybe."

"I don't think so, Sam. I think perhaps they stopped coughing when they fell asleep."[24]

Furious at her impertinence, Goldwyn hung up.

Despite their differences of opinion, Miriam admired Goldwyn and liked that he was interested in every part of his independent productions. Under his management, she felt like an individual and "never part of a great machine." Goldwyn's publicity department kept her name in the newspapers, announcing future roles, including a historical epic opposite Gary Cooper and Merle Oberon entitled *Maximilian of Mexico,* which did not pan out. Neither did *Perfectly Good Woman* with David Niven.[25]

Even her agent, Leland Hayward, wasn't sure what her future held. He covered all the possibilities in a press release: "She may make a picture, go to Europe, go to New York, stay here, go to the desert, and go to Mexico City." But he also added the likeliest option, "I think she will stay here and make another picture right away."[26] Hayward was right. She was going to make a film—an important one.

Miriam was paired again with Joel McCrea for her next picture, *Navy Born,* based on popular short-story writer Mildred Cram's article from *Cosmopolitan. Navy Born,* a story about a Navy post in the Hawaiian Islands, was bought for Miriam. As a bonus, Goldwyn planned to send the cast to Hawaii to film scenes.

That changed when Miriam ran into playwright Lillian Hellman on the Goldwyn lot, where she was adapting her controversial Broadway hit *The Children's Hour* for the screen. Miriam loved the play and asked to read Hellman's script.

Set in a girl's boarding school, *The Children's Hour* focuses on the plight of the school's headmistresses, Martha and Karen, after one of their young students, a sociopath-in-the-making named Mary Tilford, tells her grandmother the two women are having an affair. Scandal and tragedy ensue.

When Hellman's play opened on Broadway on November 20, 1934, to rave reviews, Samuel Goldwyn expressed an interest in buying the film rights. According to legend, an executive told him, "You can't do that. We'll never get it through. It's about Lesbians."

"That's all right," Goldwyn supposedly replied. "We'll make them Americans."[27]

"Americanized" or not, when the Hays office learned that Goldwyn intended to produce *The Children's Hour,* they voiced their objections. As stipulated by the Production Code, the mere implication of lesbianism was forbidden. Joseph Breen, Hays office director of studio relations, was "skeptical about its picture possibilities." If Goldwyn insisted on making *The Children's Hour*, changes would be required to satisfy the censors, including a sanitized screenplay, no mention of the play in the studio's publicity, and most importantly, a different title.[28]

Hellman's screenplay deftly avoided the lesbian theme by substituting rumors of an illicit heterosexual love triangle. Ironically, the press was not hampered by the same restrictions, so they wrote freely about the scandalous *The Children's Hour* adaptation with its mundane new title, *These Three*.

When Goldwyn learned that Miriam had read Hellman's script, he called them both into his office to convince Miriam to take the part of Martha. As they discussed the script, Goldwyn and Miriam argued and kept interrupting each other, which irritated Hellman. Finally, Miriam agreed and was somewhat placated when she was told that Merle Oberon would play Karen.

Although they were neighbors with adjoining beach houses, Miriam had first met Merle Oberon a year earlier at Goldwyn's home. At the time, Oberon was returning to New York on a trans-Atlantic voyage, so Goldwyn had to wire her that Miriam would be her costar. When her ship arrived, Miriam met her at the dock. "She had a cocktail party in my honor at her lovely home in Sutton Place," Oberon recalled, "and I don't think I have ever met so many important people at one time. They were all well-known authors, playwrights, decorators, painters, architects, and tops in their professions."[29]

Although casting wasn't complete, Goldwyn needed a director. Hellman suggested William Wyler, who was at Universal. Hellman had seen Wyler's *Counselor-at-Law* and "didn't want to work with any of the standard directors." She had met Wyler before and liked him.[30]

For the past decade, Wyler had directed a string of low-budget action films and an occasional "A" picture, including *The Good Fairy* and *The Gay Deception*. Wyler accepted *These Three* but wasn't happy with Goldwyn's cast, especially Joel McCrea. He would have preferred the prestigious Leslie Howard, but Goldwyn insisted on McCrea since he was on the payroll and was idle.

Wyler did add his input to the two schoolgirls: the bully Mary and the bullied Rosalie. For the latter, Wyler wanted a child he had seen in a Broadway play, but again, Goldwyn denied his request. Instead, he found Marcia Mae Jones, one of several show-business siblings, after meeting her on the Twentieth Century Fox back lot.

The casting for Mary was trickier. Wyler needed a young actress who could believably be spoiled like a child and coldheartedly manipulative like an adult. After testing dozens of girls, they picked Bonita Granville, the daughter of actors, who had been working in films since the age of nine.

From the first day of filming on Stage 8, Miriam knew *These Three* would be "the girl's picture," based on how Wyler was directing them. Hardly timid, she voiced her feelings so adamantly that Goldwyn was called to the set to intercede.

After a week, Merle Oberon also became concerned, and she shared her feelings with Miriam and McCrea, complaining that Bonita Granville was stealing the film. "Merle came to me, and we started talking about it," McCrea recalled, "and we agreed that I should say something to Goldwyn. . . . Now, of course, Goldwyn never listened much, but I started to explain what I was doing up in his office."

After a while, Goldwyn became impatient. He told McCrea, "I'm having more trouble with you stars than Mussolini is with Utopia," a Goldwynism referring to Italy's recent invasion of Ethiopia. Confused, and forgetting why he was there, McCrea left and returned to the set. But the problem wouldn't go away.[31]

As for Miriam and Merle Oberon, there were reports that they quarreled, but they had an exceptional relationship. Oberon raved about Miriam's wit, noting, "If you have to spend day after day on a hot set . . . , there's nothing as pleasant as having a sense of humor." Besides, they shared the same problem; Granville and Jones were stealing the picture. Miriam had no problems with her former *Barbary Coast* and *Splendor* costar, so the drama on the set was with William Wyler, who "loved her one minute and hated her the next." When both were satisfied with the scene, they once again were friends.[32]

Actors who worked with Wyler complained that he often couldn't articulate what he wanted in a scene, which led to multiple takes, sometimes as many as fifty. "He used to make her do more takes," McCrea recalled. "With Merle and I, he would say, 'Print the thing' after about the third, but he'd work maybe about an hour with Miriam."[33]

Miriam, of course, made several attempts to rewrite the script—a tendency that earned her the nickname "Helpful Hopkins" among the crew. Her "helpfulness" agitated Wyler. "Many directors were overwhelmed by her suggestions," said author George Eells, "which, when rejected, could cause Miriam to throw a tantrum that ended with her stalking off the set and retreating to her beach house until whatever displeased her had been rectified." Miriam's reputation had preceded her, and Goldwyn knew what he had signed on for, but her antics bored him.[34]

The principal actors on *These Three* became good friends after sharing private moments with each other. Every morning at the crafts table, Joel McCrea recalled the latest about his newborn son, David, but Miriam would interrupt with tales of Michael's most recent deeds.

When Michael visited the studio, he bounded onto the soundstage, and even when the cameras were rolling, Miriam would shout, "Hello, son!" and filming would stop. If Michael saw his mother first, he yelled, "Miriam, here I am!" innocently interrupting the scene. Wyler would smile indulgently, admiring Miriam's affection for her child, but the ruined scene still had to be reshot.[35]

During his childhood, Michael rarely was in the public eye, nor did Miriam allow him in studio publicity. Miriam was concerned about kidnapping, a fear in Hollywood at the time. She was renting Goldwyn's Santa Monica beach house at 602 Ocean Front Avenue, a private enclave enclosed by a high board wall where Michael could play in absolute safety. Besides, his nanny and the servants were always around, as was Michael's constant companion and protector, a Saint Bernard named Aesop. However, the dog was always running off, so Miriam "sent him away to school—a progressive school—to learn manners."[36]

Miriam's friends were amazed at how Michael, with his fair skin, big blue eyes, and blonde hair, copied his mother's mannerisms. He was spoiled, but Miriam loved "to see him happy." Besides, a few more years remained to indulge him before he learned that life is not all play.[37]

During those formative years, Miriam hoped Billy would step in as a father figure. He tried to build a relationship with the boy, but "Uncle Billy," as Michael called him, only gave him a silver baby cup engraved with, "It's a long time between drinks." Miriam was forced to be mother *and* father, raising Michael with his nanny Mademoiselle with a great deal of common sense. She protested that he called her Miriam or Maw-Maw and not "Mummy or Mumsey or something nice and Galsworthy." In any case, she insisted it was "charming."[38]

His life was going to be as normal as possible. No doubt Michael received more pampering than the average child, but Miriam recognized she had "money enough to give him the things that enrich life like education and travel. It will be awfully thrilling to watch him grow and develop."[39]

The entire cast of *These Three* was reunited on Louella Parsons's radio show *Hollywood Hotel* to publicize the film's upcoming release. But moments before going on air, Miriam and the director argued about how much airtime Bonita Granville and Marcia Mae Jones would be allowed. According to Jones, when they couldn't agree, Miriam walked off the set.

The behind-the-scenes drama made the eleven-year-old Jones a "nervous wreck," especially when Parsons said, "Bring on the stand-in," an actress that was waiting in the wings to read Miriam's lines. But at the last minute, Parsons convinced her to go on. When "they pulled the drapes, and Miriam Hopkins walked out," Jones was impressed.[40]

Next, Miriam took a plane to Mexico City without telling Goldwyn or anyone at the studio. The scheduled preview for *These Three* was coming up at the Hollywood Pantages, and Goldwyn insisted that she be there. In time, the publicity department found her and sent several frantic wires, but she was flying over Central America, then on to Panama, and possibly South America. After many threats, she returned to Burbank on February 21, the day of the *These Three* preview, and was driven directly to the Pantages.

The audience's reaction to *These Three* was astounding. Not since 1925's *Stella Dallas* was a Samuel Goldwyn film received so enthusiastically. There were three sustained outbursts of applause, and as expected, Granville's and Jones' performances were standouts. Telegrams of congratulations flooded Goldwyn's West Hollywood office.

"Superb picture," wrote David O. Selznick. "Handling of this most difficult subject with little or no loss of the value of the original play." Jesse Lasky, Goldwyn's former associate, congratulated his friend: "*These Three* destined to be great box office. Audience deeply moved and fascinated by superb performances of everyone in [the] cast."

"Picture simply great," added Irving Thalberg. "Everybody fine but picture as a whole one of the most interesting and audience-warming I have seen in years."

After the world premiere of *These Three*, the reviews were equally good. Critics called attention to William Wyler's direction and Gregg Toland's photography.

Miriam had excellent reviews, as did McCrea and Oberon. With all its effusing about the film, the honored *New York Times* said, "Miss

Oberon gives one of her finest performances and Miss Hopkins, and Mr. McCrea are no less impressive." Likewise, the *Los Angeles Times* credits the film's reality to "the excellence of Miriam Hopkins, Merle Oberon and Joel McCrea in the featured roles."[41]

But, as expected, both girls received the highest accolades, with the *Los Angeles Times* stating simply: "Of primary importance are Bonita Granville and Marcia Mae Jones."[42]

These Three showcased Miriam's finest moments, but according to Hank Potter, Goldwyn was losing faith in her star power. "Miriam was great in *These Three,* but I wouldn't say the picture was a blockbuster. It got admiring, intelligent reviews, but it didn't appeal to the lowest common denominator. And when the critics saw Miriam's portrayal, they didn't say, 'Here's the new Jean Harlow or Marilyn Monroe.' Because it wasn't that kind of part. But you knew there was a sense of disappointment around the studio at her reception."[43]

As for Miriam, she was bored. Goldwyn was providing fewer opportunities than Paramount had. She told a relative that she was "fed up with Hollywood" and asked Goldwyn for time off. For a while, he ignored her request since it would postpone her next project *The Princess and the Pauper* (working title) that husband-and-wife screenwriters Sam and Bella Spewack were adapting.[44]

After her coaxing and sweet talk, Goldwyn surrendered, but to hasten her quick return, he offered her the role of Drina, who dreams of escaping her miserable life of poverty in Sidney Kingsley's *Dead End.* Goldwyn had acquired the hit Broadway play for $165,000, an exorbitant amount, but Miriam had reservations.

Goldwyn suggested that she see the play at the Belasco Theater before leaving for Europe. "I came to New York after making *These Three* fully prepared to write a piece entitled 'Suffer the Little Children to Come unto Me Nevermore,'" she told the *New York Times,* "and this morning I was determined, furthermore, that I would never play in *Dead End.* But I guess I will because I've been wrong so many times about these things in the past."[45]

It's true; Miriam had a track record for rejecting parts that were successes for other actresses. Carole Lombard appeared in *Twentieth Century* and *Bolero,* both films that were offered to Miriam. But the part she most regretted turning down was the runaway heiress Ellie in *It Happened One Night.* When Columbia mogul Harry Cohn gave the green light for the film, director Frank Capra and screenwriter Robert Riskin began casting the female lead. Capra's first choice was Myrna Loy, but she wasn't interested. Margaret Sullavan was next, but she declined.

"We resorted to clandestine approaches," Capra recalled. "A friend of a friend casually slipped a script to Miriam Hopkins. The friend of a friend returned it, hinting Miriam was insulted. 'Not if I *never* play another part,' she was reported as saying. Riskin and I stopped laughing."[46]

In the end, her former costar Claudette Colbert accepted the role and won the Academy Award for Best Actress. To Miriam, *It Happened One Night* would make a charming little program picture; she told screenwriter Robert Riskin, it "was just a silly comedy."[47]

"So I guess I'm no judge of movie scripts," she admitted, "and anyway by the time the directors get through with them they're usually transformed into something I never figured on. So I'll probably do *Dead End* after all if they still want to when they get around to making it—but I'm not going to enjoy it."[48]

As it turned out, she had no reason to worry. Goldwyn postponed the film for another year, and by then, he was having second thoughts about her. Instead, Sylvia Sidney took the part.

For now, Goldwyn could proceed with his plans for *The Princess and the Pauper* in May—if he could get a script he liked.

On March 21, 1936, Miriam and longtime friend Libby Holt sailed for Europe on the French liner *Paris* for a five-week vacation. Michael remained at Sutton Place with his nanny, Mademoiselle.

In Paris, Miriam and Libby checked into the Hotel George V, where the press mobbed them. A few days later, Miriam reunited with Gertrude Stein and Alice B. Toklas at their Paris residence, before traveling to Versailles as the guest of Lady Mendl.

Miriam was unknowingly witness to the militarization of Europe. In Berlin, on Adolf Hitler's birthday, she watched from her hotel room as children marched carrying bayonets and crying "Heil Hitler!" On a Nazi square, she listened as the German leader stirred the crowds with his oratory skills.

Her friend Libby, not as mindful of current events, was bored and complained, "I'm so tired of Berlin. We don't know any men here—let's go to London where we can have a good time." Annoyed by her apparent lack of interest, Miriam snapped, "You're seeing history in the making! Isn't that enough for you?" Then in a softer tone, she admonished her, "Forget men for a little while. There is always plenty of time."[49]

The following week, in Italy, at the great court beneath the Palazzo Venezia in Rome, she listened as Hitler's Italian counterpart, Benito Mussolini, shouted his Fascist propaganda.

On a lighter note, the American ambassador in Munich entertained her, and for ten days in Budapest, she partied with friends of Ernst Lubitsch. Then, it was off to Russia, where she attended a performance at the Moscow Art Theatre. "I wouldn't take anything for those experiences," she said. "Some were stimulating and some terrifying. I felt I had a front seat to history in the making."[50]

Disappointed that her trip was ending, she cabled a frustrated Sam Goldwyn, insisting that he extend her vacation, since she had cities yet to visit.

While she traipsed across Europe, back in the States, a book was making its mark on the literary scene: Margaret Mitchell's *Gone with the Wind*. A romantic novel set during America's Civil War and Reconstruction era, the book told the story of Scarlett O'Hara, the spoiled daughter of a prosperous plantation owner.

Because of the novel's enthusiastic reception, Katherine Brown, the East Coast story editor for independent producer David O. Selznick, mailed him a detailed synopsis. "This is Civil War story and magnificent possibility for Miriam Hopkins or Margaret Sullavan," she advised, and she asked that he give it his prompt attention. Selznick considered it a "fine story" but was hesitant because he had no suitable female stars under contract. After some thought, Selznick wisely changed his mind and paid $50,000 for *Gone with the Wind*.[51]

Meanwhile, in London, British producer and director Victor Saville was searching for an actress to play opposite Conrad Veidt in *Dark Journey*. At the time, several European newspapers were following Miriam's sojourn and noted that she was returning to Paris. Saville knew she would be a lure to the much-needed American market, so he flew to Paris to offer her the role of Madeleine. Miriam liked the screenplay and went with Saville to London, where they would discuss it further.

However, when they arrived, producer Alexander Korda, Saville's boss and the founder of London Films Productions, had a script that was more suited to Miriam's talents. According to Saville, Korda then "commenced a first-class Hungarian charade."

Korda had not read the *Dark Journey* screenplay but told Saville that Miriam was wrong for it and was a better fit for his project. Saville's *Dark Journey* didn't have a star. Korda's solution: Vivien Leigh, an actress who played Laurence Olivier's romantic interest in his recent film *Fire Over England*. Even though she wasn't familiar to the American market, Saville believed Leigh "had all the qualities and rare beauty to become a world star."[52]

Back in Hollywood, the screenplay for *The Princess and the Pauper* was still giving Goldwyn headaches. If he couldn't iron out its many problems, he planned to reteam Miriam and Merle Oberon in the Hungarian dramatist Ferenc Molnár's *Angel Making Music*, about a frustrated love affair in Venice. Either way, he wanted Miriam back at the studio. Then, he received a telegram from Alexander Korda (a member of United Artists' board of directors), asking to borrow Miriam for his film with the working title *Triangle*. Reluctantly, Goldwyn agreed.

The British press had already announced Miriam's involvement with *Dark Journey*, but one newspaper wrote that she had insisted on script changes that Saville refused to make and had walked away from the project. It wasn't true, but it made good copy, considering Miriam's reputation. Miriam wanted to make *Dark Journey*, but when she arrived in London, "there was Mr. Korda with a long list of water-tight assignments—and I found myself listening."[53]

Her five weeks abroad were turning into several months, so she sent for Michael and Mademoiselle to join her in London. For comfort, she leased an old rose-covered cottage in Denham, a community about nineteen miles northwest of London. As a companion for Michael, she bought a Bedlington terrier, or "lambie dog," named Rhumba.

At Denham Studios, filming began on *Triangle*, now titled *Men Are Not Gods*, a line from Shakespeare's *Othello*. Sebastian Shaw, Rex Harrison in one of his earliest roles, and the London and Broadway musical star Gertrude Lawrence were Miriam's costars.[54]

The Austrian-born director and screenwriter Walter Reisch wrote and directed *Men Are Not Gods*, an original and intelligent comedy-drama with a theater setting. "I sat down and wrote a story about an actor who played Othello and wanted to kill Desdemona during a performance," Reisch later said.[55]

The first day of filming got off to an ominous start. As Reisch was blocking a scene, a microphone boom hit Miriam's head, making a cut that would leave a tiny scar. The following weekend, Miriam's car skidded off the road, throwing her into the windshield. Although she was not seriously hurt, she nursed a stiff shoulder for several days.

Rex Harrison, Miriam's love interest, found her to be "very beauti-ful" and considered her acting effortless. "I remember while I was still totally unversed in the art of film acting and scared like hell of the cam-era," the stage-trained Harrison recalled, "watching Miriam doing a silent scene, standing at a window and just turning on the tears. I thought it was marvelous."[56]

That summer, London was teeming with American elite, includ-ing Miriam's old beau Bennett Cerf, who, before leaving for Europe, had given Miriam a letter of introduction to Jamie Hamilton, the half-Amer-ican half-Scottish founder of the book publishing house Hamish Hamil-ton Limited. Cerf cabled Hamilton, an impressionable young man, and warned him that Miriam would contact him. "You're going to be crazy about Miriam because she's fascinating," Cerf cautioned. "Don't make one terrible mistake. Don't fall in love with her. She's great fun, but god help you if you fall in love with her." But sure enough, when they met, Hamil-ton became smitten, whereas for Miriam, it was merely another fling; she reserved their "time together" for when it was convenient.[57]

But if Hamilton was a mere pastime, Miriam took her royal activities seriously. One day she lunched with the Duke and Duchess of Kent and then dined at St. James Palace at the invitation of King Edward VIII and his companion, Mrs. Wallace Simpson. Miriam considered Mrs. Simpson "a vivid and intensely vital personality, always eager to go places and do things." When questioned by the press about her evening with the king and Mrs. Simpson, her reply was "no comment."[58]

Men Are Not Gods premiered at London's Piccadilly Theatre and was well-received because of the popularity of its stars: the foreign Miriam Hopkins and the native Gertrude Lawrence. "A considerable bit of acting from Miriam Hopkins," reported one English critic. "It has a lively cine-matic story with a triangle basis," wrote *Variety*, "and an excellent perfor-mance from Miriam Hopkins in a part which calls for a delicate blend of broad comedy and high drama."[59]

As for the British press, Miriam treated them as she did their Ameri-can counterparts. Near the end of her London stay, she had an interview scheduled with a British magazine, but she canceled it because she was tired. She rescheduled but then went to London instead. Again, the mag-azine set another time, but history repeated itself. She agreed to see the reporter the following day, her last chance before sailing for home the next Tuesday. The reporter waited thirty-five minutes, but Miriam failed to show. He telephoned her later, pointing out the importance of "attention to business." Her excuse was she "had to count the laundry."

This mindset was Miriam's response to the press. The London reporter used the opportunity to question why Miriam Hopkins, who was such a "talent and a phenomenon," was taking so long to become a bigger star. Was it sour grapes on his part? Perhaps, but it was still a fair question.

Miriam had the unique qualities to be a successful film actress: looks, talent, vitality, an intuitive sense of character, and a quick intelligence. Yet, being a potentially successful actress is one thing; becoming a great star is another. To claim a spot in the star roster, she had to play the game of stardom by abiding by the rules; most of the time, she wasn't willing.

Miriam was the master of her career and made it difficult for others if circumstances didn't go her way. Michael considered her a "perfectionist" and understood why people thought of her as difficult, "because any perfectionist can get on people's nerves"; she was accustomed "to being in charge." Tom Hopkins agreed. He remembered his grandmother as a dominant personality; a "difficult person, which may be why she didn't get more parts." He regretted that she couldn't compromise, but as he said, "she was very uncompromising."[60]

With her European adventure over, it was time to return to New York to jump-start her professional life—and, unexpectedly, her private life as well.

10

Tola

Before sailing for the United States on the SS *Normandie* from Southampton, Miriam said goodbye to her English admirer, the publisher Jamie Hamilton, who was enamored enough to fly his private plane to buzz the ship, zeroing in dangerously over the smoke stacks. Miriam stood at the ship's rails, watching her impulsive suitor swooping overhead while beside her, watching Hamilton's stunts as intently, was an impeccably dressed man with prematurely graying hair. "Who is that fool?" the man said with a distinct Russian accent. "What is he doing? He's going to kill himself."

Miriam, enjoying the attention, smiled and said, "That's for little me."[1]

As Hamilton's plane soared above her head, Miriam and the handsome stranger flirted. After several minutes, they retreated to the *Normandie*'s smoking room for coffee. Meanwhile, Hamilton was still buzzing the ship, but Miriam was busy elsewhere, getting to know the handsome stranger, Russian director Anatole Litvak. At the time, he was basking in the popularity of his latest French film *Mayerling*, starring Charles Boyer and Danielle Darrieux.

The son of a Jewish bank manager, Litvak studied philosophy at the Saint Petersburg State University and later was an assistant director and set designer. In 1925, he left Russia for Berlin, where he was an assistant editor on Georg Wilhelm Pabst's *The Joyless Street*, one of Greta Garbo's early films.

Leaving Germany in 1932, he lived briefly in London before moving to Paris, where he made *Mayerling*. It was such an international success that American producers sought him out.

This trip would be Litvak's second to America. The year before, he had come to Hollywood at the urging of independent producer Walter Wanger, who wanted to make *Joan of Arc* at Warner Bros. with Claudette Colbert; the project never happened. Instead, Litvak rubbed elbows with influential people, but he was lonely and disillusioned with nothing to do, so he returned to Europe.

But now, Hollywood beckoned again. At RKO's invitation, he returned to remake *L'Équipage* (Flight into Darkness), another of his French hits about a World War I love triangle starring Annabella.

Miriam was impressed with *Mayerling*, but until now, she had known Litvak by reputation only. She admired his talent, but he was merely a curiosity. Litvak, however, fell in love at first sight. They spent time together on the trip over, and soon she was calling him Tola, a nickname used by friends. Then, on the last day of their voyage, out of the blue, Litvak proposed marriage. Miriam laughed.

When the *Normandie* docked in New York, Miriam called Bennett Cerf to tell him about Litvak. "She had another beau," Cerf recalled. "By this time, I was getting bored with her damned beaux. They changed too fast. But we made a date to have dinner together at the Maisonette, which is downstairs from the St. Regis Hotel. They specialize in Russian dishes. That's when I met Tola. He proved to be delightful."[2]

On autumn evenings, they walked the streets of the East Side. Miriam never led him on or gave him false hope. When it was time to return to California, she told him, "Tola darling, you're sweet. When we arrive in Hollywood, try to meet a young man, Jean Negulesco. He knows me well. He can help you."

Miriam never explained how Negulesco could help, but Litvak felt like a castoff. In Hollywood, several weeks later, the two men met. "So you're Jean Negulesco?" Litvak said sardonically.

Puzzled, Negulesco replied, "Well, yes I am. Why?"

Litvak explained how he had met Miriam while crossing the ocean on the *Normandie* and that he had proposed.

"Good God, why?" Negulesco asked.

"Because I love her."

"That's kind of Miriam," Negulesco replied, knowing that Miriam wanted him to enlighten Litvak about her. "I loved her for years, and I don't pretend to know one thing about her. She's one of the most exciting ladies I ever loved. She was kind to choose me—temporarily among so many admirers. But to know her, never."[3]

When she returned to America, Miriam learned she was leading in newspaper polls as the favorite to play Scarlett O'Hara in the film adaptation of *Gone with the Wind*. Living in Europe all those months, she hadn't read the book and wasn't aware of how popular it was. It piqued her interest, but her obligation now was to Sam Goldwyn.

Miriam's career wasn't progressing as she had hoped. In December, Goldwyn tested her for a remake of *Stella Dallas* with Joel McCrea penciled in as the male lead, but he gave the roles to Barbara Stanwyck and John Boles.

In the meantime, Litvak was in talks with Katharine Hepburn for his film *The Woman I Love* (the English version of *L'Équipage*). When negotiations stalled, he asked for Miriam. "When I returned, after meeting Tola on the boat coming back," she recalled, "he wanted me to be in his first American picture. I saw the French version of it and knew the part was unsuited for me, but he seemed sweet and I thought even if it was bad for me it couldn't matter much, and it would help him."[4]

As the start of filming approached, Miriam had not yet replied to Litvak, so she asked Goldwyn to be "allowed to play in it." Goldwyn warned her it was a terrible script, but since *The Princess and the Pauper* wasn't ready, he gave his approval.[5]

Problems continued to plague *The Princess and the Pauper*, now titled *The Woman's Touch*. Popular husband-and-wife writing team Sam and Bella Spewack had written the original screenplay. After reading a rewrite authorized by Goldwyn, the Spewacks "refused to have their name connected with it"; they offered to return their salary. Eric Hatch, an author and *New Yorker* contributor, was asked to revise the script, but he too declined. Frustrated, Goldwyn borrowed Dorothy Parker and her husband, Alan Campbell, from David O. Selznick to give it an overhaul. Until someone at Goldwyn could smooth out its kinks, Miriam reported to RKO.[6]

The Woman I Love begins on the night Lt. Jean Herbillion (Louis Hayward) joins the French flying squadron and meets and falls in love with Helene (Hopkins), who, unbeknownst to him, is the wife of his pilot, Lt. Claude Maury (Paul Muni).

Because Charles Boyer owed them one film, RKO was hoping to get him for the lead, knowing that Litvak worked well with him. Instead, producer Albert Lewis negotiated a "loan-out" deal with Warner Bros. for his close friend Paul Muni. Joining them in the cast was Louis Hayward (*Anthony Adverse*), and *Frankenstein*'s Colin Clive, in his last film role. On December 14, 1936, filming began at RKO's San Fernando Valley ranch.

That morning, as Miriam was leaving her Beverly Hills home, her chauffeur-driven sedan collided with the car of Phyllis Astaire, the wife of dancer Fred Astaire—coincidentally, an RKO star. Miriam badly bruised her nose and dislocated her shoulder. Her maid, Yvonne, had two fractured ribs; Astaire's injuries were minor. Miriam would be confined to bed for three days.

Albert Lewis had briefly worked with Miriam before, when he produced *No Man of Her Own*. "Miriam Hopkins, with whom I had an unfortunate experience at Paramount when she defected from a Gable picture, was suggested by the studio to play the wife," Lewis recalled many years later. "She was now under contract to RKO, and over my objections, she was set." Because of their past animosity, the two barely spoke during the shoot.[7]

Paul Muni had his own problems. The film's success was important to both Miriam and Litvak—with whom she was falling in love—so Miriam tried influencing Muni's performance. At lunch, she scribbled suggestions for Muni and other cast members. She rehearsed, planned action, and tampered with the dialogue. Muni was infuriated by her "ideas." Albert Lewis declared that she "again proved herself a disturbing element during the shooting."[8]

A carnival scene was ready to film, and tensions were running high. A mechanical problem left Miriam and Louis Hayward suspended in midair on a Ferris wheel. At first, Miriam thought it was a prank, but as time wore on, she lost her temper. Litvak convinced her it wasn't a gag; a motor pulley had broken and there were no spare parts.

As they waited, a grip set up a ladder so they could climb down, but Miriam was wearing a dress and declined. Hoping to calm her frazzled nerves, Louis Hayward remained on the Ferris wheel. They were stranded for three hours until the problem was repaired and filming resumed. For reasons unknown, Litvak cut the scene from the final picture.

Litvak did his best to support Miriam. They were together, on the set and off. Before Litvak, Miriam rarely went to nightclubs, but now they were seen rapt in conversation at various Derbys, at the Trocadero, or the Clover Club. When asked where their relationship was heading, her clearly well-prepared response was, "Mr. Litvak is a charming and distinguished man, and the type who makes friendship such a delightful experience."[9]

On the set, Litvak was a nervous man. He seldom remained still, pacing the floor between scenes. Instead of yelling "Cut!" he blew a gold whistle he had fastened to his lapel. He favored rehearsals, which pleased

Miriam. But he could overdo it, with ten or more, which led to arguments. In many ways, he reminded Miriam of William Wyler, who, like Litvak, would rehearse a scene many times.

One day, Miriam had difficulty finding the right mood for a scene with Elizabeth Risdon. After several takes, she snapped, "I'm trying, Tola, I'm trying. Please tell me what to do." Litvak took her aside, calmed her, and shot the scene again. Finally, he was satisfied, but noise from an adjacent stage ruined the take. During a break, Miriam puffed on a cigarette and giggled as she whispered something provocative in Litvak's ear. He blushed. Filming resumed, and they repeated the scene again, and when it was over, they kissed.

Despite their intimacy, Litvak had difficulties controlling Miriam, and she tried to control everything else. One day, Miriam crossed the line with Paul Muni; he refused to tolerate her behavior any longer. Albert Lewis was prepared to fire her, but Litvak stepped in and threatened to resign in protest. "It was a miracle that the picture was finished at all," Lewis admitted. Nevertheless, hurt feelings were calmed, if not healed, and filming continued.[10]

Since her return from Europe, Miriam had been renting Marlene Dietrich's former Beverly Hills house on Rodeo Drive. She considered Hollywood a perfect place to make pictures, but it was "no good as a permanent residence." However, she owed the federal government $55,000 in back taxes, so she desperately needed a write-off. Her lawyers suggested buying a house in Los Angeles. When she had purchased Sutton Place a few years earlier, she formed a corporation, saving her thousands of dollars on taxes. A California home would give her a necessary exemption.[11]

In January 1936, John Gilbert, Miriam's former lover, died from complications of alcoholism. Although she knew he was ill, his passing came as a shock. Now, Gilbert's executors listed for sale the actor's hilltop property, a house Miriam knew well.

One day, she inspected the property, which sat on Tower Grove (now Drive), a winding road off Benedict Canyon. The house stood on a high hill a short distance from the Beverly Hills Hotel, the late Rudolph Valentino's Falcon Lair estate, and Pickfair. King Vidor, who had a house nearby, had persuaded Gilbert to buy the land in 1924. In those days, the property's remoteness suited the reclusive screen idol. Gilbert hired interior designer Harold Grieve to create his hideaway—a Spanish colonial house painted blood red.

Miriam loved the property and its provenance. On January 4, 1937, she bought it for $42,500, telling friends it was a bargain with a "superb location." But mostly she liked the "feeling of a home, my own, my own earth under my feet."[12]

Miriam hired the original designer, Harold Grieve, to guide the redecorating. Scattered on the floor of her dressing room were wallpaper pieces, door paneling squares, and swaths of fabric. She studied and compared samples, one against the other, asking only Grieve for advice. Every detail had her individualized touch on it, from tearing out Gilbert's vaulted ceilings to matching samples of linens to handwoven rugs.

Near the end of December 1936, Warner Bros. was negotiating with producer Guthrie McClintic and playwright Owen Davis Sr. for the film rights to their Broadway dud *Jezebel*. McClintic was willing to sell, but Miriam, who was also a part owner, was not so eager.

Within a week, newspaper accounts reported that she was negotiating with the studio for the starring role, but that seems unlikely. Top Warner Bros. producer Hal Wallis had mentioned the possibility of her repeating her role in the film, but it went no further than a casual conversation.

As executives tried to close the deal, Miriam ignored their inquiries. "I gather that Miriam Hopkins' signature is also necessary?" noted Warner Bros. story department worker Walter MacEwen. McClintic assured Wallis that Miriam wasn't a concern, yet the legal department asked about the delay.[13]

But Miriam *was* holding out. She would sell her share of *Jezebel* only if Jack Warner gave her the role. MacEwen told her they were considering her, but only when there was a suitable screenplay, giving the impression that she was their first choice. But MacEwen was lying. Based on that lie, Miriam conceded and sold her share of *Jezebel* for $12,000. Unbeknownst to her, MacEwen was developing the story for Bette Davis, telling Wallis that Davis would "knock the spots off the part of a little bitch of an aristocratic Southern girl." Miriam believed that she had *Jezebel*, but no one would tell her the truth.[14]

The *Hollywood Reporter* once said: "Sam Goldwyn never has an easy time with any of his endeavors because he goes at them the hard way."[15]

No less than seven screenwriters had tackled Goldwyn's sole venture into screwball comedy, the recently renamed *The Woman's Touch*.

Goldwyn called William Wyler back to Hollywood from a London vacation, intending for him to direct *The Woman's Touch*. But Wyler assumed that it was for *Dead End,* so when Goldwyn dumped *The Woman's Touch* in his lap, Wyler was surprised.

Wyler rejected the script but gave in to Goldwyn's pleas to work on it. He tried, but nothing could improve it; it was hopeless. Wyler even offered to refund his three weeks' salary *and* the $25,000 bonus for *Dodsworth* and *Come and Get It* if Goldwyn would take him off the film. Not only did Goldwyn accept Wyler's naive offer, but he also placed him on suspension. Wyler was stunned.

When Miriam read the script, her reaction was the same: She told Goldwyn, "No way." After several threats, she agreed to do it if director Gregory LaCava, fresh off his *My Man Godfrey* success, would direct. Goldwyn got LaCava, but when the director read the script, he secretly drove off the lot. With pressure from her upcoming contract negotiations and from Litvak, Miriam gave in and accepted the role.

Problems continued. Goldwyn contract player Andrea Leeds said she would starve before taking a supporting role in the film. He placed her on suspension. An executive committee provoked him further when they tried to persuade him to write off the $100,000 he had invested in the picture and move on. He ignored them.

As rebellion spread throughout the studio, Goldwyn's fortitude increased. He hired a new team of contract writers, changed the title to *Woman Chases Man,* and persuaded prolific director John Blystone to helm the picture—and filming began.

The result was a story about a wily, unemployed young woman (Hopkins) who meets an elderly, bankrupt promoter (Charles Winninger) with a wealthy son (Joel McCrea) who refuses to give his wasteful father any more money. Miriam and Winninger plot to get McCrea's signature on a check to fund the old man's latest building project.

During the filming of the final scene, Miriam climbs onto a limb of the magnolia tree outside of McCrea's window. She meows, and McCrea throws a shoe at her before climbing onto the limb. Miriam dangles from the top branch of the tree; for safety, a strap is twined through the hem of her robe. But just as she was about to say her line, the strap broke, and she fell to the studio floor, tearing her diaphragm muscles. She was laid up in bed for four days.

Miriam possibly held the record for the most injuries and illnesses on film sets. Over her career, among the inflictions she suffered were an ear infection, an abscess on her tonsils, bronchitis, singeing her arm on an open flame, being hit on the head with a mike boom, injuring her back after a costar dropped her, two car accidents, and spraining her ankle, twice.

After she had healed, Miriam was in Goldwyn's makeup room one day preparing for a scene, when Joel McCrea tossed a folded copy of that morning's *New York Times* onto her lap. "Congratulations," McCrea said.

"For what?" she asked as she unfolded the paper and read the headline aloud: "Miriam Hopkins and Gable Slated for Leads in *Gone with the Wind*." In the article, a source close to David O. Selznick reported that the producer had cast Miriam and Clark Gable as Scarlett O'Hara and Rhett Butler. Miriam was doubtful. "This is news to me," she said. "David hasn't asked me to test for it yet."[16]

Miriam had not auditioned for Selznick despite what the press had reported. According to documents in the Selznick archives, Tallulah Bankhead was the only established actress to have been considered and tested for the role at that time. Selznick's representatives pleaded ignorance when asked about the *New York Times* article. Yet, the newspaper's source stood by their story.

Miriam was in the unusual position of being cast as Scarlett O'Hara by everyone but the man making the film. She consistently led in the polls and was the choice of fans across the country.

In her native Georgia, the civic-minded ladies of Atlanta campaigned for her. "We, the women of the Atlanta Women's Club," wrote their president, Mrs. W. F. Melton, "wish to endorse most heartily Miriam Hopkins as the actress most suitable to play the part of Scarlett O'Hara in Margaret Mitchell's screen version of *Gone with the Wind*." The Dixie Club of New York, a group Miriam's mother served as vice-president, and who likely led the campaign, lined up solidly behind her. In their opinion, the selection of Miriam "would be most-gratifying to all Southerners."[17]

Marian Spitzer Thompson, the wife of producer Harlan Thompson, had known Miriam since her days in vaudeville. She agreed with public opinion. "When I read *Gone with the Wind*, I immediately thought of her. She was Scarlett O'Hara before the book was written."[18]

But the most noteworthy support came from the novel's author, Margaret Mitchell. "Miriam Hopkins has been my choice from the beginning," Mitchell wrote to a friend, "but I know what I had to say wouldn't matter so [I] said nothing. She has the voice, the looks, the personality and the sharp look."[19]

Once, at a party, the conversation centered on the *Gone with the Wind* casting wars. Everyone knew Miriam was a favorite, so they asked her who should play Scarlett. Before she could answer, David O. Selznick walked in, and she asked him, "Who should play Scarlett?" Selznick admitted that "some unknown, but capable actress should do it." The trouble, he explained, was he "ha[d]n't been able to find the right unknown."[20]

Miriam understood then that the most coveted role in Hollywood would never be hers. Some sources claim that Selznick screened *Becky Sharp* and allowed her to read for the part, but she didn't make a test. He was impressed by her intensity, but he was looking for something else. Even two hundred thousand letters from southerners—half of which, Selznick claimed, said, "Give us Miriam Hopkins as Scarlett"—could not change his mind. But the public opinion in her favor forced Selznick to tell her privately that he would have to use one of his actresses or someone he could build into a star.[21]

While the widely publicized search went on, other actresses came to the forefront as possible contenders: Paulette Goddard, Anita Louise, Bette Davis, Frances Dee, Jean Arthur, and Joan Bennett, among them. It would be more than a year before Selznick found his Scarlett: minor British actress Vivien Leigh.

Miriam was disappointed and regretted losing the role. Had she played Scarlett, she may have been, relatively speaking, a "name" today.

While Miriam worked with interior designer Harold Grieve on the Gilbert house, Sam Goldwyn was ironing out a deal to loan her to Warner Bros. Jack Warner wanted to pair her with Errol Flynn in his new comedy *The Perfect Specimen*, but Miriam hated the script and let them know she would have no part in the film. Warner's producer Hal Wallis was alarmed over her response, but Goldwyn reassured him that this reaction was typical at the beginning of every Miriam Hopkins film. Even if that were true, Miriam was adamant this time. *The Perfect Specimen* was wrong for her. The only news she wanted to hear from Warner Bros. was confirmation that she had landed the lead in *Jezebel*.

By telegram, Goldwyn ordered her to report to Warner Bros. on April 26. Instead, she drove with Litvak to Pebble Beach, five hours north of Los Angeles. Infuriated, Goldwyn reminded her that according to her contract, he could loan her to any studio he chose. Warner's had put up substantial expenditures. "We are reluctant to believe that you will not report at said studio," Goldwyn demanded. "Your failure so to do will undoubtedly result in a claim against this company by Warner Bros. for damages incurred as a result of your non-reporting. In such event, we desire to advise you that it will be necessary for us to hold you accountable for any damages or loss suffered by us without in any way waiving any other rights granted to us under your contract with us."[22]

Litvak may have convinced her to rethink the situation, for two days later she told a reporter she was "doing a new picture for Warner Brothers as soon as I get back," but added, in case Goldwyn thought she was mellowing, "in a week or two."[23]

When she returned, she attended the press preview for *The Woman I Love* on an RKO soundstage. While there were no whistles or shouts of "Bravo" from the visiting journalists, the *Hollywood Reporter* spoke highly of the film, calling it "brilliantly conceived and brilliantly executed" and praising both Muni and Miriam for giving "impeccable performances that well sustain their high repute."[24]

At the preview, Miriam had a tearful reaction to her performance and the distressing finale. When a reporter asked her "how she liked Miriam Hopkins," Miriam replied with a smile, "I enjoyed her very much." However, she later changed her view and called *The Woman I Love*, which lost $114,000 at the box office, a "bad picture" and said, "Goldwyn blamed me."[25]

A few days later, the studio previewed *Woman Chases Man* at New York's Loew's Sheridan Theatre. A Goldwyn executive noted there was "continuous laughter from the very beginning to final fadeout." The audience comment cards hinted that the picture was a "sure box office hit." But on its world premiere, the reviews were mixed. According to critics, the laughter ceased halfway through, and the ending was a disappointment. "Three top-flight players simply run out of material," *Variety* reported, "and, towards the end, Hopkins and McCrea literally find themselves, somewhat inebriated, up a tree."[26]

The news about *Jezebel* was even more discouraging. Goldwyn broke the news that Bette Davis, under contract to Warner's, had gotten the part. Davis wouldn't play Scarlett O'Hara, so Jack Warner gave her *Jezebel* as a consolation prize. Miriam suspected some deception on Warner's part and wasn't amused. "They lied," she told a friend some years later. "Bette stole that picture, but yet she always made me out to be the villain."[27]

Miriam was more determined not to appear in *The Perfect Specimen*. RKO had offered her a Dudley Nichols comedy script, *She Married for Money* (produced as *The Next Time I Marry*), which she was considering.

In the end, Jack Warner surrendered and cast Joan Blondell in *The Perfect Specimen*. Whether a guilty conscience played a role in Warner's decision remains unclear.

To take her mind off *Jezebel*, Miriam continued redecorating her new Beverly Hills home. Her new neighbors were John Barrymore, Mary Pickford, Academy Award–winning writer Frances Marion, Universal mogul Carl Laemmle, and comedian Harold Lloyd. A winding, precipitous road off Benedict Canyon led up to the property, which, covered with trees and hanging vines, gave the impression of a secluded refuge.

The house was private and eccentrically designed. Harold Grieve redid the house in the art moderne style, describing his plan as "very simple and very contemporary." He removed Gilbert's boxed-in beamed ceiling, carvings, and frills and installed a new mantle. He originated the soft blue color scheme from a pair of eighteenth-century Chinese vases that Miriam had in her dressing room. She told Grieve she "simply had to get a house to go around them." In the living room, Miriam's extensive and eclectic collection of books lined the walls on either side of the fireplace.[28]

A few years later, Gilbert's daughter, Leatrice Gilbert-Fountain, made an unannounced visit to her father's former home. "My mother was entertaining guests from France," Gilbert-Fountain recalled, "I think the husband was a baron or some such title. The French visitors expressed a desire to see my father's house, where I had not been since his death some years before. I took them up behind the Beverly Hills Hotel to Tower Road as it was called then. We stopped on the very steep hill, and they gazed at the pretty, rather small Spanish house he had helped design.

"I pulled into the driveway, and the caretaker came out. He was an old Dutchman whom I remembered from my father's time. He recognized me, and on meeting the French couple agreed to let us into part of the house as Miss Hopkins was in New York. The interior was utterly changed. Father had decorated in a Spanish style with hardwood floors, Oriental rugs, and oil paintings. Miss Hopkins had redecorated the living room in soft beige, carpets, curtains, and upholstery. It was very elegant and in perfect taste. There was a wall of books to the right of the entrance to the room. The French baron was attracted to them and looked them over carefully. He was impressed to find a collection of Schopenhauer's essays along with several scholarly biographies and some classic novels. 'Miss Hopkins obviously has a mind,' he remarked."[29]

Miriam planned a house warming that doubled as a thirty-fifth birthday party for Anatole Litvak. Miriam's parties were legendary, as they were often impromptu affairs; a simple invitation would go out—"Won't you stop over?"—and half of Hollywood would show up. At a late hour, Miriam would call her Czechoslovakian-born cook Anna to tell her that six guests were coming for dinner, and then twenty-four would arrive. Anna would shake her head and miraculously roast a turkey stuffed with truffles and a dozen other dishes to feed the unexpected arrivals.

A Russian orchestra would sometimes entertain, but mostly the guests entertained themselves. George Gershwin would play the piano. Grace Moore would sing. Screenwriters would tell stories, and from that improvisation, another movie would be born. These gatherings, modeled after Theodore Dreiser's soirees from a decade earlier, would continue in Beverly Hills and New York, for years to come.

Until she met Anatole Litvak, Miriam had little interest in politics. She kept up with current events and prided herself on being well-read, but she refrained from sharing her political views. When she did, she usually argued on the conservative side. But as ex-lover Patrick Kearney and ex-husband Billy Parker had molded her mind on literature and the arts, so Anatole Litvak mentored her politically.

The seeds of "political rightness" were planted in October 1933, when Eddie Cantor gave an impassioned speech to a group of eight hundred actors gathered at the El Capitan Theatre. In the end, he convinced them that the Academy of Motion Picture Arts and Sciences was unable to represent their "full interests." Inspired and moved, Miriam was one of five hundred actors who "flocked to the stage" to become members of the new Screen Actors Guild.[30]

Miriam's subsequent exposure to liberalism came at a fund-raiser at Fredric March's home. March was hosting a viewing of Dutch filmmaker Joris Ivens's propaganda film *The Spanish Earth*. Among those attending were Robert Montgomery, Luise Rainer, Dorothy Parker, F. Scott Fitzgerald, Fritz Lang, Ernst Lubitsch, Lillian Hellman, King Vidor, Dashiell Hammett, Errol Flynn, Donald Ogden Stewart, and Marc Connelly. After the screening, author Ernest Hemingway spoke about the suffering of Spanish soldiers and the bombing of innocent citizens.

Fitzgerald was captivated by Hemingway's enthusiasm and noted the author "raised $1,000 bills won by Miriam Hopkins fresh from the gaming table; the rumor is $14,000 in one night." German director Fritz Lang, a close friend of Litvak's, confirmed in a letter to Soviet agent Otto Katz, confiscated by the FBI, that "Hemingway has shown the film about Spain . . . and Miriam Hopkins, [name redacted], Dorothy Parker, I, and many others have given him money."[31]

The film moved Miriam, and since she had a movie screen and projector in her new house, she asked Lang to host another screening, raising more money for the cause. She enjoyed her new political awareness, but unbeknownst to her, because of the people she associated with, she was on the FBI's radar.

Miriam and Litvak had been discussing marriage for weeks—while the press had been predicting it for several months. In August 1937, they decided to elope. The evening before the planned nuptials, Litvak was working late at Warner Bros. on *Tovarich* while Miriam was playing poker with friends. She apparently lost big (compared to the small ante she usually betted) and was so depressed she called off the marriage. Accustomed to her wildly erratic moods, Litvak didn't argue, knowing she would eventually have a change of heart.

The following evening, after attending a performance at the Hollywood Bowl with Fritz Lang and Mady Christians, the wedding was back on. Lang and Christians would witness for them.

The next day, Miriam was Louella Parsons's guest on her radio show; afterward, she told the columnist of their marriage plans. "She said she wanted me to have the 'beat,'" Parsons said. "Then, immediately after the broadcast, when she and Tola were preparing to elope, she discovered that a rival paper had the story."

Parsons was upset. The newspaper reported the couple was eloping, so Miriam changed her plans and gave Parsons an exclusive. "Greater love hath no woman for a reporter!" Parsons exclaimed. Miriam waited until September 4, 1937, and chartered a private plane from Santa Monica's Clover Field to Yuma, Arizona, where they could obtain a marriage license without waiting for three days.[32]

With the temperature running 112 degrees in the shade, they were married by a justice of the peace in an air-conditioned Yuma hotel room. After the ceremony, Lang and Christians flew back to Hollywood while the bride and groom honeymooned at the Hotel del Coronado near San Diego.[33]

Back at Tower Grove, Litvak took on a fatherly role. Michael adjusted, and according to Tom, Litvak treated Michael "as a son, giving him the attention her other husbands didn't." Michael, who Miriam christened the "king of the mountain," was starting his first year in the Beverly Hills public school system. His visits to the studio, "to watch Mummy work," were limited.[34]

During Michael's years on Tower Grove, his circle of friends included his best friend, Bob Potter, the son of director H. C. (Hank) Potter, Michael's godfather. He also spent time with Bing Crosby and his sons, and with the sons of David O. Selznick, Danny and specifically Jeffrey, who was a close friend.

Miriam returned from her honeymoon and reported to RKO for *Female of the Species*, now titled *Wise Girl*, the studio's attempt at screwball comedy. Costar Ray Milland, who had started out in British films a decade earlier, was Miriam's love interest in a romance combining the sophistication of Park Avenue with the Bohemian lifestyle of Greenwich Village. There's little more to *Wise Girl*; one critic conceded that Milland and Miriam "do well with the slim material assigned to them."[35]

Next, Miriam accepted the Theatre Guild's invitation to appear in their production of *Wine of Choice*, a play by S. N. Behrman. The theme of the play concerned the sociopolitical changes going on in the world. Miriam was impressed: "It's so smart and so chic to be with the Theatre Guild. And in a Behrman play." Since Goldwyn had nothing for her, he gave her the time off. Litvak went as far as New York and then traveled to Europe for business and family visits in Russia.[36]

The prestigious Theatre Guild was a theatrical society whose sole purpose was to produce noncommercial works by American and foreign playwrights. Miriam claimed that *Wine of Choice* "seemed good on the story they came to Hollywood and told me." Lawrence Langner, a cofounder of the Guild and producer of *Wine of Choice*, admired Miriam's acting, calling her "one of the more versatile actresses of the stage and screen, with a gift for rapid-fire dialogue, both on and off the stage."[37]

Despite having Behrman's name on the play, the version of *Wine of Choice* that opened at Chicago's Erlanger Theatre on December 13, 1937, was so ill-constructed that the rewriting required became drastic, and the Guild threatened to close the play. As rehearsals progressed, Miriam grew unhappy and didn't hesitate to express herself.

After the Chicago tryouts, they moved the play to Pittsburgh; there Litvak joined her after returning from Europe. Each morning Behrman greeted the cast with sheets of rewrites. Langner recalled that when he discussed Behrman's modified pages with Miriam and Litvak over dinner,

Miriam "would comment until the small hours of the morning on how unfavorably her part had been affected."[38]

In Pittsburgh, *Wine of Choice* premiered to a capacity audience at the Nixon Theatre. Despite the terrible writing, Miriam received enthusiastic reviews. "Miriam Hopkins, as the girl desperately trying to lift herself out of inevitability into the power of making a *choice* all hers, plays brilliantly and shrewdly," wrote the critic for the *Pittsburgh Press.*[39]

The play finished in Pittsburgh but would sit idle until its scheduled January reopening in Baltimore. Until then, Behrman turned in another rewrite. While Langner waited, Miriam read Behrman's revisions in her sitting room at Pittsburgh's William Penn Hotel. Finally, she informed Langner "that under no circumstances would she play the part in New York," and she gladly handed in her resignation.[40]

Miriam returned to New York, where she met with Billy, who had taken an option on Ernest Hemingway's play *The Fifth Column.* Like *This Spanish Earth,* it revolved around the Spanish Civil War. Producer Jed Harris, recently responsible for the hit Broadway play *Our Town,* had planned to finance it but disagreed with Hemingway on the revisions, so he dropped out. Billy was returning to Los Angeles and wanted Miriam to collaborate on the play with him. She would join him in a few days.

Although no longer married, Miriam and her ex-husband remained bonded. "You observe Billy and me, we are good friends, the best in the world," Miriam once remarked. "It took a little time for the vaccine of marriage to wear off and friendship to 'take' but once the first reaction fireworks of I'll-show-you-how-attractive-I-am-to-others wore off, a delightful relationship took place. There is nothing for Billy to learn about me, nor I about him, that can disillusion or dismay."[41]

On March 20, 1938, Billy was working on the play at Miriam's Tower Grove house while having Sunday breakfast alone. With no warning, Billy collapsed and was rushed to Good Samaritan Hospital. Miriam was across town at the time, and when she arrived at his side, Billy was dead from a brain hemorrhage.

The funeral was held the following Tuesday—a funeral of "no sadness, no mourning, and no ceremony," according to his written instructions. Miriam and a group of Billy's friends, including writer Sy Bartlett, actors Brian Aherne and Ronald Colman, and director Monta Bell, assembled to remember him at Pierce Brothers Mortuary.[42]

Wearing a gray sports ensemble, Miriam spoke with reporters to explain the service before viewing Billy's silver casket. "The letter Mr. Parker wrote in which he requested this funeral was only a paragraph long—but it was a beautiful letter. If you had known him the way we knew him, you would realize he merely wanted his close friends to come and sit around, just as we would in a living room, and talk about what a swell guy he was. And that is what we are doing."

Billy had addressed a letter to Rex Cole, his business manager, but Cole wouldn't reveal the text. "It was read to his friends in the room by Ronald Colman. He asked that there be no eulogies, no sadness, and no singing."[43]

In an adjoining room, a pianist played selections from Chopin and Debussy. After the service, his body was cremated and returned to Helena, Montana, for burial in the family plot. Overcome with emotion, Miriam collapsed outside the mortuary and was taken to Cedars of Lebanon Hospital, where doctors treated her for exhaustion.

Austin "Billy" Parker was one of the few men in Miriam's life who could handle her lightning-fast, rapier-sharp wit, follow her on flights of fantasy, and understand her moods and whims; he enjoyed sharing them, as she enjoyed sharing his. Their friendship had endured to his death, unmarred by the experiences of marriage, separation, and divorce.

Anatole Litvak had always perceived Miriam and Billy's relationship as an obstacle to his marriage; it was unnatural to him. He felt jealous and neglected. Yet, Billy's death would not change that.

11

West Hollywood to Burbank

When Miriam returned to Goldwyn Studios, she had concerns about her career. Her last film, RKO's *Wise Girl*, had been released more than a year earlier, at the end of 1937. The film lost $144,000, and the reviews were hardly raves. Also, the box office for her four Goldwyn films was middling at best. There were many reasons for this. Goldwyn, as an independent producer, distributed his films through United Artists, whose exhibition market was smaller than that of the major studios; hence, Miriam had less screen exposure countrywide.[1]

What's more, the year before, a poll of theater managers across the country ranked Miriam in the third tier of top moneymaking stars. Goldwyn was shocked.

During her recent contract negotiations, Leland Hayward had worked out a lucrative deal for his client, getting her six films at $75,000 each. To minimize his future losses, Goldwyn panicked and convinced Jack Warner to take four of her pictures for his Burbank studio. RKO also agreed to take one, leaving one film for him. Goldwyn would still be in control of Miriam's contract until it expired in April 1942.

Miriam expected Goldwyn to give her a powerful picture or two to reinforce her slipping box office and to offset the fallout of her earlier films, especially his own *Woman Chases Man* and RKO's *Wise Girl*. When she returned after Billy's funeral, Goldwyn explained his new deal with Jack Warner and RKO. Stunned at Goldwyn's betrayal, she decided to devise a plan to resurrect her career.

Anatole Litvak, now at Warner Bros., convinced executives to acquire the rights to the 1934 Broadway play *Dark Victory*, starring Tallulah Bankhead. It had received good reviews and critics praised Bankhead's performance, but it was not a commercial success. Litvak, however, said the young, pleasure-seeking socialite who develops a brain tumor would be perfect for Miriam. Miriam agreed. She wanted *Dark Victory* as her first picture for the studio, followed by *Juarez*, another script the studio owned.

But within the week, newspapers reported that *Dark Victory* was assigned to Bette Davis, as was *Juarez*. Miriam was still upset with Davis for usurping her role in *Jezebel*, and now she had taken *Dark Victory* as well, a property recommended for her by her husband. Even though she seemingly had lost both plum roles to Davis, she continued to fight for them until cameras rolled.[2]

While Miriam was still in negotiations, her husband's career at Warner's was developing remarkably. After finishing *Tovarich*, starring Claudette Colbert and Charles Boyer, Litvak directed *The Amazing Dr. Clitterhouse*, with Edward G. Robinson. He was now working on *The Sisters*, with Errol Flynn and Bette Davis.

Until a better role came along, Hal Wallis offered Miriam a B-programmer called *Curtain Call*, a Bette Davis reject that Davis had called "weak tea." Miriam insisted that Jack Warner intended using up her contract "the way they did Kay Francis, to make money for them in their second-rate productions." If that were Warner's plan, then Miriam's career would suffer. She asked producers Hal Wallis and Henry Blanke if she had talent. Both reassured her she did. But their best stories couldn't be reserved for her, a freelancer under a short-term agreement, when it was in the studio's long-term interest to boost Davis's career.[3]

Not satisfied, Miriam stated it would be impossible to do a film in which she had no interest. She insisted on talking to Jack Warner directly, but the mogul made excuses. For months, he told executives that she was wrong for his studio at the salary he was paying her. After a week, with no response, Miriam teased him with a deal to save his studio $200,000 on her contract. She hoped that would get his attention.

Leland Hayward had left the Selznick organization in the middle of negotiations to produce plays. Instead of letting Myron Selznick take over as her agent, Miriam offered to meet with Warner without representation. Selznick told her it was a "bad idea." Miriam, undeterred, made a not-so-veiled threat against the mogul: "How can I make concessions and give up money without having an audience with you. I will not discuss the matter with anyone but you personally but if you refuse . . . , I shall be compelled to heed the advice of my agent and business manager and forget all thought of concessions."[4]

Warner responded. It was not his intent to ignore her, but with Hal Wallis on vacation, he was exceptionally busy. He reminded her of their past meetings and regretted they could not come to an agreement before Hayward left. "In view of the fact, however, that we have extended considerable money in production preparation, assigned a director, lined up the cast, and you have already commenced wardrobe preparations for *Curtain Call*, to which you have been assigned, I am sure it would be useless at this late date to try to work out anything with respect to your first picture."[5]

Once again, Warner had only excuses. Four days after receiving his letter, Miriam was hospitalized for an acute infection of the spine and wouldn't be available for two weeks or more. Since hospitalization could change her appearance, they suspended her from *Curtain Call* for "physical incapacity." Kay Francis, once again dumped into a subpar product, replaced her in the retitled *Comet over Broadway*.

Miriam Hopkins was the proverbial thorn in Jack Warner's side—and she hadn't made her first film yet. When her health improved and nothing was available at Warner's, she tried RKO, whom she owed one film. They offered her *Trailer Romance*, originally on Ginger Rogers's schedule but now available after the studio postponed it at the last minute.

After Leland Hayward left Selznick, Miriam moved to talent agent Charles Feldman at Famous Artists. Feldman was Myron Selznick's main rival. In fact, many of Selznick's clients were signing with Feldman, who "took a cool and integrated approach to business." Feldman was friends with many of the studio moguls, including Twentieth Century Fox's Darryl Zanuck, Samuel Goldwyn, and Miriam's current boss, Jack Warner.[6]

In mid-July, Feldman reopened contract negotiations with Jack Warner on Miriam's behalf. Instead of $300,000, Miriam preferred to be paid $100,000 for two pictures, but she would "choose the stories, directors, etc.—in other words, the setup." She was certain Jack Warner would accept her offer if he talked to her. She and Feldman prodded the head of Warner Bros. until he finally had no choice but to meet with her face-to-face.[7]

In his autobiography, Edward G. Robinson wrote that during *Barbary Coast*, Miriam's political beliefs were similar to those of Howard Hawks, Joel McCrea, and Walter Brennan, emphasizing "they were *not* liberals."

Her views had changed after meeting Anatole Litvak, who introduced her to left-wing politics.[8]

Then, in the spring of 1938, she met actor Melvyn Douglas. Douglas, known as a "liberal," convinced her to become more involved in politics. At the end of one two-hour conversation, Douglas asked her to cohost a "registration party" at his home, to encourage those in the business to vote in the upcoming August primary.

Frank Merriam, the Republican governor of California, was running for reelection, and many Hollywood liberals hoped to defeat him for a second term. During his first run at the governor's office, the studio moguls coerced their stars to contribute to Merriam's campaign, but some more socially minded actors rebelled and joined his opponent, Upton Sinclair.

Using the studio's resources, a smear campaign was begun against Sinclair, describing him as "a most dangerous Bolshevik beast." MGM and Fox produced newsreels showing "random" interviews with California voters: Solid, well-heeled citizens articulated support for Merriam, while advocates for Sinclair were "unshaven, poorly dressed and obviously uneducated."[9]

At a cocktail party at Fredric March's home, Irving Thalberg admitted to making those films. March rebuked him for the studio's unfair treatment of Sinclair. "Nothing is unfair in politics," Thalberg told him. In the end, Frank Merriam won reelection.

According to screenwriter Allen Rivkin, during Merriam's run for governor in 1938, "a group met at Miriam Hopkins' house and, led by Mel Douglas, we set up the 'Studio Committee for Democratic Political Action,' which soon switched to the title, 'Motion Picture Democratic Committee (MPDC).'"[10]

Miriam hosted meetings and became a supporter of the MPDC, a pro-Roosevelt, pro–New Deal organization touted as "the voice of Hollywood political liberalism." *The Studio Call*, the official newsletter of the Conference of Motion Picture Arts and Crafts, stated: "The Motion Picture Democratic Committee is a progressive political organization which should have the support of every employee of the motion picture industry." Its members included writers Dashiell Hammett, Philip Dunne, Dudley Nichols, and Allen Rivkin, directors Frank Tuttle and John Ford, and actors Paul Muni, Gloria Stuart, and Melvyn Douglas's wife, Helen Gahagan Douglas.[11]

Some called Miriam a "radical." Many believed that Americans were not interested in the political views of actors. "It's none of my business," wrote Hedda Hopper about the MPDC in her column, "but actors are entertainers, who make their living from the public, and I don't believe [the] public is interested in their political, racial or religious affiliation."[12]

Not surprisingly, the conservative Hopper didn't apply her view about actor's political opinions to herself; she openly expressed her beliefs, in her column and elsewhere. Her right-wing views a decade later would destroy the lives and careers of many artists caught in the notorious blacklist era.

Miriam's participation in the MPDC had the attention of the FBI. For more than the next thirty years, they tracked her activities, political and otherwise, as they did those of many people in public life. J. Edgar Hoover considered the MPDC "a front for Stalinist fundraising." An unnamed informant for the FBI said it was "conceived and delivered by the Los Angeles County Political Commission of the Communist Party." Before long, Miriam was implicated as a Communist supporter, having been identified in an article as a member, like Bette Davis, of the League of Women Shoppers, an organization reportedly organized by Communists.[13]

In August 1938, she was publicly linked to the Communist Party, along with Robert Taylor, Clark Gable, James Cagney, Bette Davis, and even Shirley Temple, for sending first anniversary greetings to the French newspaper *Ce Soir*, which the FBI believed was "owned outright" by the Communists. James B. Matthews, a former Communist organizer, testified before the House committee investigating un-American activities, that he hoped no one would claim "any of these persons, in particular, is a Communist." He explained it was unfortunate that "most of them unwittingly served" the purposes of the Communist Party since their names had a "definite propaganda value" that the party would quickly exploit.[14]

Miriam had no idea the FBI was documenting her movements. It would be a decade before Communism would even slightly impact her life, and the lives of many others, in Hollywood.

For now, though, she was concentrating on Jack Warner. Charles Feldman and Hal Wallis discussed the chances of canceling Miriam's four-picture deal with Sam Goldwyn. If canceled, she could enter into a new freelance contract with Warner Bros. for two relevant pictures at $50,000 each. The new agreement would save the studio $200,000. But before they could decide, Warner's lawyer told Sam Goldwyn about the deal; Goldwyn's attorney composed a letter: "We were advised this afternoon by Mr. Obringer that some understanding has been entered into between yourselves and Mr. Feldman, representing Miss Hopkins, to the effect that Miss Hopkins' contract is to be suspended pending the negotiation of some deal between yourselves and Miss Hopkins. You are, of course, aware that Miss Hopkins is under contract to us and that we have certain obligations under said contract."[15]

Goldwyn's lawyer reminded them that a new agreement between Warner Bros., Miriam, and Charles Feldman wasn't binding unless Goldwyn canceled the original contract.

Besides her career troubles, Miriam was having difficulties with her marriage. Between mourning Billy's death, the man who was arguably the love of her life, and her fights with Jack Warner, she was heading for a nervous breakdown. But Litvak had complaints of his own: Miriam was ignoring him, giving all her time to rescuing her fading career.

In mid-August, Bette Davis invited the Litvaks to a fund-raising banquet for the Tailwagger's Association, a pet advocacy group. An animal lover, Davis was their president, and the Tailwagger's were honoring Howard Hughes, with whom Davis was having an affair at the time.

Nothing suggests that Miriam had been in contact with Davis since their stint in Rochester a decade earlier. Nevertheless, Miriam was a dog lover too and decided to forgo her feelings from *Jezebel* and support the event at the Beverly Hills Hotel.

Oddly enough, their roles were now reversed. Bette Davis was a bigger star in Hollywood and Miriam was struggling to find a good part. The switch in their standing added to Miriam's resentment of Davis. In any case, things went well that evening, and surprisingly the two women were inseparable, reminiscing and chatting as they held hands and giggled like two schoolgirls.

Those feelings changed in a few days when Miriam heard rumors that her husband had carried on a weekend fling with Bette Davis. Embarrassed and outraged, she confronted him, but as Miriam told Becky Morehouse years later, Litvak denounced what he called the words of "ignorant and narrow-minded gossips."[16]

Davis's past affairs with William Wyler, George Brent, and Howard Hughes were well-known, so Miriam refused to accept Litvak's denial. She referred to Davis as a "greedy little girl at a party-table who just had to sample other women's cupcakes. First, she wanted my husband and then she wanted Hepburn's boyfriend [Howard Hughes], and her own husband was all but forgotten."[17]

Miriam was about to file divorce proceedings and name Davis as corespondent, but Jack Warner intervened, and there was also Michael to consider. Litvak was a father figure, so until some peace could return to their lives, he moved to his Malibu beach house to allow Miriam some time alone to calm down.

That same week, after haggling with Miriam's legal entourage, Goldwyn and his lawyers agreed to cancel her original four-picture loan to Warner Bros. A similar agreement was made with RKO, of which she received $25,000 to release her. While Goldwyn refused to give up the one picture she owed him, since he was no longer controlling her beyond that engagement, she could be a free agent and work directly with Hal Wallis, who promised to find her two good pictures.

One of them, and most likely the first, would be an adaptation of the James Hilton novel *We Are Not Alone*. As for the second film, Miriam was still campaigning for *Dark Victory*, even though Bette Davis was scheduled to begin shooting in a few days. Charles Feldman assured Jack Warner that Miriam wasn't being difficult by insisting on it, telling the mogul, "Miss Hopkins is enormously fond of Hal [Wallis] and you, Jack, and the nice attitude you have both shown."[18]

On a side note, Feldman brought to Wallis's attention an unproduced screenplay languishing in Paramount's vaults. He enclosed the synopsis and added, "In my opinion, this would be a delightful subject for Bette Davis and Miss Hopkins. Why not look into this as a possibility for the second photoplay? I am sure both of these girls would love to do it."[19]

The story was based on Edith Wharton's 1924 novella *The Old Maid* and on a Pulitzer Prize–winning 1935 Broadway play by Zoë Akins, starring Judith Anderson and Helen Menken. Paramount had planned to star Ann Harding and Claudette Colbert and then possibly assign the title role to Irene Dunne, but all three actresses declined. Paramount had invested $100,000 before abandoning the project and putting it on the market.

When Feldman suggested the story, Wallis asked Casey Robinson, a former director and one of Warner's top screenwriters, if it would suit Davis and if he would write the screenplay. After reading Akins's play, Robinson called the story too saccharine but said he would add a new element, one that would make it suitable—hatred. Based on Robinson's assessment, Warner Bros. paid Paramount $75,000 for the rights.[20]

For the past several months, Miriam's income had come from ten radio shows and RKO's payoff of her contract, an amount that barely supported her mother and sister and Michael's boarding fees. She also owed $26,806 in taxes to the government on her 1937 income. She hoped 1939 would be more prosperous.[21]

At one point, Miriam believed that Dudley Murphy, her old flame from *24 Hours*, had the answer. He asked her participation in a unique experiment: Murphy would produce legitimate plays on Broadway and simultaneously film them at the old Astoria lot using the original cast. "That's how I plan to work with Miriam Hopkins," Murphy said in an interview, "whom I've signed for the lead in a film and play derived from the novel, *They Shoot Horses, Don't They?*"[22]

The idea fascinated her. It would combine her love of the stage and give her film exposure, where most of her fan base originated. But neither Broadway nor Hollywood was interested. The idea floundered, presumably because of a lack of investors, so Miriam returned to playing the Warner Bros. waiting game.

As far as Miriam knew, *We Are Not Alone* was still on her schedule. Producers were searching for the right actor to play opposite her, but it was a difficult part to cast. Paul Muni's name continued to be on the short list, but he couldn't decide if he wanted to work with Miriam again after their experience on *The Woman I Love*. The project was on hold.

While she waited, Miriam accepted the role of Delia in *The Old Maid* opposite Bette Davis. But according to Miriam, she wasn't anxious to be in a picture with Warner Bros.'s major female star, "knowing she would get all the publicity breaks and the best of it. But I had seen the play, and it was a good character part, the kind I liked, and I had to start working, so I said yes."[23]

The part brought her into open competition with Bette Davis on her home lot. The Davis-Hopkins feud has been written about ad infinitum, but mainly from Davis's point of view. In her autobiography, *The Lonely Life*, Davis wrote that Miriam was "a perfectly charming woman socially. Working with her [was] another story."[24]

Davis could be forthright about her feelings—especially later in life. In an interview on a morning news show shortly before her death, Davis talked about working with difficult actors. When the host mentioned Miriam, she replied, "Miriam Hopkins. She was a real bitch! She was the worst, unprofessional-behaved person. She was a terribly good actress, I did two films with her, but she was terribly jealous."[25]

Michael, who met Davis on the set of *The Old Maid* when he was seven years old, was watching that morning. "What dismayed me about Bette Davis was I didn't see the point. Mother had passed away, and she couldn't defend herself. My mother, to my knowledge, never publicly went on record saying she hated anyone."[26]

Throughout her life, Miriam denied her stormy relationship with Davis. "It wasn't a real feud," she told columnist Erskine Johnson in 1950. "The studio thought it would be good publicity. But it was Bette's studio, and I think I fared badly. It made me look downright rude." Miriam had many opportunities to speak negatively about Davis but rarely said anything. With no lack of irony, she also confessed to Johnson that she would make another picture with Davis, adding, "But I wouldn't get down on my knees and ask to."[27]

One morning in February 1939, Miriam read in Edwin Schallert's *Los Angeles Times* column that Davis wanted to play a dual role in *The Old Maid*—as Charlotte *and* as her illegitimate daughter, Tina. Charles Feldman told Roy Obringer that "if Miss Davis is to play a dual role, as she reads in the papers she is to do, that would change everything."[28]

Contrary to Schallert's report, Davis wanted to play both cousins, including Delia, Miriam's role. For Davis, it would be an acting coup to play two such distinct personalities. The producers humored her, allowing her to think it would happen, but after Davis's repeated requests to read the script, Obringer shared his concerns with Hal Wallis: "I am wondering whether or not when Bette Davis gets a script and finds out she is not to do the dual roles we will have any trouble with her."[29]

Surprisingly, when Davis read the script, she said nothing about Miriam playing the role. Miriam had no idea of Davis's real plan and knew only about the "leaked" rumor in the *Los Angeles Times*. It was by then a moot point, as Wallis assured Feldman and Miriam there was no truth to the reports. But Davis would get her wish to play dual roles in two later films: *A Stolen Life* and *Dead Ringer*.

Still, other contractual points needed clarifying, including final script approval. Miriam also insisted that her name be displayed on the same line and in the same size type as her costar's. Once this demand was met, she signed a modified contract on February 13, 1939, to star in *The Old Maid*.

Next, problems arose concerning Miriam's makeup. For the preliminary tests, she brought her own orange filter to enhance the color of her eyes. But the filter had an unintended effect: it distorted her look in the tests. On Saturday, February 18, Wallis complained about the tests to associate producer Henry Blanke, who telephoned Miriam to discuss the problem. Miriam was dissatisfied as well but wanted to go to San Francisco. She would return on Thursday and make one test after another until everything met with their approval. Blanke approved Miriam's request because Davis was making her tests on Tuesday and "this will help avoid their running into each other—which I think, in general, will help the situation."[30]

The world would know the outcome of Davis's *Jezebel* nomination on Thursday evening after the Academy Awards ceremony. The top personnel at Warner Bros. knew that Miriam believed Davis stole the role, and given their other differences, they deemed it a priority to keep them separated until they had announced the results.

On Thursday, when Miriam returned from San Francisco, she intended to listen to the show on the radio, but coverage was banned that year. Instead, a friend called from the Biltmore Hotel, where the ceremonies were held, and informed her that Bette Davis had won the Best Actress Oscar for *Jezebel*. Miriam went into a rage, trashing everything until Litvak stopped her.

If Miriam believed her problems with George Raft and Paul Muni were stressful, she was about to find out that they were minor quibbles compared to what was to come. And so would the cast and crew of *The Old Maid*.

12

"Perfect Little Bitches"

Variously described as a "woman's picture," a "tearjerker," and a "soap opera," the melodrama has been a standard since the early days of the silent cinema. The maternal melodrama, a subgenre featuring plots of self-sacrificing, loving mother figures who suffer adversity, best describes Miriam's first film at Warner Bros., *The Old Maid*. Similar films include *The Sin of Madelon Claudet, Imitation of Life*, and the twice-filmed *Stella Dallas*.

In the late 1930s and into the following decade, Bette Davis was a staple in the melodramatic maternal film. Along with *The Old Maid's* director Edmund Goulding, executives paired him with Davis in the 1937 film *That Certain Woman*, about a self-sacrificing mother following an annulled marriage. Then, two years after *The Old Maid*, Davis and Goulding made *The Great Lie*, wherein newly widowed Davis offers to bring up the child of her husband's pregnant ex-wife (Mary Astor). *The Old Maid* shared a similar plot line: Davis as a cynical "old maid" spinster who gives her illegitimate child to her self-centered cousin (Hopkins) to raise.

Filming began on Wednesday, March 15, 1939, with Edmund Goulding directing. According to Goulding's biographer, film historian Matthew Kennedy, the British-born director was multitalented, taking on "multiple functions on each set. Though he didn't usually take credit, he co-wrote many scripts, composed incidental music, produced, even consulted on makeup, costumes, and hair styling."[1]

Goulding knew Davis well, having directed her in two films at Warner's: *That Certain Woman* and *Dark Victory*, the film Miriam had hoped would be hers. But he had known Miriam longer, beginning with the New York social circles in the late 1920s, and later at Astoria Studios, where they both were making films.

The first day, the cast reported to the sound stage at nine o'clock, but

Miriam was ten minutes late, wearing a replica of a dress Davis wore in *Jezebel*. Davis claimed that Miriam hoped she would "blow [her] stack at this."[2]

Both Miriam and Davis suggested to Goulding how they could improve their roles. At first, unit manager Al Alleborn reported that each one had "little suggestions in the working out of scenes and getting the characterizations of their parts which did cause a slight delay on the first day, but company is now going smoothly." Any disturbances were short-lived.[3]

The first two days, Goulding filmed the original opening scene in Mr. Painter's lingerie shop, where the cousins and their grandmother are buying Delia's trousseau. However, Davis wanted to enhance her role at Miriam's expense. William Wyler had taught her that an actor's first appearance in a film established their character. When they completed the lingerie shop sequence, Davis wanted to cut the scene. Instead, the opening sequence would be Delia's wedding day.

The following day, Friday, March 17, Miriam was on Stage 15 at nine o'clock, an hour earlier than Davis. Assuming that she had already established her character in the lingerie shop, Miriam played the wedding scene at a lower register. She had no idea that this scene would be the audience's first glimpse of her. So when Davis entered, excited and enthusiastic, people noticed.

A month later, when Goulding cut the lingerie shop scene, Miriam sensed what Davis had done. By then Miriam was using "every trick in the book" to rile her costar. Davis was fascinated, "watching [the tricks] appear one by one." Miriam's scene-stealing stunts were endless: a button would come undone, or a hairpin would fall out. She would change her position in close-ups and then inch her way upstage so Davis would have to turn away from the camera, sometimes at the expense of losing her light.[4]

Considering Miriam needed this film to salvage her career, this unprofessional—and costly—behavior was risky. She was fighting to be popular with audiences but was allowing her loathing of Bette Davis to rule her emotions.

Davis admitted that Miriam was a good actress and was perfect for the role, so it baffled her why she behaved as she did. Did Davis know that Miriam was seeking revenge for her transgressions, including stealing *Jezebel* and the Academy Award that went with it and the weekend fling with her husband? It's unlikely. Instead, Davis played dumb and acted the victim, claiming she controlled her temper during the day but at night "screamed at everybody."[5]

The Davis-Hopkins thespian duel threatened to absorb innocent bystanders as well. Rand Brooks, who that year also appeared in the classic *Gone with the Wind,* played Delia's son, Jim Ralston Jr. He later recalled that both actresses had tried directing him. "One would tell me one thing, (and) then the other would say something else. They were both so anxious to look good and be better than the other. Edmund Goulding just stood by and was amused by the whole thing."[6]

Goulding tried to be a mediator. He respected Davis, but he was Miriam's friend. To his credit, he tried keeping the peace. "Whatever respect they had for each other as professionals was quickly thrown out of the window when one or the other didn't get her way," Goulding said of the two women. "If it wasn't lighting, it was costuming or camera angles or lines. There were times they behaved like perfect little bitches, but I loved them both, and I think the admiration was likewise."[7]

Unit manager Al Alleborn acknowledged Goulding's struggles. "Working with two impossible people like Davis and Hopkins, many things have to be ironed out. . . . Goulding has a tough job on this picture with these two girls. Not that they want to cause him any trouble or worry, but each one is fighting for a scene when they go into it."[8]

Casting the secondary roles, especially that of Clem Spender, the object of both cousins' desires, also presented problems. Gilbert Roland was the studio's first choice, but Goulding wanted to borrow David Niven—with whom he had worked with on *The Dawn Patrol* the year before—from Sam Goldwyn. Since neither actor was available, they gave the role to Humphrey Bogart.

After filming for two days, Hal Wallis, Henry Blanke, and Goulding viewed the scenes between Bogart and Davis at the train station. Bogart's acting was unconvincing, and he appeared thin and unattractive in his uniform. In a memo to Hal Wallis, Goulding wrote that he wished to replace Bogart with George Brent. "In the present stress and with the general line-up, I do feel that the picture needs George," he wrote, emphasizing the part required someone with strength and personality that audiences would remember, someone they would believe could be important to both women's characters.[9]

After two more days, Bogart convinced everyone, including Jack

Warner, that he had no sex appeal. When Wallis fired him, Bogart reportedly shrugged and walked off the set.

On April 1, Miriam was ill and told production manager Tenny Wright that if she went home and rested over the weekend, she would return on Monday feeling better. *The Old Maid* set was at a standstill.

Within a week, the delays were affecting the shooting schedule. The crew was ordered to rush through scenes so Davis could start her next film, *The Private Lives of Elizabeth and Essex*. Everyone worked to speed things along—from shooting out of continuity to arriving early and staying late. Scenes were partially rewritten, causing more delays. The front office ordered Goulding to make up for the time lost.

One morning, Miriam arrived twenty minutes late and had problems with her makeup. "We cannot argue with her," Al Alleborn reported, "but we have lost the time anyway. She always has a reason for being a little late, and we are pushing her along as fast as we can to get her on the set in the mornings."[10]

Davis contributed to the delays as well. On April 17, she fainted on Stage 22 and was sent home to rest. The following day she didn't come to work, and filming was moved to the Ralston home on Stage 12. On Davis's third day of absence, Miriam reported to the studio, washed her hair, and was made up for the day's work. Minutes later, she developed chills and asked to leave for the day. She promised Al Alleborn she would go to bed and return the next day. "I talked to Miss Hopkins, as well as Jack Sullivan, the assistant," Alleborn told Blanke, "and Sullivan and I both feel that she is sick as she shook all the time we were talking to her." When contacted by telephone, both women assured Alleborn they would report to the studio the next day.[11]

The rumors about friction on the set spread. The Warner's publicity department concocted a scheme that Davis and Miriam agreed to. Davis told a reporter, "Hoppy [her nickname for Miriam] and I are going to get a couple of pairs of boxing gloves and pose for a picture glowering at each other like a couple of fighters in their corners. It's the only answer we can make to all the nonsense about how we can't get along."[12]

In their silk dresses and bodices and shawls, they donned boxing gloves and posed for a picture with a worried-looking Edmund Goulding between them. Hedda Hopper reported that the actresses had a sense of humor. Even so, she "never knew two blondes yet who were real palsie-walsies!"[13]

Miriam's sense of humor was waning; the staged photograph made matters worse. "Now they call me 'Hardboiled Hopkins.' I'm not," she insisted. "I'm not temperamental and not hard to get along with. It's those boxing gloves that caused all the trouble. But everyone forgot it was just a gag. They took it seriously."[14]

Hal Wallis, who witnessed their antics, confirmed that their hatred for each other was real. "It was an incredible feud, just fantastic," Wallis claimed in an interview years later. "They would each prolong their arrival on the set, trying to make the other wait. I think later the studio tried to claim it was all just publicity, but it was the real thing. Those girls hated each other."[15]

The Old Maid was nearing completion, but problems continued to plague the set. On Saturday, April 29, Miriam fell ill again. Alleborn found her shaking and nervous. She had had trouble sleeping the night before and wanted to leave, promising to be ready on Monday. It meant delays and additional expenses for the studio, Alleborn explained. Miriam understood, but she had been ill for several days and had come to the studio against her doctor's orders. She worked as long as she could, but the illness was unbearable.

Finally, on May 6, 1939, principal filming on *The Old Maid* was completed. Those who witnessed these two highly strung stars battle compared their performances to a duel. Their seven weeks vis-à-vis became a contest, with each actress demanding, and getting, her full share of dramatic moments. Both women were good actresses and should have limited their rivalry for the benefit of the film, but they were unwilling to do so.

Now that she had completed *The Old Maid*, Miriam was ready for her next picture, *We Are Not Alone*. Jack Warner promised that it would be a starring vehicle for her and that the male role would no more than equal hers. As Milton Krims's screenplay took shape, it became evident that Jack Warner was lying. Several "off the record" sources told her that a revised version of the screenplay was in development and that the female lead's screen time had been significantly cut. Concerned, Miriam asked to read the new script and meet with producers and the writers to avoid obstacles. Miriam asked Warner if he understood "how vital it is to me and my future career that this picture and my part in it be terribly important." As usual, Warner waited.[16]

In June, Miriam flew to New York with Michael, joining Litvak at Sing Sing prison, where he was filming *Castle on the Hudson*. After several days, she returned to the city, taking in plays, including *The Philadel-phia Story*, with Katharine Hepburn, and *The Little Foxes*, with Tallulah Bankhead. Friends were using the Sutton Place house, so she rented a suite at the Hotel Pierre. When Litvak completed filming, he joined them for a few days before returning to Burbank.

One day she lunched with journalist Dorothy Thompson, known for her monthly column for *Ladies Home Journal*. She introduced Miriam to the German writer and playwright Carl Zuckmayer. Zuckmayer had studied at the universities of Frankfurt and Heidelberg, where he formed friendships with bohemian intellectuals and political leftists. He had written several plays, including *The Captain of Köpenick*, a 1931 comedy satirizing German militarism and bureaucracy in an attempt to warn Germans of the rising threat of Nazism. He also scripted *The Blue Angel*, launching Marlene Dietrich in Hollywood, who was banned in Nazi Germany in 1933, as were all the Jewish Zuckmayer's works.

Miriam was attracted to the handsome and intelligent German writer. They shared similar political beliefs and could discuss multiple subjects. Although both were married, they began an "unavoidable" tryst, according to Zuckmayer, having "gigantic dimensions in line with all things American, surrounded by blue lightning's of catastrophe."

Zuckmayer's wife, Alice (nicknamed "Jobs"), had "no inkling" of the affair. Whenever he rendezvoused with Miriam, his wife believed he was meeting with producers, directors, and publishers. Within the week, Zuckmayer left for Barnard, Vermont, where he made his home. But, he could not deny his feelings for Miriam, admitting he "fell in love with a—pardon me—film actress, a movie star."[17]

While she enjoyed her time with Zuckmayer, Miriam wanted to get back to Burbank to start *We Are Not Alone*. There was no decision about her leading man, but the columns reported that Paul Muni was on the list. Muni had read the script but called it "chicken shit." Producer Henry Blanke brought in the novel's author, James Hilton, to work with Milton Krims on the revisions. When Muni read the revised script, he agreed to do it provided Warner removed his former *The Woman I Love* costar from the project.[18]

Jack Warner bluntly told Miriam that Muni didn't want her and she was out. Miriam was stunned. "In decency and justice it can't be taken from one player and laid in the lap of another," she wrote in a lengthy letter to Warner.[19]

Miriam questioned why he didn't tell the New York office, Paul Muni, and everyone involved that this was a committed property. Warner complained it was hard to run a studio, so would she try to understand; would she cooperate? "I promise to, and I did," she assured him.[20]

Miriam reread several scripts but found nothing that suited her. Davis had already made the top two films on her list, *Dark Victory* and *Juarez*, and a mediocre story wouldn't do, considering her financial sacrifices. Then, they suggested one of their B pictures—a remake of *One Way Passage*, a 1932 Kay Francis film the studio retitled *'Til We Meet Again*.

In a June 9, 1939, memo to Charles Feldman, Warner's legal counsel Roy Obringer expressed disappointment that Miriam was "reluctant, or should I say, refuses, to consider *One Way Passage* as the basis of her picture for us." Instead, Obringer convinced Warner to submit another script for her approval, *Three Strangers*, written by the well-respected John Huston, albeit another Bette Davis reject.[21]

In the meantime, a recently purchased property had piqued Miriam's interest. Litvak raved about a marvelous new novel he found. "It's going to make a wonderful movie for Bette Davis and a radio play for you."[22]

"I knew the marriage was over then," she later said.[23]

The new property, *All This, and Heaven Too*, was based on the bestselling novel by Rachel Field about a French governess who falls in love with her employer before being indicted for his wife's murder. Although Warner bought it for Bette Davis, it was removed from her schedule since she had appeared in two costume pictures in a row—*The Old Maid* and *The Private Lives of Elizabeth and Essex*. It was agreed that a similar picture would suffer at the box office. For now, *All This, and Heaven Too*, would lay dormant.

Miriam wouldn't let that stop her. On June 20, she had Charles Feldman contact Warner to have *All This, and Heaven Too* replace *We Are Not Alone*. She wanted to begin on September 15, or October 1, 1939, at the latest. If the studio stalled longer, she might miss out on a Broadway play or a film at another studio. "Miriam absolutely insists upon it," Feldman told his associate Ralph Blum, who relayed Miriam's demands to Jack Warner.[24]

She also wanted her choice of directors. Hungarian-born director Michael Curtiz, known mostly for his adventure films, was first on her list (Warner said he would assign him to *One Way Passage*), but if he was engaged, she wanted Edmund Goulding or William Dieterle, or they could bring in Rouben Mamoulian.

That afternoon, Jack Warner agreed to everything except the October 1 starting date; he suggested November 1. Charles Feldman explained that her "entire year was practically ruined" because of their indecision casting her for parts. She was humiliated by the adverse media when they reported her in one film and retracted it the following week. To counteract what she called "offensive and embarrassing publicity," she insisted that they give her their full support. In a bold move, she wanted Jack Warner to sign the contract before she did. She was testing the limits of her studio contract—and of Jack Warner's patience.[25]

That afternoon, Ralph Blum discussed Miriam's additional demands with Warner. Reluctantly, he agreed on the October 15 starting date, but publicity wouldn't start until Bette Davis had completed her current picture, to avoid obstacles associated with having them at the studio at the same time.

After a heated argument with Feldman, Warner agreed to sign the contract in advance. On June 22, 1939, it was official: Miriam would star in *All This, and Heaven Too*, in the role of Henrietta. Warner assigned George Brent as her costar and Edmund Goulding would direct, all with Miriam's approval. When it was her turn to sign the contract a few days later, she wrote in longhand: "Which role shall be the most important role in said photoplay," wording studio lawyers had omitted from the original text. She initialed it, as did Roy Obringer.

Even though Edmund Goulding was approved, the contract confirmed that Miriam could have her choice of directors and that if none were available, "then we agree to *make every reasonable effort* to secure an outside director of equal importance and ability." In heavy pen strokes, Miriam scratched out "make every reasonable effort." The negotiations were complete.[26]

The studio had a special preview of *The Old Maid* on July 28, 1939, at Warner's Beverly Theater, a month before its official opening. Miriam was invited but sent her regrets because she would be in New York. Bette Davis was also absent. Nevertheless, Edmund Goulding attended along with seventy-eight members of the film's crew, who were curious enough to buy their own tickets.

Edwin Schallert of the *Los Angeles Times* reported that *The Old Maid* was "moving in the highest degree, reaching a powerful climax, which never overdoes but beautifully understates." Despite the problems experienced while making the film, *The Old Maid* would earn $6.6 million at the box office (equivalent to $198.7 million today) and was the thirteenth highest grossing film of the year.

Davis, a remarkable actress, complimented by film historians for her performance in *The Old Maid* in particular, had earned the well-deserved moniker of "legend" by the end of her career. Yet, critics in 1939 gave Miriam equal or higher praise. The fairest description of their ambitious efforts was a "dead heat," with neither Davis nor Miriam losing a millimeter of professional stature. "Miriam Hopkins, another estimable actress, and one who delivers a performance as telling as that of Miss Davis," wrote the *Hollywood Citizen News*. Other critics were more flattering. The *Hollywood Reporter* wrote that Miriam's performance "will cause her stock to soar high once again. In the progression of the story, she gains stature and is never overshadowed. It is a superb enactment of a difficult role."[27]

Edwin Schallert continued in his *Times* review that "Miss Hopkins may be said to surpass almost anything she has played since the days of *Dr. Jekyll and Mr. Hyde*. It is a remarkably sensitive impression she evokes." Louella Parsons called her performance "magnetic" and "a revelation." And Hedda Hopper said: "*The Old Maid* will hang up another box office record, with Miriam Hopkins giving Bette Davis a photo finish. Swell stuff casting those two in the same picture. Like steel striking steel. Miriam now bigger than ever."[28]

The Old Maid demonstrated that Miriam could play a complex character under challenging circumstances. It also proved that despite her nine years as a leading lady, she could share the spotlight with another star of like candlepower and come out undimmed.

While she enjoyed the praise, being a continent away didn't prevent the gossips from spreading stories about her husband's alleged infidelities with his *Castle on the Hudson* leading lady, Ann Sheridan. In August, Litvak and Sheridan attended a joint birthday party for Jack Warner and Dolores del Rio. A few days later, they were seen at the Hollywood Pantages premiere of the Irene Dunne melodrama *When Tomorrow Comes*. Miriam had doubts about the marriage from the beginning, saying it was "as impossible as the stories I was appearing in."[29]

But what mattered most to Miriam were the rumors insinuating that Litvak was intimate with Sheridan. Miriam was humiliated. After all, she was having an extramarital fling with Carl Zuckmayer but kept it from the columns. She would end her two-year marriage to the Russian director. When Litvak learned of his wife's intentions to divorce him again, he called her to discuss it, but she refused to speak with him. He took a flight to New York, but she wouldn't see him.[30]

After appearing on *The Chase and Sanborn Hour* radio program, Miriam said goodbye to Zuckmayer (who returned to his wife in Vermont), and with Michael, she flew to the West Coast to obtain a Reno divorce, which required a six-week residency. For added support, Kay Francis would join her.

Louella Parsons broke the news in her column: "I had hoped they might settle their difficulties. Miriam said yesterday that until a few days ago it seemed as if the whole thing would be worked out satisfactorily. I am fond of Miriam, and I am disappointed that she and Anatole couldn't work out their domestic difficulties. I believe that her director husband is really in love with her, but of course, she knows best, and she says with two pictures to make for Warner's and one for Samuel Goldwyn, she feels she must be free to live her own life."[31]

Miriam dashed off a note to Parsons's competitor, Hedda Hopper, explaining they had tried to work out a life. "But divorce seems the only intelligent remedy. This is dull copy for you, darling because neither of us are leaping into anything else. Thank goodness, son Michael and Kay Francis are with me."

Hopper understood Miriam's reasons for ending her marriage (except the one about her affair with Zuckmayer—or did she?), but she admitted that the rumors of Litvak and Sheridan's affair were a "little far-fetched."[32]

All This, and Heaven Too would begin on October 15, leaving Miriam with barely enough time to satisfy the Nevada divorce requirements. When they landed in Burbank, Kay Francis was waiting, and the trio left quietly on the United Airlines flight to San Francisco. From there, they would catch a connecting flight to Reno.

As they waited for their flight in San Francisco, a gang of reporters surrounded them. Miriam was abrupt about why she was getting a divorce. "We just couldn't get along," she replied tersely, and she then dismissed them with an outburst that she'd be "damned glad" if they were out of her sight.

After midnight, when their plane landed in Reno, reporters again mobbed them as they disembarked. Francis did her best to run interference, explaining that Michael was ill and his mother was anxious to get him to bed. Miriam growled some obscenities over Francis's explanations and screamed, "I am not here for publicity!" She rushed Michael outside through the airport waiting room into a station wagon to take them to Zephyr Cove, a resort on the east side of Lake Tahoe, approximately sixty miles from Reno.[33]

Litvak, who was still in New York, confirmed the divorce rumors to a reporter on Park Avenue. Yes, Miriam was divorcing him, but he refused to comment further. However, the Warner Bros. publicity department released a statement explaining that "the temperaments of each trying to make a career" didn't mix with marriage.[34]

Rumors spread that once Litvak was divorced, he would marry Ann Sheridan, but Sheridan emphatically denied it. "Why should I have the house fall on me twice?" she asked, referring to her divorce proceedings with her husband, Eddie Norris. "But why pick on him [Litvak]? I went out with numerous other men."[35]

If Litvak and Sheridan were intimate, as Miriam believed, it was never confirmed publically. Years later, Jean Negulesco revealed that Sheridan "really fell for Tola, as deeply and seriously as a simple girl could fall for a foreign charmer." The affair, however, was short-lived. Litvak still had feelings for his ex-wife and confessed his love for her for many years.[36]

The following day, Anna and Miriam's dog Flush arrived at the Reno train station. Kay Francis stayed a few days and then returned to Los Angeles, so Miriam waited out her Nevada residency with Michael, taking walks by the lake, reading during the day, and listening to reports on the radio about the new war in Europe.

Miriam was enjoying her time with Michael. She had recently discharged his nanny, Mademoiselle, who had returned to her homeland in France. At seven years old, Michael was too old to associate with "movie brats," so she was sending him to the private Arizona Desert School in Tucson. "I felt he was awfully young to go away until I saw him in camp, and how important it was for him to have male companionship."[37]

It was easy to give him too much. Michael attended private school in Beverly Hills and then went to public school, which Miriam said was better, but even then he had fantastic ideas. One day, he asked for a servant. He argued that one of his playmates had two, and he wanted one to boss around. "That may seem funny," Miriam admitted, "but it was an awful blow to his mother. I said there weren't such things as servants. I reasoned that Mademoiselle worked for us, but we didn't boss her around."[38]

Miriam believed that Michael should be with children his age and living under a strict regime, getting bossed—not doing the bossing. "He has been with me the six weeks here and is unbelievably companionable. I loved Mademoiselle, but she stayed one year too long. She unconsciously, and through her love for him, kept him rather babyish and a little sissy. Since camp, that is gone completely."[39]

In the meantime, Miriam looked for ways to save money while she battled the studio. *The Old Maid* was her first film in almost two years; she was heavily in debt. Sixty cents of every dollar she earned went for federal and state taxes, with an additional ten percent to her agent. Rather than sell $40,000 worth of stock, or mortgage the New York house or the one in California, which she owed $12,000 on, it was wiser to borrow from the bank.

In the interim, she would rent out both homes. "You know, up to this year, I kept up a house in California and one in New York, too. Then I suddenly woke up and said to myself: 'Who do you think you are anyway —a movie star?' And so I got myself some tenants."

Even though she had loaned Sutton Place to friends in the past, businessman Richard Rheem was the first to lease it for $600 a month until the following September. That amount would cover the taxes and the upkeep for both houses, with some remaining. She still owed the government and the bank around $45,000. "That sounds scary but it isn't at all," she wrote to her aunt, Minnie Hopkins, in Syracuse. "I shall do three pictures this winter, and it will be paid."[40]

Although financially strapped, she continued sending a $200 check to her mother, one to Ruby, and another check to Minnie. Michael's tuition was an added expense. During her Nevada stay, Ellen asked for an additional $100. In a letter to her mother, Miriam explained her financial situation and obligations, including her support of Ruby and Minnie. If she didn't make another film soon, it would be impossible to send anyone a full check. Ellen didn't understand. She threatened to send Miriam's letter to Minnie so she could see how badly her niece was doing, but before Ellen could do that, Miriam decided to quote portions of Ellen's letter to Minnie herself.

Ellen's letter began:

"When you spoke to me of sending a monthly check to Minnie, I raised no objection, feeling, of course, you had plenty of money, but since then, the summer you went to Europe, I remained in a hot one-room apartment all summer. Now you speak of our living on borrowed money from the bank and cannot send me, at least, one hundred dollars extra.

It is time you discontinued sending a monthly check to any members of the Hopkins family. Minnie has three grown nephews, her brother's sons, who should help her if she needed help. You and Ruby owe nothing to any member of the Hopkins family; they should have helped me to take care of you but didn't. And if you continue to give it to her and deprive me, no good can come of it."[41]

Typically, Miriam wouldn't have discussed finances with her mother, but now she had no choice. Ellen reasoned that since Miriam paid her rent with checks from Pioneer Royalty, Miriam's corporation, she couldn't be living on borrowed money. No doubt she had investments, annuities, and so on, like other actresses who made fortunes.

To be helpful, Miriam suggested ways her mother could earn extra money. Why not be a receiving hostess in a hospital, as a friend had done, or take appointments at Elizabeth Arden's? She could be a hostess at the chic hat salon John-Fredericks or take on any "pleasant and utterly dignified" positions that would occupy her time and divert her mind from "all her personal vanities."

Instead, Ellen blackmailed her. "What would the world think if I didn't live in the proper environment and in the manner the world expects of the mother of a girl successful in the movies."

Miriam warned her aunt about Ellen's letter, while reminding her that hers was the "one check I sign out of love and not duty."[42]

In the meantime, Miriam wasn't feeling any love for Jack Warner and his Burbank cronies. Unbeknownst to her, Warner Bros.'s lawyers were plotting how they could get out of their commitment to her without having to see the inside of a courtroom.

13

All This, Jack Warner, and Bette Davis, Too

While Miriam played the waiting game in Nevada, the Warner Bros. legal department was working on what they referred to as the "Miriam Hopkins situation." Contract or no contract, the studio postponed filming of *All This, and Heaven Too* but were uncertain of how Miriam would react. Days earlier, Germany had invaded Poland, stopping all big budget pictures at the studios; Warner Bros. used that as the reason to cancel *All This, and Heaven Too.*

Miriam had a moral and lawful agreement, but Warner's legal team debated whether she still had the right to appear in their film or whether they could pay off her contract. Her contract wasn't the standard agreement; for a reduced compensation, she could appear in two "quality" films. But now, Roy Obringer said it was "doubtful if any court would give us the right to merely pay Hopkins the remaining $50,000 due her under her contract and thereby relieve ourselves from further obligation."

Even so, if they paid Miriam the $50,000 instead of making *All This and Heaven Too*, she would "undoubtedly claim breach of contract and bring a lawsuit." After wrangling with legal counsel and top Warner's executives, they finally told Charles Feldman that the film was no longer on the studio's schedule.

On September 21, Miriam received a letter from Feldman explaining the studio's decision. The possibility of a European war and the one million dollars necessary to make the film were their justifications. Miriam wasn't sure how to proceed. Her isolation at Zephyr Cove complicated communications with Feldman. "It's so difficult handling all this five hundred miles away with the nearest telephone ten miles away in a general store," she complained.[1]

That night, leaving Michael with Anna, her cook, she drove eleven hours to Los Angeles, where she met with Feldman and Hollywood attorney Barry Brannon. She questioned whether Warner Bros. could be forced to make the film. They could not, according to Brannon, and nor could an actress be compelled to appear in a picture. She could sue for damages, but a lawsuit might last a year or more, and the studio would most likely appeal the decision. Based on his counsel, Miriam decided to take legal action only as a last resort.[2]

Upon returning to Zephyr Cove, she wrote a lengthy letter to Jack Warner explaining that her situation was unlike anything she had experienced. He promised her two relevant pictures, not any B-picture script. "Jack, we have a contract," she wrote. "I entered into it in good faith: I thought you did the same. Now Jack, first it was Mr. Muni [regarding *We Are Not Alone*]—now it's Mr. Hitler. I'm very sorry but [on] October 15th I'll be in Hollywood to fulfill my contract."[3]

A few days later, after speaking to Feldman from the general store, she learned the situation had improved. Warner read her letter and had a meeting with Feldman that morning. Feldman advised Warner that Miriam was "adamant" that if she didn't make *All This, and Heaven Too*, or at least one of her conciliatory films, she would bring a suit against the studio for damages or the rescission of her contract. If the lawsuit were successful, her original Goldwyn contract would be reinstated, including her $300,000 salary. After much discussion, they came to a compromise, promising that when he made *All This, and Heaven Too*, Miriam would play the lead role. "That would be fair," she agreed, "and I only hope it works out."

In concluding her letter to Jack Warner, Miriam expected, "rather childishly," she supposed, "that because the press said I was all right in *The Old Maid*, you would be rather pleased and think it was nice to have me with your studio. And I breathed a sigh of relief that all the petty arguments were over—it seems they have just begun. I repeat, as I started this letter, I really don't understand it."[4]

While at Zephyr Cove, Miriam had contact with Carl Zuckmayer through letters and telephone calls. At her insistence, Charles Feldman arranged a writing job for him at Warner Bros. "Circumstances drove me westward," Zuckmayer wrote to a friend. "Behind the scenes, my movie star had been busy arranging for a big Hollywood firm to send me the travel check."

But first, Zuckmayer promised to visit her in Nevada. When his plane landed in Salt Lake City, Miriam was waiting. They returned, driving back through the Utah desert and over the Sierras to Lake Tahoe; there she rented him a cabin near hers. He would stay with her until the divorce was final.

Two weeks later, Miriam completed her self-imposed exile. On October 11, behind the locked doors of the Reno District Court, she severed her marital ties to Anatole Litvak. The judge granted the divorce on the grounds of extreme cruelty. Litvak's attorney filed a cross-complaint charging desertion but offered no evidence. Afterward, the divorce papers were sealed.

Miriam escaped by the courthouse back stairs to avoid photographers. A chauffeur drove her and Zuckmayer to the train station where Michael, Anna, and Flush boarded a train to Pasadena. Miriam and Zuckmayer rented a car for Hollywood, via Sacramento, San Francisco, and the Pacific coast, arriving in the film capital four days later. Zuckmayer wasn't impressed: "But that city is as ugly as one imagined, and if one had to live there for any length of time, one could go packing." The following day, Zuckmayer signed a seven-year writing contract with Warner Bros.[5]

Miriam's lawyer claimed in a press release that she had several films waiting for her at Warner Bros., but in reality there was nothing. Instead, she followed through on her earlier threat. She cabled Hal Wallis that she was "ready willing and able" to start work on "the photoplay entitled *All This, and Heaven Too*." She reminded him of her contract, underlining the amendment promising her the picture.[6]

The day before her thirty-eighth birthday, she met with several Warner Bros. executives. As a result, Miriam agreed to drop *All This, and Heaven Too*. In its place, she was given a part opposite Errol Flynn in the studio's latest western, *Virginia City*. She gave no explanation for her change of heart, but there was more to her decision than she let on.

The truth came out years later, when Miriam confided to Becky Morehouse that Jack Warner had found out about her affair with Zuckmayer. He knew of Miriam's aversion to bad publicity and had hinted that if certain information "became public," it might be detrimental to her already teetering career.

Miriam was at a stalemate. Most likely it was an empty threat, but her insecurities overruled her. If she fought for *All This, and Heaven Too*, in her mind she might lose everything. Career even trumped her feelings for Zuckmayer, who claimed that when "publicity became involved," their relationship suffered.[7]

For now, Jack Warner had won. "That son-of-a-bitch had me and he knew it," Miriam told Becky. If true, she had no choice but to accept Warner's offer and bow out of *All This, and Heaven Too*; and *Virginia City* was an imperfect substitute.[8]

Although hardly a starring vehicle, *Virginia City* was a high-budget production starring Warner's top leading man, Errol Flynn. The director was Michael Curtiz, one of Hollywood's best and on her first-choice list of filmmakers.

Jack Warner also left the door open for the *One Way Passage* remake; either that, or Miriam could accept *January Heights*, based on Polan Banks's novel of two women who vie for the affections of the same man. As a bonus, Warner added another film to her contract, possibly *All This, and Heaven Too*. However, both Miriam and Warner knew that was unlikely.

Virginia City was considered a sequel to Errol Flynn's recent western hit, *Dodge City*. Olivia de Havilland, Flynn's costar in that film, was fitted for wardrobe and makeup tests, but at the last minute, Hal Wallis removed her from the cast. Olivia de Havilland was playing a southern woman in the soon-to-be-released *Gone with the Wind*, and Wallis believed she shouldn't be in two southern roles in a row, so Miriam took over.

Besides Flynn, in the film was Randolph Scott, Miriam's original love interest, and in a miscast role, Warner Bros. tough guy Humphrey Bogart, who played a Mexican bandito.

Virginia City focused on gold smuggling during the final days of the Civil War. Captain Kerry Bradford (Flynn), a Union intelligence officer, escapes from a Confederate prison and learns of a conspiracy to smuggle $5,000,000 worth of gold out of Virginia City to aid the South. He falls in love with Julia Haynes (Hopkins), who, unbeknownst to him, is a Confederate agent masquerading as a dance hall girl.

Miriam had problems with the script, but she was a last-minute addition to the cast and time was running out. At the final costume fittings with Curtiz and designer Orry-Kelly, she let her "shoulders slouch and stuck out her rear," distorting the look of the dress. Knowing that Curtiz might "accuse him of inferior work," Orry-Kelly grabbed Miriam and straightened her posture. "This lady just wants the script rewritten," he complained to Curtiz. When Miriam cried that he was hurting her, Orry-Kelly replied, "Not half as much as you're hurting my reputation."[9]

A week later, filming began at Flagstaff, Arizona, about seventy miles south of the Grand Canyon. Miriam hoped that several weeks away from Carl Zuckmayer would rekindle their affair. But while Zuckmayer waited for a writing assignment, he indulged himself, having expensive meals and attending parties. But overall, Hollywood was a disappointment. He met with producers, visited Wolfgang and Gottfried Reinhardt, the sons of Max Reinhardt, and lunched with famous people, but nothing came of it.

When Miriam lost *All This, and Heaven Too*, Zuckmayer lost interest, especially when she mentioned marriage. She waited for an answer, but the pressure on him ended their relationship. "Women get this strange idea too easily that one has to make a 'decision,'" Zuckmayer explained. "My God, how I hate decisions. They bring all conflict into the world. Without them, life could be so much more beautiful."[10]

Production on *Virginia City* began at Oak Creek Canyon. Per the script, the Wells Fargo Overland Stage transporting Flynn and Miriam is stuck in the middle of the turbulent river. In take after take, Flynn carried Miriam through the freezing water to the safety of an overhanging tree. Later, back at camp, Miriam nursed a headache and sighed, "All day long I have been afraid that Errol would drop me in the water. Perhaps it would have been better if he had."[11]

Flynn was, in all likelihood, tempted. Their dislike for each other was well-known, but no one knew the source of the bad blood between them. Stories abounded, including one that claimed Flynn would eat gorgonzola cheese with onions and beer before their love scenes. "He didn't," Miriam insisted. "That tale is a—a falsehood. It makes me out a sorry one, doesn't it? But it does more injustice to Flynn. He wouldn't do a thing like that. What do you call that kind of a story? I know. Apocryphal."[12]

Apocryphal or not, *Virginia City* screenwriter Robert Buckner told author Ronald L. Davis that Miriam was "a very difficult person, and everyone in the industry knew it."

"They simply couldn't stand each other and were at swords point all the time," Buckner continued. "One time we were on location, and they had to play a love scene. They weren't speaking to each other. The night before, each one got a typewriter in their room and rewrote the scene with themselves having all the lines. It took us three days to unscramble that."[13]

According to eyewitness accounts, the *Virginia City* set was a war zone, not unlike the set on *The Old Maid*. John Hilder, a correspondent for *Hollywood* magazine, reported that "tempers flared, and feuds raged. For one memorable weekend, it appeared the cast was about to choose sides—the blues and the grays—and re-fight the Civil War with bare hands, rocks or practical bullets."[14]

Columnist Sidney Skolsky wrote that, according to his spies, several quarrels were going on simultaneously: "Errol Flynn and Humphrey Bogart are feuding, Flynn and Miriam Hopkins are feuding, and Mike Curtiz and Miriam Hopkins are feuding."[15]

Twelve-year-old Dickie Jones, who played Cobby, didn't recall the stress, even between Miriam and Errol Flynn. "On the set [Errol] was all professional," Jones remembered about his favorite actor. "I didn't socialize with him, so I don't know about the other things that he did, or so they claimed, but I liked him."

Jones was also fond of Miriam and recalled that she "talked *to* me and not *at* me." To a young boy, she made an impression. He reasoned the temperament rumors were "professional jealousy. A youngster can pick out someone that's nice and someone that isn't, and not just by their attitude and the way they talk."[16]

Jones's feelings were not unusual. Unseasoned actors and children appreciated Miriam's willingness to help them, unlike the experienced players that rejected her "well-meaning suggestions."

Even though she thought of Carl Zuckmayer, she had almost daily telephone conversations with Anatole Litvak, encouraging rumors of reconciliation.

In Burbank, Zuckmayer was adapting Arnold Zweig's novel, *The Fight over Sergeant Grischka*, which was challenging. But soon, they reassigned him to Errol Flynn's next film *The Sea Hawk*. Not surprisingly, he declined it, knowing Warner would fire him, and he did.

With no more prospects, Zuckmayer bid farewell to Miriam and returned to New York, where he lectured at the New School for Social Research. "All this was regal," said Zuckmayer recalling his visit to California:

> But after a few months of this exceptional state of affairs in Hollywood, she [Miriam] turned again into a movie star and lived there a royal façade of a life in a palais-like façade of millionaire's mansion, and even though the swimming pool pleased me to no end, and the wine cellar bulged over with Pommery and

Chambertin, it became soon a piss of a life, particularly since publicity got involved, and the return route to Jobs [his wife] and to my own proper life and my better self had to be taken swiftly, after all these escapades. I had a contract in Hollywood in order to earn a little money and not to live only as prince regent.

Miriam was unhappy about Zuckmayer's departure and his refusal to marry her.[17]

The *Virginia City* cast returned to Burbank, where Curtiz held dance rehearsals for the so-called cancan number. Miriam fought with Michael Curtiz, who caused anxiety for everyone. He was demanding and had low opinions of nearly all actors. Bette Davis once refused to work with him after he called her a "goddamned nothing no good sexless son of a bitch."[18]

Miriam called Curtiz "a madman—mad and adorable." For twelve weeks they yelled and disagreed on rehearsal time and the song she was to sing, "Marching through Georgia," an 1865 ballad familiar to the Union Army. As a southerner and a Georgian, she thought the choice was offensive. "'Marching through Georgia' was a song wrung from the heartaches and suffering of the people of my home state," she said. Not wanting to start another civil war, Curtiz used "The Battle Cry of Freedom" instead.[19]

But Miriam's "battle" with Curtiz continued. "It becomes tougher every day to handle Hopkins and Mike Curtiz together," reported Frank Mattison to production manager Tenny Wright, "for each shows their utter contempt and disregard for each other. [I] am only hoping that we can get her through this picture without any further blowups."[20]

Miriam's demands were clear: Until Curtiz allowed more time for rehearsals, she wouldn't prerecord "The Battle Cry of Freedom" or film the dance number. Her confidence was low; except for some minor steps, she hadn't danced in a decade. To save time, Curtiz let her rehearse on Stage 9 with dance director Bobby Vreeland.

That evening, Miriam practiced until ten o'clock and recorded the song for playback. The next day, she "squawked about coming in" and refused to "accept the call until 10 a.m.," Mattison reported.[21]

During rehearsals on December 23, Miriam dislocated her hip and collapsed in pain. They applied first aid in the studio's emergency hospital and sent her home. She was bedridden over the holiday, yet managed to attend the *Gone with the Wind* premiere at the Carthay Circle Theater with Michael and Bennett Cerf, who was visiting from New York.

On January 11, with her hip injury healed, she walked onto Stage 11 to film the cancan dance number. It was the last scene to be shot. That morning, she arrived late and hid in her portable dressing room. After two hours, Curtiz remarked, "Now, either she dances or else," lightly tapping on her dressing room door. Miriam stepped out wearing a black, laced bodice and a ruffled skirt. "Let's get this over," she said smiling. Miriam took her place in line with the other girls, raising her ruffled skirt in typical cancan fashion. The prerecorded music began. Determined to finish the scene, Miriam and her chorus girls kicked vigorously to the music until Curtiz was satisfied. *Virginia City* was a wrap.[22]

After the New Year, Warner Bros. approved *All This, and Heaven Too*, but not surprisingly, Bette Davis had the lead. Hal Wallis had not yet cast the supporting role of the Duchesse de Praslin, so he suggested, "Let's not drop consideration [for Hopkins] altogether for the Duchesse, but keep her in mind." Anatole Litvak, the newly assigned director, agreed, saying, "The Duchesse de Praslin is a heartless and venomous bitch. Miriam will be perfect." Miriam, however, would have refused the offer. She wouldn't have supported Bette Davis or have accepted her ex-husband's directions. The part went to Barbara O'Neil, earning her an Academy Award nomination.[23]

Miriam instead accepted *January Heights* with her costar Fred Mac-Murray. Then, producers Lou Edelman and David Lewis told Wallis they were shelving the film. It wasn't "a criticism of the work" they said, but the script required revisions and the right director.[24]

With lots of free time, Miriam flew to New York, ostensibly for a rest; instead, she met with a large manufacturer about sponsoring a radio program, saw a designer about redecorating a room at Sutton Place, and wrote down stories for Ward Morehouse's new book. She spoke disparagingly to a fan magazine writer about *Virginia City*: "If you want to see me look tragic you must take a peek at my new picture—I just finished it —whoof!"[25]

Miriam's schedule was tight. She rushed back to Los Angeles, where Orson Welles paired her with William Powell for a radio adaptation of *It Happened One Night.* Later, she attended a party for classical pianist Arthur Rubinstein at Basil and Ouida Rathbone's home.

Two days later, she returned to New York and learned that Carl Zuckmayer was also there. She called him at two o'clock one morning complaining that she was lonely and unhappy. She needed company. "And this I could not resist," Zuckmayer recalled, "so I came [to her hotel] for seven

Miriam Hopkins, two years old, circa 1904. (Courtesy of Michael Thomas Hopkins)

Hopkins as a child with her grandmother Mildred Cutter, her mother, Ellen, and her older sister, Ruby (1905). (Courtesy of Michael Thomas Hopkins)

Hopkins's grandmother Mildred Middleton Dickinson Hines Cutter (1900). (Courtesy of Michael Thomas Hopkins)

With school friends at Goddard Seminary in Barre, Vermont (1919).

A painting of a young Miriam Hopkins by New York artist Harry Stoner (1920). (Courtesy of Michael Thomas Hopkins)

Hopkins, center, in her first Broadway production as one of Irving Berlin's "Eight Little Notes" in the *Music Box Revue* (1921).

With Fredric March in *Puppets* (1925) at the Selwyn Theatre (now the American Airlines Theatre). (Courtesy of Joseph Yranski)

Miriam's second husband, author and writer Austin Parker (1935).

With Eliot Cabot in the Theatre Guild production of *The Camel through the Needle's Eye* (1929) at New York's Martin Beck Theatre.

The cast of Miriam's first film, Paramount's *Fast and Loose* (1930). From left: Carole Lombard, Frank Morgan, Herschel Mayall, Charles Starrett, Miriam, and Henry Wadsworth. (Courtesy of Joseph Yranski)

With *The Smiling Lieutenant* (1931) costars, Maurice Chevalier and Claudette Colbert. (Courtesy of Joseph Yranski)

Fredric March, Miriam, and director Rouben Mamoulian at a table read for *Dr. Jekyll and Mr. Hyde* (1931).

Fredric March in makeup as Hyde in *Dr. Jekyll and Mr. Hyde* (1931).

At an RKO film premiere with husband Austin "Billy" Parker (1931).

Hopkins and her adopted son, Michael (1932). (Courtesy of the Academy of Motion Picture Arts and Sciences)

Miriam Hopkins in a rare moment in her backyard. (Courtesy of Michael Thomas Hopkins)

With legendary actor Lionel Barrymore in MGM's *The Stranger's Return* (1933).

With Gary Cooper, Fredric March, and director Ernst Lubitsch outside the *Design for Living* (1933) stage at Paramount.

Hopkins with Gary Cooper on Rudy Vallee's *Fleischmann's Yeast Program*, rehearsing the radio version of *Design for Living* (1933). Robert Shayne (far left) portrayed Fredric March's role.

Hopkins in a Paramount
publicity photo (1933).

Jack La Rue and James Eagles in the corncrib before the rape scene in *The Story of Temple Drake* (1933).

With Jack La Rue in the sensational *The Story of Temple Drake* (1933).

Jezebel's (1933) program cover. (Courtesy of Joseph Yranski)

Onstage in *Jezebel* (1933) at the Barrymore.

Hopkins and crooner Bing Crosby in the musical *She Loves Me Not* (1934).

Michael's French nanny, Christiane Deveraux, whom they called "Mademoiselle." (Courtesy of Michael Thomas Hopkins)

With Michael on the SS *California*, arriving in New York from Los Angeles
(1934).

Signing her four-year contract in August 1934 with producer Samuel Goldwyn, as Goldwyn star comedian Eddie Cantor looks on.

With Frances
Dee in the first
Technicolor
full-feature
film, *Becky
Sharp* (1935).

Rouben Mamoulian directing Miriam in *Becky Sharp* (1935).

With Edward G. Robinson in her first film for Goldwyn, *Barbary Coast* (1935).

Hopkins and her son, Michael, in 1935.

With Merle Oberon in Lillian Hellman's *These Three* (1936).

At play behind the scenes of *These Three* (1936) with Merle Oberon, producer Samuel Goldwyn, Joel McCrea, and comedian Eddie Cantor.

With Rex Harrison in *Men Are Not Gods* (1936), a film she made in England.

In the living room of her newly decorated Tower Grove house, former home of John Gilbert, in Beverly Hills (1937).

In the drawing room of her Sutton Place townhouse. A portrait of Michael hangs on the wall behind her (1936).

With Joel McCrea in *Woman Chases Man* (1937). During this scene, the strap in Miriam's robe snapped and she fell to the stage floor, tearing her diaphragm.

Being directed by future husband Anatole Litvak on the set of *The Woman I Love* (1937).

With Theodore Newton in S. N. Behrman's play *Wine of Choice* (1937) at Chicago's Erlanger Theatre.

Hopkins and director Fritz Lang at the *Faust* premiere at the Pilgrimage Theatre in Hollywood on August 24, 1938.

Anatole Litvak spending time with Michael at his beach house in the summer of 1938. (Courtesy of Michael Thomas Hopkins)

With former Paramount boss Jesse L. Lasky and talent contestant Camille Patty on Lasky's 1939 radio program, *Gateway to Hollywood*.

With Bette Davis at the Tailwagger's Association fund-raiser in mid-August 1938 at the Beverly Hills Hotel. It was Hopkins's first meeting with Davis since they costarred in George Cukor's *Excess Baggage* a decade earlier.

Hopkins attending the premiere of *Confessions of a Nazi Spy* (1939) with her husband, and the film's director, Anatole Litvak.

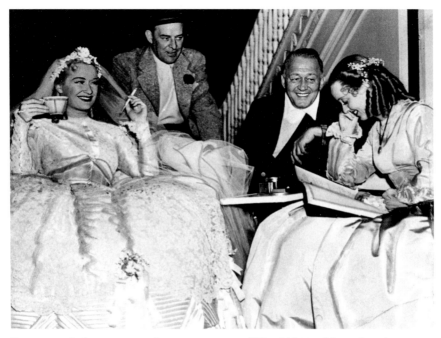

Enjoying a lighter moment between scenes of *The Old Maid* (1939) with assistant director Jack Sullivan, director Edmund Goulding, and Bette Davis.

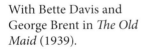

With Bette Davis and George Brent in *The Old Maid* (1939).

With Ralph Morgan and Henry Hull in Atlantic City in August 1939, during a
jurisdictional dispute between actors and stagehands.

With her son, Michael, Kay Francis, and Geraldine McDonald on August 29, 1939, at the San Francisco airport, waiting to board a flight to Reno to divorce her third husband, Anatole Litvak.

Miriam in the Tower Grove house with her dog Flush (1940).

Performing in a *Campbell's Playhouse* radio broadcast of *Air Mail to Red Riding Hood* with Humphrey Bogart on November 12, 1940.

With Errol Flynn in *Virginia City* (1940).

Toasting Bette Davis in the final scene of *Old Acquaintance* (1943).

Onstage at the
Plymouth Theatre in
Thornton Wilder's
The Skin of Our Teeth
(1943). (Courtesy of
Joseph Yranski)

With her fourth and final husband, journalist and author Raymond Brock, on their wedding day, October 23, 1945, in Alexandria, Virginia.

With Mady Christians in a scene from *Message for Margaret* (1947) at New York's Plymouth Theatre. Miriam and Christians lost money on the play, ruining their friendship. They never spoke again.

Rehearsing a scene on the set of *The Heiress* (1949) with Olivia de Havilland, Montgomery Clift, William Wyler, and Ralph Richardson.

Michael visiting the set of *The Heiress* (1949) with his mother and director William Wyler. (Courtesy of Michael Thomas Hopkins)

The cast and crew of *The Heiress* (1949). (Courtesy of Michael Thomas Hopkins)

Hopkins, in 1951, with her mother, Ellen, and son, Michael. (Courtesy of Michael Thomas Hopkins)

Michael in uniform after enlisting in the Air Force in 1951. (Courtesy of
Michael Thomas Hopkins)

Gig Young, Anthony Quinn, and Hopkins in a scene from television's *Pulitzer Prize Playhouse* adaptation of "Ned McCobb's Daughter" (1951).

Hopkins and Thelma Ritter in *The Mating Season* (1951).

Hopkins and her half-sister Katherine Hopkins Cox with their father, Homer Ayres Hopkins, in 1951. (Courtesy of Michael Thomas Hopkins)

Michael and his wife Christiane with their newborn son, Tom, in 1951. (Courtesy of Michael Thomas Hopkins)

Hopkins and Andrew Prine in *Look Homeward, Angel* (1958) at the Ethel Barrymore Theatre. (Courtesy of Michael Thomas Hopkins)

Relaxing in her dressing room during the road tour of *Look Homeward, Angel* (1960).

With Shirley MacLaine in *The Children's Hour* (1961).

With Leticia Roman and Cara Garnett in *Fanny Hill* (1964).

Miriam Hopkins's Upper East Side townhouse at 13 Sutton Place, New York.

Hopkins's last television appearance, in *The Flying Nun* (1969), starring Sally Field. She played the Mother Superior.

Hopkins with her longtime friend H. C. Potter (Michael's godfather) and writer Becky Morehouse at the Museum of Modern Art's showing of *The Story of Temple Drake* on July 12, 1972. The last known photograph of Miriam Hopkins.

nights." That was their last meeting. Despite Miriam's clinginess, Zuck-mayer had pleasant memories of his mistress: "She is one of the nicest and smartest women I ever met and has helped me discover this country like no one else could have managed or would have wanted to."²⁶

Miriam flew to Hollywood to begin *January Heights*. She knew nothing of the story, other than that her role was a pianist who "performs with a philharmonic orchestra." At the last minute, the film was shelved.²⁷

Miriam was broke and desperately needed work. She never handled her finances moderately, and at any given time, she could be dreadfully broke or abundantly wealthy. Once, after returning from the Bahamas with Billy, she met Ward Morehouse at the dock and yelled to him from the gangplank, "Oh, darling—I'm so glad. Have you got $20? We haven't five cents to do any tipping." But when money was plentiful, she enjoyed buying gifts for friends: at Christmas, during the making of *Splendor*, David Niven gave her two handkerchiefs—she gave him a Studebaker.²⁸

This time she wasn't concerned about her current lack of funds. Columbia wanted her for *Singapore* opposite Melvyn Douglas. After that, she would reunite with Edward G. Robinson in Warner Bros.'s *A Dispatch from Reuter's*. In June, she would return to the Goldwyn lot to satisfy her contract obligations. However, for whatever reasons, none of these projects materialized: Goldwyn's script wasn't ready, and her usual excuse—she "didn't like the screenplay"—had her backing out of the Columbia and Warner's projects.

She had promised Jack Warner she would attend the star-studded premiere of *Virginia City* in Reno, but at the last minute, she was hospitalized with the flu and an ear abscess.²⁹

The reviews for *Virginia City* were mixed. Many critics cited the lack of chemistry between its leading stars. "Weakest sequences have to do with Mr. Flynn's making love to Miss Hopkins," the *Dallas Morning News* reported, "with Miss Hopkins reading her lines poorly for her and Mr. Flynn reading his very well for him but still poorly. The lines probably never should have been written in the first place."³⁰

While recovering in the hospital, she was invited by the Theatre Guild to do a summer play of her choice for Bela Blau, producer of her 1931 Broadway production, *The Affairs of Anatol*. She passed on several scripts, including *Design for Living* and *Tomorrow & Tomorrow*, and finally agreed on Ferenc Molnár's *The Guardsman*. She received a $750 weekly salary and 20 percent of the gross over $3,750.

In *The Guardsman*, Miriam plays a vivacious and temperamental Viennese star who falls in love with a guardsman. She asked for Italian actor Tullio Carminati for the title role: "I had seen him play, and, besides, he was a friend of mine."[31]

Still under a doctor's care when she arrived for rehearsals, she was given a shot before the first table reading; it dulled her senses and caused hallucinations. Seemingly confused, she claimed to hear "Mussolini speaking with Hitler" on the radio, and he "declared war"—so, she surmised, she "must have been sleepy."

Right then, she overheard Carminati, a man with Fascist sympathies, admiringly discussing Mussolini and Fascism. Offended by his remarks, Miriam rebuked her costar. "Mussolini may have taken the smells out of the Venice canals," she sternly warned Carminati, "but he was certainly stinking up the rest of the world. Not only do I refuse to appear on the same stage with you, but I also refuse to be in the same room with you. Leave."[32]

Enraged by her outburst, Carminati walked out. With the opening in a few weeks, Blau had to find a new leading man.[33]

When she recovered, she apologized to Blau and offered to pay the expenses caused by the delays. He told her it wasn't necessary, but oddly enough, a few days later she received a letter from Actors Equity informing her that Blau was suing her for the delay. He was asking for $3,000 in damages.

For the sake of the play, Blau rescheduled *The Guardsman*'s premiere for White Plains, New York. Kent Smith, who would stand out in the horror classic *Cat People*, was hired to replace Carminati. Miriam blamed the medication for her outburst. "I couldn't remember what I said, but Mr. Carminati seemed very glum." As for her lawsuit, Miriam settled with Blau for less than $1,000, a third of what he sued her for.[34]

When *The Guardsman* opened at the Ridgeway Playhouse, Miriam received glowing reviews. "Miss Hopkins performance is smooth and accomplished and utterly feminine," reported Sidney B. Whipple of the *New York World-Telegram*. "Her radiant loveliness, however, is an asset unimpaired by Hollywood's demands during these last ten years, and the seeming coldness of her characterization made this beauty all the more tantalizing."[35]

During *The Guardsman*'s run, the Theatre Guild sent Miriam another play written by a young, untested Mississippi playwright. For many,

Tennessee Williams's *Battle of Angels* was a combination of *The Grapes of Wrath* and *Tobacco Road*. The story is set in a small rural Mississippi town, where the love-starved owner of the local dry goods store befriends a virile young drifter; soon, his charisma draws out her underlying sexual passion.

Williams wrote the play for Tallulah Bankhead, but she declined it, so the Guild considered Joan Crawford. But she too turned it down, calling it "low and uncommon." Williams was pleased; Crawford's casting "appalled" him, calling her "such a ham!" He conceded that Miriam "would be magnificent in the part" but admitted he would "have to take what they give me."[36]

Lawrence Langner, a Theatre Guild producer, told Williams that Miriam was "prodded" about the play. Hoping to convince her, Williams went to *The Guardsman*'s opening to deliver the script. Their meeting was "cordial," and Williams added it would be "wonderful if they could get her," but Miriam informed him she was "tied up with the movies" until Christmas.[37]

The movie she was "tied up" with was the Warner Bros. biopic *Lady with Red Hair*. The film, her third for the studio, was a consolation from Jack Warner for stealing *All This, and Heaven Too*. Bryan Foy, the eldest of the "Seven Little Foys" and son of the famed vaudevillian Eddie Foy, would produce.

Miriam starred as the late stage actress Mrs. Leslie Carter, née Caroline Louise Dudley. To spite her ex-husband, a Chicago millionaire, she used her married name as a stage name. Miriam met Mrs. Carter during the making of *Becky Sharp* and called her "a grand dame of the theatre, old and irascible," though she noted that she had "an aura of glamour still about her."[38]

Broadway impresario David Belasco was played by Claude Rains, who Miriam costarred with in the 1929 Broadway production *The Camel through the Needle's Eye*. Belasco was instrumental in Carter's rise to fame. Since their last meeting, Rains had made a name for himself as a Warner Bros. supporting actor, appearing in such classics as *The Adventures of Robin Hood*, *Juarez*, with Bette Davis (with whom he would appear in three more films), and Columbia's *Mr. Smith Goes to Washington*, for which he would receive an Academy Award nomination for his role as a crooked senator.

After reading the *Lady with Red Hair* script, she suggested through

Charles Feldman that Milton Krims or Howard Koch should improve the writing. Jack Warner would have none of it. He told Brian Foy that he didn't want "Hopkins to cut the script down," nor would she "have anything to say other than 'yes' or 'no.'"[39]

Curtis Bernhardt (billed as Kurt Bernhardt) was selected to direct the film. When the German expatriate had arrived in Hollywood the year before, he had a dozen or more films to his credit in his native Germany and also in France. Because of the success of his 1938 French film *Carrefour*, he had his choice of contracts with Warner Bros. or MGM—he chose Warner's. To date, he had directed one American picture, *My Love Came Back*, with Olivia de Havilland and Jeffrey Lynn. The film opened to decent reviews and good box office, but somehow Bernhardt upset the front office and was put on suspension. In any case, for *Lady with Red Hair*, Bernhardt was given a $482,000 budget and a strict twenty-four-day filming schedule. With Miriam back at his studio, Warner waited.

Miriam's tarnished reputation at Warner Bros. extended beyond her costars and the crew. The studio's messenger staff, a group of young men ranging in age from mid-teens to mid-twenties, also disliked her. Twenty-two-year-old Stuart Jerome, who later wrote dozens of television scripts, called his studio cohorts "a motley crew, sometimes irresponsible, usually irreverent, and always prejudiced."[40]

The boys disliked many Warner Bros. executives including Jack Warner, but they reserved their total disrespect for Hal Wallis, whom they called the "coldest, unfriendliest executive of them all." Miriam was also on that list. "If temper, arrogance, and lack of common courtesy had been the prime requisites of stardom," said Jerome, "Miriam Hopkins might have been The Greatest."[41]

On her first day, messenger Larry Dannenberg escorted her to her dressing room. Her limousine edged its way along Dressing Room Row, and Dannenberg walked with it to the end, but her bungalow was still half of a short block away. "This is ridiculous," Miriam mumbled. "At Paramount, I would always be driven right up to my dressing room door."

Paul Muni, who had recently left Warner Bros., was the dressing room's former tenant. Darkly decorated with old furniture, it had the mood of a gothic novel. "Lord have mercy," she exclaimed as she entered the dank and depressing suite. "They've given me the dungeon."

As Dannenberg was leaving, Miriam searched through her purse for a quarter. He thanked her for the thoughtful gesture, but explained, "We're not allowed to accept tips." She congratulated him for resisting that "very demeaning practice" as she dropped the coin back into her purse.[42]

In the opening of *Lady with Red Hair*, Mrs. Carter (Hopkins) loses her son Dudley (Johnny Russell) through an unjust divorce. To get him back, she comes up with a plan to be a successful stage actress, moving with her mother (Laura Hope Crews) to a theatrical boarding house in New York. There, Mrs. Carter pushes her way into the offices of famed producer and playwright David Belasco (Rains). From there, the story revolves around her transformation into a star, her emotional breakup with Belasco, and their reconciliation.

Bryan Foy hired Lou Payne, Mrs. Carter's second husband, as technical advisor. Jeffrey Lynn, who was Bernhardt's leading man in *My Love Came Back*, was his choice to play Payne, but Foy cast the British-born Richard Ainley instead. Payne was "haunted" watching Ainley portray him, and also noted that Miriam didn't "look like Mrs. Carter, and she doesn't imitate her, but her reactions are the same."[43]

Casting Miriam Hopkins as Mrs. Leslie Carter was called life imitating art. Carter was a great actress but, not unlike Miriam, was noted for her rancor and venomous temper. Still, Miriam was careful not to let her performance go over the top. She asked Lou Payne if she was portraying Mrs. Carter as "too excitable." Payne told her, "I doubt if you can make Mrs. Leslie Carter too temperamental. Go to it."[44]

Filming was off to a good start. On August 26, Bernhardt filmed the Chicago custody scenes. Bryan Foy, pleased with the rushes, told Miriam she looked "wonderful. Everything is swell."[45]

It wasn't long, though, before there were problems; but not every crisis was Miriam's fault. First, eight-year-old Johnny Russell had difficulties learning his lines. Bernhardt worked with him for two hours and eighteen takes. By early evening, the boy was in tears, intimidated and not able to continue. Jack Warner was livid. "I know there was talent breakdown, and he was working with a kid, but why 18 takes? This cannot go on as I will not stand for it. You can tell this to Bernhardt for me in no uncertain terms."[46]

Richard Ainley, who was acting in his first American film, was also causing difficulties. According to assistant director Eric Stacey, Bernhardt believed that Ainley was talentless, with "so much rehearsing and so many takes." One scene required ten takes and a fifty-two-minute discussion, followed by more rehearsals. There were another five takes before Bernhardt was satisfied.[47]

At this point, Miriam had minor problems, such as not having time to schedule her costume fittings with Milo Anderson and trouble with the six red wigs she wore (she stayed overnight at the Vitagraph lot to correct it). Stacey reported: "Miss Hopkins is most cooperative and has been less trouble in this picture than on any other and [I] do not anticipate trouble." That was about to change.[48]

For starters, in one scene, Mrs. Carter has a curtain call and bows two or three times to the audience before shouts of "Belasco" brings Claude Rains on stage. Bernhardt was in the back holding a button that raised or lowered the curtain. "At the second curtain, the extras clapped and shouted Mrs. Carter's name," Bernhardt recalled. "The curtain went down and up again and then somebody shouted 'Belasco.'" But the script called for *two* curtain calls *without* Belasco. Miriam was enraged. She walked to the footlights and shouted, "Who is the idiot that called out 'Belasco'?"

"Gazing at the poor extra who had made the unwitting mistake, she began to abuse him," Bernhardt said. "She screamed so much that I pressed the button, bringing the curtain down in front of her nose, and all you could hear were muffled sounds coming from behind it."[49]

David Belasco's former press agent read about Miriam's antics and offered to help. He wrote to Foy that he had "survived the most temperamental redhead of all time," adding "Little girls like Miriam Hopkins are duck soup to me."[50]

Kurt Bernhardt could relate. "I had a wonderful time making that picture," he recalled. "Although I like Miriam Hopkins' performance— she conveyed the hysterics and tenseness of a temperamental stage actress effectively—she was terribly difficult to work with. In fact, she was so tense that it overlapped into real life."[51]

Because of her "star" standing, payback wasn't an option to most. But one group could slip into the shadows unnoticed and wreak havoc: the studio's messenger boys. The actors' perks included a stockpiled pantry complete with roast beef, ham, pâté, fruit and cheese, and an assortment of wines. Like the Phantom of the Opera, the messenger boys helped themselves to treats from whatever the actors had.

Miriam's refrigerator had a rare prime rib roast beef that three of the boys sampled on three separate occasions until nothing remained but slivers of fat and denuded bones. Later that day, Miriam returned to her dressing room, tired and ravenous, to find only the remains of her roast beef. Infuriated, she reported to security that her suite had been burglar-ized, implying that valuables were missing.

Blayney Matthews, a former FBI agent and one-time chief investiga-tor for the Los Angeles district attorney, was the head of Warner Bros. security. He investigated Miriam's allegations. Under his questioning, she admitted only a roast beef had been stolen—or eaten, in this case—so he turned the matter over to Fred Pappmeier, the messenger boys' boss. He deduced they were the likely culprits, having access to the dressing room's master keys.

Pappmeier gathered the boys and told them that whoever took Miss Hopkins's roast beef should "man up" and confess. After threatening to fire "the whole bunch," the matter was dropped. But their hatred for Mir-iam was reinforced, so they plotted revenge. "You know the way she likes to have some wine every afternoon," one of them remarked. "Let's piss into one of her wine bottles." At first, they were enthusiastic, but someone pointed out that if she became ill, the studio would lose money. Cooler heads prevailed that day, but they continued to pilfer food and items from the stars' dressing rooms, except for Miriam's. "Fuck Hopkins," they said. "Figuratively, that is," added Stuart Jerome.[52]

While Miriam was filming *Lady with Red Hair*, Warner Bros.'s execu-tives decided to produce *January Heights*. Bette Davis and George Brent were now on the project, and Edmund Goulding was directing. They still considered Miriam for the supporting role of the famous concert pianist, which didn't go over well with Davis. It took some work, but Davis per-suaded Mary Astor to accept the part of Sandra Kovak, the concert pia-nist, pushing Miriam out. The producers changed the film's title to *The Great Lie*, and for her performance, Astor won the Academy Award for Best Supporting Actress.

Davis's casting strategy opened Miriam's schedule to consider the Tennessee Williams's Theatre Guild play *Battle of Angels*. Williams had asked a mutual friend, Bennett Cerf, to exert his "influence, moral or oth-erwise," upon Miriam, anything "short of abduction from the studio lot."[53]

The Guild's Theresa Helburn told Williams that Miriam had expressed some interest. After discussing it, Miriam accepted, telling friends, "It will either be a terrific flop, or it will win the Pulitzer Prize." Williams was pleased: "Now here is a woman who could take my frequently overwrit-ten speeches and match them with an emotional opulence of her own that would make them not only natural but tremendously moving as well!"[54]

Miriam felt the play needed improving, but she was impressed with the young playwright's first effort. She invested money in the play, assuring her the lead if *Battle of Angels* made it to Broadway. As soon as she completed *Lady with Red Hair*, she would fly to New York to meet with producers and discuss the play with Williams.

While *Lady with Red Hair* was wrapping, Miriam was hitting the night spots with ex-husband, Anatole Litvak. The gossip columns predicted they would resolve their differences and remarry within the year, though both were dating other people.

But any hopes of the two reuniting ended when a now legendary incident occurred at Ciro's nightclub on the Sunset Strip. The incident involved actress Paulette Goddard, recently separated from her husband, Charlie Chaplin. Author Julie Gilbert, in her biography of Goddard and her last husband, writer Erich Maria Remarque, wrote that Litvak was "supposedly mad for Paulette." One evening at Ciro's, Gilbert writes, "Paulette's shoulder strap popped, her bodice slipped down, Litvak held up the tablecloth to shield her, she slipped prankishly under the table, he followed, and they carried on."[55]

Another version of the incident claimed that Goddard's breast was exposed and that Litvak kissed it before covering her with the tablecloth. Then, Litvak slipped under the table and allegedly performed oral sex on the actress in view of those at the neighboring tables.[56]

The rumors flew. According to columnist Jimmy Fidler, a bit player telephoned him in the middle of the night, breathlessly reporting that "Anatole Litvak just went down on Paulette Goddard!" Fidler was skeptical until calls started coming in, all confirming the young lady's report. The gossip columnist couldn't resist. In his column, Fidler discreetly stated it was "quite a 'show'" that Goddard and Litvak put on for the celebrity-studded audience at Ciro's.[57]

Miriam and Litvak's mutual friend Jean Negulesco and his date, model and would-be actress Alice Eyland, were witnesses that evening. Negulesco wrote in his autobiography: "Paulette dropped one of her earrings under the table. Tola—quite drunk by now (as was Paulette), but still the perfect gentleman—disappeared under the table to find it."

Litvak was under the table "beyond the time limit of a prank," according to Negulesco, until Goddard moaned convincingly. The crowd laughed and whispered encouragement to Litvak. "They felt they were witnessing a free and bold Hollywood scandal," Negulesco remarked. After fifteen minutes, Litvak appeared from under the table "to the applause of the amused audience," straightening his hair with "just the right amount of embarrassment," as flashbulbs and rumors exploded.[58]

In Litvak's defense, his friend, playwright and screenwriter Arthur Laurents, didn't believe the rumors. "Litvak was too straight-laced, too formal," Laurents recalled. "I just couldn't see him doing that under a table or anywhere else." Decades later in a *Vanity Fair* article, director Billy Wilder said that Goddard's husband, Erich Maria Remarque, told him "on his oath and he swore that her shoulder strap just slipped, and all he did was kiss her on the breast."[59]

Something happened that evening at Ciro's, and by the following morning, the gossip was spreading. According to Becky Morehouse, Miriam shared what she knew of her former husband's antics. At the Vitagraph lot the next morning, no one would tell Miriam what supposedly had happened, but the extras and crew still whispered and giggled behind her back.

While he didn't always agree with Miriam, Claude Rains hated the gossip-mongering at her expense. To prevent a scene, Rains invited her to his dressing room. She sensed something was wrong and confronted Rains. He stammered, so she blurted out, "Oh for Christ's sake Claude, say it." He explained what he knew of the rumor. "Surprisingly," Becky recalled, "Miriam held her temper, thanked Claude for his candor and returned to the soundstage—embarrassed, but calm."[60]

As for Litvak and Goddard, they both denied the stories, but it turned serious when the State Department received complaint letters. Litvak was forced to testify that it was a misunderstanding. As for Goddard, she slipped away to Mexico until the journalistic free-for-all subsided. The truth about that evening depends on which story you believe.

Lady with Red Hair wrapped sixteen days behind schedule and $16,000 over budget; the domestic box office was around $1.92 million ($57.9 million today).

Garnering mixed reviews, the *Los Angeles Times* called the film a "captivating presentation," yet complained about the "plot and purpose." Miriam received good notices, such as she "meets the demands of a difficult role efficiently," while her portrayal of Carter was called "vivid and fascinating" and "beautifully done." But it was Claude Rains's tyrannical and withal lovable performance as David Belasco that received the bulk of the praise. The *Hollywood Reporter* noted, "It is to Claude Rains . . . that top honors must be accorded."[61]

Most critics, while complimenting the film's performances, panned the story, especially for misrepresenting facts about Carter's life to suit the screenwriter's vision. It was surprising for Warner Bros., a studio having a desirable standing as film biographers, especially with their recent hits *The Story of Louis Pasteur*, *The Life of Emile Zola*, and *Juarez*, among others.

Miriam was still a capable actress and managed to be a marquee name, yet *Lady with Red Hair* did little for her career. There were no film offers from Warner's or any studio after that. Fortunately, she was returning to the stage. That fall, she would be in New York discussing the first efforts of a young man who would become one of the country's most talented playwrights.

14

Angels Battle in Boston

It had been seven years since Miriam appeared on Broadway, in *Jezebel*; each year she insisted she would "be back next season," but "next season" never came. There were plays, but nothing that made it to Broadway. Her starring role and investment in *Battle of Angels* would prove to her nay-sayers that she was still an audience draw.[1]

Mississippi's Delta is the setting of Tennessee Williams's *Battle of Angels*. The Theatre Guild's Lawrence Langner and Theresa Helburn hired director Margaret Webster to oversee the production. Webster, who was once popular on the English stage, was the daughter of actress Dame May Whitty and the lover of actress Eva Le Gallienne. She was currently staging the Shakespearian play *Twelfth Night* on Broadway.

Webster, who never traveled farther south than Washington, DC, thought Williams's play "wasn't, and never would be a very good one, but that there was power in it and some splendid, multicolored words." She believed the author would live up to his "obvious potential talent and write a real dazzler."[2]

Langner agreed and hoped rewrites would "straighten out its defects." For two weeks, Williams stayed at Langner's Connecticut farm to improve it.

In early November, Miriam met with Tennessee Williams and Margaret Webster in Miriam's suite at the Ambassador Hotel on Park Avenue and East Fifty-First Street. Webster found Miriam to be "lively, restless, [and] stimulating." Williams arrived an hour late, wearing "pebble-thick glasses" and a "shabby corduroy jacket and muddy riding boots." Miriam asked if he had had a pleasant ride, but he replied he never went riding, he just liked boots, and he placed both mud-covered feet on the hotel's pristine yellow chaise lounge.[3]

The champagne dinner went well, but when they discussed the play,

Miriam "raised the roof" about her role. "I think she wants to do a solo performance," Williams wrote to his family in Mississippi. "Would like to cut everything in the play except her own speeches." Williams had heard that Miriam's mother and sister were "mental cases" and considered her outbursts unavoidable; he ignored her.[4]

Frustrated by his lackadaisical attitude, Miriam chastised the young playwright. Williams had had enough. "As far as I can gather from all this hysteria," he prefaced his returning fury with. Miriam was speechless. No one had dared talk to her like that, above all a southerner. Webster, too, was shocked, but Williams didn't intend to be rude. He was terrified— of Miriam and of his current circumstances. "We should have realized," Webster later recalled, "that he was, in fact, stupefied by the maelstrom of the Broadway theatre into which he had been flung quite suddenly and unexpectedly." But, by the end of the evening, both the star and the playwright had made peace, temporarily.[5]

During casting, Miriam wanted Raymond Massey in the role of her lover, Val, but he was unavailable. Instead, Langner chose Robert Allen, a B-movie actor known for westerns. Williams described Val as having "a fresh and primitive quality, a virile grace, and freedom of body, a strong physical appeal."[6]

During preparation, Miriam worried about her character, Myra, a lonely woman trapped in a loveless marriage to an older, dying man. As rehearsals progressed, she became increasingly uptight. With every suggestion or change, she told a frustrated Tennessee Williams, "That's impossible!"[7]

Once, when told of a script change, she threw the manuscript at Langner, missing his head. He claimed that Miriam "wanted only what was best for the play." To Williams, the problem was evident: "She is afraid of slipping." One thing Langner knew, Miriam was an "excitable girl," and he was ready to "duck when [the] occasion called for it."[8]

Miriam's anxiety forced the Guild to cancel the New Haven tryout and go directly to the Boston opening; many believed that was a mistake. Williams had written a "sex play with cosmic overtones," and Boston audiences were considered snobby and prude. Langner foolishly ignored Williams's warnings.

But moving the opening to Boston only made Miriam more anxious. Ten days before the premiere, she wanted to replace Robert Allen. Wesley Addy, who was under contract to the Guild in *Twelfth Night*, was Allen's replacement. Webster had worked with Addy before and knew he could learn his lines quickly.

Absentmindedly, Miriam raced around the stage, picking up props and putting them in the wrong place. She demanded that Langner cut another actress's long speech and worried that the ending—calling for the store to burn to the ground—was wrong. "Do something!" she pleaded to Williams. The Guild producers asked for changes to satisfy Miriam, who, according to Williams, "wanted to remain on the stage all the time and consequently twisted the script around quite a bit."[9]

Williams wrote a new scene the day before the Boston opening but had no time to integrate it into the play. He insisted he could rewrite the entire play by avoiding the "dervish frenzy," his words for Miriam's panic-stricken rants; but it was too late. He told Margaret Webster to "take what there is and do what you can with it!"[10]

Battle of Angels opened at Boston's Wilbur Theatre on December 30, 1940. That evening, Miriam wired a peacemaking message to Williams: "Dear Tenn, so deeply hope, for your sake, you will be as happy after the performance as the day you sold the script. Fondly, Miriam."[11]

The audience, however, showed no fondness for the play. Any religious tolerance the audience had entered the theater with vanished when a painting of Jesus Christ with Val's face placed over it was smashed and stuffed into the belly of a stove. "I never heard of an audience getting so infuriated," Williams recalled. "They hissed so loud you couldn't hear the lines, and that made Miriam so mad that she began to scream her lines above the hissing." The audience stamped their feet, and many left the theater. In bohemian, worldly New Haven, would it have been an altogether different reaction?[12]

The ending called for the main characters to die in a fire, but in the final run-through the night before, the special effects failed, so smoke pots were substituted. Before the final curtain, "wisps of evil smelling smoke began to drift onto the stage" and roll into the audience. "It was like the burning of Rome," Williams said. "To an already antagonistic audience, this was sufficient to excite something in the way of pandemonium. Outraged squawks, gabbling and spluttering spread to the front rows of the theatre. Nothing that happened on the stage from then on was of any importance. Indeed the scene was nearly eclipsed by the fumes. Voices were lost in the banging up of seats as the front rows were evacuated."[13]

The following day, some critics were indifferent and others were less than pleased. They praised Miriam's acting and Webster's direction amid all the smoke and seat-banging but saved their worst reservations for the play itself. The *Boston Globe* imagined the audience had the "sensation of being dunked in mire" and called the play an "embarrassment." Elinor Hughes of the *Boston Herald* reported, "Miriam Hopkins gives an excellent performance of the repressed wife," and prophetically recognized the playwright's ability, saying "a few years in the theatre and Tennessee Williams should add craftsmanship to imagination and produce important work."[14]

The principal cast members met to discuss the play's future. Both Langner and Helburn agreed that continuing the play would prolong the hysteria without solving their problems. "We also felt that the play needed some recasting as well as rewriting, so we reluctantly withdrew it," Langner said.[15]

Langner announced that when *Battle of Angels* completed its two-week commitment in Boston, it would close. "Oh, but you can't do that!" Williams cried. "Why, I put my heart in this play." Everyone was silent. Webster gave Williams some Shakespearean advice: "You must not wear your heart on your sleeve for daws to peck at."[16]

The Boston City Council called an emergency session to make sense of the public complaints, voting to send representatives to investigate. After the performance that evening, the delegates met with producers and management and denounced the play as "putrid," "dirty," and "a crime"; but they would allow the play to continue if Williams expunged certain lines.[17]

Miriam was outraged. She called a press conference and laughingly suggested the Boston City Council be thrown into the harbor, "the way the tea once was." She defended Tennessee Williams, saying it was "an insult to the fine young man who wrote it," and reiterated that the play was "not dirty."

"I haven't got to the point where I have to appear in dirty plays," she added. "The dirt is something in the minds of some of the people who have seen it. They read meanings into it according to their own suppressed feelings."[18]

Miriam's defense of Tennessee Williams and his play endeared her to the playwright despite the headaches she caused during rehearsals. Williams would tell a friend, "She is amusing enough to be pardonable." When *Battle of Angels* ended, Williams gave Miriam a gold disc with the word "Impossible" engraved on one side, recalling her fervent cries of "That's impossible!" It was the beginning of a lifelong friendship.[19]

In retrospect, everyone agreed that opening the play in Boston was a mistake. Audiences may have appreciated *Battle of Angels* in Philadelphia, Washington, or New Haven, but not Boston, where "Banned in Boston" meant censorship. The Theatre Guild postponed and then canceled the Washington engagement and abandoned the Broadway run. With the Guild's backing, Williams retreated to Florida to rewrite *Battle of Angels*, which was produced sixteen years later on Broadway as *Orpheus Descending.*

Miriam saw the new version and lamented that the original couldn't have been a success. "There was so much that was good about that play," Miriam said about *Battle of Angels*, "that I still feel very badly that it didn't turn out better on the stage. Much of the dialogue I can still remember for its unusual imagery and depth of feeling, but Tennessee was very young at the time—only 24—and he was still just feeling his way. . . . The new version is much better, so much so that I'll do it again for him if he wants, but I think he's more interested in going forward than looking back."[20]

Miriam, who discussed new roles during *Battle of Angels*, was unemployed again. Director Fritz Lang wanted her for an adaptation of the Harlow Estes book *Hildreth,* but nothing came of it. There was talk of RKO starring her opposite Ronald Colman in *My Life with Caroline,* about a married woman who falls in love with another man. Instead, they went with British import Anna Lee, who was a decade younger than Miriam.

Following the failure of *Battle of Angels* and the loss of several film roles, Miriam's faith in her talent was shaken. In February 1941, gossip columnist Sheilah Graham reported that Miriam was in Los Angeles hoping a producer would offer her a film. "I can't remember when I've seen Miriam looking so sad," Graham wrote to her readers. "The flop of her play cut deeply. And another cause for depression is that Miriam is minus a lead man in her life, and this is quite essential for Miss Hopkins' happiness."[21]

Miriam loved men. Her infatuations could be long-lasting or spontaneous and short-lived. On a train trip to New York one Christmas season in the late 1930s, Miriam met Fritz Lang. Lang asked her to dine by candlelight, seducing her for hours. Following after-dinner drinks, Miriam asked the director, "How would you like me for a Christmas present?" Both had one "unforgettable" night in a sleeper car, as Lang later boasted, "nestling close as they crossed the American West on the Twentieth Century."[22]

No matter the length of a relationship, Miriam was a creature of impulse; when a romance was over, it was over, and the break was usually dramatic.

According to Ward Morehouse, she once quarreled with a lover about the end of their affair. To make her point clear, she threw a diamond-studded wristwatch, a gift he had offered to convince her to stay, from the twentieth floor of the Hotel Pierre. Another time, she grew tired of having playwright Edwin Justus Mayer around, so she impulsively threw a glass of scotch in his face, telling the stunned playwright to leave. Remarkably, she remained friendly with many of her ex-admirers.

While her past career was unimportant, she delighted in reminiscing about old romances. "When I can't sleep, I don't count sheep. I count lovers," she alleged. "And by the time I reach thirty-eight or thirty-nine I'm asleep."[23]

Reportedly, she advised her teenage son, Michael, that the worst thing a man could be was a bad lover. Michael contemplated that and asked what she did when a man didn't live up to her expectations. "I kick him out of bed," she responded frankly. Michael later claimed the story wasn't true. "Things like that are jokes. We never had a conversation about sex," he explained, while adding, "although it sounds like something my mother would say."[24]

Miriam filled her loneliness with a succession of influential men. The gossip columns associated her with such companions as writer Eugene Solow, Capt. Owen Cathcart-Jones of the RCAF, and San Francisco aristocrat Whitney Warren Jr.

Adding to her self-esteem problems, the *Harvard Lampoon* editors selected Miriam as its "least desirable companion on a desert island." Making light of the situation, she called the Harvard boys "excellent students of psychology" and was surprised at their "keen insight into human nature." She assured them that "in my New York apartment or in some quiet restaurant, well—I really would not be bad at all."[25]

A few weeks later, she received a call from her old boss, Sam Goldwyn. Since she still owed him one film, he considered casting her in the Regina Giddens role of the Lillian Hellman play *The Little Foxes*. Tallulah Bankhead, who originated it on Broadway, was also in the running, as was their mutual competitor, Bette Davis. Miriam had seen the play in New York and knew she could sink her teeth into the role of the greedy and calculating Regina. But unbeknownst to her, Jack Warner had agreed to loan Davis for the part. One week before filming began, Sheilah Graham reported that Goldwyn had a "change of heart," and Miriam would not be getting the part.[26]

Further disappointments followed. Republic Studios planned to cast her opposite John Wayne in *Lady for a Night* but gave the part to Joan Blondell. Then, Universal, at the time a relatively minor studio with a handful of productions each year, signed her for their B western *Badlands of Dakota*. That was better than no work, but when she found out that twenty-two-year-old Robert Stack was to be her love interest, she balked because of the age difference. She asked for John Wayne, but Wayne was busy. In the end, she bowed out and was replaced by the much younger MGM loan-out, Ann Rutherford.

She refused *The Law of the Tropics* at Warner Bros. for the same reason. With a seven-year difference in their ages, she was too old to be the lover of up-and-coming leading man Jeffrey Lynn. Constance Bennett, three years younger than Miriam, replaced her.

But her biggest disappointment was losing the Maria Tura role in Ernst Lubitsch's comedy *To Be or Not to Be*. The film, a satire about a troupe of actors in Nazi-occupied Warsaw, starred comedian Jack Benny. Both Lubitsch and United Artists wanted Miriam—especially Lubitsch, with whom she had a great rapport in the early 1930s.

After reading the script, Miriam wanted her role enhanced and a larger share of the funny lines. When Benny found out, he lobbied producer Alexander Korda for Carole Lombard. Korda let Lubitsch decide, but the director passed it back to Korda. Benny took Korda out for a night of drinking and convinced the inebriated producer to hire Lombard.

But according to the American Film Institute's files, when Miriam complained to Carole Lombard that she was unhappy with the role, Lombard urged her to withdraw, leaving the part open for her. Whether it was Benny or Lombard, Miriam walked out after Lubitsch refused to revise the script. Later, she admitted it was another "error in judgment," along with turning down "that god-damned *It Happened One Night* that will haunt me 'til the day I die."[27]

Miriam's "rewriting the script" strategy had worked a decade earlier, but now she needed a quality role no matter its size. Had she allowed Lubitsch to guide her performance, as he did in *The Smiling Lieutenant* and *Design for Living*, *To Be or Not to Be* might have revived her career.

Instead, she looked for something on the stage. Ward Morehouse discussed with her taking over New York's Little Theatre and having a year-round stock company. "It was a wonderful idea, really," she laughed. "I wanted to have a straw hat in New York, as they call them. I wanted only the best people in the world. Everybody would get the same salary, and we'd all change about, playing maids one week and leads the next. I haven't given up on the idea—I certainly haven't."[28]

Desperate to find her niche, Miriam thought of doing a radio series playing a roving foreign correspondent. But that went nowhere, so she accepted her only offer: the lead in independent producer Edward Small's film production of *Heliotrope Harry*.[29]

In *Heliotrope Harry* were Brian Donlevy, her former *Barbary Coast* costar, and Preston Foster, a supporting actor with a list of impressive films. Miriam plays Flo Melton, an utterly cruel villainess. "It's a part you can get your teeth in," she said. "She's worse than Becky Sharp. A thoroughly reprehensible woman." Her husband, Harry Melton (Donlevy), is a jewel thief with the nickname Heliotrope, his favorite flower. After murdering his wife's lover, Donlevy agrees to surrender if the judge (Foster) will adopt his baby girl.[30]

"The effect," Miriam said, "is the same, except now I have to run away by myself on account of Mr. Reed [her lover] being dead." Years later, Flo returns and tries to ruin her daughter's happiness. Upon learning what his ex-wife is planning, Melton escapes from prison and gets his revenge against Flo. "An awful woman," Miriam purred, "and one I've been very happy to play."[31]

According to the crew, Miriam was "swell, does anything you ask, is always on time, never keeps you waiting." Miriam was tired of "that 'difficult Miriam' story" that followed her "from studio to studio."

"You don't work twice with the same director if you give him trouble. Do you?" she questioned. "Would I have been asked back by Lubitsch, by Mamoulian, if I were troublesome?"

Miriam believed that working more than once with the same people proved her case: Her hairdresser was with her for eight years, her maid for five, and her butler for ten. This reasoning confirmed her feeling that "you can't keep people with you if you're—er—tough," but she admitted that there was a period when she could be difficult: "That's before I start a picture."[32]

Before its premiere, Edward Small changed the film's title to *A Gentle-*

man after Dark. Miriam received decent reviews. The *Hollywood Reporter* wrote that she "wisely asks no sympathy for her portrayal of an unnatural mother," and the *New York Times* called her "unutterably poisonous (which is what she is supposed to be)." However, the *Dallas Morning News* gave a backhanded compliment, noting "the lady is still something of an actress though close-ups do not exactly give her the best of it. Time, unfortunately, has a habit of marching on."[33]

With no offers coming in except for an occasional play in stock, Miriam returned to her first agent Lyman Brown, whom she hadn't worked with since their separation in 1934. "Here I am again with the same old question," Brown wrote, "prompted by numerous inquiries as to whether you will consider any appearance in the summer theater."[34]

Summer theater was all right, but she was hoping for something on Broadway. Brown sent her a John Patrick script, *The Willard and I*, for the next season. "Hope you like it," Lyman cabled. She didn't.[35]

Meanwhile, finances were running low, so she rented Sutton Place to RKO screenwriter Garson Kanin and his wife, actress Ruth Gordon. Katharine Hepburn, who was leasing the Tower Grove house, left the place "shining like a newly scrubbed baby." The income from both houses covered her lease at 3141 Coldwater Canyon, with enough for expenses.[36]

The money situation was about to improve. Warner Bros. owned the rights to the John Van Druten play *Old Acquaintance*, a sentimental comedy about two sophisticated female novelists, and producer Henry Blanke was preparing it as a starring vehicle for Bette Davis. Van Druten had collaborated with director Edmund Goulding on the screenplay, and both agreed that the role of Millie, a successful writer of romance novels, should be an actress of "great physical force and strength for her outbursts, and her scenes of hysterics." In their minds, the part was tailored to a type and personality, that only one actress could play it.[37]

15

"This Is Pure Hopkins"

Warner Bros. paid $75,000 for the film rights to *Old Acquaintance*. Of the two women writers, one is a success in the commercial market and the other writes more erudite, and unpopular, fare. They live by different standards. Their commonality is that they attended the same school.[1]

Since their infighting on *The Old Maid*, Bette Davis had not been idle. The Warner Bros. star was still the studio's most lucrative asset, appearing in nine films (compared to Miriam's three) and racking up three Oscar nominations. Off the lot, Davis had had a short stint as the first woman president of the Academy of Motion Picture Arts and Sciences, had cofounded the Hollywood Canteen, had divorced her husband, and had rejected George Brent's proposal of marriage.

Both Edmund Goulding, director of *The Old Maid*, and John Van Druten thought of Miriam for the role of Millie, the thoughtless, selfish, ambitious friend of Kit, portrayed by Davis. Goulding's twelve-year friendship with Miriam inspired many of the nuances, dialogue, and characterizations in the screenplay. Throughout the writing, Goulding would say, "This is the kind of thing Hopkins does so well," or, "This will be swell for Hopkins" or, "This is pure Hopkins." He knew it would "not be easy on set," but, he reasoned, "we managed before" and he believed they would again.[2]

When producer Henry Blanke read Goulding's treatment and vision of Millie's character, he agreed "only Hopkins can play it." In a memo to Goulding, Blanke stated, "The more I read of it, the more I can see 'Milly' [*sic*] only Miriam Hopkins playing it. I am thinking of Miriam Hopkins— the comedienne she was in the Lubitsch comedies—and I wonder how you feel about this. I would go to Jack Warner and try to ascertain the possibility of Hopkins for the part."[3]

Jack Warner wasn't convinced. Miriam could test for the part, he conceded, but he would rather have Mary Astor or Constance Bennett. Blanke argued that Bennett would "be completely miscast" and was "not the actress Hopkins is." Also, Bennett and Davis were too similar in type, and there wouldn't be the contrast that Miriam could provide. Warner's hesitation to reunite the two actresses was due to the problems on *The Old Maid*.[4]

Warner's short list for Millie included Janet Gaynor, but when Blanke told Van Druten, he disagreed. "In the first place, Millie is a strong 'character' part, needing a definite character comedienne," Van Druten explained to Blanke. "I do not feel that Gaynor is quite that. Second, Millie is a bitch. I do not feel the bitch a possible quality in Gaynor's sweetness."

"Hopkins is a good actress and a good comedienne," Van Druten added. "Millie must be played by a skilled comedy actress to whom Bette Davis can play 'straight,' or a great deal of the script's best values will be lost."[5]

While Miriam's casting prompted many objections, the loudest came from an expected source: Bette Davis. Before they made a final decision, she insisted that they offer the role to Norma Shearer. But when Goulding told Shearer that Davis wanted her for Millie, "the bitch who writes the trash," she declined. Goulding had a heartfelt talk with Davis. While she disliked the notion of working with Miriam again, she admitted she was "the only woman who can play the part of Millie."[6]

Blanke wanted to act before Miriam started another picture or play. "I don't believe there is anybody who likes to be working with Hopkins," said Blanke, adding, "but, for the best interests of the picture, we all agree on the one point that Hopkins should play the part of Millie."[7]

Reluctantly, Jack Warner conceded, signing Miriam for a one-picture deal. Arthur Lyons, her agent, asked for $10,000 a week for the estimated seven weeks of production—twice as much as Davis was earning. Also, she wanted control of her makeup, wardrobe, and hairstyling. Warner balked at these demands but offered her the same salary as Davis. After much thought, Miriam agreed to $5,000 per week. Because it was a prestige picture, she also decided to be billed second.

After the unpleasant experiences she had had with Orry-Kelly on *Virginia City*, Miriam hoped for a civil reunion with the designer. According to Orry-Kelly, she embraced him, kissing his cheek and crying, "Darling."

"Please, Miriam, we don't like each other," Orry-Kelly bluntly said, pushing her away. "I'll do my best to dress and please you, but no kissy-

kissy, please." She transformed into Becky Sharp. "Aren't I awful, Orry-Kelly?" she purred. "Now what are you going to do with a belle like that?" In all likelihood, Miriam remembered his behavior on *Virginia City* and was ridiculing him.

The following day, Orry-Kelly received a bonnet Miriam sent to use in the picture, but he threw it on the floor and stomped on it. To have as little interaction as possible, he assigned Milo Anderson to handle her fittings. Despite such animosity, Orry-Kelly admitted in his autobiography "difficult or not, I think she was an exceptionally fine actress."[8]

As for Goulding, he dreaded working with Miriam and Davis again, and his interest in the film was fading. There were problems. Davis insisted on using cameraman Sol Polito, who had worked on *Dark Victory*, but Goulding wanted Tony Gaudio because he had worked on *The Old Maid*. Blanke promised Goulding he could have Gaudio, but instead he assigned Polito to the project. Goulding fired off a telegram to Jack Warner and asked if he was "working for Warner Brothers or Miss Davis and there is a difference." He urged Warner not to confirm Polito until they could discuss it. Otherwise, it would put him in a position of "Davis, Hopkins, moods, fads, and nonsense."[9]

Dealing with Davis's demands about cameramen, in addition to Miriam's late-night telephone calls complaining about her salary and her frosty reception at the studio, Goulding's health suffered. In October, he developed the flu and was admitted to Good Samaritan Hospital, where he recovered, only to suffer a relapse in December. Rumors abounded that he had feigned a heart attack, but according to Goulding's biographer Matthew Kennedy the director was not faking. "It's true that he left *The Old Acquaintance* set with nary a backward glance," Kennedy wrote, "but he was genuinely sick."[10]

Goulding's health crisis notwithstanding, filming was scheduled to begin in a few weeks; Hal Wallis was forced to look for a replacement. The first Hopkins-Davis teaming was still fresh in everyone's mind, so the job was turned down by several directors. "I might be able to work with Hopkins," one director admitted, "and I might be able to work with Davis. But together? Never!"[11]

Wallis handed the screenplay to Vincent Sherman, a former stage actor who had recently directed Ida Lupino in *The Hard Way*. "Goulding was supposed to do this," Wallis told him, "but he has had a heart attack, and he can't do it." After reading the script, Sherman considered it "lightweight" and "women's magazine stuff." He told Wallis he would like to work with Davis but not on this project.[12]

Irving Rapper, who directed *Now, Voyager*, was next, but he was joining the navy and wouldn't be available. Frustrated, Wallis went back to Vincent Sherman and demanded that he direct the picture.

With no choice, Sherman started with the preproduction work completed by Goulding. The cast included Warner's contract player John Loder as Millie's husband, Gig Young as Kit's younger lover, and ingenue Dolores Moran as Millie's daughter. When Sherman looked over the cast, he wanted to replace Moran with fast-rising Warner's contract actress Eleanor Parker, but Jack Warner intervened, telling Henry Blanke, "If she's good enough for Goulding, she's good enough for him." Sherman chose not to complain since this was his most important assignment to date.[13]

Production was to begin, but Davis was in Palm Springs vacationing. Sherman was told to start without her. On November 11, he filmed scenes with Miriam and John Loder.

Miriam and fellow Georgian Sherman had a mutual admiration. "She was an expert comedienne," Sherman said, "and it was a pleasure to work with her." At one point, though, he made the mistake of reading a line for her the way he wanted it. Miriam did as he asked, but snapped, "The only other director I'd allow to read a line for me is Ernst Lubitsch."[14]

After four days, Davis returned from Palm Springs with her agent, Lew Wasserman. From the edge of the set, they watched Sherman direct Miriam in a scene. Sherman assumed she was there to view the rushes. He knew if the footage didn't please her, she could have him dismissed. An hour later, Davis called from the projection room. She thought the footage was "marvelous" and asked how he got Miriam to "do all those things, they were wonderful."[15]

When Davis joined the cast the following day, Sherman recalled that the peace between the two women "lasted approximately twelve minutes." The first thing Miriam did was blow smoke into Davis's eyes.[16]

As the production continued, Sherman noticed a change in Davis's mood and asked if something was bothering her. She recalled many of the arguments she had had with Miriam on *The Old Maid*. "You watch her," she explained. "She's always pulling little tricks, trying to upstage me."[17]

Although he was familiar with the studio gossip, Sherman wasn't concerned. That is, not until he noticed how preoccupied Miriam was with the placement of the camera. She also did small things that Sherman questioned. While these things were trivial, each day it would be something different. "She'd straighten a picture or rearrange flowers in a vase when she should be concentrating on what Bette was saying to her," Sherman said. Alarmed, he discussed it with Henry Blanke, who advised him to ignore it as Goulding had done and "regard it as amusement."[18]

One day, Miriam recommended that her character use a long cigarette holder. Sherman thought it was an innocent request and allowed it. Then, as both actresses were sitting on the sofa, the camera panned across Miriam's shoulder toward Davis. Miriam puffed on her cigarette and held it so that it blocked Davis's face. Sherman stopped the scene and chastised her, but she defended her actions, saying that she was "just trying to match up" what she did before. These little tricks may have worked on the stage, but in films, an editor could remove them from the final picture, and she knew it. Apparently, she intended to distract Davis and hinder her performance.[19]

Miriam may have been the worst offender, but Davis wasn't blameless. During a shared two-shot, she cast shadows on Miriam's face, and in another scene, she changed her dialogue to confuse her. During Miriam's close-ups, Davis would shout to the grips, interrupting her concentration.

Lastly, according to a report from *Time* magazine, Davis accused Henry Blanke of favoring Miriam because her portable dressing room was closer to the set than hers. To solve it, an assistant director measured the distances between both dressing rooms and the set and arranged them "so they were precisely equidistant."[20]

One day as Sherman was blocking a scene, Miriam suggested that she and Davis do it themselves. Sherman agreed. Both women walked to the center of the room and stood there, waiting for the other to make the first move. Davis took several steps, but with each step, Miriam took a parallel one. For the rest of the scene, they stood motionless, delivering their lines. When the scene was over, Sol Polito laughed. Sherman shook his head. "Thank you, ladies," he told them, "that's just right, you stood right in the center of the room and didn't move for five pages." After an uneasy pause, Davis burst out laughing, but Miriam failed to see the humor. Sherman reshot the scene.[21]

Davis claimed she never lost her temper, but that isn't true. In other productions, she didn't bother with camera angles or lighting, but on *Old Acquaintance* she fought Miriam point-for-point on every suggestion.

Sherman lost his patience and yelled, "Ladies, sometimes I feel I'm not *directing* this picture, I'm *refereeing* it!"[22]

Filming was nearing completion, and neither actress was speaking to the other. Sherman was the arbitrator and listened to their grievances separately. "Well, I know Bette doesn't like me," Miriam would say, and afterward, Sherman would walk to Davis's dressing room, and she would predict what trick Miriam would pull next.[23]

Davis complained about Miriam's makeup. "That bitch," Davis said, "you look at *Old Maid*. I get older, and she gets younger. And she's doing the same damn thing here. I'm going to be looking old; she's going to be looking younger than she looked at the beginning."[24]

The time frame of *Old Acquaintance* spans twenty years; to show the progression, Davis dyed a lock of her hair gray. Ironically, one day as Davis was having her hair done, her stylist exclaimed, "Why, Miss Davis, you have a gray hair." Bette replied, "Let's name it Miriam because I'm sure she's responsible for it."[25]

Davis leaked Miriam's resistance to aging to Hedda Hopper. Hopper reported: "Miriam has to make up as a 42-year-old woman, and she doesn't like it. Bette says, 'I can't understand it because to me older women are so much more interesting than young ones.'"[26]

The Warner Bros. publicity machine leaked tidbits about the apparent unrest on the set. Miriam was upset. She never admitted to having problems—in fact, she denied them. When asked for her side, she told a reporter, "There never was a feud. Of course, arguments always are possible when two actresses of some reputation are working together in parts which they have been led to believe are of equal importance. Even so, we had no outbreaks of temperament, Bette and I, or of temper."[27]

Luckily the other actors were not recipients of the Hopkins-Davis wrath. John Loder said Davis was "responsive" and enjoyed working with her on *Old Acquaintance*, more than on *Now, Voyager*. As for Miriam, he considered her a fine actress, "very stimulating and responsive, but I made the mistake of telling Bette that, and she didn't speak to me for a week!" Loder's wife, actress Hedy Lamarr, understood her husband's predicament. "You can imagine what is left of John after working with Miriam and Bette!" Lamarr said. "We will probably see an ear, or if we're lucky, his back, in the picture."[28]

The conflict between them affected the film's shooting schedule, but delays were also caused by script rewrites. "See you're up to your old tricks again," Jack Warner wrote in a memo to Sherman: "Received this morning 14 pages rewrite on *Old Acquaintance*. Why don't you stop rewriting this script? It was damn good when you started. You are 16 days behind your schedule. Now make some of this time up and get through with this production."[29]

Also, the combined illnesses of the two stars caused multiple delays. In December, Davis had the flu. Then, one morning in January, Miriam arose early to meet Michael at the train station. In the shower, she slipped on a bar of soap and fell, head first, on a steel fixture. "I split my ear and cracked my head," she wrote to a friend. "Don't worry, I shall live—that old Hopkins luck, but the doctor says I must be flat on an ice bag for about a week."[30]

Later that month, Davis was out for three days; the following day, Miriam was ill. The day after, Miriam returned, but Davis called in sick. For seven consecutive days, the women alternated their absences.

Finally, Jack Warner had had enough. The picture was thirty-six days behind schedule and in production for three months. On January 29, Warner gave Henry Blanke a week to complete the film. "The picture has been going on long enough," Warner complained, "irrespective of the problems of all the artists, which I have taken into consideration."[31]

To show the seriousness of the situation, Warner's assistant, Steve Trilling, threatened to turn the matter over to the Screen Actors Guild and bar both women from working. They tearfully denied there were problems but promised to finish the film amicably. That spirit of cooperation was short-lived.

The climactic scene wherein Kit shakes Millie was on the schedule. Word leaked out, and *Life* magazine asked to document it. "I had no objection," Sherman said, "but Warner said it was not his idea of good publicity and denied them access to the set."

The day before, Davis warned Sherman that Miriam would try something to avoid being shaken by her, even though, Davis declared, "that's exactly what I intend to do." Sherman reassured her he would film the scene as written.[32]

The next day, crowds of curious onlookers filled the rafters above the set. "It was rather like a prizefight ring below," Davis noted. Before starting, Miriam summoned Sherman to her dressing room. "Vincent, dear," she said, "I know Bette is supposed to shake me, but I'd appreciate it if you'd ask her not to be too violent. . . . You see, I slept badly last night, and this morning I have a little crick in my neck." Sherman promised he would speak to her.[33]

"I knew it!" Davis screamed when she heard. "I knew she'd come up with something!"[34]

On the set, Sherman rehearsed the dialogue and blocking but not the shaking. He hoped they would get it in one take.

During rehearsals, Miriam's eyes darted around the set, and her body wandered from Davis to every corner of the stage. Davis stopped her. "Miriam!" she said. "If I have to sit on top of the piano to look into your face for this speech, I will."[35]

At last, the cameras rolled.

To absorb a blow realistically, the actor would stiffen her body. When Davis placed her hands on Miriam's shoulders to shake her, Miriam relaxed, and her head bobbed unnaturally, like "a doll with a broken neck."[36]

"She just went limp," Davis yelled, before storming off the stage. Sherman took Miriam aside and quietly explained that it would look odd because her head was wobbling. "Well," she said defensively, "I didn't want to fight her; I just wanted to let her do it." With tempers calmed, everyone returned to the set and tried the scene again.

According to the script, Kit says to Millie, "If I don't get out of here, I'll do something I'll be sorry for." Millie responds with more insults before screaming, "Well, why don't you go?" Kit is about to leave but sets her package down, grabs Millie by the shoulders, and shakes her violently, before pushing her onto a nearby sofa. Davis's final line was, "Sorry, but I've been wanting to do that for a long time." Instead, she only says, "Sorry," and leaves, which is how it is in the film.[37]

Sherman was pleased with the results, and the scene was over. "I can only report that it was an extremely pleasant experience," Davis said about shaking Miriam. That morning, Miriam wept, which Davis assumed was a last attempt to upset her.[38]

Miriam reported late the next day, keeping Davis waiting for hours. When she arrived, she apologized, claiming she was not feeling well. "I could have thrown her off the roof for that one," Davis said, but added, "Yes, Miriam is a caution, but [a] good actress she is."[39]

On her last day, Miriam apologized to Vincent Sherman for the trouble she had caused, admitting her insecurities. "But because this is Bette's home lot," she added, "I was sure you'd favor her over me since I'm only a guest star."[40]

For the rest of her life, Miriam insisted she had no ill-will toward Bette Davis on *Old Acquaintance*. "The more we saw of each other, the better we got along," she would say. However, she claimed that she lost eight to ten pounds during filming.[41]

Bette Davis spoke openly about her feelings for Miriam. "When Miriam Hopkins said she lost ten pounds playing in a picture with me— *Old Acquaintance*—she isn't mentioning half of it," Davis told the *Boston Globe*. "I lost weight, too, but I lost my mind as well. Anyway, Miriam Hopkins could afford to lose ten pounds—she needed to, to be as thin as I am. You know me—I get along with practically everyone. But this is the last time—positively. She is about the limit."[42]

Davis had one more blowup over *Old Acquaintance* when she saw the cover of the film's sheet music, which showed both women toasting each other with champagne. The content of the song concerned her: Two lovers drift apart and one of them finds a "new" acquaintance. The song had nothing to do with the story.

When Davis saw the cover and read the words, she screamed "bloody murder!" According to studio memos, she was "practically hysterical" and feared the "dirty implications of [the] lyrics and [the] still of two women toasting each other" would suggest they were lesbian lovers. Davis's outbursts apparently fell on deaf ears, since Warner Bros. published the sheet music with no changes.[43]

The reviews for *Old Acquaintance* were excellent. James Agee wrote in the *Nation*: "The odd thing is that the two ladies and Vincent Sherman directing, make the whole business look fairly intelligent, detailed and plausible."

Critics called Miriam's performance a "lethal portrayal," "wonderful," and "vibrant and shrill." The *Hollywood Reporter* added, "Miss Hopkins has the better acting assignment and takes every advantage of the intentionally unpleasant character of her role." Likewise, Philip Scheuer of the *Los Angeles Times* said Miriam had the "more spectacular of the two; hers is the showier role." He added if it was exaggerated, "it is exaggerated legitimately."[44]

Despite the glowing reviews, Miriam was through with Hollywood after three months with Bette Davis on *Old Acquaintance*. Tired of the questions about a feud, she would smile in her best southern belle way and through clenched teeth, and with possibly a touch of sarcasm, reply, "Where in the world did the idea ever come from that Bette Davis, and I was feuding? Simply ridiculous. We've always been just like sisters."[45]

The reasons for her hatred of Bette Davis were blurred. It was not their introduction in Rochester or Davis's "stealing away" *Jezebel* and the Academy Award that went with it. It wasn't even her weekend affair with Anatole Litvak. Miriam was envious. Bette Davis was at the zenith of her career, while Miriam was struggling to secure good parts.

Despite her talents, Miriam Hopkins lacked confidence. In her mind, she had to fight for what was best for her—and maybe she did. But according to Miriam, Davis wasn't the reason she said goodbye to Hollywood. "Oh, I was keyed up," she finally admitted. "There was tension on the set. But Bette didn't drive me out of town. I had made up my mind to go back to the theater. Ward Morehouse told me that I couldn't keep making movies and talking about the day when I would be doing plays again. He made me realize that it had to be one or the other. So I left Hollywood."[46]

For five years, except for a rare film offer that never materialized, Miriam made her home on the Broadway stage or traveling across the country in one play or another. According to Miriam, she had no regrets. Hardly any.

16

To New York and Back

In February, Miriam returned to New York for a rest. Sutton Place—exclusive, architecturally unblemished, and impressively stamped with good breeding—was a far cry from her perception of Hollywood. On that serene byway, she was neighbors to a Vanderbilt (Lillie Havemeyer, a Vanderbilt sister) and a Morgan. While Miriam was in Burbank making *Old Acquaintance*, Katharine Hepburn was renting Sutton Place, but now it was hers again.

Miriam wanted to keep the house. She loved New York and wanted to live there for a part of every year. "I have a house in California and a lot of pictures and furniture travel from coast to coast. There is a Renoir painting that I particularly love and a red chair."[1]

Michael, now eleven, was attending Chadwick, a California boarding school, and would join her later. "It's a splendid school," she raved, "progressive without being phony. I think he'll have a good time in New York."[2]

Since her return to New York, Miriam had been romantically involved with journalist John Gunther, known for his "Inside" series of books in the late 1930s. He would gain more fame in 1949 when he wrote the acclaimed *Death Be Not Proud*, based on his teenage son's struggle to overcome a brain tumor.

Gunther traveled in the same social circles as Miriam, hobnobbing with many of New York's upper crust, such as journalist and novelist Vincent Sheehan, *Time* magazine cofounder Henry Luce, photographer Margaret Bourke-White, and opera singer Grace Moore.

Miriam enjoyed being with Gunther and wasn't looking for work. But Broadway producer Michael Myerberg asked her to replace Tallulah Bankhead in Thornton Wilder's Broadway hit *The Skin of Our Teeth*, then enjoying its run at the Plymouth Theatre. Directed by Elia Kazan, the controversial, allegorical farce was one of the most talked about theatrical works in years.[3]

Despite the play's success, Bankhead wanted out. Publicly, she left because of health issues. She planned to return after an eight-week rest, even though "backstage rumblings" with Myerberg were the actual reason she was leaving. Miriam's former costars, husband and wife team Fredric March and Florence Eldridge, were also departing (they wanted to return to their farm in Connecticut), reinforcing the "backstage rumbling" rumors.

Miriam, who hadn't appeared on Broadway since *Jezebel* ten seasons earlier, was advised not to take the role. Myerberg evidently was a taskmaster. John Gunther agreed, but for a different reason: It was a bad career move to step into a play made famous by another actress.

Miriam, however, never followed advice. "Follow your own decisions," she would tell friends. "I believe that no one can make up their mind, but the person involved. That is why I never take advice without making up my mind before I consult others—then I listen gratefully to them and convince myself that I am right, or wrong. Sometimes I am changed."[4]

Despite the naysayers, Miriam accepted and signed on for eight weeks at $1,500 ($20,000 today) per week. When she finished her run, Bankhead would return. Since she was in talks with Warner Bros. for an unnamed film, the timing was perfect.

Lizabeth Scott, a sultry, gravel-voiced actress who would make her mark in film noir roles, was Bankhead's understudy. Scott appeared in a midtown New York stock company when she auditioned for Sabina in *The Skin of Our Teeth*. She didn't get the part but left an impression and was asked to be Bankhead's understudy. When Miriam replaced Bankhead, Scott was disappointed. "I felt I should have inherited the role of Sabina," Scott recalled. "Being a very young girl, I did not comprehend the realm of economics. 'The marquee must have star power.'"[5]

In his column, Burton Rascoe, the drama critic for the *New York World-Telegram,* was critical of Bankhead's replacement. Miriam would be "the last actress in the world" he'd choose for the part, and he couldn't "see her acting for dust." Her mannerisms annoyed him and he "wouldn't even go to see a Walt Disney picture of a double bill in which Miss Hopkins also appeared, out of fear of catching her in the tag end of a feature."[6]

Many harshly criticized Rascoe for his remarks. Tallulah Bankhead called it offensive to prejudge Miriam's performance before rehearsals had started: "Why it's an outrage for a critic to do a thing like that; it's uncritical; it's unethical. It's a dreadful thing to do to that poor child and not only that, but it's liable to create sympathy for her, and the little so-and-so will get good notices."[7]

Miriam had two weeks of rehearsals before taking over the role on May 31, 1943. Lizabeth Scott remained as the understudy, and on the first day, Miriam invited her to her dressing room. "She asked me if I had any suggestions for her interpretation of the role of Sabina," Scott said. "I was astonished, speechless and honored. I left her dressing room with a sweet impression of Miriam Hopkins."[8]

Despite Miriam's considerate attitude, Scott was still disappointed and left the play shortly after. Elia Kazan brought in another ingenue, Gloria Hallward, a nineteen-year-old blonde who would change her name to Gloria Grahame the following year. However, just as Lizabeth Scott never filled in for Bankhead, Grahame never would for Miriam.

Soon, rumors spread that Miriam and Bankhead didn't get along during the transition. One story claimed that Bankhead had locked up her costumes so Miriam couldn't copy them. Miriam had had enough. When asked if the reports were true, she posed, "What you can do for me is to deny that I'm always feudin' with somebody." The so-called Bankhead dispute added fuel to the tales still circulating about her feud with Bette Davis, and they wouldn't let up until *Old Acquaintance* was released six months later. "I want to get this off my chest because I'm really bored with it, always making people say, 'She's difficult, she's tough,'" Miriam clarified. "Tallulah and I are not close friends, but there has always been a perfectly polite relationship between us."[9]

"Actually," she went on to explain, "I sent flowers to Tallulah and a note saying I must have lost my mind to say so casually that I'd try to do the role after she left. She sent me flowers, too. Not the phony way that some women do. She also lent me her maid for the first four performances to be with my maid and help me on all those quick changes."[10]

The truth was, Miriam detested Bankhead, and the feeling was mutual. At Bankhead's parties, guests would imitate someone they didn't like. Miriam was often the first on Bankhead's list.

During Miriam's run in *The Skin of Our Teeth,* Bankhead checked in on an evening performance. Miriam's costume had several metal buttons and braids. When an actor was speaking, she would delicately twist the brass buttons to reflect light into the audience, diverting their attention to her. Later that evening, Bankhead entertained several young men at a party and re-created Miriam's attention-diverting trick. Everyone laughed; Miriam wouldn't have.[11]

Many celebrities dropped in at the Plymouth Theatre to catch Miriam's performance. Backstage one evening, the assistant director handed her a dinner invitation from former Republican presidential nominee Wendell Willkie. Miriam accepted. As a Roosevelt Democrat, Willkie piqued her curiosity.

After dinner, Willkie escorted her to the front door of Sutton Place. As they said good night, Willkie mumbled something about "fires burning deep inside." Before she could close the red lacquered door, Willkie lunged at her, forcing them both inside the foyer. Shocked by his advances, Miriam grabbed the nearest object, a lamp, and smashed it over Willkie's head, knocking him unconscious.

Envisioning the headlines, she called her neighbor Eliot Janeway, a journalist for *Time* and *Fortune* magazines and an economic advisor to President Roosevelt. "Eliot, I think I've just killed the next president of the United States," she cried in her deepest southern drawl. According to Michael Janeway, his father rushed over and "revived Willkie with cold water and coffee."

Potential memories of a tainted affair a few years earlier motivated Willkie to end the evening. Janeway was tempted to call the story in to his *Time* editor, but he had to "protect his friend Miriam Hopkins." He "discreetly" escorted Willkie to the street and into a cab.[12]

Tallulah Bankhead was scheduled to return to *The Skin of Our Teeth* in August but surprised everyone by quitting the show. Miriam's eight-week commitment was over, but she extended her stay by a few weeks, until Myerberg replaced her with Gladys George, known mostly for her film work.

Myerberg was prepared to cast Miriam in the comedy *Star Dust*, a farce about dramatic schools written by Walter Kerr. She called the play "nice" but wasn't interested. She wanted a "darling play," something like *The Philadelphia Story*. "Yes. . . . I'm going to talk to Phil Barry," she pondered. "He doesn't have to write all his plays for Hepburn, does he?"[13]

Miriam followed Tallulah Bankhead in a role that was tantamount to chasing a hurricane, but she wasn't looking for sympathy. According to some critics, she didn't surpass Bankhead's performance, but many said she mimicked it. One critic claimed she followed Bankhead "so closely that she seems a rather tidy carbon copy—no smudging, but not as clear as the original."[14]

Many years later, Miriam bumped into Bankhead at a party and recalled *The Skin of Our Teeth*. "I was trembling in my shoes at following you."

"You should have been," Bankhead replied, and added, "I was trembling myself."[15]

For Miriam, the sting of Hollywood was wearing off, and she wanted to make a film, but discussions with Warner Bros. never came to fruition. She remained in New York for a radio broadcast of *The Philadelphia Story*, followed by episodes of *Inner Sanctum* and a bit with Bert Lytell in the *Stage Door Canteen* series. Miriam loved doing radio and wasn't bothered that the medium relied on sponsors. "It is curious, but Helen Hayes and I were talking about just that thing the other day, and we decided that the play, not the pills—be they what they may—is all that need concern us."[16]

John Gunther had been in Europe and had recently returned to host Miriam's forty-first birthday party at Sutton Place. Newspaper columnist Elsa Maxwell loved Miriam's parties, recalling they "couldn't be more inspiring, gay, charming or interesting. Everybody talks at once, nobody listens—and very few care."[17]

Maxwell could remember when Elisabeth Marbury and Elsie de Wolfe lived and entertained there and meeting "Maurice Barres and Sarah Bernhardt." Maxwell named Miriam a worthy successor, dubbing her the "modern Elisabeth Marbury" and noting that "people of substance and parts, of brains and talent" still streamed into that house.[18]

Writer John O'Hara, known for his novels *BUtterfield 8* and *Pal Joey*, was a frequent guest at Miriam's "unique" gatherings, where he met his idol, broadcast journalist Edward R. Murrow: "Most of her guests were chosen from the world of the intellects, novelists, playwrights, musicians, composers, painters, sculptors, directors, government officials. They were there because Miriam knew them all, had read their works, had listened to their music, (and) had bought their paintings. They were not there because a secretary had given her a list of highbrows."[19]

It's a shame that "highbrow" or not, her friends could not get her a good film or stage role. Since no offers were coming her way, Miriam returned to Hollywood for two *Lux Radio Theatre* adaptations, *The Hard Way*, with Henry Fonda, and *Old Acquaintance*, not with Bette Davis—

that would never happen—but Alexis Smith, who re-created the role of Kit while Miriam reprised her role of Millie, the successful trash novelist.

Miriam was leasing a bungalow at 21112 Malibu Road when New York producer Cheryl Crawford, a founding member of the Group Theatre, sent her the new Samson Raphaelson play, *The Perfect Marriage*. Cast in it was Victor Jory, Martha Sleeper, and child actress Joyce Van Patten.

Raphaelson wanted Miriam but "chose her against the advice of others, including Cheryl Crawford." He did have one key supporter: former Hollywood powerhouse agent and Miriam's ex-lover, Leland Hayward, the play's chief backer.[20]

Still, Miriam wasn't convinced. She demanded a summer leave of absence to do films if the play were a success and insisted that Crawford "not engage another actress to replace her" during that time. Crawford agreed, and Miriam took the role.[21]

The Perfect Marriage is the story of Jenny (Hopkins) and Dale (Jory) Williams, who are celebrating their tenth wedding anniversary. As they ready for a romp in the hay, tempers flare up. Husband and wife talk it out and hear some unpleasant things about themselves, but in the end they are awakened to the real love they have for each other, which they had been neglecting.

One evening, Miriam and Martha Sleeper were in the middle of a scene when a man from the audience cried out, "You stink!" Everyone was quiet. "What the *hell* are they doing up there?" the man, apparently drunk, yelled. After this second outburst, audience members shouted for him to "shut up."

"Don't tell *me* to shut up," the drunk man yelled, hurling more insults. Victor Jory walked to the footlights and asked the heckler if he would "please go?" The drunk heckled him again. People yelled, "throw him out," and then applauded when a police officer grabbed the man and dragged him out of the theater. Miriam returned to her mark and continued with the play. "It lasted only a minute or so," Miriam later told a reporter, "but it was like an hour to your nervous system."[22]

The play's critical reaction was similar, though Raphaelson was blamed for its shortcomings when the *New York Times* called it "not his best." Despite that, *The Perfect Marriage* fared well at the box office. The play cost about $34,600 to produce, and ninety-two performances later, the backers made a profit.

"It was not exactly a box office failure," Raphaelson said, "however, perhaps because Miriam Hopkins starred in it. But she was also one of the mistakes I made." He never expounded on why "Miss Hopkins did not enhance the part," but he added, "I might have survived the reviews if I could have put the blame only on my not too bright choice of star. But I knew that the play itself had missed."[23]

Miriam believed that the poor reception was due to Victor Jory, who was likable but miscast. Coincidentally, he believed the same about her. According to Joyce Van Patten, who played Helen, the couple's ten-year-old daughter, Miriam was a problem "from the get-go." "She was never on time for rehearsals, and it got so bad that they were going to stand up to her," Van Patten recalled. Crawford considered replacing her, but Miriam found out; her plan to stay in the play was shrewd but misplayed.[24]

On opening night, as they had rehearsed it, Jory let his hand slip from Miriam's waist to her bottom. "She patted my hand," Jory recalled, but "as the curtain went up, she whispered, 'Victor, I'm going to faint,' whereupon she went limp." To save the scene, Jory ad-libbed and carried her to the bed until she came around, but "it killed the scene."

Before opening night, Miriam had sent telegrams to several critics, apologizing for her poor performance and fainting. "Any person who attains a certain plateau of success has to fight to maintain it," Jory admitted. "But she'd sent the telegrams before she came to the theater—*before* she fainted. It was a little too much."[25]

Critics found Miriam to be schizophrenic, alternating her acting styles between "Miss [Gertrude] Lawrence, Tallulah Bankhead and Miriam Hopkins. In those moments when she can be herself, she brings some fire and enthusiasm to the stage, but those moments do not make up the greater length of the play."[26]

Crawford planned to take *The Perfect Marriage* on tour when it closed on January 13, 1945, but conflicts with Victor Jory's schedule prevented it. Raphaelson peddled the film rights to the studios, and Joan Crawford was considered for Miriam's role. Miriam was never asked. Instead, Paramount cast Loretta Young with costar David Niven.

With so much time and distance separating her from John Gunther, Miriam ended their relationship. Finding herself with the spare time, she attended the United Nations International Conference in San Francisco as the guest of CBS radio host Helen Sioussat. There, she was introduced to former *New York Times* war correspondent Raymond Brock. The Texas-born Brock, a pudgy, apple-cheeked young man, had covered police court for the International News Service eight years earlier. In 1940, he was in Belgrade and Ankara for the *New York Times* and gained recognition for his story of the Serbian coup d'état of March 27, 1941, which was perceived as a heroic defiance of the Nazi juggernaut. But because of editing disagreements, he resigned and was now freelancing.

Miriam, who was eleven years Brock's senior, was attracted to the Ernest Hemingway look-alike. "I think the newspapermen, the foreign correspondents, are the world's glamour boys," she told a friend. "Yes, I do like those slouch hats, you know, that they wear, and the wonderful stories they tell. It is hard to resist them, isn't it?"[27]

When Miriam returned to New York, Brock tagged along. One evening, screenwriter George Oppenheimer and fashion designer Muriel King were dinner guests at Sutton Place. Miriam met them at the door and told them she had a "little man you're going to meet who knows all about Yugoslavia. He's absolutely fascinating. Now when I give you a little signal at dinner, ask him about Tito."

Midway through dinner, Oppenheimer felt a kick and, as instructed, asked Brock about the Yugoslavian statesman. But before Brock could respond, Miriam jumped in and spoke for half an hour, not giving Brock a chance to speak. "Brock was furious," Oppenheimer recalled. "But that was Miriam. She didn't know a goddamn thing about it. She was just quoting him."[28]

After a five-month romance, the couple drove all night from New York to Alexandria, Virginia, where they were married at a Methodist Church on October 23, 1945. "Sometimes eloping is more sensible than getting dressed up and standing before a phony altar in somebody's house," she said. This was her fourth marriage (Brock's second) and her fourth elopement. When Ellen heard the news, she remarked, "If you marry again I hope you'll let me know beforehand. I always read about your marriages in Winchell's column."[29]

There was no time for a honeymoon. Miriam wanted to do a film before appearing in the stage version of Vera Caspary's crime drama *Laura*, which starred Twentieth Century Fox actress Gene Tierney onscreen. At the same time, she declined a generous four-year contract from MGM executives, not wanting to be tied to one studio. However, she added, "I'll be glad to sign for individual pictures."[30]

While waiting on *Laura*, the Tower Grove house was rented to David O. Selznick for $1,500 a month. Selznick needed a hideaway while his estranged wife, Irene, decided whether to grant him a divorce and while his number one star, Jennifer Jones, considered his marriage proposal.

While *Laura* was in preproduction, Miriam accepted an offer to do a stage adaptation of Miklós László's *St. Lazare's Pharmacy* at Montreal's His Majesty's Theatre for producers Eddie Dowling and Louis Singer. The play was about a French-Canadian pharmacist in the village of St. Lazare who has inherited a pharmacy from his father. The son is resentful of his dull life of pills and prescriptions and is about to desert the store for the lure of Montreal when a woman (Hopkins) arrives whose uncanny knowledge of both family and shop leave him puzzled.

The popular Canadian comedian Fridolin was cast as both the father and the son. Miriam suggested that the roles be played by two actors instead of one. Dowling disagreed. To make her point, she boycotted rehearsals for two days until he threatened to call her "before Equity on charges of unprofessional behavior." Then, she collapsed with pleurisy, which she recovered from within the week, but a relapse forced the cancellation of several performances.[31]

St. Lazare's Pharmacy received mixed reviews. The *Montreal Gazette* called it a "frail story, but one which can hold theatrical life." One critic said Miriam "brought to it the charm of her blonde and temperamental personality, underscored each soliloquy and through sheer technique held the audience in her quieter moments," whereas Ken Johnstone of the *Montreal Standard* dismissed her performance as "hammy."[32]

Johnstone, who also free-lanced for *Variety*, learned that Chicago theater critics were going to pan Fridolin. When the play opened there, Fridolin received similar warnings, hinting at a conspiracy. Indirectly, Johnstone accused Miriam of plotting it, angering Ray Brock, who wrote an open letter to the newspaper defending his wife. He called Johnstone's accusations "shockingly vicious . . . , slanderous . . . , filthy and cowardly" and added, "You are a fourth-rate cub, Johnstone, and I strongly advise you to mind your manners."[33]

On December 23, the play moved to Chicago's Studebaker Theatre, where Wesley McKee took over as director. At a cast meeting, McKee told Miriam, "With your interpretation of the role, the play will be slaughtered in New York. You are not trying." After an evening performance later that week, McKee complained again about her acting. The audience was still exiting the theater and heard the ensuing argument backstage. Miriam screamed that she was "tired of taking criticism from a second-rate son of a bitch."[34]

Two days later, Miriam developed pneumonia. Several performances were canceled before her understudy, Joy Lafleur, took over the role. Rumors that Miriam faked her illness could not be stilled, but nothing conclusive was proven.

St. Lazare's Pharmacy closed in Chicago after ten weeks of decent attendance and split reviews. Miriam's illnesses and moving the show from theater-to-theater decreased the number of performances and financially burdened the show's backers. Nevertheless, the play had been given a terrific build-up before its Chicago opening and grossed around $14,500, because of the acting and staging, which received good reviews from critics who nevertheless panned the script. "The setting, acting, and staging cover up for weakness of dialog and theme," reported *Billboard*.[35]

Tennessee Williams's agent sent him the Chicago reviews along with a "withering attack" on Miriam and producer Louis Singer. "The latter pleased me," the playwright said, "but I was sorry for Miriam." Fridolin denied any strife between him and his costar, adding, "Whatever may have gone wrong with her relations with the management did not concern me because we are the best of friends."[36]

The last straw came when Miriam, who was unhappy, argued with Louis Singer about the characters' development. She wanted Edwin Justus Mayer to rewrite her part, and when they couldn't agree, Miriam left the play. It was a last-minute decision, so when Eddie Dowling couldn't find a star of Miriam's caliber to replace her, he closed the play.

In the meantime, producer Hunt Stromberg Jr. was ready with *Laura*. To accommodate Miriam, rehearsals were held in Chicago under Michael Gordon's direction. She read the book and had seen the film and was surprised to see Gene Tierney playing the part of "an innocent young girl who couldn't possibly be accused of murder."

"But as Vera Caspary wrote Laura," Miriam pointed out, "she was a successful business woman in her early 30's who was hard enough to commit a crime, very possibly, but who was also charming, gay and attractive enough to interest four different types of men. There's a mystery right here—did she, or didn't she, kill the girl found dead in her apartment!"[37]

Laura opened at the Playhouse in Wilmington, Delaware, on April 19, 1946. Comparisons to the film were inevitable, but *Variety* called the play "good entertainment, definitely on the sophisticated side." The daily said that Miriam's performance brought "brittle charm and expertness in throwing dialog across the footlights," adding, "even her mannerisms fit the character."[38]

While touring the country in *Laura*, Miriam sold the Tower Grove house to David O. Selznick for $75,000—ten years after she had bought the property for $42,000. Selznick loved the house and had made Miriam an offer. She had given up on her film career and was tired of maintaining two homes three thousand miles apart. "After all, my bridegroom's work is in the East," she remarked, "my son Michael's school is in the East, and I expect to appear in the theater in the East."[39]

Even though *Laura* was scheduled to open on Broadway on September 10, 1946, it closed in August because of poor responses in Boston, Baltimore, and other cities.

Tired from her grueling schedule, Miriam returned to Sutton Place amid rumors that her marriage was in trouble. While there were periods of separation, the couple always reconciled. Hoping to grow closer, they formed a theatrical firm called Miriam Hopkins-Ray Brock Productions. They expected to stage a series of shows during the next season, but their growing differences stalled any progress and their budding entrepreneurial attempt fizzled.

Several weeks later, producer Stanley Gilkey sent Miriam a script for *Message for Margaret*, the James Parish play about two womens' worldly struggle for the memory of a man they both loved. Miriam liked the role and suggested that her friend Mady Christians appear with her. Miriam invested in the play and encouraged Christians to do the same. But when the play opened, critics weren't impressed; *Message for Margaret* was unanimously panned, with the *New York Times* calling it "some old-fashioned clap-trap."[40]

Miriam shrugged. She'd been there before and admitted it was hard to judge a play, and especially hard for an actor to tell the difference between a good script and a good part. "*Message for Margaret* was one of those cases," she explained. "So many intelligent people liked it and thought it would duplicate its English success here—I did, too. But in performance, it just didn't work out that way—laughs came in the wrong places and the whole thing became an embarrassing disappointment."

Miriam and Mady Christians lost their investment and also ended their friendship. They never spoke again, and *Message for Margaret* closed after five performances.

After vacationing with Tennessee Williams in Key West, Miriam returned to New York hoping to produce and star in a summer play. She looked over several, including *Romance*, but it had a cast of thirty-five and used eight sets. *Reunion in Vienna* was not much better—a long cast and three large sets would be impractical for a summer company. Finally, she chose the John Van Druten play *There's Always Juliet* because of its one set and four cast members.[41]

Rehearsals were held at Sutton Place in Miriam's living room, which the scenic designer patterned the set after, even using several of her Jean Negulesco paintings as props. "Negulesco," she explained, "is now a Hollywood director, but whose work sells for enormous prices. I have pictures by Degas, Renoir, Picasso and John Carroll, among others, but these Negulesco paintings seemed just right to dress up a modern, small apartment."[42]

The ten-week tour began in Princeton, but Miriam was unhappy with the set's furniture. "I can't act on this second-hand junk," she told the play's director, Harold Kennedy. "Don't you have a truck?" They did, so she had them go to New York and take the furniture from her apartment. But first, Miriam called her maid and warned that if her husband was "asleep on the couch, which he usually is, be sure to get him off it before they move it. We don't need him down here."

After all these years, Miriam still practiced her scene-stealing tricks. Harold Kennedy, besides directing the play, also had a small but good part with many funny lines. During a run-through, as he was about to deliver one of those lines, he saw Miriam hovering around, dusting the piano. "Are you going to do that?" Kennedy asked her.

"Well, I have to do something."

"You might just stand still and listen."

"Suppose I don't want to?"

"Don't forget I am also the director of this play. If you move on one of my laugh lines, I simply raise a finger and the entire bank of pink lights goes out."

Miriam was shocked. She loved her pink lights, which made her look younger. After she called Kennedy a "bitch," Kennedy told her she could "bet [her] ass" those irreplaceable pink lights would go out. Miriam had met her match. She fell, laughing, into Kennedy's arms and her behavior "was heaven ever after."[43]

With a strong director, usually there were no problems. But if the director was weak and submitted to her demands, there was no end to the troubles she would create. Miriam admitted to telling more than one director how to do their job, saying, "They'd spread their hands to the heaven and ask why I couldn't be made to shut up."[44]

Audiences and critics alike raved about *There's Always Juliet*. For one critic, Miriam "turned in a polished and thoroughly effective performance." It was the same all over; in Marblehead, Massachusetts, audiences threw roses at her feet and cheered. *There's Always Juliet* was a huge success. "We broke records," Miriam recalled with pride, "and, on salary and percentage, I suppose I made quite a bit."[45]

17

"A Little Off-Center"

It had been nearly four years since Miriam's last film, and she was certain she had "burned her Hollywood bridges," at least metaphorically. Her career was on the stage, she believed, Broadway or elsewhere.

Jezebel producer Guthrie McClintic asked her to appear with English stage and screen actor Brian Aherne in *Penelope*. Miriam hoped her old *Dr. Jekyll and Mr. Hyde* and *Becky Sharp* director Rouben Mamoulian would supervise. "You know I would love to do a play with you," Mamoulian wrote, "but *Penelope* does not appeal to me personally. Sorry and hope someday soon we will do a show together."[1]

Discouraged by Mamoulian's refusal, Miriam, too, declined the play. She was, at the time, also distraught by Ernst Lubitsch's death in Hollywood. Miriam loved and respected Lubitsch and credited him with her success on the screen. "No, he didn't help my career," she insisted. "He made my career."[2]

The following week, she was going to produce and star in J. B. Priestley's *Ever Since Paradise*, about love and marriage. The prospects looked promising until Christmas Eve of 1947, when, on her way home from shopping, she tripped on a bus step and injured her spine. She was hospitalized for seven weeks and "didn't go out for months after that."[3]

Confined to bed, Miriam had only her maid and Ray Brock with her at Sutton Place. Brock's drinking was placing a strain on their marriage. He encouraged her to drink with him, which concerned Michael: "I think his drinking hurt her, causing a lot of problems." One result was that Brock let Miriam pay the bills, costing her "a mint—like all of them, except Billy."[4]

Looking ahead, Miriam contacted theatrical agent Alan Brock (no relation to her then husband), who was a bit player in her third film, *24 Hours*. Brock, who had offices in the old Palace Theatre, represented older film stars wanting to return to the stage.

With Brock's help, Kay Francis had had a successful three-month run in summer stock. According to Brock, Francis brought her wardrobe and said, "These are the clothes that I just bought; this is the jewelry I have, what play goes with these clothes?" Francis, it seems, was realistic about her box office appeal and didn't desire stardom. As Brock remembered, "Kay said, 'the women are coming to see what I'm wearing, and the men are coming because the wives always decide what they're going to see.'" This approach was a success for Francis, so she recommended it to Miriam. But as Brock recalled, working with Francis's *Trouble in Paradise* costar was different. Her first question was, "What new play am I going to captivate my audience with this season?"

"Well, what old chestnut would you like to play?" Brock asked her.

Miriam wanted a *new* play, but Brock explained: "You don't do that with summer stock because you're working with kids who have to know the play." She wasn't demanding money, which Brock expected. She wanted to be treated like a star, even though, in his opinion, those days were over. After two meetings, Miriam and Brock parted company.[5]

When teaming up with Brock didn't work out, Miriam returned to Sutton Place, with no prospects. She was resigned to a season of idleness but hoped to book at least one play, possibly at Cape Cod.

Then, one evening, she had an unexpected call from William Wyler in Hollywood. Since *These Three*, Wyler had become a two-time Best Director Academy Award winner, following the critical and commercial success of two World War II dramas, *Mrs. Miniver* and *The Best Years of Our Lives*.

Now a producer and director, Wyler was prepping the film adaptation of Ruth and Augustus Goetz's hit Broadway play, *The Heiress*. Olivia de Havilland, a Best Actress Oscar winner for 1946's *To Each His Own*, had seen the play and brought it to Wyler's attention, urging him to see it. "Because of this, he and his newly founded independent film company, Liberty Films, undertook the making of the movie," de Havilland recalled. "I had, like everyone else in the industry at that time, the highest regard for Wyler and I knew that he would make of *The Heiress* a brilliant film."[6]

De Havilland would play Catherine Sloper, the titular character, while Sir Ralph Richardson and relative newcomer Montgomery Clift were cast as Dr. Austin Sloper and Morris Townsend, Catherine's lover.

The Heiress explores the relationship between a wealthy physician

(Richardson) and his daughter (de Havilland), whose gracelessness and self-abnegation he both encourages and despises. She "grows up" when her father's argument that her suitor (Clift) is after her money is proven correct; after that, poised but unhappy, she can see her father's contempt for what it is—an effort to score a victory—when, years later, the now destitute suitor returns.

Miriam was Wyler's first choice to play Lavinia Penniman, Catherine's eccentric aunt. For forty-five minutes, he captivated her, reading passages from the script.

While psychics frequently guided her, at times, she entertained respect for fate, destiny, or whatever brought opportunities her way. Her recent back injury, she concluded, was for a reason, and this was it. She eagerly accepted Wyler's offer. Besides, this was the type of role Ernst Lubitsch had advised her to take. "Never play 'just nice girls,'" Lubitsch once told her. "Always try to get parts that are a little off center."

"Lavinia wasn't the old, broken-down, shawl-over-the-shoulders kind of aunt," Miriam reasoned, "but a woman who encourages Olivia in her romance with Montgomery Clift. . . . I think Lavinia is vicariously in love with him herself."[7]

Except for an occasional visit with Adolph Zukor, Miriam's return to Paramount in April was her first time on the lot since filming *She Loves Me Not* with Bing Crosby. Producer and longtime Paramount employee A. C. Lyles recalled escorting her on an earlier trip from the famous studio gate to Zukor's office. "So many people stopped to talk to her—producers, cameramen, directors—she always had a story to tell," Lyles recalled. "I was amazed at the number of people she remembered. Hopkins considered Paramount as her home lot; she said she was at home here. I found her to be incredibly gracious."[8]

Her first meeting was with Edith Head, *The Heiress*'s costume designer. Miriam convinced Head that her character, though a poor widow, would have made up her gowns to be more attractive. When Wyler heard, he ordered Head to return the costumes to their original state. "There's only one Miriam Hopkins," Head asserted. "She's a definite person." Nevertheless, Head called her "stunning."[9]

The Heiress was Montgomery Clift's third film. To build him up, the studio wanted his character to be more likable than he was in the stage play. Clift told actress Patricia Collinge that the cast wasn't friendly, but they were polite, "like we were made of glass."[10]

219

De Havilland remembered it differently, remarking that everyone was well-mannered and that, under Wyler's "restraining influence, all went well with Miss Hopkins and me during the filming." Years later, film historian Robert Osborne asked de Havilland at a screening of *The Heiress* if she, like Bette Davis, had trouble with Miriam. She replied, "Oh no. Miriam was no problem at all—she thought the film was all about her character."[11]

It was true that there was no fraternizing going on between the cast; according to de Havilland, she saw Miriam only on the Paramount sound stages: "Both of us concentrated so fully on our work that we had few exchanges concerning anything else."

In many ways, Miriam was her old self—the Paramount crew nicknamed her "Madame Napoleon"—but Wyler managed her well. Clift did complain that Wyler allowed her to upstage him and monopolize his scenes. But as in *These Three*, Wyler guided Miriam into a controlled performance. "I think Miriam Hopkins had a great deal of confidence in Wyler (as well as she might!)," de Havilland attested, "and that he understood her talent and knew how to lead her to express it at its best."[12]

When *The Heiress* wrapped in September 1948, Miriam was offered three stage roles, two of them on Broadway. Her astrologer advised her to remain in Los Angeles to take advantage of her hoped-for return to film, and wait. When nothing turned up, she signed with the theatrical producing team Russell Lewis and Howard Young, for the Anita Loos play *Happy Birthday*. In it, Miriam showed her versatility, dancing and singing hot numbers in a comic performance that was both boisterous and genteel. The play ran for three weeks, earning Miriam decent reviews.[13]

Meanwhile, Olivia de Havilland viewed footage of *The Heiress* and suggested to Wyler that he reshoot some of Miriam's more overly dramatic scenes. After the New Year, Miriam returned to Paramount for retakes but delayed the inevitable by feigning headaches. Finally, Wyler got what he wanted.

Miriam accused de Havilland of cutting her "best monologs" and trying to manipulate her performance. When she told Becky Morehouse that many years later, Becky said she "couldn't believe Olivia would do that. Evidently, the scenes could be improved, but Miriam convinced herself of Olivia's supposed deception, and I couldn't persuade her otherwise."[14]

De Havilland appreciated Miriam's skills but recognized her imperfections. "I think Miriam Hopkins had immense talent and an abundance of nervous energy. The latter made her a rather 'high-keyed' person, intense, and sometimes over-animated. This quality occasionally endangered her work. Willie Wyler knew how to restrain this characteristic so that, under his direction, she would give a really wonderful performance."[15]

But Miriam wasn't finished with *The Heiress*. Within weeks of completing the film, she began a revival, this time playing the lead, on New York's subway circuit, opening first at Brooklyn's Flatbush Theatre. Ralph Forbes played her father, and thirty-three-year-old Efrem Zimbalist Jr. was cast as Morris Townsend. "It would be difficult for a critic to praise highly enough the performances of Miss Hopkins and Mr. Forbes without bounding in Hollywood-like clichés," reported the critic for the *Hartford Courant*.[16]

One evening after a performance, future Broadway musical historian Miles Kreuger (who was fifteen years old at the time) and his friend Harvey Grossman went backstage to meet her. "I introduced myself to Miss Hopkins and told her that I admired her work," Kreuger recalled. "She was delightful; maybe she mellowed like old brie, or maybe she just needed to protect her own interests, and the stories we heard were exaggerated."[17]

When *The Heiress* premiered at Radio City Music Hall on October 6, 1949, Miriam was performing in the play. To avoid confusion with the film, Paramount persuaded the theater to pull its publicity. Refusing to go on until Paramount backed off, Miriam called William Wyler, and he cleared it with the studio. The play went on as scheduled.

The movie version of *The Heiress* received widespread critical acclaim. The *New York Times* wrote that it "crackles with allusive life and fire" and said that Wyler gave it "an absorbing intimacy and a warming illusion of nearness that it did not have on the stage."[18]

Miriam received great reviews. The *Los Angeles Times* noted, "Miss Hopkins, while talkative and gay, never ceases to be a very real person, and appealing." The *Hollywood Reporter*, in its praise of the entire cast, noted that Miriam was "delightful as Olivia's widowed, but still youthful, aunt, with her frivolous gaiety, love of romance, shrewd knowledge of men and unfailing love and sympathy for the girl. She adds color and charm to every scene in which she appears."[19]

The Heiress earned eight Academy Award nominations and won four, including Olivia de Havilland's second Best Actress statuette. Miriam, bypassed by the Academy's Actors Branch, was nominated for her first and only Golden Globe, in the Best Supporting Actress category. She lost to eventual Oscar winner Mercedes McCambridge for her role in *All the King's Men*.

At the Golden Globe ceremonies, the forty-seven-year-old actress saw her former *Men Are Not Gods* director, Walter Reisch. She told him she was through playing leading ladies and femmes fatales. Hearing that, Reisch recommended her for the part of an ambassador's wife and mother of Gene Tierney in the film *The Mating Season*, "and she made a very funny comeback."[20]

The Mating Season is the story of a handsome young man (John Lund) from the wrong side of the tracks who falls in love with a Washington blueblood (Tierney) with a long diplomatic pedigree and a high-flying, flighty mother (Hopkins) who commutes between Paris and New York. He has ambition and a salt-of-the-earth mother (Thelma Ritter), who closes the small-town hamburger stand that put him through college to hitchhike to New York for the wedding.

Produced by Charles Brackett and directed by Mitchell Leisen, who had been with Paramount since 1933, filming began in mid-May 1950. Leisen recalled that "everything went along fine until we started shooting the scenes Miriam Hopkins was in."

Eleanor Broder, Leisen's secretary, remembered that Miriam drove Leisen "crazy," believing she was the star of the picture instead of having a supporting role. At the end of each day, Miriam would map out the pages of the following days' scenes and suggest directions herself. "Her ideas were very good," Broder admitted, "but they detracted from Gene Tierney and John Lund who were the real stars of the story."

Leisen was polite and never argued or rejected her ideas. Instead, he filmed whatever she wanted, sometimes changing the camera lens so she would be out of focus or not in the frame; in any event, the footage was never used in the film.

Once, Miriam was not in a scene that Leisen was shooting on another stage, so he led the cast in a different direction to avoid tipping her off. Another time, as Leisen was working with Tierney, Miriam grabbed the star by the shoulders and said, "I think it would be better if you stood like this."[21]

When *The Mating Season* premiered in March 1951, it was called "a thoroughly amusing and delightfully improbable comedy." The standout of the film was the performance of Thelma Ritter, who walked away with the acting honors. Miriam wasn't happy about her part and complained to Brackett. With a supporting role, she expected more screen time. Nevertheless, critics enjoyed Miriam and called her "expert in a generally first-rate cast." Her dialogue sometimes left audiences howling, but it wasn't enough to outshine Ritter, who was nominated for a Best Supporting Actress Oscar while Miriam was once again bypassed.[22]

Miriam was frustrated, but then William Wyler sent her a screenplay adaptation of Theodore Dreiser's novel *Sister Carrie*. Recently knighted Laurence Olivier and Jennifer Jones were cast in the leads. Wyler wanted Miriam for the Julie Hurstwood role, the wife of Olivier's character.

The story follows Carrie (Jones), a naive farm girl, who comes to Chicago to live with a man (Eddie Albert) who befriended her. Later, love develops between Carrie and George Hurstwood (Olivier), a wealthy restaurant manager who is unhappily married to a spiteful woman (Hopkins). He embezzles from his employer and takes Carrie to New York. They're wed, bigamously, but as Carrie soars to success on the stage, Hurstwood sinks into dissolution. It the end, he walks out.

"When Willie Wyler sent me the *Carrie* script, I thought it was fine," Miriam recalled. "But I thought the character of the wife needed more motivation. I don't mean the part was too small; size doesn't matter. But the wife needed to be understood for the good of the whole story. I made some suggestions to Willie, and he seemed to like them. But he didn't know if he would be able to work them into the script."

Budget problems arose and the studio wouldn't pay Miriam's fee. "Of course I would do the part for nothing, because of the people involved," she claimed. "But that wouldn't be wise. I wouldn't work for Paramount for under $5,000 a week. They wouldn't respect me if I did."[23]

To replace Miriam, Wyler signed actress Ruth Warrick. But according to Paramount sources at the time, screen tests proved that Warrick looked too young for the part. However, the truth was that Wyler couldn't get Warrick to evoke the cold, heartless qualities that embodied Mrs. Hurstwood, so he fired her.

That evening, Wyler asked Miriam whether she would reconsider if they paid her price. She agreed, arriving at the studio early the next morning for her first scene. Edith Head worked all night on her wardrobe, and both were so tired they took "Benzedrine tablets to keep going" and were talking "like mad all day."[24]

Although it was a small part, William Wyler was able to pull a superb, shrewish performance from Miriam that amazed the critics. "As Hurstwood's cold, greedy, terrifying wife, Miss Miriam Hopkins is the essence of malevolence," proclaimed the *Pittsburgh Post-Gazette*.[25]

While Miriam kept her Hollywood career afloat, the House Un-American Activities Committee had launched a second examination on Hollywood and Communism. Unbeknownst to her, she had been placed on the FBI's radar when a former high-ranking Communist Party member accused Miriam of being a Communist sympathizer.

18

"They Are Sure Reds"

During the 1930s and throughout the 1940s, Miriam got involved with several political and social groups that the FBI suspected of fronting for the Communist Party. Among them was the Motion Picture Democratic Committee (Miriam was its second vice president) and the incendiary League of Women Shoppers, which also counted Bette Davis among its members.

In 1945, Louis F. Budenz, a Communist Party functionary and the managing editor of the *Daily Worker*, renounced Communism and created the List of 400 Concealed Communists for the FBI. Miriam happened to be one of the four hundred. When questioned about Miriam's Communist ties on June 30, 1950, Budenz called her a "concealed Communist," or someone who is secretly involved and, if asked, would deny membership in the Party.

Budenz wrote the following about Miriam:

"During the Hitler-Stalin Pact, when I was on the commission checking the attitude of intellectuals and professional people toward the Party, I was advised officially by Alexander Trachtenberg and V. J. Jerome that Miriam Hopkins was loyal to the Communist Party. Up until about 1943 or 1944 I received official reports to the same effect from Eugene Dennis [the longtime leader of the Communist Party] and later from Jack Stachel. Although I do not recall any such reports in 1945, the official attitude of the Party toward her was still friendly."[1]

A 1939 article in *Film Fronts*, a Communist-run Paris newspaper, praised Miriam and other film stars. That year, an FBI informant told J. Edgar Hoover that Miriam had ties with an unnamed Communist organization. In a 1943 report, sources accused her of backing programs that furthered the interests of the USSR. The FBI believed she was an active sponsor of several organizations that were Communist Party fronts.[2]

On August 8, 1950, because of Budenz's testimony, the FBI placed

Miriam in the category "Pending Security Matter–C case"; in other words, she was loyal to the Communist Party. The FBI report stated that "Miriam Hopkins, a Hollywood movie actress for more than 20 years, has been active as a sponsor, member, and officer of several Communist Front Groups since the late 1930s."[3]

In her more than one-hundred-page FBI file, several informants accuse her of supporting Communism. One suspected her of espionage, but subsequent inquiries failed to prove anything. Another letter addressed personally to J. Edgar Hoover anonymously asked, "Why not investigate the following: Miriam Hopkins, Hollywood. [Screenwriter] Donald Ogden Stewart, Hollywood? They are sure Reds."[4]

Miriam knew that having Communist connections was dangerous, particularly during that time of America's history. Ronald Reagan, who was then president of the Screen Actors Guild, admired Senator Joe McCarthy and supplied him with lists of actors that he suspected of being Communist sympathizers.

One of the actors in Fritz Lang's 1952 *Rancho Notorious*, Lloyd Gough, was on Reagan's list. Miriam attended the wrap party and left in the same car with Gough, who invited her for a nightcap. As the evening went on, their conversation became politically heated. Finally, Miriam chimed in, "You really are a Communist, aren't you?"[5]

Gough replied, "That is a question that, under the Constitution, I don't have to answer—and on principle, I never will."[6]

Miriam respected his response.

Was Miriam Hopkins a Communist or a Communist sympathizer? Michael didn't believe so: "I wasn't aware of her political beliefs. I know she was interested in world affairs. She would listen to Edward R. Murrow and made sure I knew what was going on in the world. But was she a Communist? Absolutely not. But she believed that because of her friendships with many possible Communists in Hollywood, it affected her chances of getting film roles in the 1950s. Whether that's true or not, I don't know."[7]

What is the truth? Miriam believed in some liberal causes that linked her to the Communist Party. Although possibly graylisted, it's unlikely Miriam was an official, card-carrying member, like many in Hollywood were accused of being and who were the actual victims of the black list.

When Miriam and Ray Brock were married, she accepted him for "better or worse," pledging her Sutton Place townhouse as his workshop for life.

Now, six years later, she regretted her promise. Her marriage to Brock was the longest of her four marriages, yet after several breakups and reconciliations, they divorced in April 1951. She no longer remembered why she had married him, except that he "wanted me to so much."

She promised not to marry again—or maybe she would if she "found the right man," but she was "still waiting for him to come along." Men with money didn't appeal to her, nor did the young men; she was interested in "intelligent men."[8]

Now that Brock was gone, she flew to Los Angeles for a well-deserved vacation. As a favor to Alan Campbell, the husband of Dorothy Parker, she appeared in his play *Told to the Children*. Although her acting "disappointed none of her admirers," the writing moved at a "lumbering pace." It ran for several weeks.[9]

Near the end of the play's run, Miriam's psychic predicted that she would return to the screen. Within days, a Twentieth Century Fox executive contacted her about the part of Duchess, an aging prostitute in *The Outcasts of Poker Flats*. Set during California's gold rush, the adaptation of Bret Hart's short story starred Anne Baxter, Dale Robertson, and Cameron Mitchell, as the villain. In one scene, Mitchell pushes Miriam and injures her back. Critics claimed that Miriam's best scenes were on the cutting room floor, yet she walked off with "acting honors."[10]

In the meantime, Michael graduated from high school. The six-foot student's accomplishments filled her with pride, and she told everyone he was "one of the best football players at Lawrenceville." But after graduation, Michael surprised everyone, including his mother, by joining the US Air Force. "It was either do something or get drafted," Michael claimed. But to enlist, he needed his birth certificate, and for whatever her reasons, Miriam had never told Michael that he was adopted. More amazing is that no one else revealed the secret while he was growing up, even though newspapers publicized the fact widely. When Miriam finally told Michael, he took the news well. "I was surprised, but I wasn't angry. What could I do? I never wanted for anything, and I wasn't treated badly, so in my mind, there wasn't much for me to say."[11]

In 1952, Miriam and producer Ben Kranz optioned *A Night at Madame Tussaud's: A Shocker in the Grand Guignol Manner*, by playwright and screenwriter Edwin Justus Mayer. "My father wrote *A Night at Madame Tussaud's* and then put it away," said Paul Avilla Mayer, the son of Edwin Justus Mayer, "but he eventually sent it out. He was very broke and desperate for a production."[12]

The play is set during the French Revolution on the afternoon and evening of April 5, 1784, when a titled couple, the Marquis Lomenie de Brienne (Ralph Clanton) and his wife, Ninon (Hopkins), seek asylum from the mobs in the wax museum of Madame Tussaud (Viola Frayne).

Peter Lorre, who specialized in playing menacing roles, directed and played Brutus, the long-haired, pock-faced artist who assists Madame Tussaud in her macabre waxworks. Lorre had been popular on the Vienna and Berlin stages, but with luck, this would be his first Broadway play.

Madame Tussaud's began a five-week tryout at the Norwich (Connecticut) Summer Theatre, and while *Variety* noted that Broadway "could do with a good horror play," the magazine wasn't sure that this play was the one. It was a definite audience pleaser, but the pace was slow, and the suspense needed enhancing. Also, the play couldn't decide whether it wanted to be "an out-and-out horror" or a horror play "with comedy overtones."[13]

Miriam had ideas for improving the play, but animosity between Miriam and Lorre threatened to erode the comic overtones. "Lorre and Hopkins hated each other cordially," said Paul Mayer. Actor Joseph Warren said that to let off steam, Lorre would arm-wrestle anyone while muttering under his breath, "'that bitch' and so on."[14]

During the final week, their hostility reached its threshold. "Hopkins got so angry with Peter," said Mayer, "that after the final curtain, she kicked him. He took his bow hopping on one foot, certainly more for effect than from pain. He must have enjoyed that!"[15]

According to Miriam, Lorre played the first scene "wonderfully," but then she complained that she was doing most of the acting. "I don't mind working like mad playing straight for Peter," she told Rouben Mamoulian. "I did it in the beginning, to tell you the truth. But when I had a terrible cold for three nights, and didn't have tempo and pitch at the rate I usually went, played sort of like an understudy, the big laughs didn't come big, and the excitement wasn't there. I must drive like mad, then he scores, then drive like mad again and then he scores. That's fine with me. Only let me have a beautiful entrance."[16]

Broadway producer Lee Shubert saw *A Night at Madame Tussaud's* in Boston, where the play drew seven curtain calls. Shubert told Miriam that he "never had a better time in the theater." She wanted to take the play to

Broadway, so when the company arrived in York, Pennsylvania, Shubert wanted to discuss the details. Shubert said he would "completely finance the show," but if Miriam could raise money on her own, he would give her a similar interest in the producer's share of the profit.[17]

When the summer run of the play was over, Miriam returned to Sutton Place and worked for three months getting *A Night at Madame Tussaud's* in shape for Broadway. She tried to convince Rouben Mamoulian to direct the play, sending him a complete script and blueprints of the set. They shared suggestions on how to improve it.[18]

Edwin Justus Mayer wanted to buy Miriam's share of the play, but she refused. "Hopkins held the rights long enough for the Shuberts to cool off," said Paul Mayer, "long enough for Peter to go back to Hollywood, long enough for the thing to fall apart."[19]

The truth, however, was more complicated. Miriam was meeting with investors and lawyers, but she ran into obstacles. At last, she contacted Hank Potter, who brought in Victor Samrock, a theatrical business manager, to take over. Samrock wanted to leave Shubert out and assured her that raising the additional money was "no worry." Samrock gave the script to producer Roger Stevens, who liked it. Even Peter Lorre agreed, and it looked as though it was coming together.

At the last minute, Roger Stevens wanted $30,000 for his participation, the same amount earmarked for Miriam's salary. "Take my thirty thousand," Miriam said, "[after] all the work I had done putting the package together and financing the summer production." The new deal would give Miriam 6.25 percent of the profits—the same as Lorre—and Stevens would receive 27.5 percent, with the "entire package being laid in his lap," Miriam said disbelievingly.

Samrock and Miriam's lawyer, Bill Fitelson, both agreed the arrangement was "ridiculous and unfair." They reassured her that they would find another producer. Once again, she was told not to worry. However, before that, Miriam had asked Rouben Mamoulian to produce *and* direct the play, hoping it would make him decide. Without Mamoulian's involvement, there would be no joy in the "whole thing for me," Miriam admitted.

She told Mamoulian that she had "never worked so hard," yet reasoned that she was "old enough and wise enough" to know when she had found "an honest, good hit."[20]

After another failed try with Shubert, Miriam was disillusioned. "It is too tough for me otherwise," she said, agreeing to turn it over to theatrical producer Chandler Cowles, "and if he can get it going, I will be thankful." But Cowles admitted that the entire set up was "all too expensive and obviously too difficult to readjust." Hoping for a miracle, Miriam wired Mamoulian that he was needed in New York if he was "interested in directing this." But it was not meant to be. "Probably have to call everything off," she said, admitting defeat. "Put on shelf for future setup."[21]

After that disappointment, Miriam starred in a revival of the Noël Coward play *Hay Fever* at the Sombrero Playhouse in Phoenix, Arizona, before taking it on an eight-week tour.

That spring, she met with agent Alan Brock, who was working with Ben Hecht at his old Ziegfeld Theatre offices on Forty-Second Street, about a role in Dorothy Parker's new play *The Ladies of the Corridor*. However, it was a supporting part, not the lead.

Before receiving confirmation, Brock had a telephone call, supposedly from Miriam's maid, but he believed it was Miriam disguising her voice. Screaming profanities and threats, the "maid" reportedly said, "How dare you send her this piece that is unworthy of her? Miss Hopkins is a star of stage and of film."

Brock had dealt with difficult actors before, but the fierceness of this woman's rage, whoever she was, was incredible. "You would have thought I had attacked or killed her child or her mother, with the vehemence that was coming from her," Brock said. "Hopkins needed to get her face in front of the public; she was getting to the point where she was becoming, 'whatever happened to Miriam Hopkins.'"[22]

Miriam declined the role.

In May, Miriam interrupted the *Hay Fever* tour to appear at the University of Michigan's Mendelssohn Theatre in Ann Arbor, where they were trying out the Jane Bowles play *In the Summer House*. Her costar was Mildred Dunnock. "I have the most wonderful part in it," Miriam said about her role as Gertrude Eastman-Cuevas. "The action takes place in Southern California. Everybody in it is sort of insane; it's all very strange. Don't ask me the plot. I said to Jane it is really rather difficult being in a play so unusual you can't tell people what the plot is when they ask you."[23]

The local newspapers agreed, calling it a "pretentious, wordy nonsense." A Detroit critic, while not so harsh, said it was a "magnificent artistic mess." Tennessee Williams, a friend of Jane Bowles, called *In the Summer House* "original, funny, and touching."[24]

"I went to Ann Arbor to see it," Williams recalled. "This was the play in its original form, not the one that some years later appeared on Broadway: and it was, in my opinion, much the better. But it was ahead of its time and had received a disgracefully unappreciative reception from both the press and the Academic community. The author, Jane Bowles was there but in seclusion. Miriam was by no means crushed but was defiantly outraged and in full control on the stage."[25]

Behind the scenes, it appeared that "the cast didn't like her," said Steve Siporin, an assistant director of the play who also had a small part. "In the beach scene, everyone had to throw hot dogs at her, and they threw them with a lot of force."[26]

Miriam hoped to stay with the play after rewrites, when it went to Broadway. "It's the sort of play that may run two years or two nights," she said. "You never know what a play will do until you see it before an audience. It's being rewritten now to clear it up a bit, and I'm most anxious to see the results."[27]

However, when the play moved to Broadway, Judith Anderson took over the role. Tennessee Williams considered that a mistake. "Miriam Hopkins, though not so powerful an actress [as Judith Anderson], was much better in the part. She gave the greatest performance I've ever seen her give and was somehow exactly right for it. She had an off-beat humor and zany sort of extravagance that was both heartbreaking and hilarious; she was really Gertrude Eastman-Cuevas in the flesh."[28]

In April 1954, Michael was with the Strategic Air Command at the Rabat Salé Air Force Base in Morocco. The first wave of Americans stationed there after World War II were "pretty obnoxious," and while those arriving in 1953 were a different breed, the bad reputation followed them. A French girl living in Morocco and trying to be good wouldn't associate with Americans because "they only had one thing on their mind."[29]

One day, Michael and a Canadian friend attended a Moroccan tea party. There, he met Christiane Carreno, a beautiful young French girl. Michael knew what the French thought of Americans. As a child, his nanny Mademoiselle taught him to speak French, so he told Christiane he was Canadian and gave her a fake French name. Christiane, or Chris as the family called her, was attracted to the handsome young serviceman and agreed to go on a date. But, as their relationship got serious, Michael admitted, "I'm not Canadian. I'm American."

Soon, Michael told Chris the truth about his mother. By chance, *The Mating Season* was playing at a local theater. As they watched, Michael pointed to the screen and said, "See that lady there? That's my mother." After his first deception, Chris was dubious and replied, "Yeah, and the girl over there is my sister." It took a while, but Michael convinced her he was telling the truth. It wasn't long before Michael proposed marriage.[30]

Michael revealed the news of his engagement in a letter to his mother. In Los Angeles and New York, Michael had dated Linda Berlin, the daughter of Irving Berlin, and for a while, future *Bewitched* star, Elizabeth Montgomery, which likely amused Miriam because of her summer romance with her father, Robert Montgomery, some twenty-five years earlier.

Miriam couldn't attend the wedding, so her gift was an all-expense paid ten-day honeymoon. She sent telegrams to friends about Michael's engagement and asked them to send money: "[I] can't furnish apartment but Michael has done most of that himself. A cable or a small check would appreciate if you would send as he has no uncles, aunts, sisters or brothers." Her friends probably chuckled knowing that Michael had an aunt, grandmother and a cousin, but again, they considered it another of Miriam's eccentricities.[31]

Michael and Chris were married twice; first by the justice of the peace on May 7, 1954, and the following day by the Catholic Church. Before Michael, a Protestant, could be married before the church's altar, he had to promise to raise their children as Catholic. Michael agreed.

The previous year, Miriam had learned that her father was in failing health. After the death of his wife, Kate, five years earlier, Homer lived with his daughter Katherine, her husband, Garland Reid Cox, and their three daughters at their home in Kankakee, Illinois. "My father adored Homer," recalled Charlotte, Katherine's middle daughter. "He was a valued member of that household. The girls all piled into one bedroom, and he got a bedroom by himself, and we all thought that was just fine."

Besides an occasional letter or telephone call, Miriam had not been with her father since she was seven years old. Friends encouraged her to visit him, feeling that otherwise she might regret it. Their first meeting was awkward, with much soul-searching. Both were hurting. Miriam missed her father's presence growing up, and his absence deprived Homer of watching his children become young ladies. According to Charlotte, it pained him when "he wrote all these letters and she never wrote back." Soon, Homer stopped writing, and when he married Kate and started a new family, his old life was a memory.[32]

As a child, Miriam couldn't understand why her father had seemingly abandoned her and Ruby. Once they were reunited, Homer explained about the unanswered letters and blocked telephone calls. When she confronted her mother, Ellen replied, "It was for the best." Miriam was furious. Her behavior was "so low" that she was speechless: "As an individual, I have neither affection nor respect for her."[33]

According to Charlotte, Miriam believed that her father didn't care, "and I think that was a real problem for her in life." Charlotte, or Cissy as they called her, was eight years old at the time of the reunion and remembered that it was emotional: "She was extraordinarily affectionate with Homer. Of the three girls, I was in the middle, and she took to me probably because I was the most outgoing."

To show her fondness, Miriam gave Cissy the gold disc that Tennessee Williams had presented to her in 1941 during *Battle of Angels*. On one side, Williams had engraved "Impossible." Miriam had a Kankakee jeweler inscribe on the reverse, "Cissy, love Miriam."[34]

In August 1954, Miriam learned that Homer was dying. She arrived in Kankakee shortly before her father died from a coronary thrombosis. Homer was eighty-two years old and was buried in Oklahoma City's Memorial Park Cemetery next to his second wife, Kate.

The next April, Michael and Chris had a son they named Michael Thomas Hopkins; they called him Tom or Tommy. Chris and Michael had promised the priest at their wedding to raise their children in the Catholic faith, which baptizes babies shortly after birth. Michael would soon return to the States, so Miriam asked that they wait to perform the baptism. Since Miriam couldn't be in Morocco for their wedding or Tom's birth, Chris reluctantly agreed.[35]

Three months later, Michael transferred to New York City. They settled in a Brooklyn Heights apartment that Miriam found for them. But when it came time to baptize Tom, Miriam kept postponing the date. "He was almost six months old," Chris said, "so we had to do something because it was taking too long." Finally, Miriam agreed on a date. But something came up, no one remembers, and she didn't show for the baptism. Chris was disappointed. "It was painful for my family, especially my parents, not to be there for the baptism of my son," Chris remembered with much regret. "I have to say that I was somewhat resentful after agreeing to wait for her to be at the baptism, and she didn't show up."[36]

Initially, Ellen didn't approve of Michael's adoption, and according to

Miriam, she had "disliked him as a child." However, in her old age, Ellen helped care for Tom. Michael recalled that Ellen took the subway to the Catholic Church for Tom's baptism, "which unfortunately my mother did not do. She didn't care for that—she had some problems."[37] "I was thankful to grandmother for that," Chris added.[38]

For a while, Miriam was working steadily on television and the stage and was financially stable, but Sutton Place cost more than she could afford. It required two servants to run, but selling it was out of the question. Instead, she gave MCA president, Jules Stein, a four-year lease; Stein made improvements, such as installing air-conditioning and adding a laundry. He offered Miriam $175,000 for ten more years, but she declined. "I might want it myself in that time," she thought. She wasn't about to leave New York, so she moved to a charming, windswept penthouse at 230 East Forty-Eighth Street.[39]

During much of the decade, Miriam appeared on television, guest starring on shows such as *The Texaco Star Theatre, The Philip Morris Playhouse, Studio One,* and *The Whistler.* One standout performance was as Norma Desmond in an adaptation of *Sunset Boulevard* for the *Lux Video Theater.* For Miriam, television was offering better opportunities. She enjoyed the teleplay *Long Distance,* also for *Lux Video Theater.* "It was a 24-minute monologue," she explained. "I was a wreck at the end of it, but I loved it." Her performance was well received, and audiences demanded that she repeat it.

Furthermore, many of Miriam's old Paramount and RKO films were showing on the small screen. For her to watch them was a surreal experience. One afternoon, several friends telephoned that *The Richest Girl in the World,* which she had made twenty years earlier, was on television. "I thought I wouldn't bother watching at first," she said, "but about the third phone call, I changed my mind. I switched on my television set, and there was a close-up of a girl lying on a bed, looking a little like Marilyn Monroe. My first thought was an amazed 'Did I look like that?' My next thought was to sign up for a series of facials. Seriously, though, I'd been disassociated with the film for a sufficiently long time to find it an amusing little picture, quite funny, really. It was like watching someone else, Miss Jones or Miss Brown."

Viewing her films on television was different than watching rushes in a studio screening room or the latest television drama. "You watch a new television play that you've done," she said, "and you worry about everything from the way you acted a scene to the angle at which you held your chin. But watching an old movie you find a horrible hairdo or a dreadful dress something to laugh at. It's all very impersonal."[40]

For now, though, television would wait. A stage role was about to be offered to her that would bring raves and the satisfaction she had yearned for her entire career.

19

"How Many Times Can You Come Back?"

For a period, Miriam was dividing her time between television and road tours. In the spring of 1958, she was in Phoenix, appearing in Arthur Laurent's play *Time of the Cuckoo* as a lonely American secretary in search of romance in Venice. A few years earlier the play had been adapted into a film titled *Summertime*, with stars Katharine Hepburn and Rossano Brazzi.

One afternoon, Miriam received a call from Ketti Frings, the screenwriter of *The File of Thelma Jordan* and *Come Back, Little Sheba*, asking if she would take over Jo Van Fleet's role in the current Broadway hit *Look Homeward, Angel*. Frings had adapted the play from author Thomas Wolfe's 1929 largely autobiographical novel of the same name.

Van Fleet was leaving the play after more than six months (and a Tony nomination), as were two of its other stars, twenty-five-year-old Anthony Perkins, a film and stage actor who originated the role of Eugene Gant, and Hugh Griffith, the father who runs a sculpture shop housing his prize possession, an angel. Both actors were leaving the play to appear in films: Perkins in *Green Mansions* opposite Audrey Hepburn, and Griffith as Sheik Ilderim in William Wyler's remake of *Ben-Hur*.[1]

Set in North Carolina in 1916, *Look Homeward, Angel* recounts the early life of Eugene Gant: his first love affair, the death of his brother, and his relationship with his drunken father and stingy mother, Eliza, who runs a cheap boarding house.

Wolfe's first novel received mostly positive reviews upon its publication. The *New York Times* referred to it as "strikingly original," but it would be nearly thirty years before Frings adapted the book into a play. Ironically, Miriam's former costar, Bette Davis, was initially cast as the miserly mother, but a fall on her Bundy Drive basement stairs resulted in a broken back and four months of healing, forcing her to back out. Jo Van Fleet, whose success was mainly on the stage and who received a Tony Award for 1954's *A Trip to Bountiful* and a Best Supporting Actress Oscar the following year for *East of Eden*, had replaced Davis.

When *Look Homeward, Angel* premiered on November 28, 1957, at the Barrymore, John Chapman at the *New York Daily News* called it a "truly magnificent play of stifling beauty and wild, lusty humor." Likewise, Brooks Atkinson at the *New York Times* called it a "solid drama" played with "great passion and tenderness." The play won a Pulitzer Prize and for Ketti Frings the New York Drama Critics' Circle Award.[2]

But now, the three top principals wanted to move on. *Look Homeward, Angel* had been sold out for months, so producer Kermit Bloomgarden (his hit show *The Music Man* was also playing on Broadway) had to find replacements as quickly as possible. Character actor Ed Begley replaced Griffith, but the most challenging of the three roles to fill was Eugene and Eliza Gant.

It had been several years since Miriam had appeared in a film or a Broadway play, yet her name was consistently in the public eye with multiple television appearances and road tours across the country. In both, she drew large audiences, receiving rave reviews and bringing in solid box offices. In Bloomgarden's opinion, she could repeat that success with Broadway audiences.

Miriam was familiar with the novel, so after reading the script, she accepted the role. Also, Miriam had kept up with theater casting and would have known that this was a role that Bette Davis was cast for and wanted. The experience could reap her prestige and popular success, besides giving her great satisfaction over her old adversary, whom she blamed for stealing many critically acclaimed parts in the past.

Producers now searched for their Eugene Gant. Among the more than two hundred young men auditioning for the role was a newcomer, twenty-two-year-old Andrew Prine, whose only acting job had been a small role in television's *United States Steel Hour*. Bloomgarden liked Prine but was hesitant about his inexperience, so he asked him to read again to be sure "we weren't making a mistake."[3]

Bloomgarden ended up hiring him, but he and director George Roy Hill, who would gain fame and an Oscar for directing *The Sting*, wanted Prine to be in the theater every night. Not wanting Anthony Perkins to influence his performance, Prine rebelled and skipped several shows, expressing that he wanted the role "to be my own." Both Bloomgarden and Hill told him, "Do the role, say the words. We don't need another interpretation." From then on, the stage manager made sure Prine was in the audience for every show.[4]

Bloomgarden and Frings had faith in Miriam, but because she had been without a recent hit on Broadway or the screen, and was now following Van Fleet's memorable performance, even close friends didn't believe she would make much of the role. Ward Morehouse told his wife, Becky, that Miriam "won't be as good as Jo Van Fleet," but he was hopeful, knowing his old friend needed a comeback. But "comeback" wasn't in her vocabulary. She would ask, "How many times can you come back? It's such a tacky phrase. It sounds like you've been in a home for destitute actors and somebody has dragged you out."[5]

Miriam wasn't "destitute," but she did need a suitable role, and Eliza Gant did not disappoint. When the new cast debuted on June 30, 1958, critics who saw the drama for the second time showered her with praise. The well-respected *New York Post* theater critic Richard Watts Jr. wrote: "Miss Hopkins is giving a brilliant portrayal, one of the ablest of her career, and nothing stands in the way of her force and skill." Nearly everyone agreed that she gave a controlled presentation in an unglamorous role. Even Ward Morehouse gave her the highest praise: "Miriam Hopkins is giving the finest performance of her career in Broadway's best play, *Look Homeward, Angel.* She's in a class with Bernhardt."[6]

Eliza Gant would prove to be the high point of Miriam's stage career, so she was protective of the character: "Someone said that Eliza Gant is mean. I don't think that at all. She has great strength, and she has a great love for her children, but she is unable to express it. She always says the wrong thing, and there's something pitiful about that."[7]

Every performance was a reason to celebrate, with Andrew Prine joining her for drinks in her dressing room; they would "get half lit and hang out." Decades later Prine recalled that he "loved the shit out of" his *Angel* costar, adding that she was a "super bright, cultured, educated person." They took a great liking to each other.[8]

While Miriam's ire was not directed toward him, Prine quickly learned that Miriam could be "spirited," at least with the rest of the cast. For example, Arthur Hill, who later gained fame as the titular lawyer in the television series *Owen Marshall*, played Prine's brother Ben, who dies in the second act. Several times during his death scene, Miriam would be backstage hacking and coughing loud enough to be heard on West Forty-Seventh Street. It drove Hill crazy, because she seemingly had no regard for the other actors when they were onstage.

At times, an audience "distraction" also proved that Miriam was not reticent about "breaking the fourth wall." One evening, a woman in the front row was repeating the dialogue to a friend, who was apparently hard of hearing. Miriam stopped the show, walked to the apron edge, and said to the woman, "Would you shut up?'" Spinning around, she returned to her mark and continued with the scene.

Prine admired Miriam's tenacity and learned from it: "She was five feet tall, and she could stomp a hole in the stage floor if she didn't like what was going on. She would let people know."

Soon, he would learn other lessons.

When Miriam invited Prine to his first star-studded cocktail party at her East Forty-Eighth Street penthouse, he bought a brand-new sixty-dollar suit. That evening he met "some heavyweight people—Ward Morehouse, Bennett Cerf, and whoever the hell they were." But he was mostly impressed with playwright Moss Hart drinking alone at the bar. Wanting to be "cool," Prine joined him and ordered himself a drink. Moss looked him over, leaned toward him, and whispered, "You know, the tag is still on your sleeve?"

"And I just fucking died," Prine recalled with great embarrassment. "'Cause there it was." Hart borrowed a knife from the bartender and cut the tag off Prine's sleeve. "Don't let this bother you," Hart said, trying to appease the humiliated young actor. "Some days I can't even open a door."[9]

That Prine was a young, unsophisticated Georgian could be why Miriam mothered him. Prine admitted that he was "undisciplined" in his early years and was going on "emotions." But then, it was Miriam's custom to take new, inexperienced actors under her wing and watch over them; Andrew Prine was no exception.

By January 1959, *Look Homeward, Angel* had played at the Barrymore for more than a year. Miriam had been with the show for six months, and attendance was still decent. However, the company's lease on its theater was expiring, and they had to move out for the play, *A Raisin in the Sun*, starring Sidney Poitier. Kermit Bloomgarden temporarily rented the Fifty-Fourth Street Theatre but after a month decided to take the show on the road. *Look Homeward, Angel* closed on Broadway on March 9, 1959, having run for a respectable sixteen months and 564 performances.

Miriam agreed to go on the road tour, but Andrew Prine decided to say "goodbye"; he had had it. The tour would open the following October in Wilmington, Delaware, but Miriam had a film commitment on the West Coast, so she agreed to take *Look Homeward, Angel* to the La Jolla Playhouse at the end of June. As a favor, Prine reprised his role as Eugene Gant for that week's showing.[10]

On July 26, Miriam checked into the chic Chateau Marmont, an elegant hotel in the Hollywood Hills overlooking the Sunset Strip. The following day she reported to the former KFI radio studio on N. Vermont Avenue, where independent producer Bill Ferris was filming *Ma Barker's Killer Brood*, a fictionalized account of the infamous, real-life gangster and the mother of more than a few hoodlums who ran the Barker gang.

At costume fittings, they dressed her as the plain, shoddy Ma Barker, and her transformation was akin to the one she undertook to play Eliza Gant. Even though her clothes suited the role, she insisted on a contemporary look, causing the wardrobe mistress to remark, "Miriam came in for so many wardrobe fittings and changes, sloppy old Ma Barker was starting to look like a Dior model."[11]

On the first day of shooting, production coordinator Phil Giriodi, who had never seen Miriam before, was at the Chateau Marmont to drive her to the studio. "As I sat in the lobby I saw an aging but wonderfully preserved woman walking to me," Giriodi recalled decades later, "and by the regal manner in which she walked, I knew it had to be Miss Hopkins." As Giriodi rose and introduced himself, Miriam smiled a "little devilish" grin and offered her hand. He was charmed. "She didn't reveal her name, but of course everyone was supposed to know who she was."

Filming went well, but on the second day, Miriam drove to the studio alone, arriving more than two hours late. The financial resources of *Ma Barker's Killer Brood* were small, so two hours of lost production ate into their budget. Bill Karn, the director, called for the first take. Giriodi recalled that Miriam forgot her lines and at times slurred her words. "Everyone on the set quietly cringed."

After consulting with Karn, Ferris told Miriam her services were no longer required. Giriodi recalled, "She took it hard, as one might. I felt very sorry for this once shining star, now humbled and unceremoniously dumped from a small 'B' film."[12]

To counter any publicity leaks, Miriam's press agent released a brief statement: "Miss Hopkins, exhausted after a long road tour in *Look Homeward, Angel,* has withdrawn after one day of shooting from the Ma Barker role on doctor's orders to take a four-week rest."[13]

Within twenty-four hours, actress Lurene Tuttle replaced Miriam. *Ma Barker's Killer Brood* did poorly at the box office and was critically panned due mainly to the weak script and direction. "It was low budget schlock at its worst," one reviewer said.[14]

In early September, once she had "rested," Miriam was back in New York for the *Look Homeward, Angel* road tour rehearsals. Producers replaced Prine with John Drew Barrymore, the son of the late actor and silent-era star Dolores Costello and father of future actress Drew Barrymore. Barrymore had appeared mostly in low-budget films such as 1958's *High School Confidential* and *Never Love a Stranger.*

During rehearsals, Miriam and Barrymore quarreled continuously. According to actress Florence Sundstrom, who played "Fatty" Perk in *Angel,* Miriam knew the play so well she was "propelling him around the stage." Barrymore was unhappy, and then one day, he didn't show up. The director of the road show asked Sundstrom to convince Miriam to stay at home for a few days while he worked with Barrymore alone. Miriam resented the implication, making excuses, but agreed. When she returned, things continued as before; she still played the part for him. This time, Barrymore walked out for good. His agent claimed he was ill, underweight, and had a skin infection.[15]

In a panic, road tour producer Ted Ritter called Andrew Prine and asked him to step back into the play. Prine wasn't happy but agreed to return temporarily, opening at The Playhouse in Wilmington the following week. He worked six weeks before his former understudy, Jonathan Bolt, replaced him.

Florence Sundstrom blamed Miriam for Barrymore's desertion of the play and told her so. Sundstrom was amazed that "she took it from me" but admitted they were like sisters, so, she said, "I think she knew I was trying to help."[16]

Growing weary of her gray wig and the drab dress she had worn for nine months, Miriam reached her limit when her four-year-old grandson, Tom, didn't recognize her after a backstage visit. So for the road tour, the gray wig was replaced with a modern beehive, and she "improved" her makeup with thick false eyelashes. Miriam knew she would be criticized about her new look, especially in Chicago by the *Sun*'s most ruthless critic, Claudia Cassidy, or as she was better known "Acidy Cassidy," "that Woman from Chicago," or simply, "that bitch."[17]

Miriam could visualize the reviews Cassidy would give her: "She's going to say, 'Miriam Hopkins, with eyelashes that swept the floor and a bouffant wig, was more Madame Butterfly than Eliza Gant.'" When Sundstrom remarked that she could avoid Cassidy's wrath by getting rid of the eyelashes and the new wig, Miriam replied, "I won't give her the satisfaction." But Miriam knew better. She wore the gray wig and left off the eyelashes on Chicago's opening night. In the morning, Claudia Cassidy gave the play a good review, calling it a "fine, strong, sensitive and powerful play." As for her portrayal of Eliza Gant, Cassidy wrote only, "Miriam Hopkins gives the mother no quarter."[18]

Subsequently, Miriam returned to the bouffant wig and long eyelashes to be the "glamour girl, the Southern belle," as Florence Sundstrom called it. When the play opened in Alexandria, Virginia, the costumes and scenery were lost in transit, so she played Eliza with her natural hair and a sexy black dress. Sundstrom recalled that she "loved doing it that way because she was pretty."[19]

The *Look Homeward, Angel* road tour ran for more than a year, traveling coast-to-coast to nearly one hundred cities. In one-night stands, college auditoriums, gyms, arenas, and wherever else it played, Miriam received rave reviews. At the tour's last stop, at Los Angeles' Biltmore Theatre, the *Times* stated: "Miriam Hopkins brings to the role of the mother the consummate skill of an expert actress, wringing sympathy and even love from a part that could have been reduced to caricature."[20]

For six months following the run of *Look Homeward, Angel*, Miriam relaxed at Sutton Place, taking a well-deserved rest. Then, one evening, William Wyler called from Hollywood. Wyler was adapting *The Children's Hour* as Lillian Hellman had written it for the stage. More than two decades earlier he had directed *These Three*, in his opinion, an "emasculated" version of the play. He was dissatisfied and told Curtis Hanson it "was not the picture I intended."[21]

These Three had starred Miriam and Merle Oberon, but now, Shirley MacLaine and Audrey Hepburn would take those roles. They had experience, both with Academy Award nominations (Hepburn had a win for *Roman Holiday*, which Wyler had also directed).

For his new adaptation, Wyler offered Miriam the Lily Mortar role, the aunt of Martha (MacLaine). As played in *These Three* by Catherine Doucet, Lillian Hellman described Mortar as "a plump, florid woman of forty-five" (Miriam was fifty-eight). A vain, egotistical woman, Mortar lived in a romanticized vision of her past achievements as an actress.

The film could have been a reunion had Merle Oberon agreed to play the grandmother, Amelia Tilford, but she declined. Instead, it was a different get-together when Wyler cast Fay Bainter, Miriam's costar from their Broadway plays *The Enemy* and *Lysistrata*. James Garner, best known for his lead role in the television western *Maverick*, played the country doctor, previously played by Joel McCrea.

Wyler scoffed at critics who said *The Children's Hour* was a remake. In his view, it was a reinterpretation. "I will not remake an old picture of mine," he insisted. "This would not make sense. Some story elements are the same. The new film is a tragedy; the other was not."[22]

Based on a true-life 1809 Scottish scandal, a schoolgirl's malicious gossip leads a small town to believe two teachers are lesbians. On *These Three*, Lillian Hellman rewrote the script to have the two women fall in love with the same man. "We never did the play the first time," Wyler said. "It could not be made as a movie in those days. I always thought it a great pity that we couldn't do so. Ever since then I have always wanted to do it right. Now the restrictions have been eased. It is not us in Hollywood who have grown up. It is the people who have grown up. The average adult knows that these things exist and we can deal with the subject just as we can do pictures about a Tennessee Williams play or about the life of Oscar Wilde."[23]

In her first film, the Houston-born Karen Balkin played Mary, the spoiled and manipulative young student who is the root of everyone's problems.

The role of Rosalie, the shy schoolgirl who is blackmailed by Mary, was skillfully handled by twelve-year-old child actress Veronica Cartwright. In the middle of her screen test, Wyler shot off a gun to see what her reaction would be. Cartwright remembered thinking, "I didn't know it was supposed to be during the war," but she continued without breaking character and won the part.

In one scene, Cartwright had to cry hysterically, but "she wasn't getting hysterical enough," according to Mimi Gibson, who portrayed one of the schoolgirls. Miriam was watching and said to Wyler, "Do you want her to cry harder?"

Wyler said, "Yeah," so Miriam slapped Cartwright's face.

"Veronica was so shocked," Gibson recalled, "her face turned red. All of us were shocked. Her mother didn't say one thing, and they went on with the scene. Of course, she was hysterical enough then. That couldn't happen today."[24]

However, Veronica Cartwright claims that Gibson's version was "such bullshit." According to Cartwright, William Wyler was discussing Karen Balkin's character, Mary, slapping her across the face. Miriam overheard and interjected, "You know, there are stage slaps where you cup your hand, and when you hit the person, it doesn't hurt." Without warning, Miriam hit Cartwright across the face, but Cartwright insists that it "was not a stage slap, let me tell you." The blow was so hard it left fingerprints on her face.

Cartwright began to tear up from the blow, but Miriam scoffed, "Oh, that didn't hurt this silly girl." To reinforce her actions, she recalled a Broadway play where an actor slapped her every evening. Then, she offered to show William Wyler how the stage slap worked. Wyler shook his head. "No thanks, I get the idea."

"It had nothing to do with the scene we were shooting then," Cartwright recalled. "Mimi was talking about the scene at Karen's house where we're in our school uniforms, and they discover I'm a kleptomaniac; that's why I have to tell the lie, and she hits me. It's funny, Miriam Hopkins wasn't even there when we shot that scene—and neither was Mimi, so what she said was totally out of context."[25]

Except for the slapping incident, Miriam's behavior was exemplary. Even so, Cartwright recalled Miriam was "a presence," telling stories and "always a bit louder than life."[26]

Miriam was "louder than life." Her words tumbled out rapidly, spiced with a wicked wit. She often bragged about her love to gab: "I could talk all the time. I just love to shoot off my head—it's so much fun, don't you think so?"[27]

William Wyler didn't believe so but openly accepted his friend's "nonstop talking" and once likened her to the old joke of "being vaccinated with a phonograph needle." Cartwright recalled that between scenes on *The Children's Hour*, Miriam would sit with Wyler (who was deaf in one ear) as he worked and "tell him stories and just go on and on" until finally he would say, "Miriam, you're on my deaf ear. Come over to my other ear" (which, in actuality, *was* his deaf ear). Now, not hearing her clearly, he could work in peace with an occasional "Uh-huh, uh-huh" while Miriam prattled on.

In any case, Miriam had a great time with her *Children's Hour* costars, calling Shirley MacLaine "great fun" and Audrey Hepburn "a dear." As for James Garner, one day she closed her eyes as he rehearsed a scene with Audrey Hepburn to see if it "rang true." Captivated, she predicted, "Yes, young man, you're going to make it."[28]

While Miriam prophesied a successful future for Garner, she couldn't do the same for *The Children's Hour*. The film opened to mixed reviews. While Hedda Hopper reported that Audrey Hepburn and Shirley MacLaine gave "two of the greatest performances I've ever seen" and called Fay Bainter and Miriam Hopkins "superb," Philip K. Scheuer of the *Los Angeles Times* said the film seemed "contrived, that it has a false air from start to finish." Still, he admitted that Wyler had pulled "sensitive professional performances" from his stars, including Miriam.[29]

Shirley MacLaine felt the film would have been more powerful had Wyler had less "trepidation" about the subject matter. "It was 1961 and nobody had done that (taken on homosexuality as a theme)," she said, recalling "scenes of brushing each other's hair or ironing clothes" that Wyler cut. In doing so, MacLaine felt it "pared the picture down a little bit."[30]

After decades of strife and recriminations, Miriam's relationship with her mother had mellowed. However, they still had little affection for one other. Nevertheless, she remained a devoted daughter—at least where Ellen's physical needs were concerned—promising that as long as her mother lived, she would "take care of her." She kept her word, but her "devotion" didn't include spending time with her mother. It did consist of a monthly stipend, the rent on an apartment in a select area of East Fifty-Seventh Street, and a maid. A friend noted that it was "very expensive for Miriam, but she never complained."[31]

"Whatever her excesses," said author George Eells, "she had breeding that instinctively caused her to do the decent thing—if it did not conflict with her career—and one of the decent things was to be nice to your family."[32]

Even at her advanced years, Ellen enjoyed good health and was active. In her mid-seventies, she considered marrying a poor Virginia farmer, and "with the income you give me," she told her daughter, "we could get along nicely." But before Miriam would give her blessing, she had the farmer vetted to be sure her mother was not making an unwise decision. In the end, Ellen didn't marry him.

At eighty-two, Ellen still danced at the Plaza Hotel, was the historian of the Virginia Society, and actively supported the Daughters of the American Revolution. On her eighty-fourth birthday, Miriam treated her to dinner at Quo Vadis, a classic, continental restaurant on East Sixty-Third Street.

Less than two weeks later, on the evening of December 10, 1962, Miriam called Ward Morehouse and his wife, Becky. Between the broken sobs and incoherent words, Morehouse deduced that Ellen was dead and Miriam was taking the body back to Georgia.

Campbell's was in charge of the funeral, holding services at the Episcopal Church of the Reincarnation on Madison Avenue, where Ellen's friends from the Daughters of the Confederacy and the Dixie Club could pay their last respects. As expected, her burial would be in the Dickinson family plot in Bainbridge, near her mother, Mildred, and her half-brother, Dixie.

In Bainbridge, Miriam had a bachelor friend, Clarke Gurley, with whom she had remained close since childhood. Each year on Dixie's birthday, she sent Gurley a check to put flowers on his grave. Gurley agreed to meet Miriam at the Tallahassee airport, the closest one to Bainbridge. For support, he brought along several friends she knew as a child to accompany her mother's body back to Oak City Cemetery.[33]

Despite their differences, Ellen's death had an unexpected effect on Miriam. When her plane landed at Tallahassee, Miriam appeared out of sorts; her friends assumed she was "ill with the flu or something." She apologized and wanted to go to a hotel, asking them to "bury her in Bainbridge" without her.[34]

"She *said* it was the flu," remarked Paul Kwilecki, a friend of Clarke Gurley's. "She went directly to a hotel in Tallahassee and was holed up in her room, and didn't come to the funeral. Clarke Gurley, who was there, said she was 'drunk as a coot.' She made the trip—a thousand miles from New York to Tallahassee—but she didn't make the forty-mile trip from Tallahassee to Bainbridge for the funeral. She turned around the next day and flew back to New York."[35]

Miriam went as far as she could for the woman that she battled with for six decades. Whether it was guilt, regret, or something else, the strain and emotion overcame her.

After the New Year, Stanley Raiff, a producer and director of summer stock and regional theater in New York, was casting a new play that was "perfect for her." Raiff called her, and she invited him to "come over and talk with me."

The play was *Riverside Drive*, conceived as two one-act plays. The first, *Damn You Scarlett O'Hara*, was about a woman who tries to carry on her husband's publishing business after his death and the other, *All My Pretty Little Ones*, concerned an actress who had lost three sons in the war. Each play required two performers. Her longtime friend, Basil Rathbone, was playing the male lead. The script interested her, but when Rathbone backed out for personal reasons, she became more involved and suggested changes in the plot and the characters' motivation.

Even though John Donovan, Raiff's companion at the time, was the playwright, Miriam insisted on handling the rewrites. For hours, she sat on the floor, cutting up the script and piecing it back together so "it suited her particular talent and style."[36]

While getting the play in shape, she also accepted a television role in the drama *Route 66*, a popular anthology series filmed on location. For this episode, it was Punta Gorda, Florida, with series regulars Glenn Corbett and Martin Milner. Miriam followed that with an outstanding performance on the popular science fiction program *The Outer Limits*. In it, Miriam plays Mary Kry, a woman whose husband disappears on their wedding night. He mistakenly unwrapped a gift labeled "Don't Open Till Doomsday" and was transported into the box, where an alien creature lurks. For thirty years, his bride waited, hoping someone would look into the box and take his place.

David Frankham, a veteran of dozens of television shows, played the youthful bridegroom but had no scenes with Miriam. "My scenes were shot before she began filming," Frankham recalled. "She did come on set to introduce herself, and I was frankly thrilled to meet somebody from Hollywood's Golden Age. She announced she was asking for script changes and would remain at her hotel until producers met her demands. So it may have been a rather turbulent shoot!"[37]

While she was away, she was often lonely and would call Stan Raiff in the early morning hours, "slightly inebriated, but wanting to talk." According to Raiff, he was "her protégé" and she was going to make him a star.[38]

When she returned to New York from Los Angeles, *Riverside Drive* went into rehearsals at the Theatre De Lys. Miriam complained about the director, Douglas Seale, and asked Raiff to replace him with Rouben Mamoulian, who would direct her "doing a tap dance on my hands with my drawers showing." But Raiff nixed that idea and kept Seale.[39]

Miriam submitted the names of several suitable actors to replace Basil Rathbone, but Raiff selected Donald Woods. Woods, who in the 1930s had the moniker "King of the Bs" for his mostly low-budget films, arrived on Christmas night 1963, in time for the first table reading.

"Right there I made a mistake," John Donovan recalled. "[Miriam] announced she should be looking at the *New York Times* instead of the *Daily News*. I tried to reason with her, pointing out it was a character part, and she said, 'But I would never buy the *Daily News*,' and I told her, 'This is not *you*. I know you would never buy the *News*, but this woman would. She no longer will make the effort to read the *Times*.' And this became such a problem that the read-through came to a stand-still. From there on it was all downhill."[40]

Then, it appeared she hadn't memorized her lines. Even though Raiff cued her, she insisted on referring to the script. The play was scheduled to open in three or four days, so Raiff said, "Miriam we have to see what this play looks like and feels like; you really have to put the sides down."[41]

What's more, if rehearsals were at 11:00 a.m., she might show up at noon. Sometimes she arrived drunk. She would wander around the stage, improvising her lines and disorienting Donald Woods until he broke out in a rash. Miriam reassured him, "Don't worry, dear, I'll take care of you." That was the final straw for Douglas Seale; he resigned, but Raiff appeased him, and he returned.[42]

Three days before the preview, Miriam called in sick. Then, she wanted to accept a television role, but Raiff told her "no." That evening at rehearsal, she still carried her sides, so Raiff canceled the preview to give her more time, but two days later she failed to show up.

It was evident to Raiff the play wouldn't be ready on schedule. Infuriated by Miriam's unprofessionalism, he called her agent and requested Sylvia Sidney to replace her. The agent told Miriam, and within the hour she was at the theater, smiling and greeting everyone as if nothing was wrong. She suggested they start rehearsing. Donovan and Seale silently backed away to allow Raiff to fire her. Not certain if she knew her lines, Raiff explained that he had to replace her. According to Raiff, she "got really pissed off" and said, "That's ridiculous, there's no reason to fire me."

Then she gave an impromptu "performance" that could have been from a movie. She told Raiff, "I will show you that I know every line in this play."[43]

Defiantly, Miriam walked the darkened aisle to the stage and turned to face her accusers. After a dramatic pause, she began reciting the lines in the play including those of her costar to prove that she knew them. "See, that's what I was trying to tell you," she screamed when she finished. "You can't fire me from some tacky little off-Broadway theater. Don't you realize who I am? I'm Miriam Hopkins!" Furious, she stormed off the stage to her dressing room.

Raiff waited for her to return, but after a few minutes, he went to her dressing room to tell her he was locking the theater. He offered to call her a taxi. Miriam ignored him as she gathered her belongings, including a bucket she had borrowed from a local bar to ice her champagne. After leaving the theater, she went to the bar, threw the empty bucket across the floor, and slammed the door without saying a word. "And that was the end of it, and she left," Raiff said. "We never spoke again."[44]

Sylvia Sidney went on as Miriam's replacement. "Curiously enough, while *Riverside Drive* obviously was not a successful evening of the theater," John Donavan said, "it was very good for Sylvia, and Miriam could have had the same kind of tremendous personal notices."[45]

Albert Zugsmith was the producer of such titles as *Female on the Beach*, with Joan Crawford, *The Incredible Shrinking Man*, and the Orson Welles thriller *Touch of Evil*. His more recent films were the exploitation titles *Sex Kittens Go to College* and *Confessions of an Opium Eater*.

In April 1964, Zugsmith contacted Miriam to make a movie for him in West Berlin. Miriam had never heard of him, but Michael was at the Nancy-Ochey Air Base in France, so she figured it would almost be a free trip to visit him and agreed. But when Zugsmith explained her role—the madam of the brothel in *Fanny Hill*—Miriam responded with a disheartened, "Oh."[46]

Fanny Hill was an adaptation of John Cleland's 1748 erotic English novel *Memoirs of a Woman of Pleasure*, which after its first publication became one of the most prosecuted and widely banned books in history. In the United States, people read the book for the first time in 1963—more than two centuries after its controversial debut—and even then it was after a prolonged court battle. Miriam had not read *Fanny Hill*, for if she had, she "would never have done the movie." She learned enough about the novel's plot to state that *Fanny Hill*, the movie, "hadn't anything to do with the book." Her part was a composite, "in other words, I'm five madams rolled into one."[47]

Fanny Hill's director, Russ Meyer, was known for low-budget sexploitation films with such titles as *The Immortal Mr. Teas* and *Wild Gals of the Naked West*, and his films frequently showed a profit. He had yet to make his better-known films such as *Faster, Pussycat! Kill! Kill!* and *Beyond the Valley of the Dolls*.

A coproduction between Zugsmith and German producer Artur Brauner (*The Death Ray of Dr. Mabuse*), *Fanny Hill* starred Leticia Roman, whose first film had been in the 1960 Elvis Presley star vehicle *G.I. Blues*. Cast in the title role, Roman would bring to life Cleland's naive farm girl who fails to realize her dearly loved "adoptive mother," Mrs. Brown (Hopkins), is, in fact, a madam and all the "friends of the family" are dirty old men after her virginal body. Included in the cast was Hollywood veteran Alexander D'Arcy and as Fanny's suitor, nineteen-year-old Ulli Lommel, a former Polish-born German child actor who would later become a frequent Rainer Werner Fassbinder collaborator.

Although cast in what amounted to a supporting role, for the first time in thirty years Miriam received top billing in a film.

On April 8, 1964, Miriam renewed her passport and two days later boarded a Pan American Airways flight to Frankfurt. From there she traveled to Berlin. Unbeknownst to her, the passport renewal was questioned by the FBI because of her past connections to alleged Communist fronts in the late 1930s and early 1940s. About six weeks later, on May 20, on a pretext redacted from her FBI file, a special agent interviewed her at the Berlin Hilton Hotel. She explained that she was making a film and would be in Germany for at least three months. The agency accepted her explanation and the incident was closed.[48]

Costar Ulli Lommel called the *Fanny Hill* experience "totally insane, totally unpleasant, total chaos." Right away, Meyer, who felt the film should have a serious tone, disagreed with Albert Zugsmith, who wanted to broaden the comedy; Zugsmith, who held the purse strings, won. Leticia Roman also became a problem, revealing after the start of filming that she was both married *and* pregnant. Compounding matters, Lommel recalled Roman "didn't want to be sexy" in what should have been her steamy scenes with him, while Miriam wandered around in "a world of her own."

Meyer, however, had no complaints about Miriam's conduct. In fact, he remembered her as "a delight" and a "real pistol of a gal"; she called him "Sonny." This more sociable behavior, atypical for her, might have several explanations: perhaps she was mellowing, or perhaps she trusted Meyer's direction.[49]

Most likely, Miriam was acquiescent on *Fanny Hill* because she didn't care. According to Becky Morehouse, with the ridiculous script and the on-the-set "drama" around her, Miriam could only "laugh and admit defeat." She had played risqué parts on Broadway and during her pre-Code days at Paramount, but *Fanny Hill* was not risqué; it was simply "ludicrous."

This laissez-faire attitude could be the reason for one of the most unusual stories about Miriam. Several years after her death, historian David Del Valle interviewed Russ Meyer on his cable access show, *Sinister Image*. Meyer narrated a story that purportedly occurred after an unusually long day of filming.

According to Meyer, Miriam asked if he would be free to "do the town." Since Meyer enjoyed having a good time, he asked what she had in mind. She looked him in the eye and said, "Russ, tonight I am looking to party with the ladies if you catch my drift." He told Del Valle that they drove into Berlin's Red Light District looking "for just the right ladies for Miss Hopkins' pleasure."[50]

Now, what would explain Miriam's out of the ordinary behavior? There is no evidence she ever had a lesbian encounter or even a sexual interest in women.

In his biography *Fasten Your Seatbelts: The Passionate Life of Bette Davis*, author Lawrence Quirk claims, without providing any sources, that Miriam was bisexual and had made advances on Davis when they first met in Rochester, adding she had girlfriends at the time. Of all of Davis's biographers, Quirk is the only one to make this accusation. In fact, Davis herself, hardly a Hopkins fan, never alluded to it.

In Russ Meyer's retelling, he never confirmed whether Miriam went through with her quest to "party with the ladies." Either way, in the event such a request was made, it would be more plausible that Miriam, who had always been a sexually liberated woman, was curious about Berlin's Red Light District. An excursion into the city's underworld could be research for her role as the madam of a brothel.

When *Fanny Hill* premiered in the United States, the reviews were mixed. Now an elderly remnant of the old Hollywood media, Louella Parsons called the title character a "female Tom Jones!" The *Boston Globe* referred to the film as a "cynically naughty story," adding that it was not the "original novel" and that Miriam played her role "with gay insouciance." Another reviewer noted that a "rather disinterested-looking Miriam Hopkins is given no chance to display either nostalgic appeal or comic subtlety."[51]

In August 1965, singer and actress Judy Garland was leasing Sutton Place, but according to Miriam she was a poor tenant, "pasting telegrams on the walls." At the same time, Miriam was forced to give up the lease on her East Forty-Eighth Street penthouse, where she had lived for the past eight years.

With no roof over her head, she was "free and foot-loose" and returned to Los Angeles. After consulting her astrologer, she perused the Sunday ads but couldn't find anything suitable to rent. Not wanting to spend her summer building bookshelves, she stored her possessions and moved into the furnished house of her friend actor Edwin Ashley. It was tropical, "like living in a corner of Trader Vic's," was beautifully decorated, with a big lanai, and was "definitely a party house."[52]

Not long after, Miriam was offered a supporting role as Robert Redford's mother in an adaptation of Horton Foote's book and play *The Chase.* She called it a "field day for actors," a story of continuous action from one afternoon through the morning of the following day.

In it, a young man (Robert Redford) escapes from prison while the sheriff (film idol Marlon Brando) pursues him. From Lillian Hellman's adapted screenplay, Arthur Penn directed. Miriam called Brando and Penn "wonderful and cooperative, they make me feel like a debutante. They've given me five of the best scenes I've ever had on screen."[53]

However, that wasn't the consensus of everyone. Arthur Penn tried to appease her and soften her exaggerated, sometimes hysterical, performances, especially where she berates Marlon Brando, believing he intends to kill her son.

During rehearsals on the courthouse set, Miriam paced through her scene. "Liar, murderer, liar, murderer," she repeated in a reserved, untried way. She was anxious, realizing she could go over-the-top, so she consulted with Penn. "I was concerned about the emotional scenes," Miriam admitted, "afraid I might get too hammy, so I asked Arthur Penn about it. He said to let go. So when I did a scene with Brando who plays on a rather low key and I came out with 'You're a murderer!' I can assure you the audience will know I'm there."[54]

Critics agreed, but not positively. That scene was pointed out in many reviews. "And Miss Hopkins goes hysterical in her big scene with enviable lung power," wrote the *Motion Picture Herald*. However, the *Saturday Review* was less than kind when they suggested it was, "well—best to avert one's embarrassed eyes from the screen when she's on."[55]

The film itself didn't fare better. At the New York preview, the "audience jeered loudly at the film's overheated dramatics and inappropriate performances," and *Life* magazine called *The Chase* a "modest failure. Thanks to the expenditure of a great deal of time, money and talent, it has been transferred into a disaster of awesome proportions."[56]

20

The Final Years

Miriam always looked for opportunities to make money and often invested in her plays, but at the time there were no prospects. She sought advice from Eliot Janeway, who two decades earlier had rescued her from the advances of former presidential candidate Wendell Willkie. On Janeway's advice, she invested in shopping malls, but something went wrong, and she lost a fortune.

To cover her losses, she sold paintings from her art collection—the Picasso, the Renoir, and the Monet. "She had many beautiful, famous paintings," Michael remembered, "so she got rid of them to live." Although she hated parting with them, it was more painful to sell Sutton Place, the home she had loved for more than three decades.[1]

At the time, actress Sheila MacRae, who gained fame on television as Jackie Gleason's wife, Alice, on *The Honeymooners*, was leasing the house after separating from her husband, singer Gordon MacRae. MacRae loved the house, so when Miriam placed it on the market, she made an offer. Dressed in black and wearing pearls and diamonds, Miriam discussed the sale with MacRae over a cup of tea. "I'll be happy if this house becomes yours," Miriam told her. "I've lived in a lot of places, but this was my favorite."

For several minutes, Miriam reminisced about "many other houses, apartments, parcels of real estate she owned here, there, and everywhere."

"I will cherish your house, Miss Hopkins," MacRae promised.[2]

Miriam sold 13 Sutton Place for $500,000; not bad considering she paid $20,000 for the property in 1934. "Miriam wasn't in poverty," Tom admitted, "but she was notched down to middle class. She lost over a million dollars in that bad investment."[3] Miriam put some belongings in storage and sent the rest to her apartment at the Shoreham Towers in West Hollywood.

Miriam had been friends with Ward Morehouse for forty-three years, ever since he was a columnist for the *Brooklyn Times* and she had her first significant Broadway role, in *Little Jessie James*. "I enjoyed something of a best-friend relationship with Miriam Hopkins," Morehouse remembered, "but even so, there were times when she became annoyed with me. During such a period, she made a point of not inviting me to a big party she was giving for theater and screen people. The next day, a little jittery and more than a little contrite, she mailed me a check for three thousand dollars as her investment in a play of mine, *Miss Quiss*."[4]

Another time, Miriam tossed his tie clasp from the top floor of the Hotel Lincoln, because she didn't like the design. Two hours later a repentant Miriam sent Morehouse a ruby-studded platinum clasp from Tiffany's.

Becky Morehouse, his fourth and last wife, suspected there was more between them than friendship. "I'm sure that they had an affair back in the 20s," Becky insisted. However, Ward Morehouse III, the writer's son by his second wife, actress June Marlowe, was not convinced. "I don't know whether they were lovers or not," Morehouse surmised, "or if he had a fling with her or was good friends. Miriam was a live wire. Even then she bubbled with enthusiasm and was the life of the party. My father was quite pointed and humorous himself. She amused him, but in her presence he let her do the talking. They were obviously at ease with each other."[5]

On December 7, 1966, Miriam was at the Shoreham preparing for dinner when she saw Morehouse's photograph flash across the television. The news anchor announced that the seventy-one-year-old writer had died. His death hit her hard. The following day, she called Becky and invited her to California for a visit. "I never knew her well before Ward died," Becky said. "I met Miriam for the first time at a party Jean Dalrymple gave for me not long after Ward and I married. And Miriam came and brought a dozen red roses for me. That's my first memory of her."

Miriam would occasionally invite Becky to visit, until finally she agreed. When she arrived, Miriam was welcoming, but Becky had misgivings until she found a big silver bowl filled with floating magnolias in her room. From then she felt comfortable, calling the gesture "incredibly beautiful and thoughtful."

It was days before press agents knew Becky was in town and asked her to do interviews. Magazine editors would call in the morning when

"'Madam' was sleeping," but when they did, the phone rang in Miriam's bedroom, "and boy she would hit the ceiling." Becky hoped that Miriam didn't regret her hospitality. To be sure it never happened again, Miriam had the telephone company fix it so the phone rang in Becky's room when the call was for her.[6]

One day, Anatole Litvak invited Miriam to the premiere of his recent film, *The Night of the Generals*, but she refused to go. She was still holding a grudge over Litvak's alleged public indiscretion with Paulette Goddard some thirty years earlier. But she wanted Becky to go and arranged for a friend to escort her. "When we got back," Becky said, "she was waiting for my report. So I thought I'd have some fun, and I said, 'Oh Miriam, I saw Mr. Litvak, and he sent his dearest love to you.' And she bought it at first, and then she realized I was putting her on; she threw a pillow at me. She was terribly funny."[7]

Another time, Miriam received an invitation to the Malibu home of actress Sally Blane, a sister of Loretta Young. Miriam gave her regrets but convinced Becky to go and again arranged for a date—a man with a convertible, and besides, Becky reasoned, "he was amusing." But after an hour, Miriam walked in the door; she had driven herself in her blue-gray Mustang. "Miriam was a terrible driver," Becky remembered. "A Los Angeles cop once told her, 'Lady, you ought not to be driving.'"[8]

In no time, they were good friends; both southern women, Georgia-born with southern accents. However, Miriam's drawl was a sensitive topic, one she couldn't accept.

During a stay in New York, they went to Quo Vadis, a restaurant where violinists serenaded the guests. As they were seated at their banquette, a couple next to them was leaving. However, when they saw Miriam, they sat back down. Later, the man came over and in a courtly manner said, "Miss Hopkins, we've been sitting here enjoying your Southern accent."

"He couldn't have said anything more inflammatory," Becky recalled.

Miriam stiffened and looked the couple in the eye: "Mrs. Morehouse has a Southern accent; I don't have a Southern accent. I can't have an accent—I'm an actress."[9]

Miriam's West Hollywood apartment was sixty miles from Riverside and March Air Force Base, where Michael was stationed. Miriam now had a unique chance to get reacquainted with her daughter-in-law, Chris. Tom recalled that his mother and Miriam had their differences. It was a "battle of wills," especially since Chris was raising Tom as Catholic.

Miriam, an Episcopalian, was private about *her* religion, but according to Tom, she believed in God, "but she never discussed it."[10]

Both women were similar. Like Miriam, Chris was intelligent and dominant. And now, two strong personalities were in Michael and Tom's life, and both wanted Tom to "know his stuff." Miriam wanted to guide Tom's upbringing and education with servants and boarding schools. Finally, Chris confronted her when Michael would not, telling Miriam, "That's not going to happen to my son." Chris respected her elders, but Miriam was interfering, so she confronted her. "I'm glad I did because it liberated me, and I became a stronger person," Chris recalled. "There's no doubt Miriam wanted things her way, but I wasn't about to do that. We had some tests, and finally, I stood up to her, and when I did, we became almost best friends; there were no more problems. But she was not going to direct me."[11]

Miriam gave in to her daughter-in-law's will but still exercised her grandmotherly prerogative by "spoiling" her grandson. For Tom, his time with Miriam was "all expenses paid"—he could do no wrong.

For Michael, however, it was hard to watch his mother spoil Tom. He remembered his childhood of private schools from the age of eight and of never getting the attention he wanted. As a toddler, Michael was with Miriam constantly. But when he reached school age, she was busy salvaging her career and sent him to a string of boarding schools. Mother and son grew apart. Miriam loved Michael, and with Tom, she tried to redeem herself, but unknowingly she caused Michael pain.

Miriam's visits to Riverside were rare. Once, when she slipped on her Shoreham bathroom's marble floor and injured her knee, Michael insisted that she stay with them. Uncomfortable in Michael's two-bedroom house on Bel Air Avenue, she checked into the nearby Mission Inn, returning only in the morning.

Michael refused to argue, so he visited her. For two Sundays a month, they drove to West Hollywood for Miriam's afternoon salons. It became a tradition and an obligation. According to Michael, Miriam's visitors were "mostly writers." With William Saroyan or Tennessee Williams as her guests, "her gatherings were interesting; it wasn't boring."[12]

Miriam orchestrated her parties by coordinating and engaging guests in conversation. She was *the* personality. "Since I'm her grandson, I might be subjective," Tom admitted. "But she had a great presence among everyone else."[13]

Actors rarely attended, yet Vincent Price, Shelley Winters, or Loretta Young might be there. Edward G. Robinson, who had tangled with her on *Barbary Coast* three decades earlier, was also a guest. Tom recalled that Robinson, a "quiet man," always talked to him. "I think he connected with me because he had problems with his son. He had a demeanor that for a teenager proved he was a fascinating person."[14]

For entertainment, Miriam used Tarot cards, discussed numerology, astrology, and the occult, and told stories of the late actor Ronald Colman, who she swore haunted her Shoreham apartment.

At one party, she insisted on reading the palm of actor and carnival barker Peter Garey, but he politely refused. A carnival palm reader once told him he would die young. Even though he wasn't a believer, he had no interest in having another reading. Miriam persisted until he gave her his palm. She gazed at it for several moments, and then told him, "Stop worrying! You're not going to die. You may have an accident that will leave you paralyzed from the neck down, but you'll live to a ripe old age." Garey wondered whether she was serious or pulling his leg.[15]

Her curiosity about mystics and the occult surprised her closest friends. Becky Morehouse never questioned her about it but admitted that Miriam "had many peculiarities. If you said you had a new apartment, she would ask what number it was, and you'd tell her, and she'd say, 'Oh that's a bad number.' Lord help us."[16]

Miriam was taught that a southern belle should believe as her mother and her mother's mother before her. But growing up independently minded, she disregarded her mother's passions and replaced them with nonconformist beliefs that she learned from her uncle Dixie, the "free thinker" of the family.

Sometimes, however, Miriam's actions contradicted her liberal convictions. Rose Hobart, her *Dr. Jekyll and Mr. Hyde* costar, recalled that at the Fiftieth Anniversary Equity Ball in 1963, she was directing the seating and had a table for people that had worked with her. One of them, she said, was "a Negro, a friend of mine." When Miriam refused to sit at their table, presumably because of Hobart's "Negro" friend, Hobart told her, "Well, don't, then, girl. Go somewhere else."[17]

Singer Lena Horne recalled meeting Miriam at Cole Porter's home, where she was invited to sing. She didn't mind performing with close friends, but "it's different when you walk into a room where you don't know anyone, and you're presented as sort of the dessert." It was awkward for her. "Miriam Hopkins was there," Horne recalled, "and she started telling me how I was different from other black people she knew in the South. She was maybe being sweet, but it was very condescending."[18]

Could Miriam have been prejudiced or was she ignorant of her actions? According to Michael, his mother never spoke disparagingly of African Americans, at least not in his presence, and nor did she discriminate.

At the time, she had two African American manservants—Perry in New York and Charles in Los Angeles. According to Michael, they may have been employees, but they were also her friends.

Florence Sundstrom, Miriam's *Look Homeward, Angel* costar, celebrated Thanksgiving one year at Sutton Place. "[Miriam] arranged the tables so that Mama [Ellen] was sitting with three other people," Sundstrom remembered. "And she said to me, 'Flo, I've invited Perry as a guest today. You don't mind if he sits with us, do you?' I said, 'Of course not,' because Perry was a friend."

Ellen, however, was bothered that Perry was eating at their table. "She was still a Southern belle," Sundstrom said, "and finally Mims turned around and withered her with, 'Mother, this is Thanksgiving, and Perry has just as much right to be thankful as you do.'"[19]

At the Shoreham, Charles Whitfield cared for Miriam. Charles was her butler, cooked her meals, and chauffeured her blue-gray Mustang, yet theirs was a hot-tempered bond that people likened to marriage. Becky Morehouse knew both Perry and Charles. She recalled a party Miriam gave for her one evening at the Shoreham:

"Before everyone arrived, she [Miriam] walked over to the bar and said, 'Come over and let's have a glass of personality.' And Charles, I think he had a couple of glasses of personality himself. When the Edward Ashley's arrived—they were good friends of Miriam's—Charles announced them as the Duke and Duchess. British royalty in other words. Miriam was furious. 'I'm going to break your neck,' she told him. She thought it was rude."[20]

Another evening, the phonograph was not working, and Miriam fiddled with it, trying to get it to play. "Charles, you broke this," she shouted at him in front of her surprised guests. He said, "I did not. You broke it!"

"They were literally screaming at one another," said director Curtis Harrington, a friend who was at the party. "She turned on her heel and headed for her bedroom."

"Are you going to leave your guests?" Charles yelled after her.

"Yes," she shouted and slammed the door.

"Now we all sort of made polite conversation from three to five minutes," Harrington said, "and suddenly she emerged from the bedroom as if nothing had happened."[21]

After their fights, Charles would sometimes walk out, leaving Miriam to fend for herself, which she couldn't do. Then, someone would mediate and convince Charles to return, prompting Miriam's apology and a promise to behave; it was a routine they repeated. But it was clear they cared for one another, and Charles took his responsibilities seriously.

At sixty-seven years old, Miriam wanted people to remember her. Stan Raiff, who fired her from *Riverside Drive*, believed that recognition was important to her: "At that point in her life she wasn't a household name anymore, not everyone would instantly recognize her. I think that annoyed her."[22]

Years earlier, when she was traveling with Ward Morehouse and his second wife, actress Joan Marlowe, to his vacation home in the Thousand Islands, they stopped for gas and, as a joke, Morehouse told the station attendant that a movie star was outside and to ask for her autograph. Two women were in the car: Marlowe who was pretty and barely twenty years old, and Miriam, in her early forties. Morehouse didn't tell him which woman was the movie star, so when the attendant asked for Marlowe's autograph, Miriam nearly "blew a gasket."

"I'm going back to New York; this is outrageous!" Miriam screamed from the back seat. "I'm the movie star in this car. Don't you know who I am? I'm Miriam Hopkins." When she calmed down, the apologetic and terrified attendant got her autograph as well.[23]

Miriam was growing more pessimistic about her life and career. When she sold Sutton Place, Sheila MacRae asked her, "Was it ever fun in Hollywood when you were there, way back when?"

"Miriam sat quiet for a long time," MacRae recalled, "then with a shrug of her shoulder and a shake of her head said, 'There is no Hollywood any more. It's just a post office and a phone no one ever answers.'"[24]

She was pleased when Curtis Harrington offered her a part in his new Universal project. She liked his latest film, *Games*, and after reading the new script agreed to do it with one stipulation. "But my price was set by *The Chase*," she told him. "I get five thousand dollars a week, and I have a limousine pick me up in the morning and take me home at night. If you can't pay it, there's no use discussing it. We'll just be friends."[25]

As she aged, her priorities reversed; money became important, more so than the script. Regrettably, her salary demands were beyond Harrington's budget. For Miriam, when Hollywood did answer, the price had to be right.

Even so, Miriam didn't remain idle. In June 1969, she was invited to be on the popular television sitcom *The Flying Nun*. In the episode "Bertrille and the Silent Flicks," she played Sister Adelaide, a nun who once was a glamorous silent movie star famed for her sultry role in the film *Desert Madness*, which contained the longest kiss on record. "We're delighted to get such a famous star for this role," said Jon Epstein, the producer. "It was the script which convinced her to do it. It's a delightful role and a charming story."[26]

When asked why she took the role, she said it was "interesting. I only do things that interest me. This did."

By all accounts, she impressed a young Sally Field. "It really was amazing working with her. It gave us a new awareness, a new insight into professionalism. Miss Hopkins was always prepared, even if the order of scenes was changed. She was much too polite to say so, but I think she considered our work very easy because there are so many short scenes."[27]

When *The Flying Nun* episode aired, director, producer, and writer Donald Wolfe was casting *The Comeback*, a low-budget independent film. Wolfe, who had made one other film nine years earlier, was searching for an actress to play an aging movie star whose career had ended. The actress lived in her crumbling Hollywood mansion surrounded by an odd group of people who tended to her every need. When Wolfe saw Miriam on *The Flying Nun*, he knew he had found his star.

Wolfe envisioned his screenplay as a cross between *Sunset Boulevard* and *Whatever Happened to Baby Jane?* and this is how he pitched it to Miriam. He reminded her how successful *Baby Jane* had been for Bette Davis. She accepted the part without reading the script, because Wolfe met her salary demands.

Filming began in November 1969, with location photography at a mansion that many believed was the former estate of the silent film actress Norma Talmadge. The credits at the end of the film confirm this, but there's no evidence that Talmadge ever lived there. In any event, the walled and gated villa, built in the late 1920s, had fallen into disrepair but was still an impressive sight. It was perfect for the film.

Miriam reported to Producers Studio on Melrose and Bronson,

across from Paramount. For the supporting cast, Wolfe hired old-time actresses Minta Durfee Arbuckle, Florence Lake, and 1936's Best Supporting Actress Oscar winner, Gale Sondergaard (*Anthony Adverse*), who Miriam hadn't seen in more than twenty years.

In the role of the psychopathic serial killer who preys on middle-aged women, Wolfe cast David Garfield (billed as John David Garfield), the son of the late Warner Bros. star John Garfield, who Miriam knew casually from her political efforts in the 1930s. Up to that point, Garfield had been in a handful of minor stage, television, and film roles, but he had never clicked with audiences.

The Comeback, retitled *Savage Intruder* for the video market, could be filed under the so-bad-it's-good film. It was not the same quality of either *Sunset Boulevard* or *Whatever Happened to Baby Jane?* and not worthy of Miriam's talent or of Gale Sondergaard's.

The film has many camp moments, such as when Miriam's character, actress Katharine Packard, is drunk, sitting on a float in the Hollywood Christmas parade. A reporter asks what she thinks of the event, and she replies, "Hollywood used to be a great town full of glamour; now it is full of fags and freaks." In another scene at a hippie drug party, a midget dealer offers her LSD. She tells her host, "The only trips I take are to Europe."[28]

It's possible that *Savage Intruder* was never released to American theaters, as there are no reviews in *Variety,* the *New York Times*, or any recognized periodical. Reportedly it was shown at private Hollywood parties from 1970 to possibly 1973 before being released on video. "Deliciously seedy and sadistic," wrote Fred Beldin for the *All Movie Guide,* "with wild LSD flashbacks, convincing bloodshed and near-nude scene from aging star Miriam Hopkins. . . . Too sluggishly paced to be a lost classic, nonetheless an unsettling obscurity that might be worth a look for its period atmosphere and nasty disposition."[29]

It is doubtful that Miriam saw the film and probably better that she didn't. She cashed her check and moved on. However, it's regrettable that this is her last feature film.

At her age, men no longer mattered. Dating ended for her when a former flame stopped calling without an explanation. She was devastated. "I feel as if I'd been put down the disposal with the cold water running." While parties no longer held their appeal, she had several gay friends, such as Jim White, an importer from New York, to serve as escorts. After all, a southern woman should never arrive at a party alone.[30]

Instead, she preferred her bedroom at the Shoreham, blackout shades pulled, listening to the music of her former *The Smiling Lieutenant* costar Maurice Chevalier while drinking champagne and reading. She slept all day and stayed up all night, and when she was bored, she would telephone friends no matter the hour. "She was a night owl," Becky recalled. "Sometimes she'd call friends in New York around 11 o'clock when everyone was asleep. Jim White called her 'The Midnight Caller.'"[31]

Ruby also received many late-night calls. Margot recalled: "I learned early if the phone rang at midnight it would be Miriam. Either way, my routine was the same. I'd shuffle sleepily into the kitchen, make a big pot of tea which I'd put down in front of mom and shuffle on back to bed while she sat patiently listening and sipping her tea."[32]

When friends would visit, they dined in her bedroom. Her excessive drinking and odd eating habits worried some. She suffered from emphysema and dental problems, and many believed her heart ailment was mild, despite the nitroglycerine she kept in her purse and in a bottle on her bedside table.

The years of sun worshipping had taken its toll on her skin. "She was crazy about the sun and having a tan," Becky said. "She would use one of those reflecting mirrors. If she hadn't done that she would have looked better; she ruined her skin."

For some time, Miriam contemplated moving from the Shoreham but couldn't decide whether to stay in California or return to New York. She would go back and forth. "She liked to go to fortune tellers and psychics," Becky remembered. "I went with her a couple of times and her first question would always be, 'Should I move to California or New York.'"[33]

Until she decided, or a psychic decided for her, Miriam watched television until the early morning hours, read the latest best sellers, and essentially became a recluse.

21

"If I Had to Do It Over Again"

In the beginning months of 1972, Becky Morehouse was in Los Angeles attending several press junkets and conducting interviews. When United Artists learned she was visiting Miriam, they asked she bring her to a luncheon they were hosting. Becky tried with her "tremendous persuasive qualities" to get Miriam to go, but she would not go. "Oh boy, she could be like that—stubborn. 'Why would I go to that?' she would say."

At the luncheon, tables seating ten or twelve packed the room. It was an awkward situation; no one was talking or making an effort to be friendly, including Becky. Then, Miriam walks in and heads for Becky's table. "You all look like dumb statues. I'm Miriam Hopkins, what's your excuse for living?" She joined them, and right away, everyone had a marvelous time. Afterward, she lectured Becky: "You can't sit with people and say nothing. It's just not civilized. It's not—Southern."[1]

In late spring, Miriam was invited to a sixtieth anniversary retrospective tribute to Paramount Pictures, to be held on July 12, 1972, at New York's Museum of Modern Art. *The Story of Temple Drake*, the scandalous 1933 adaptation of William Faulkner's sensational novel *Sanctuary*, was chosen for the festival's opening. The committee asked Becky to arrange for Miriam's trip to New York.

On the day she was to leave Los Angeles, Miriam fainted, delaying her departure an extra day. Becky panicked. "I was afraid she wasn't going to show. I had to alert everyone to postpone for a day. Then, at the airport, our first glimpse of her was in a wheelchair. Everyone's heart sank."[2]

At Miriam's request, Paramount put her at the Alrae, a residential hotel on East Sixty-Fourth Street. On opening night, all was in order. Miriam wore an elegant black dress and a huge pink satin stole. To avoid speaking, Miriam asked to sit on the aisle two-thirds of the way back. Even so, the committee director invited her to say a few words. Reluctantly, she briefly introduced the film and then gave credit to Ernst Lubitsch and Rouben Mamoulian for her career. She added that Paramount was the most creative of all the studios, and she was happy to be a part of their history. Then, the lights dimmed, and on-screen was a surprise short subject with Ginger Rogers and chorus girls in bellhop costumes.

"Who's that?" Miriam asked Jim White, her escort that evening, in a loud stage whisper. He was certain she recognized Rogers, but she insisted she did not. After the third song, she muttered, "I guess they changed their minds."

Finally, *Temple Drake* started. It had been several decades since she had last seen the film, and it was one of her favorites. But for Miriam and the audience, the years had not been kind to the movie. John Kobal, a writer and film historian, recalled that "the sophisticated, supposedly knowledgeable audience, jammed in for the company of stars and the food-and-wine binge that followed, sat, looked and laughed indiscriminately as the film unrolled."[3]

According to Becky, MoMA should have consulted Miriam about their choice of films. "She was disappointed in the picture. She thought it didn't stand up very well. When we got in the ladies' room, there were lines of women at each cubicle, and she announced, 'I've suffered more than any of you. So let me in.' And they laughed and let her in."[4]

At the champagne supper in the museum's outdoor sculpture garden, guests mingled, table-hopped, and listened to a jazz combo plunking out old Paramount hits such as "Isn't It Romantic" and "That Old Black Magic."

As people ate, Bill Kenly, a Paramount publicist, introduced the silent film actress Carmel Myers. "Hank" Potter was there, as were pop icon Andy Warhol and actresses Gloria Swanson, Sylvia Miles, Estelle Parsons, and Maureen Stapleton, who was a fan.

"I felt we would be friends," Stapleton later recalled to Tennessee Williams. "I mean as a child, watching the movies she was in. She was so beautiful and elegant, but smart, a little pissy, tough. I never dreamed I'd meet her, and then I did. And she liked me. Figure that out! Listen, I don't think it's too much to say that I survived childhood because of several movie stars, and one of those is Miriam Hopkins."[5]

Another guest Miriam "liked," and who liked her, was Andy Warhol. As guests arrived, Warhol took Polaroid shots of Gloria Swanson wearing a safari outfit, and she took candid shots of him. Sylvia Miles, who sat at Miriam's table asked, "Do you want to work, Miss Hopkins? Sometimes people don't want to do anything after a while."

"I want to work if I find the right part," Miriam replied coolly.

Then, Andy Warhol, Warhol collaborator Paul Morrissey, and John Kobal approached her table. Warhol handed Sylvia Miles a Polaroid snapshot of Miriam he had taken earlier that evening. "Miss Hopkins, I want to show you a beautiful picture Andy Warhol took of you. Andy wants you to autograph it just for him." As Warhol nodded, Miriam took a swig of champagne but refused to sign the Polaroid until she had a print of her own. Not discouraged, Warhol knelt next to her with his video camera. "If only I could make movies like that," he told her, referring to *Temple Drake*.[6]

"Well, of course, it's an old film," she told the three men standing admiringly around her. "I mean, we couldn't do the book the way we wanted to. . . . It wasn't easy. You know, Paramount was terrified of the censors." John Kobal reassured her she had been superb and the "film couldn't have been made any better or any more forcefully since."[7]

Miriam appeared uncomfortable at the flattering comments. For her, the evening was not proceeding as she had expected. These well-meaning, fawning types irritated her. Their praise felt empty. Here she was, at nearly seventy years old, in ill health and unable to find work. And her film, which at one time she considered "the best film I ever made," was laughed at by many of these same people.

The one bright spot that evening was Andy Warhol; he was interesting. This odd-looking, white-haired man knelt quietly beside her for the longest time "while she talked and talked and talked." Donald Oenslager, the set designer for the stage version of *Jezebel*, who had also decorated Miriam's Sutton Place townhouse, saw them together and asked Jim White if she knew who Andy Warhol was. "Not the foggiest," White replied. Miriam overheard their remarks and told them both to "shut up."[8]

After Warhol left, Miriam asked Becky, "Who was the young man with the white hair." Becky was floored. "My God, here's a woman with an art collection and all that. She'd been in California too long. She didn't know who he was. She was being obliging."[9]

Obliging or not, according to Jim White, she "loved Warhol." She talked a "blue streak" and would do so with anyone willing to listen to her talk nonstop. "Of course," he added, "if she'd seen him the next day, she wouldn't have recognized him. She never recognized anybody."[10]

All through the evening, a thickening circle of admirers formed around Miriam's table. It comprised not just friends and old fans but many young, avant-garde film lovers to whom she could only have been a statistic in another film age.

John Kobal was not about to let this opportunity pass; he asked Miriam for an interview. For a moment, she hesitated. She didn't understand people's interest in her career or anyone's career for that matter. Her director friend Curtis Harrington once described it as "something she had been a part of and it was not, in her opinion, worth discussing."[11]

Even the publicity, photos, and news clippings from that evening were of no interest. She admitted she had no "scrapbooks, clippings, or old photographs, or anything from my career." Becky concluded she had "no vanity," but it was, in all truthfulness, the "ultimate vanity." She didn't regret her career, even though she once remarked, "If I had to do it over again, I'd do everything different." She preferred looking to the future. Miriam knew she had a place in film history. The work she performed on both the screen and the stage was worthwhile, but then she forgot about it. According to Becky, she had no desire to "talk about it or read about it or to dwell on it at all."[12]

Reluctantly, Miriam agreed to Kobal's request. Even though there could be a better use of her time, she enjoyed talking, and she enjoyed the company of a young man. Kobal scheduled the interview for the following Sunday at her suite at the Alrae. The six hours they spent that day was not an interview, Kobal said, but a "performance."

"She directed my questions to the shores she wanted to step out on. She breathed theater and drama with every syllable; every so often lighting a cigarette, taking a swig of what she called 'tonic water' (though I remember she had said that vodka was 'mother's milk' to her), and erupting with bursts of laughter that took the place of intermissions as she fixed her eyes on me to be sure I was following her, and required me to define what it was I wanted."[13]

Miriam reminisced about her Paramount beginnings and about Lubitsch and Mamoulian, among other things. She spoke about Miss Davis and their long drawn-out feud and, as Kobal remembered, she called her "'Bette' with a frosting on her voice that suggested that while centuries of water might have flowed under the bridge, they hadn't washed away *that* sore."[14]

Sometimes she confused the facts, such as the year that one of her films was made, which is understandable. Her most puzzling misstatement was that she received "ten Academy [award] nominations," one of them for "Champagne Ivy," the dance-hall prostitute in *Dr. Jekyll and Mr. Hyde.* In reality, Miriam earned one nomination, for *Becky Sharp,* so her claim of multiple nominations was odd, unless it was the "tonic water" speaking. Surprisingly, Kobal did not challenge her but instead asked if she placed any emphasis on the Oscars. Her answer was confusing: "Listen, I don't know anything about whether I do or not. It seems like some people that get two or three. . . . I don't know—I never think about it. And other people, they sometimes had hired press agents to *plug* them. I don't mean that everybody does, but I mean some people. I don't know any of that."[15]

The interview ended on her favorite subject, poetry, and a private performance of the works of William Cullen Bryant and a recitation of a Christina Georgina Rossetti poem she once gave under a table in the Anita Loos play *Happy Birthday.*

That summer, Miriam stayed in New York at the Alrae as a guest of Paramount. Then, in mid-August, she had a mild heart attack and was admitted to the Harkness Pavilion of the New York-Presbyterian/Columbia University Medical Center. It had been more than sixty years since her exposure to rheumatic fever, and with the abuses to her body over the years from smoking, drinking, and overeating, her heart was giving out.

On September 9, she was discharged and returned to the Alrae. The doctor insisted she have a private nurse while staying at the hotel. The first night Ruby called and discovered the nurse had not arrived yet, so she insisted on going into the city and staying with Miriam until then, even though it was extremely late.[16]

Miriam still had not decided whether to live in New York or return to California to live somewhere other than the Shoreham. Becky was weary of Miriam's indecisiveness. "She was ill, and this particular night I said, 'If you're to get an apartment here [New York], call tonight, or you'll have to pay another month's rent.'" Becky waited as she made the call to relinquish her apartment at the Shoreham. No longer would she spend lonely nights drinking champagne and communing with the ghost of Ronald Colman. Visibly distraught, she lamented that she no longer had "a home anywhere now."[17]

According to Becky, for as many evenings as she could, she dined with

Miriam at the Alrae. At Miriam's insistence, they sometimes talked until the early morning hours. One night Becky found herself on the street at three o'clock in the morning. "I thought I must be crazy."[18]

On the evenings when Becky was not available, Ruby would travel into the city from Forest Hills to sit with her. They reminisced about their childhood in Savannah and Bainbridge and agreed that neither of them, at least in their minds, had become their mother.

Miriam's health was slowly deteriorating. She agreed to return to the hospital for more tests, but the evening before she was to be admitted, she collapsed in her suite. The nurse called Ruby, but Miriam quickly grabbed the telephone and explained she hadn't "really collapsed"; the doctor had examined her heart and said it had "slumped a little." He was going to call an ambulance, but Miriam would "definitely *not,* be seen on a stretcher." Instead, he ordered that she have no visitors or phone calls for a week, and then she could go to the hospital "in a civilized manner." Miriam, however, refused to follow the doctor's orders and received visitors at all hours and continued making late telephone calls.[19]

On the evening of October 8, 1972, Becky and Ruby were visiting and stayed late, until two o'clock the following morning. They discussed Miriam's seventieth birthday, which was approaching in ten days. Reaching seventy years was a significant milestone, and Miriam wanted to celebrate with plenty of guests, but considering her health, Becky suggested a much quieter affair.

After Becky and Ruby had gone and she was alone, except for the nurse in another room, Miriam called Michael in California, where it was past midnight. Michael was sleeping, but Chris asked if she wanted to wake him. "No, no, no I want to talk to you." They spoke for an hour, primarily about Miriam's illness. Chris asked why she didn't tell them she was ill, saying, "We would have come." According to Chris, it was because she "didn't want to burden anyone, that's the whole thing."[20]

At four o'clock, concerned that Ruby had arrived home safely, Miriam called her apartment. "Hello, hello," Margot answered, awakened from a deep sleep. Miriam was silent. "Mom, is that you?" she asked. Receiving no response, Margot hung up.[21]

An hour later, presumably after some light reading, Miriam headed to her bedroom. The sun was barely rising over the New York skyline, and if she was following her normal routine, she was preparing for bed. Then, the nurse was awakened by a noise outside her room. Concerned, she called out, "Miss Hopkins?" When there was no reply, she rushed out and found Miriam on the floor, dead from a massive coronary.

The nurse notified Miriam's lawyer before calling Ruby, who had arrived home just a short time earlier. "Miriam was dead," Margot recalled. Ruby dressed and made the trip back into the city.[22]

Later in Riverside, Michael was told of his mother's death. Tom was at Notre Dame High School but heard the news later that day. He said, "It was the first time I saw my father cry."[23]

Within hours, Miriam's death was reported on radio and television. The first print obituary that evening, in the *New York Post*, reported her place of birth incorrectly, as Bainbridge instead of Savannah, as did every obituary in every newspaper the following day. As the day progressed, the news of her death spread quickly to friends and acquaintances.

Jean Negulesco, her longtime friend whom she met during the making of *The Story of Temple Drake*, was in London with his wife, Dusty, when the news broke: "Today—in the *Herald-Tribune*—I read the heartbreaking news. I still cannot accept our loss. I respected Miriam, I admired Miriam, I loved Miriam. And, with the years, our relations remained deep, closer than ever, and sometimes absence of years did not alter at all our closeness. And I'll never forget her rare quality to respect, admire and love each other more as our relations became more intimate."[24]

Rouben Mamoulian, Miriam's friend for more than four decades, heard of her death on his car radio as he was returning to his Beverly Hills home: "It was my privilege not only to have worked with her in films but also to have her for a dear friend. Her friendship, like her talent, was true blue. As we mourn her passing, let us rejoice in the happy reality that through her portrayals on the screen, she is still with us. A superb actress, she lives in the present and will live in the future."[25]

To the end, Bette Davis held a grudge. Miriam's longtime nemesis and former costar was in Los Angeles when author Roy Moseley called her with the news. Her response: "God has been good to us. He's taken Miriam." In contrast, Miriam's *Look Homeward, Angel* costar, Andrew Prine, was heartbroken. "She was indestructible. She was going to live forever."[26]

That evening, Tennessee Williams was watching the CBS newscast when a picture of Miriam flashed on the television screen. He instantly knew what had happened. "The shock of grief that I felt," he would later write, "made it clear to me the depth of my regard for this unique actress who had starred in my first fully professional production, *Battle of Angels*."[27]

Eager to honor his friend, he expressed his feelings in a two-page tribute he hoped the *New York Times* would publish. Williams asked Becky Morehouse to use her influence with Seymour (Sy) Peck, the editor of Sunday's Arts and Leisure section of the *Times*. She did, but Peck did not like it. When theatrical costume designer Bob LaVine told Becky that Peck had rejected the tribute, she wrote the editor urging him to reconsider. He replied: "As an old fan of Miriam Hopkins and a responsible editor, I would very much like to have seen a tribute to her. I, too, looked forward greatly to getting one from Tennessee Williams. However, the fact is that his tribute was surprisingly off-base in a number of respects, and we just couldn't see our way to printing it. I, therefore, returned it regretfully. It's really too bad, and I'm sorry about the whole thing."[28]

Becky asked LaVine to send the piece to the *Los Angeles Times*, hoping they might publish it, but she heard nothing from them. In part, Tennessee Williams said about his friend:

> Unfortunately, these great stage performances do not survive except in a few recollections of those whom they moved deeply. What we are left of her art is in her films. As in the case of Garbo, the screen star nearly always was of more importance than the material she worked with. But this fact will not seriously impair the living image of Miriam Hopkins on the screen any more than the genius of Garbo was obscured by the inadequacy of most of her vehicles.[29]

Up to the end, Miriam could not decide where she wanted to live, but she died in New York as she had predicted to Sam Goldwyn four decades earlier—not at her beloved Sutton Place townhouse, but in New York all the same.

Campbell's handled the funeral arrangements. A large crowd attended the memorial service at Madison Avenue's Church of the Incarnation, the same church that hosted Ellen's service. Michael, Chris, and Tom flew to New York. Hank Potter, another longtime friend and Michael's godfather, gave the eulogy:

> Today is a day of heartfelt mourning for all of us who have loved

her. Today must also honor the lasting impact that Miriam's vibrant personality made, not only on those of us who knew her well but also on the many thousands who sincerely believed they knew her well through her work on stage and screen.

Miriam's most outstanding quality was her radiance. Miriam needed no arc-light to follow her around. She generated her own. It literally flowed from her. She was . . . radioactive. She glowed. Today, the operative magnetism may have left us. But I can't help feeling that her radiance still shines. And will remain in our hearts.[30]

When she died, Miriam's affairs were in order. However, one important aspect was neglected: her burial. After the funeral, her body was cremated, but no one was sure where to place her cremains. It was suggested that somewhere in New York City would be appropriate, possibly Woodlawn Cemetery in the Bronx or the East River off Sutton Place.

For reasons the family no longer remembers, they buried her in the family plot at Bainbridge's Oak City Cemetery. Michael believed his mother would have wanted her "ashes spread," but instead, her remains were placed near her mother, her grandmother, and her uncle Dixie. For more than forty years, Miriam had not visited her hometown. Truth be told, Bainbridge may have been the last place she wanted to end up. Nevertheless, Michael, along with Chris and Tom, flew to Georgia carrying his mother's ashes in a bag.[31]

A few weeks later, a memorial service was held in California at St. Alban's Episcopal Church in Westwood. Among those attending were the William Wylers, the Rouben Mamoulians, Norman Foster and his wife, Sally Blane, Mrs. Clyde Beatty, Mary Anita Loos, Johnny Mercer, and Florence Sundstrom.

Edward Ashley gave the eulogy: "She was made of fire, trial circumstances, and honey. She was a sprig of rosemary." He ended by quoting Shakespeare, "We are such stuff as dreams are made of, and our little life is rounded with a sleep."[32]

Sometime later, at Oak City Cemetery, Miriam's grave was covered with a double slab of marble inscribed simply with her name and her birth and death dates. The epitaph Miriam chose herself was a paraphrased Shakespearean quote from Hamlet: "Good night sweet princess and flights of angels sing thee to thy rest."

Epilogue

MIRIAM HOPKINS advised her niece, Margot Welch, when she started as an actress, that there were five things a young person needed for a successful acting career: talent, training, good luck, persistence, and heart (or guts). Margot asked which one was the most important. "Heart," Miriam told her. "If you have that, anything is possible."

Ruby said that her sister "had all five qualities in large measure, but she had a double portion of the last. To the end of her days, Miriam had an enormous zest for living; she was the most alive person I have ever known—she also had more nerve than anyone I have ever met."[1]

Hopkins's will was probated in Manhattan Surrogate's Court on October 17, 1972, one day before her seventieth birthday. Her assets, estimated at between $200,000 and $350,000, were left to Michael, along with personal property and income from a trust fund comprising the bulk of her estate. A sale disposing of her earthly possessions was held on December 7, 1972, at the Plaza Art Gallery on East Seventy-Ninth Street.

MICHAEL HOPKINS, her adopted son, and his wife, Chris, continued to live in Riverside, California, after his mother's death. When asked how she would want fans to remember her, he replied, "She would like to be recognized as an artist with a mind." Toward the end of his life, he suffered from Parkinson's disease and diabetes. Michael Hopkins died on October 5, 2010, in a Riverside convalescent home; he was seventy-eight. He was interred at nearby Riverside National Cemetery.[2]

CHRISTIANE CARRENO HOPKINS, Michael's wife of fifty-six years, survived him by nearly six years and passed away on July 3, 2016.

MICHAEL (MIKE) THOMAS HOPKINS followed in his father's footsteps and joined the military, serving in the navy for twenty-two years before retiring and working for the Department of the Navy. "Miriam was another lifetime ago," Tom recalled. "So much time has passed. I can't relate to the stardom Miriam once had. I never knew her that way. What I remember about her is this elderly lady sunning herself on a beautiful deck patio overlooking the city. She had a book of poetry or a novel and would talk about those things and about new plays, new playwrights, and new people she considered talented. She had great respect for individuals who knew how to create and to write. Those are the things I remember about my grandmother."[3]

RUBY HOPKINS WELCH spent her final years in Forest Hills, New York, working as a writer and publicist. For years, she worked with the renowned concert manager Arthur Judson and music and ballet impresario Sol Hurok. She was active in many animal welfare and environmental organizations. Occasionally, she returned to the local stage and summer stock productions, appearing with her daughter, Margot, in such roles as Amanda in Tennessee Williams's *The Glass Menagerie* and the Empress in *Anastasia*. Ruby died on December 3, 1990, in Forest Hills at the age of eighty-nine. She was buried at Bainbridge's Oak City Cemetery, with her mother and sister. Her epitaph is a paraphrase from Thoreau's *Walden*: "Let her step to the music she hears."[4]

MARGOT MIDDLETON WELCH appeared in countless stage plays and lives in Forest Hills, New York.

KATHERINE HOPKINS COX, Hopkins's half-sister, died in Oklahoma City on May 21, 2004. She was buried in the family plot at Memorial Gardens Cemetery with Homer and her mother, Kate. She was seventy-seven.

CHARLOTTE COX SMITH, Hopkins's niece, is a retired schoolteacher living in Texas.

ANATOLE LITVAK, Miriam's third husband, had a successful career after their divorce, directing such acclaimed films as *The Long Night*, *Sorry, Wrong Number*, and *The Snake Pit*, which earned Litvak an Academy Award nomination for Best Director and its star, Olivia de Havilland, a nomination for Best Actress.

Litvak married once more, to fashion designer Sophie Steur. In 1949, he returned to Europe to make films, among them *Anastasia*, earning Ingrid Bergman her second Best Actress Oscar. His last effort was the 1970 drama *The Lady in the Car with Glasses and a Gun*, starring Samantha Eggar and Oliver Reed. Anatole Litvak died in Paris after a long illness on December 15, 1974, surviving his ex-wife by two years. He was seventy-two years old.

RAYMOND BROCK, Miriam's fourth and last husband, wrote several books, including the successful *Blood, Oil, and Sand* about the Middle East conflict. Brock died from a heart attack in Orangeburg, New York, in February 1968. He was fifty-four.

BENNETT CERF, who was married briefly to Hopkins's friend, actress Sylvia Sidney, wrote a series of joke books published by his company, Random House. Beginning in 1951, Cerf appeared on the weekly game show *What's My Line?* until its run ended in 1967. Cerf remained friendly with Hopkins until his death in 1971 at age seventy-three.

ROUBEN MAMOULIAN was Hopkins's good friend and always defended her in interviews when asked how difficult she could be. After *Becky Sharp*, Hopkins tried desperately to work with the director again, but there was never a project that they could agree on. Mamoulian continued working in theater and films until he was fired from *Cleopatra* in 1963 (he was previously fired from *Laura* and *Porgy and Bess*). Mamoulian lived until the age of ninety-seven, dying in 1987 at the Motion Picture & Television Country House and Hospital in Woodland Hills, California.

JEAN NEGULESCO, who hinted at being intimate with Hopkins at one time, became a successful director and screenwriter with such films as *Johnny Belinda* and *How to Marry a Millionaire*. He remained close until her death, even though he was living in Marbella, Spain, where he died in 1993. He was ninety-three years old.

SAMUEL GOLDWYN continued making films from his West Hollywood studios for another twenty years after handing off Hopkins to Jack Warner. Along the way, Goldwyn won a Best Picture Oscar for *The Best Years of Our Lives* (1946) and was honored with the Irving G. Thalberg Memorial (1946) and the Jean Hersholt Humanitarian (1957) Awards. Goldwyn made his last film, *Porgy and Bess*, in 1959. He died at the age of ninety-four at his Los Angeles home and was interred in an unmarked grave in a private garden at Glendale's Forest Lawn.

CARL ZUCKMAYER, the German writer and playwright, returned to his wife in Barnard, Vermont, after his affair with Hopkins. When World War II ended, Zuckmayer became an American citizen and traveled through Germany as the US cultural attaché. Zuckmayer continued writing, including many German screenplays. In 1958, he moved with his wife to Saas-Fee, Switzerland, where he died on January 18, 1977. He was eighty years old.

JACK WARNER continued to run Warner Bros. with an iron fist. Hopkins had one final encounter with the mogul in 1969 as one of many invited guests at his retirement party on a Warner Bros. soundstage. Afterward, Warner remained an independent producer, one of his last films being an adaptation of the Broadway musical *1776*. In 1974, a stroke left him blind and debilitated, and over time he would lose the ability to speak or be responsive. Jack Warner died on September 9, 1978, at the age of eighty-six.

BETTE DAVIS complained about Miriam Hopkins practically until the day she died. But over the years, their intense hatred for each other was surpassed by Davis's feud with costar Joan Crawford on the set of *Whatever Happened to Baby Jane?* Hopkins, however, was a stronger sparring partner than Crawford and also made a second film with Davis, while Crawford could not. Davis's career experienced many ups and downs after her encounter with Hopkins, but she retained her deserved "legend" moniker until the end. Plagued by cancer in her final years, Davis died at France's American Hospital on October 6, 1989 at the age of eighty-one. She was interred at Forest Lawn-Hollywood Hills in a grand marble sarcophagus that sits on a high hill overlooking Warner Bros. Studios.

TENNESSEE WILLIAMS, in contrast to Bette Davis, loved Hopkins her entire life. Williams's personal and professional life went through many good and bad spells, but it was the death of a lover in 1963 that plunged him into depression and continuous drug use. Williams died alone in his suite at New York's Hotel Élysée at the age of seventy-one. Bizarrely, an autopsy confirmed that Williams had choked to death on the plastic cap of a nasal spray bottle.

REBECCA (BECKY) FRANKLIN MOREHOUSE lived on New York's Upper East Side, writing hundreds of stories for *Time* magazine, the *New York Times*, *Playbill*, and other publications. Before her death, she finished a book on proper English usage. She died on January 7, 2010, at an assisted living facility in Statesboro, Georgia, and was buried with her husband, Ward Morehouse, at Eastside Cemetery. She was ninety-five years old.

Miriam Hopkins's films survive her. Her first, *The Home Girl*, is stored at the UCLA Film and Television Archive but has deteriorated and cannot be viewed.

As for her other films, for decades, *The Smiling Lieutenant* was in litigation and was considered lost until researchers found a print in Denmark in the 1990s. King Vidor's *The Stranger's Return* was not seen in years but was recently restored, having its premiere at the 2014 TCM Classic Film Festival in Hollywood.

In 1941, MGM bought the rights to *Dr. Jekyll and Mr. Hyde*, when they remade it with Spencer Tracy and Ingrid Bergman. They locked up the March/Hopkins film for several decades, so it couldn't be compared to their inferior version.

In 1958, Universal bought the films that Paramount made between 1929 and 1949 and has controlled them ever since. One-third of Hopkins's films are languishing in Universal's vaults, many not exhibited since they were first released or shown during television's early days. What are available to the public are inferior bootleg copies.

Trouble in Paradise wasn't permitted to be reissued under the enforced Hays Code and wasn't seen again until 1968. *The Story of Temple Drake* was viewed only in mediocre prints or at rare festival showings until it was restored and shown in 2011 at Hollywood's Grauman's Chinese Theater during TCM's Classic Film Festival.

Turner Classic Movies broadcasts her Goldwyn, RKO, and Warner Bros. films and many are available on DVD. These include her Lubitsch films, her two with Bette Davis, and several of her later supporting films such as *The Heiress*, *Carrie*, and *The Children's Hour*.

Tennessee Williams said at the time of her death: "I know that Paramount Pictures must be aware of her value, the value of her unique talent and personality, and I trust that there will be continual revivals of her films in motion picture houses and on television screens. She has the quality of which a 'cult' could emerge comparable to the 'cults' of Garbo, Marlene Dietrich, and Katharine Hepburn."[5]

Acknowledgments

In my ten years of research, I gained the cooperation and support of Miriam Hopkins's son, Michael, his wife, Christiane, and their son, Michael Thomas (Mike) Hopkins. Besides sharing their family history, they also provided photographs and encouragement. In addition, I corresponded with Miss Hopkins's niece, Margot Welch, the daughter of Ruby Hopkins Welch, and spoke with Charlotte Cox Smith, the daughter of Hopkins's half-sister, Katherine Hopkins Cox.

Special thanks go to authors Cari Beauchamp (who offered much-needed hand-holding and advice) and André Soares (who read and edited early editions) and to historian Joseph Yranski (who provided photographs) for their valuable help with getting this book ready. To Paulo Rosario, thank you for crawling around the bleachers at the Hollywood Bowl to take my author's photo.

I appreciate those who gave advice or shared their memories, including Hopkins's surviving costars, friends, acquaintances, and their children: Kitty Carlisle, Veronica Cartwright, Olivia de Havilland, Doris Eaton Travis, David Frankham, Beverly Garland, Leatrice Gilbert-Fountain, Samuel Goldwyn Jr., Brook Hayward, Sybil Jason, Dickie Jones, Marcia Mae Jones, Dickran Kouymjian, Miles Kruger, Paul Kwilecki, Arthur Laurents, Suzanne Leworthy, Nicola Lubitsch, A. C. Lyles, Paul Avila Mayer, Rebecca (Becky) Franklin Morehouse, Ward Morehouse III, Andrew Prine, Stanley Raiff, Francesca Robinson Sanchez, Barbara Rush, Aram Saroyan, Lizabeth Scott, Marian Seldes, Daniel Selznick, Steve Siporin, Belinda Vidor, Joyce Van Patten, Michael Westmore, Judith Wyler Sheldon, and Jane Withers.

I am grateful to authors and film historians who shared insights on Hopkins's career: Michael G. Ankerich, Jimmy Bangley, Robert Birchard, Margaret Burk, Lisa Burks, David Chierechetti, Anne Edwards, Joe Franklin, Laurie Jacobson, Lise Jaillant, Fay Kanin, Lynn Kear, Terry Kingsley-Smith, Richard Lamparski, Mick La Salle, Emily Leider, Pat McGilligan, Gregory Mank, Scott O'Brien, James Robert Parish, Peter

Acknowledgments

Riva, Anthony Slide, Sherri Snyder, Sam Staggs, Stone Wallace, and Mark A. Vieira.

Others who shared knowledge or encouragement include: Patrick Agan, Ron Bowers, Dianne Busch, Christopher Connelly, Crit Davis, Richard DeNewt, Richard Evans, Lee Frazer, Weimer Gard, Bill George, Lee Gerstmann, Stuart Hands, William (Bill) Lamson, Barry Lane, Richard McLeod, Dennis Mahoney, Peter Panholzer (Zuckmayer letter translations), Mauro Piccinini, Anna Pollock, Renee Saunders, Lynn Stover, Gabriella Wagner, Nancy Wickes, and Dennis Yancey.

During my research for the book, I examined thousands of rare newspaper and magazine articles that detailed Hopkins's private life, her career, and her times, including several letters from Hopkins. Through the Freedom of Information Act I gained access to Hopkins's one-hundred-page-plus FBI file documenting her so-called Communist and other political associations throughout her life.

The staff at libraries and institutions who generously helped with information include Alison Bentley, reference archivist, the Georgia Historical Society; Hilda Bradberry, the Brewer Library, United Daughters of the Confederacy; Emily Carman, Warner Bros. Archives (USC); Ned Comstock, USC; Rorri Feinstein, the Samuel Goldwyn Company; Allison Francis, Margaret Herrick Library (AMPAS); Barbara Frieling, the University of Georgia; Jere Guldin, UCLA Archives; Barbara Hall, Margaret Herrick Library (AMPAS); Dorinda Hartmann, Wisconsin Center for Film and Theater Research; Carolyn Iamon, *Bainbridge Post-Searchlight*; Marty Jacobs, curator of theatre, Museum of the City of New York; Sue Kane, Margaret Herrick Library (AMPAS); Barbara Knowles, Billy Rose Theatre Division (New York Public Library for the Performing Arts); Sandra Joy Lee, Warner Bros. Archives (USC); Kathryn Lillethun, Bainbridge Library; Linda Mehr, Margaret Herrick Library (AMPAS); Maryalice Mohr, archivist, Spaulding Library, New England Conservatory of Music; Mary O'Brien, reference archivist, Syracuse University Archives; Robert Osborne, Turner Classic Movies; Jenny Paxson, Library of Congress; Will Pettite, Paramount Archives; Jenny Romero, Margaret Herrick Library (AMPAS); Margaret Smith, the New Georgia Encyclopedia; Tameka Thomas, *Bainbridge Post-Searchlight*; Joan Tinklepaugh, historian, Hollis Historical Society (New Hampshire); Andrew D. Voisvert, archivist of the Old Colony Historical Society, Taunton, Massachusetts; and Cheryl Weber, director of alumni relations, New England Conservatory of Music.

Acknowledgments

In addition, I've researched collections at several institutions: the Los Angeles Public Library; the American Film Institute; the Library of Congress; the Museum of Television and Radio, in Beverly Hills; and the Church of Latter-Day Saints' Family History Center.

Special thanks go to the staff at the University Press of Kentucky for their guidance and patience, especially Anne Dean Dotson, and Patrick D. O'Dowd, and Penelope Cray.

Friends and old acquaintances who supported me along the way include James Bazen, Mike Francis, Deanna Good, Stella Grace, Anne Han, Michelle Horrigan, Steve Kane, Adam Kersh, Mary Mallory, Robert Murdoch, Joan Myers, Nicca Panggat, Annie Salmorin, Lisa Sevilla, Jim Shippee, Steve Troha, Marcus Tucker, Mark Umbach, Carrie Vardaman, Laura Wegter, and Arlene Witt.

Appendix

Stage Appearances

The Fascinating Fanny Brown (1919). Goddard Seminary. *Cast:* E. Miriam Hopkins, William Flanders, Percy Pitkin. Opened April 29, 1919.

Music Box Revue (1921–1922). Broadway. Music Box Theatre. Staged by Hassard Short. *Cast:* Virginia Dixon, Helen Clare, Betsy Ross, Claire Davis, Miriam Hopkins, Jeanne St. John, Richard W. Keene, Joseph Santley. Opened September 22, 1921. 440 performances.

Steppin' Around (1922). Vaudeville.

The Tavern (1923). Vaudeville.

The Sheik's Favorite (1923). Vaudeville.

Little Jessie James. Broadway. Longacre Theatre. Staged by Walter Brooks. *Cast:* Carl Anderson, Herbert Bostwick, Bobbie Breslau, James B. Carson, Loretta Flushing, Roger Gray, Nan Halperin, Winifred Harris, Miriam Hopkins. Premiered August 15, 1923. 385 performances.

High Tide. Pre-Broadway. Shubert-Belasco Theater (Washington, DC). Produced by L. Lawrence Weber. Staged by William B. Friedlander. Book by Eleanor Holmes Hinkley. *Cast:* Miriam Hopkins, Louis Calhern. Premiered December 15, 1924.

Puppets. Broadway. Selwyn Theatre (now the American Airlines Theatre). Produced by Brock Pemberton. Staged by Brock Pemberton. Book by Frances Lightner. *Cast:* Dwight Frye, C. Henry Gordon, Miriam Hopkins, Fredric March. Premiered March 9, 1925. Fifty-four performances.

The Enemy. Pre-Broadway. Shubert Theater, New Haven, Connecticut. Fired during tryout.

Lovely Lady. Broadway. Belmont Theatre (demolished). Produced by Wagenhals and Collin Kemper. Staged by Collin Kemper. Book by Jessie Lynch Williams. *Cast:* Lily Cahill, Miriam Hopkins, Charles Newsom, Elizabeth Risdon. Premiered October 14, 1925. Twenty-one performances.

The Matinee Girl (1925). Pre-Broadway. Quit during tryouts.

Gentlemen Prefer Blondes (1926). Broadway. Fired during rehearsals.

The Home Towners (1926). Pre-Broadway. Four Cohans Theatre (Chicago). Produced by George M. Cohan. Staged by John Meehan. *Cast:* Thurston Hall, Robert McWade, Miriam Hopkins. Premiered May 10, 1926.

Appendix

An American Tragedy (1926). Broadway. Longacre Theatre. Produced by Horace Liveright. Book by Patrick Kearney from Theodore Dreiser's novel. Staged by Edward T. Goodman. *Cast:* Morgan Farley, Miriam Hopkins, Katherine Wilson. Premiered October 11, 1926. 216 performances.

Thou Desperate Pilot (1926). Broadway. Morosco Theatre. Book by Zoë Akins. Staged by Rachel Crothers. *Cast:* David Hawthorne, Helen Ware, Roberta Beatty, Miriam Hopkins, Percy Ames, Ullrich Haupt. Premiered March 7, 1927. Six performances.

The Last of Mrs. Cheyney (1927). Cukor-Kondolf Company (Rochester). Lyceum Theatre. Written by Frederic Lonsdale. Staged by George Cukor. *Cast:* Miriam Hopkins, Minor Watson, Roberta Bailey, Esther Fairchild. Premiered April 18, 1927.

Is Zat So? (1927). Cukor-Kondolf Company (Rochester). Lyceum Theatre. Staged by George Cukor. *Cast:* Miriam Hopkins, Minor Watson. Premiered April 24, 1927.

The Patsy (1927). Cukor-Kondolf Company (Rochester). Lyceum Theatre. Staged by George Cukor. *Cast:* Miriam Hopkins, Minor Watson. Premiered May 1, 1927.

The Poor Nut (1927). Cukor-Kondolf Company (Rochester). Lyceum Theatre. Staged by George Cukor. *Cast:* Miriam Hopkins, Minor Watson. Premiered May 9, 1927.

Applesauce (1927). Cukor-Kondolf Company (Rochester). Lyceum Theatre. Staged by George Cukor. *Cast:* Miriam Hopkins, Minor Watson. Premiered June 6, 1927.

The Ghost Train (1927). Cukor-Kondolf Company (Rochester). Lyceum Theatre. Staged by George Cukor and Arthur Wood. *Cast:* Miriam Hopkins, Minor Watson, Robert Montgomery. Premiered August 8, 1927.

The Garden of Eden (1927). Broadway. Selwyn Theatre (now the American Airlines Theatre). Produced by Arch Selwyn. Written by Avery Hopwood. Staged by Edwin H. Knopf. *Cast:* Alison Skipworth, Miriam Hopkins, Douglas Montgomery, Doris Rankin. Premiered September 27, 1927. Twenty-three performances.

Excess Baggage (1927–1928). Broadway. Ritz Theatre. Produced by Barbour, Crimmins, and Bryant. Written by John McGowan. Staged by Melville Burke, Paul Dickey. *Cast:* Frank McHugh, Eric Dressler, Doris Eaton, Miriam Hopkins. Premiered December 26, 1927. 216 performances.

John Ferguson (1928). Experimental theatre. Theatre Masque (now John Golden Theatre). *Cast:* Miriam Hopkins, Marion Kerby. Premiered January 17, 1928. Three performances (limited).

Excess Baggage (1928). Cukor-Kondolf Company (Rochester). Temple Theatre. Staged by George Cukor and Arthur Wood. *Cast:* Miriam Hopkins, Frank McHugh, Wallace Ford, Bette Davis. Premiered October 1928.

Flight (1929). Broadway. Longacre Theatre. Produced by Laura D. Wilck. Written by Susan Meriwether and Victor Victor. *Cast:* Eleanor Woodruff, Miriam Hopkins, Henry Wadsworth. Premiered February 18, 1929. Forty performances.

The Camel through the Needle's Eye (1929). Broadway. Martin Beck Theatre (now the Al Hirschfield Theatre). Produced by the Theatre Guild. A comedy by Philip Moeller from the Czechoslovakian of Frantisek Langer. Staged by Philip Moeller. *Cast:* Helen Westley, Henry Travers, Claude Rains, Miriam Hopkins, Catherine Calhoun-Doucet, Eliot Cabot. Premiered April 15, 1929. 196 performances.

The Bachelor Father (1929). London West End. Globe Theatre (now the Gielgud Theatre). Produced by Thomas M. Reynolds. Written by Edward Childs Carpenter. Staged by Ernest Pierce. *Cast:* Miriam Hopkins, C. Aubrey Smith. Premiered September 23, 1929. Twenty performances (102 performances total run).

Ritzy (1930) Broadway. Longacre Theatre. Produced by L. Lawrence Weber. Written by Viva Tattersall and Sidney Toler. Staged by Sidney Toler. *Cast:* Ernest Truex, Miriam Hopkins. Premiered February 10, 1930. Thirty-two performances.

Lysistrata (1930). Pre-Broadway. Walnut Street Theatre (Philadelphia). (see credits below). *Note:* Lysistrata was played by Fay Bainter.

Lysistrata (1930). Broadway. 44th Street Theatre. Produced by Philadelphia Theatre Association, Inc. Written by Aristophanes; book by Gilbert Seldes. Staged by Norman Bel Geddes. *Cast:* Violet Kemple Cooper, Miriam Hopkins, Louise Closser Hale, Jose Limon, Ernest Truex, Sydney Greenstreet. Premiered June 5, 1930. 252 performances.

His Majesty's Car (1930). Broadway. Ethel Barrymore Theatre. Produced by Lee and J. J. Shubert. Adapted by Fanny Hatton and Frederic Hatton. *Cast:* Theodore St. John, Gertrude Maitland, Miriam Hopkins, C. H. Croker-King, Edward Crandall, Marcella Swanson. Premiered October 23, 1930. Twelve performances.

Lysistrata (1930). Broadway. 44th Street Theatre. (See credits above). Hopkins rejoined the cast on November 15, 1930, replacing Nadia Westman. Lysistrata was played by Blanche Yurka.

Anatol (1931). Broadway. Lyceum Theatre. Produced by Bela Blau, Inc. Written by Arthur Schnitzler. Adapted by Harley Granville-Barker. Staged by Marc Connelly and Gabriel Beer-Hoffman. *Cast:* Walter Connolly, Joseph Schildkraut, Patricia Collinge, Miriam Hopkins, Ruthelma Stevens. Premiered January 16, 1931. Forty-five performances.

Jezebel (1933). Broadway. Ethel Barrymore Theatre. Produced by Guthrie McClintic and Katharine Cornell. Written by Owen Davis. Staged by Guthrie McClintic. *Cast:* Cora Witherspoon, Lew Payton, Miriam Hopkins, Joseph Cotten,

Owen Davis Jr., Helen Claire. Premiered December 19, 1933. Thirty-two performances.

Wine of Choice (1937). Pre-Broadway. Erlanger Theatre (Chicago). Produced by
the Theatre Guild (Lawrence Langner). Written by S. N. Behrman. Staged by
Philip Moeller. *Cast:* Miriam Hopkins, Leslie Banks, Alexander Woollcott. Premiered December 13, 1937.

Battle of Angels (1940). Pre-Broadway. Wilbur Theatre (Boston). Produced by the
Theatre Guild. Staged by Margaret Webster. Written by Tennessee Williams.
Cast: Doris Dudley, Wesley Addy, Miriam Hopkins. Premiered December 30,
1940. Twelve performances.

The Skin of Our Teeth (1943). Broadway. Plymouth Theatre (now the Gerald
Schoenfeld Theatre). Produced by Michael Myerberg. Written by Thornton
Wilder. Staged by Elia Kazan. *Cast:* Miriam Hopkins, E. G. Marshall, Viola
Frayne, Dickie Van Patten, Conrad Nagle. *Note:* Miriam Hopkins replaced the
original star, Tallulah Bankhead, on May 31, 1943.

The Perfect Marriage (1944). Broadway. Ethel Barrymore Theatre. Produced by
Cheryl Crawford. Written by Samuel Raphaelson. Staged by Samuel Raphaelson. *Cast:* Victor Jory, Miriam Hopkins, Martha Sleeper, Joyce Van Patten. Premiered October 26, 1944. Ninety-two performances.

St. Lazare's Pharmacy (1945). Pre-Broadway tour. His Majesty's Theatre (Montreal). Produced by Eddie Dowling and Louis Singer. Miklos Laszlo's play adapted
by Eddie Dowling. Staged by Eddie Dowling. *Cast:* Miriam Hopkins, Fridolin
(Gratien Gelinas). Premiered December 6, 1945.

Laura (1946). Pre-Broadway tour. Playhouse (Wilmington, Delaware). Produced
by Hunt Stromberg Jr. Written by Vera Caspary and George Sklar, based on the
book *Laura*, by Vera Caspary. Staged by Michael Gordon. *Cast:* Miriam Hopkins, Otto Kruger, Tom Neal. Premiered April 19, 1946.

Message for Margaret (1947). Broadway. Plymouth Theatre (now the Gerald
Schoenfeld Theatre). Produced by Stanley Gilkey and Barbara Payne in association with Henry Sherek Ltd. Written by James Parish. Staged by Elliott Nugent. *Cast:* Mady Christians, Roger Pryor, Miriam Hopkins. Premiered April
16, 1947. Five performances.

There's Always a Juliet (1947). Road tour.

Happy Birthday (1948). Road tour.

The Heiress (1949). Road tour.

Told to the Children (1951). Road tour.

A Night in Mme. Tussaud's (1952). Road tour.

Hay Fever (1953). Road tour.

In the Summer House (1953). Pre-Broadway. Ann Arbor Drama Festival (University of Michigan). Produced by Roger Steven and Olive Smith. Written by Jane

Bowles. Staged by John Stix. *Cast:* Miriam Hopkins, Mildred Dunnock. Premiered May 18, 1953.

The Old Maid (1957) Road tour (with Sylvia Sidney and Miriam's niece, Margot Welch).

The Matchmaker (1957). Road tour.

Time of the Cuckoo (1958). Road tour.

Look Homeward, Angel (1958). Broadway. Ethel Barrymore Theatre. Produced by Kermit Bloomgarden. Written by Ketti Friggs, based on the novel by Thomas Wolfe. Staged by George Roy Hill. *Cast:* Miriam Hopkins, Ed Begley, Andrew Prine.

Look Homeward, Angel (1959). Road Tour.

Riverside Drive (1964). Off-Broadway. (Fired during rehearsals.)

Filmography

The Home Girl (1928). Paramount Famous Lasky Corporation. Short. Directed by Edmund Lawrence. Based on a story by Edna Ferber. *Cast:* Miriam Hopkins, Otto Kruger, Vincent Lopez. Released December 1, 1928. A print is stored at UCLA Archives.

Unknown Short. Warner Bros./Vitaphone short. Directed by Bryan Foy. *Cast:* Miriam Hopkins. Produced at Vitaphone's Brooklyn plant. Source: *Film Daily,* April 14, 1929.

Fast and Loose (1930). Paramount Pictures (as Paramount Publix Corporation). Directed by Fred Newmeyer. Scenario by Doris Anderson, Jack Kirkland, and Preston Sturges, based on the play *The Best People,* by David Gray and Avery Hopwood. *Cast:* Miriam Hopkins, Carole Lombard, Frank Morgan, Charles Starrett, Henry Wadsworth, Ilka Chase. Seventy minutes. Released November 8, 1930.

The House That Shadows Built (1931). Paramount Pictures. *Cast:* Groucho Marx, Harpo Marx, Chico Marx, Zeppo Marx, Sarah Bernhardt, Clara Bow, Lon Chaney, Ruth Chatterton, Maurice Chevalier, Claudette Colbert, Douglas Fairbanks, William S. Hart, Miriam Hopkins, Harold Lloyd, Herbert Marshall, Mary Pickford, Wallace Reid, Charles Ruggles, Sylvia Sidney, Gloria Swanson, Lilyan Tashman. Fifty-five minutes. Released 1931.

The Smiling Lieutenant (1931). Paramount Publix Corporation. Directed by Ernst Lubitsch. Scenario by Ernest Vajda, Samson Raphaelson, and Ernst Lubitsch, based on the novel *Nux der Prinzgemahl,* by Hans Müller, and the Operetta *Ein Walzertraum,* by Leopold Jacobson and Felix Dörmann. *Cast:* Maurice Chevalier, Claudette Colbert, Miriam Hopkins, Charles Ruggles, George Barbier. Ninety-three minutes. Released July 10, 1931.

Le lieutenant couriant (1931). Paramount Publix Corporation. French language version of *The Smiling Lieutenant.* Same cast and crew.

Appendix

24 Hours (1931). Paramount Pictures. Directed by Marion Gering. Scenario by Louis Weitzenkorn, based on the novel by Louis Bromfield and the play by Will D. Lengle and Lew Levenson. *Cast:* Clive Brook, Kay Francis, Miriam Hopkins, Regis Toomey, George Barbier, Lucille La Verne. Sixty-six minutes. Released October 3, 1931.

Dr. Jekyll and Mr. Hyde (1931). Paramount Publix Corporation/A Rouben Mamoulian Production. Directed by Rouben Mamoulian. Scenario by Samuel Hoffenstein and Percy Heath, based on the novel by Robert Louis Stevenson. *Cast:* Fredric March, Miriam Hopkins, Rose Hobart. Ninety-eight minutes. Released December 31, 1931.

Two Kinds of Women (1932). Paramount Pictures. Directed by William C. de Mille. Scenario by Benjamin Glazer, based on the play *This Is New York*, by Robert E. Sherwood. *Cast:* Miriam Hopkins, Phillips Holmes, Irving Pichel, Wynne Gibson, Vivienne Osborne, Josephine Dunn. Seventy-five minutes. Released January 16, 1932.

Dancers in the Dark (1932). Paramount Publix Corporation. Directed by David Burton. Scenario by Herman J. Mankiewicz, Brian Marlow, and Howard Emmett Rogers, based on the *Jazz King*, by James Ashmore Creelman. *Cast:* Miriam Hopkins, Jack Oakie, William Collier Jr., Eugene Pallette, Lyda Roberti, George Raft. Seventy-four minutes. Released March 11, 1932.

The World and the Flesh (1932). Paramount Publix Corporation. Directed by John Cromwell. Scenario by Oliver H. P. Garrett, from the play *On the Black Sea*, by Ernst Spitz and Philip Zeska. *Cast:* George Bancroft, Miriam Hopkins, Alan Mowbray. Seventy-four minutes. Released April 22, 1932.

Trouble in Paradise (1932). Paramount Publix Corporation. Directed by Ernst Lubitsch. Scenario by Samson Raphaelson, from the play *A Becsuletes Megtalalo* (*The Honest Finder*), by Aladar Laszlo. *Cast:* Miriam Hopkins, Kay Francis, Herbert Marshall, Charlie Ruggles, Edward Everett Horton, C. Aubrey Smith. Eighty-three minutes. Released October 21, 1932.

The Story of Temple Drake (1933). Paramount Pictures. Directed by Stephen Roberts. Scenario by Oliver H.P. Garrett, Maurine Dallas Watkins (uncredited), from the novel *Sanctuary*, by William Faulkner. *Cast:* Miriam Hopkins, William Gargan, Jack La Rue, Florence Eldridge, Sir Guy Standing, Irving Pichel, Jobyna Howland, William Collier Jr. Seventy minutes. Released May 6, 1933.

The Stranger's Return (1933). Metro-Goldwyn-Mayer. Directed by King Vidor. Scenario by Brown Holmes and Philip Stong, from the novel *Stranger's Return*, by Philip Stong. *Cast:* Lionel Barrymore, Miriam Hopkins, Franchot Tone, Stuart Erwin, Irene Hervey, Beulah Bondi. Eighty-nine minutes. Released July 28, 1933.

Design for Living (1933). Paramount Pictures. Directed by Ernst Lubitsch. Scenario by Ben Hecht and Samuel Hoffenstein, from the play *Design for Living*, by

Noël Coward. *Cast:* Fredric March, Gary Cooper, Miriam Hopkins, Edward Everett Horton, Franklin Pangborn. Ninety-one minutes. Released December 29, 1933.

Hollywood on Parade No. B-1 (1933). Paramount. Short.

All of Me (1934). A Paramount Picture. Directed by James Flood. Scenario by Sidney Buchman and Thomas Mitchell, from the play *Chrysalis*, by Rose Albert Porter. *Cast:* Fredric March, Miriam Hopkins, George Raft, Helen Mack. Seventy Minutes. Released February 1, 1934.

She Loves Me Not (1934). A Paramount Picture. Directed by Elliott Nugent. Scenario by Benjamin Glazer, from the play by Howard Lindsay and the novel by Edward Hope. *Cast:* Bing Crosby, Miriam Hopkins, Kitty Carlisle, Edward Nugent. Eighty-five minutes. Released August 31, 1934.

Richest Girl in the World (1934). RKO Radio Pictures/A Pandro S. Berman Production. Directed by William A. Seiter. Scenario by Norman Krasna, Jerry Hutchinson, Glenn Tryon, and Leona D'Ambry. *Cast:* Miriam Hopkins, Joel McCrea, Faye Wray. Seventy-six minutes. Released September 21, 1934.

Becky Sharp (1935). RKO Radio Pictures/Pioneer Pictures Corporation. Directed by Rouben Mamoulian. Scenario by Francis Edward Faragoh, from the play by Langdon Mitchell and the novel by William Makepeace Thackeray. *Cast:* Miriam Hopkins, Frances Dee, Cedric Hardwicke, Billie Burke, Alison Skipworth, Nigel Bruce, Alan Mowbray. Eighty-four minutes. Released June 28, 1935.

Barbary Coast (1935). The Samuel Goldwyn Company/ United Artists. Directed by Howard Hawks. Scenario by Ben Hecht, Charles MacArthur, Edward Chodorov, Stephen Longstreet. *Cast:* Miriam Hopkins, Edward G. Robinson, Joel McCrea, Walter Brennan, Brian Donlevy. Ninety-one minutes. Released September 27, 1935.

Splendor (1935). The Samuel Goldwyn Company/United Artists. Directed by Elliott Nugent. Scenario by Rachel Crothers, from her play. *Cast:* Miriam Hopkins, Joel McCrea, Helen Westley, Billie Burke, David Niven, Arthur Treacher. Seventy-five minutes. Released November 22, 1935.

These Three (1936). The Samuel Goldwyn Company/United Artists. Directed by William Wyler. Scenario by Lillian Hellman, from her play *The Children's Hour*. *Cast:* Miriam Hopkins, Merle Oberon, Joel McCrea, Catherine Doucet, Alma Kruger, Bonita Granville, Marcia Mae Jones. Ninety-three minutes. Released March 18, 1936.

Men Are Not Gods (1936). London Film Productions/United Artists. Directed by Walter Reisch. Scenario by Walter Reisch, G. B. Stern, and Iris Wright. *Cast:* Miriam Hopkins, Gertrude Lawrence, Sebastian Shaw, Rex Harrison. Eighty-two minutes. Released November 26, 1936 (UK).

The Woman I Love (1937). RKO Radio Pictures. Directed by Anatole Litvak. Scenario by Mary Borden, from the novel *L'Équipage*, by Joseph Kessel. *Cast:* Paul

Muni, Miriam Hopkins, Louis Hayward, Colin Clive, Elisabeth Risdon, Mady Christians. Eighty-five minutes. Released April 15, 1937.

Woman Chases Man (1937). The Samuel Goldwyn Company/United Artists. Directed by John Blystone. Scenario by Joseph Anthony, Mannie Seff, David Hertz, based on the original story by Lynn Root and Frank Fenton. *Cast:* Miriam Hopkins, Joel McCrea, Charles Winninger, Broderick Crawford. Seventy-one minutes. Released May 7, 1937.

Wise Girl (1937). RKO Radio Pictures. Directed by Leigh Jason. Scenario by Allan Scott and Charles Norman. *Cast:* Miriam Hopkins, Ray Milland, Margaret Dumont. Seventy minutes. Released December 31, 1937.

The Old Maid (1939). Warner Bros. Directed by Edmund Goulding. Scenario by Casey Robinson, from the play by Zoë Akins and the novel by Edith Wharton. *Cast:* Bette Davis, Miriam Hopkins, George Brent, Donald Crisp, Jane Bryan, Louise Fazenda. Ninety-five minutes. Released September 2, 1939.

Virginia City (1940). Warner Bros. Directed by Michael Curtiz. Scenario by Robert Buckner, Howard Koch, Norman Reilly Raine. *Cast:* Errol Flynn, Miriam Hopkins, Randolph Scott, Humphrey Bogart. 121 minutes. Released March 23, 1940.

Lady with Red Hair (1940). Warner Bros. Directed by Kurt Bernhardt. Scenario by Charles Kenyon, Milton Scrims, N. Brewster Morse, Norbert Faulkner, from the memoirs of Mrs. Leslie Carter. *Cast:* Miriam Hopkins, Claude Rains, Richard Ainley, Laura Hope Crews, Helen Westley. Seventy-eight minutes. Released November 30, 1940.

A Gentleman After Dark (1942). United Artists/Edward Small Productions. Directed by Edwin L. Marin. Scenario by Patterson McNutt, George Bruce, from the story "A Whiff of Heliotrope," by Richard Washburn Child. *Cast:* Brian Donlevy, Miriam Hopkins, Preston Foster, Phillip Reed, Gloria Holden. Seventy-four minutes. Released April 16, 1942.

Old Acquaintance (1943). Warner Bros. Directed by Vincent Sherman. Scenario by John Van Druten, from his play, Lenore Coffee, Edmund Goulding. *Cast:* Bette Davis, Miriam Hopkins, Gig Young, John Loder, Dolores Moran. 110 minutes. Released November 27, 1943.

The Heiress (1949). Paramount Pictures. Directed by William Wyler. Scenario by Ruth Goetz, Augustus Goetz, based on their play, and the novel *Washington Square*, by Henry James. *Cast:* Olivia de Havilland, Montgomery Clift, Ralph Richardson, Miriam Hopkins. 115 minutes. Released October 6, 1949.

The Mating Season (1951). Paramount Pictures. Directed by Mitchell Leisen. Scenario by Charles Brackett, Walter Reisch, and Richard Breen. *Cast:* Gene Tierney, John Lund, Miriam Hopkins, Thelma Ritter. 101 minutes. Released January 12, 1951.

The Outcasts of Poker Flat (1952). Twentieth Century Fox Film Corporation. Directed by Joseph M. Newman. Scenario by Edmund H. North, from the story by Bret Harte. *Cast:* Anne Baxter, Dale Robertson, Miriam Hopkins, Cameron Mitchell. Eighty-one minutes. Released May 16, 1952.

Carrie (1952). Paramount Pictures. Directed by William Wyler. Scenario by Ruth Goetz and Augustus Goetz, from the novel *Sister Carrie*, by Theodore Dreiser. *Cast:* Laurence Olivier, Jennifer Jones, Miriam Hopkins, Eddie Albert. 118 minutes. Released July 17, 1952.

The Children's Hour (1961). Mirisch Corporation/United Artists. Directed by William Wyler. Scenario by John Michael Hayes, from the play *The Children's Hour*, by Lillian Hellman. *Cast:* Audrey Hepburn, Shirley MacLaine, James Garner, Miriam Hopkins, Fay Bainter, Karen Balkin, Veronica Cartwright. 107 minutes. Released December 19, 1961.

Fanny Hill: Or, Memoirs of a Woman of Pleasure (1964). Central Cinema Company Film (CCC)/Pan World. Directed by Russ Meyer. Scenario by Robert Hill, from the novel *Fanny Hill: Or, Memoirs of a Woman of Pleasure*, by John Cleland. *Cast:* Miriam Hopkins, Leticia Roman, Ulli Lommel, Alexander D'Arcy. 104 minutes. Released March 10, 1965.

The Chase (1966). Columbia Pictures Corporation. Directed by Arthur Penn. Scenario by Lillian Hellman, from the play and novel *The Chase*, by Horton Foote. *Cast:* Marlon Brando, Jane Fonda, Robert Redford, E. G. Marshall, Angie Dickinson, Miriam Hopkins, Martha Hyer, Robert Duvall. 135 minutes. Released February 17, 1966.

Savage Intruder (1969). Congdon Productions. Directed by Donald Wolfe. Scenario by Donald Wolfe. *Cast:* Miriam Hopkins, John David Garfield, Gale Sondergaard, Virginia Wing, Florence Lake, Joe Besser, Minta Durfee. 100 minutes. Released: unknown.

Television Appearances

The Chevrolet Tele-Theatre (NBC). "Hart to Heart." November 21, 1949. (Season 2, episode 10). *Cast:* Donald Curtis, Miriam Hopkins, Charles Martin.

This Is Show Business (CBS). December 11, 1949. Clifton Fadiman. *Guests:* Miriam Hopkins, George S. Kaufman, Harvey Stone, Hal LeRoy.

The Ken Murray Show (CBS). April 1, 1950. (Season 1, Episode 7). Ken Murray. *Guests:* Miriam Hopkins, John Sebastian.

Pulitzer Prize Playhouse (ABC). January 12, 1951. "Ned McCobb's Daughter." (Season 1, Episode 15). Sidney Howard (writer/play). *Cast:* Miriam Hopkins, Anthony Quinn, Gig Young.

Lux Video Theatre (CBS). "Long Distance." March 12, 1951. (Season 1, Episode 24). Directed by Richard Goode. Teleplay by Harry W. Junkin. *Cast:* Richard Abbott, Helen Donaldson, Earl George, Miriam Hopkins, Lila Lee. The episode was repeated on April 23, 1953.

Betty Crocker Star Matinee (ABC). "Farewell to Love." December 29, 1951. (Season 1, Episode 9). *Cast:* Miriam Hopkins, Maria Rubenstein.

Lux Video Theatre (CBS). March 24, 1952. "Julie." (Season 2, Episode 31). Directed by Buzz Kulik. Teleplay by John Taintor Foote and William Kozlenko. *Cast:* Gene Blakely, Jerome Cowan, Miriam Hopkins.

Curtain Call (NBC). July 18, 1952. "The Party." (Season 1, Episode 5). Directed by Clark Jones. Based on a story by F. Scott Fitzgerald. *Cast:* Miriam Hopkins.

The Milton Berle Show (NBC). October 14, 1952. "Texaco Star Theater." (Season 5, Episode 4). *Cast:* Milton Berle, Gertrude Berg, Miriam Hopkins, Veronica Lake.

The Milton Berle Show (NBC). December 9, 1952. "Texaco Star Theater." (Season 5, Episode 10). *Cast:* Milton Berle, Miriam Hopkins, Caesar Romero, Teresa Brewer.

The Philip Morris Playhouse (CBS). December 10, 1953. "Serenade in Manhattan." (Season 1, Episode 11). *Cast:* Donald Cook, Miriam Hopkins, Everett Sloane.

Lux Video Theatre (CBS). February 4, 1954. "The Small Glass Bottle." (Season 4, Episode 14). Directed by Richard Goode. Teleplay by David Hill. *Cast:* Ken Carpenter, George Chandler, Ann Doran, Miriam Hopkins, Selmer Jackson.

General Electric Theater (CBS). June 20, 1954. "Desert Crossing." (Season 2, Episode 24). Directed by Frank Wisbar. Teleplay by Herbert Little Jr. and David Victor, based on a story by Dana Burnet. *Cast:* John Agar, Faith Domergue, James Dunn, Miriam Hopkins.

The Whistler (Syndicated). November 25, 1954. "The Return." (Season 1, Episode 9). Directed by Will Jason. Teleplay by Adrian Gendot and Joel Malone. *Cast:* Miriam Hopkins, Virginia Christine, William Schallert.

The Whistler (Syndicated). December 9, 1954. "Grave Secret." (Season 1, Episode 11). *Cast:* Pamela Duncan, William Forman, Robert Griffin, Miriam Hopkins, Hal Taggart, Murvyn Vye.

Lux Video Theatre (CBS). January 6, 1955. "Sunset Boulevard." (Season 5, Episode 20). Directed by Buzz Kulik. Teleplay by Richard P. McDonagh. *Cast:* Miriam Hopkins, James Daly, Nancy Gates, Lee Milar, James Mason, Ken Carpenter.

The Ray Milland Show (CBS). April 28, 1955. "The Molehouse Collection." (Season 2, Episode 33). *Cast:* Ray Milland, Miriam Hopkins.

Studio One in Hollywood (CBS). May 2, 1955. "Summer Pavilion." (Season 7, Episode 33). Directed by Paul Nickell. Teleplay by Gore Vidal. *Cast:* Miriam Hopkins, Charles Drake, Elizabeth Montgomery, Joseph Sweeney, Wyatt Cooper, Betty Furness.

Climax! (CBS). May 30, 1957. "The Disappearance of Amanda Hale." (Season 3, Episode 29). Teleplay by Katherine Albert and Dale Eunson. *Cast:* Lloyd Bridges, Verna Felton, Miriam Hopkins, Carolyn Jones, Alexander Scourby.

Matinee Theatre (NBC). September 4, 1957. "Woman Alone." (Season 3, Episode 3). Teleplay by Elizabeth Hart. *Cast:* Miriam Hopkins, John Conte.

Play of the Week (NET). February 27, 1961. "No Exit/The Indifferent Lover." (Season 2, Episode 23). Directed by Silvio Narizzano. Teleplay by Paul Bowles, based on a story by Jean Cocteau and Jean-Paul Sartre. *Cast:* Dane Clark, Colleen Dewhurst, Miriam Hopkins, Diana Hyland.

The Investigators (CBS). November 2, 1961. "Quite a Woman." (Season 1, Episode 5). Directed by Joseph H. Lewis. *Cast:* James Franciscus, Miriam Hopkins, Otto Kruger, Alan Mowbray.

General Electric Theater (CBS). March 11, 1962. "A Very Special Girl." (Season 10, Episode 24). Directed by Ida Lupino. Teleplay by Jameson Brewer. *Cast:* Ronald Reagan, Miriam Hopkins, Quinn O'Hara, Barbara Rush, Jane Withers.

Route 66 (CBS). May 17, 1963. "Shadows of an Afternoon." (Season 3, Episode 30). Directed by James Sheldon. Teleplay by Leonard Freeman and Alvin Sargent, based on a story by Leonard Freeman and Eric Scott. *Cast:* Martin Milner, Glenn Corbett, Ralph Meeker, Miriam Hopkins, Richard Mulligan, Greg Mullavey.

The Outer Limits (ABC). January 20, 1964. "Don't Open Till Doomsday." (Season 1, Episode 17). Directed by Gerd Oswald. Teleplay by Joseph Stefano. *Cast:* Miriam Hopkins, John Hoyt, Buck Taylor, Nellie Burt, Melinda Plowman, David Frankham, Ben Johnson.

The Flying Nun (ABC). November 26, 1969. "Bertrille and the Silent Flicks." (Season 3, Episode 11). Directed by Harry Falk. Teleplay by Leo Rifkin, based on a story by Michael Morris and novel by Tere Rios. *Cast:* Sally Field, Madeleine Sherwood, Alejandro Rey, Shelley Morrison, Miriam Hopkins.

Notes

Prologue

1. Milly S. Barranger, *Margaret Webster: A Life in the Theater* (Ann Arbor: University of Michigan Press, 2004), 110.

2. "Miriam Hopkins Afoul of Boston Censorship," *Montreal Gazette*, January 8, 1941.

3. Unidentified and undated quote. All quotes and clippings cited as "unidentified" and/or "undated" belong to a collection purchased by the author and now in the author's possession. Much of the material in this collection is unidentified and/or undated.

4. "Miriam Hopkins Returns to the Screen After Ten Years," *Reading Eagle*, August 26, 1961.

5. *Follies of God by James Grissom*, "Miriam Hopkins: Southern Divinity." (jamesgrissom.blogspot.com).

6. "Miriam Hopkins Returns to the Screen After Ten Years," *Reading Eagle*, August 26, 1961.

1. "From a Fine Old Family"

1. Letter from Miriam Hopkins to Minnie Hopkins Keever, September 30, 1939.

2. "Two Shows Star Georgia Girl," *Bainbridge Post-Searchlight*, October 26, 1972.

3. George Eells, *Ginger, Loretta and Irene Who?* (New York: G.P. Putnam's Sons), 1976.

4. James E. Dickinson's home was at the corner of Planter and Clay Streets. It was later owned by Judge Byron B. Bower, who married Ellen Tallulah Dickinson, James's daughter and great aunt of Miriam Hopkins. At Bower's death in 1923, the house passed to his son Byron Bower II, who lived there until it was sold to R. L. Rich for the site of Rich Chevrolet Company.

5. Ralph Hastings Cutter was born in Louisville, Kentucky, on November 4, 1835, the second of nine children of John Hastings and Susan (Pool) Cutter.

6. To commemorate Ruby Cutter's short life, a plaque in her memory hangs in St. John's Episcopal Church in Bainbridge.

7. An article appeared in the *Atlanta Constitution* showcasing Ellen's talent at

a Gainesville social event, December 5, 1897; Maryalice Mohr, archivist, New England Conservatory of Music to Allan Ellenberger.

8. The office of Hopkins & Hines represented the Prudential and the New Amsterdam Casualty Company Insurance carriers.

9. Ruby Middleton Hopkins was born on April 1, 1900, in Savannah, Georgia.

10. Joan Tinklepaugh, Hollis Historical Society to Allan Ellenberger.

11. Record of Persons supported at Taunton Lunatic Hospital; Joan Tinklepaugh, Hollis Historical Society.

12. Eells, *Ginger, Loretta and Irene Who?* 84–84.

13. Becky Morehouse to Allan Ellenberger, October 28, 2008.

14. 1910 United States Census, Savannah, Georgia. National Archives.

15. "Two Shows Star Georgia Girl," *Bainbridge Post-Searchlight*, October 26, 1972.

16. Paramount Biography, circa 1932.

17. "Miriam Hopkins Has High Ambition," *Boston Daily Globe*, September 14, 1924.

18. Ibid.

19. Eells, *Ginger, Loretta and Irene Who?* 84.

20. Ibid.

21. Miriam's boyfriend, Royce Pitkin, later returned to Goddard as its president in 1936, after the seminary was converted to a college.

22. "Tiniest Star of the Stage," *New York American*, undated clipping.

23. "Fanny Brown was Fascinating," *Barre Daily Times*, April 30, 1919.

24. The Knickerbocker Theatre Building was located at 1400 Broadway.

25. "To Film Stardom," unidentified and undated clipping.

26. "Miriam Hopkins Will be Welcomed Here in the Stellar Role of Laura," *Daily Boston Globe*, April 28, 1946.

27. "The Greatest Thrill I Ever Experienced," by Miriam Hopkins, Paramount Pictures.

2. Broadway Bound

1. Eells, *Ginger, Loretta and Irene Who?* 86.

2. Ibid.

3. "To Film Stardom," unidentified and undated clipping.

4. Joseph Hergesheimer, "The Music Box Theatre Takes a Bow at 50," *New York Times*, September 23, 1951.

5. "More About Miriam," unidentified clipping, January 1933.

6. *New York Times*, September 23, 1921.

7. *True Confessions*, March 1935.

8. Becky Morehouse to Allan Ellenberger, October 28, 2008.

9. Ibid.

10. Letter from F. Scott Fitzgerald to Anne Ober, July 26, 1937.

11. Eells, *Ginger, Loretta and Irene Who?* 87.

12. The dance company was founded the previous year by Desiree Lubovska, born Winniefred Foote, and was supported by Langdon Greer, L. S. Rothafel, and actress Lillian Gish (who served on the board). The troupe would be performing in Argentina, Peru, Chile, and Brazil and sailed on February 4, 1922, on the SS *Van Dyke*; U.S. Passport Applications, January 30, 1922.

13. "Accidents Come in Handy for Miriam Hopkins," *Los Angeles Times*, October 15, 1933.

14. "The Human Side of a Menace," *Modern Screen*, February 1940.

15. *New York Times*, August 16, 1923; *New York American*, undated clipping.

16. "Miriam Hopkins Has High Ambition," *Boston Daily Globe*, September 14, 1924.

17. "Miriam Hopkins Deserted 'Art' to Thrill Mystery-Mad Crowds," *Boston Daily Globe*, May 12, 1946.

18. Ward Morehouse, *Forty-Five Minutes Past Eight* (New York: Dial, 1939), 71–72.

19. "Velvet Dynamite," *Picture Play Magazine*, March 1935.

20. "Along Broadway with Dixie Hines," *Evening Independent*, August 1, 1924.

21. "Belasco," *Washington Post*, December 16, 1924; *Washington Star*, December 16, 1924.

22. Marion Tanner (1896–1985) lived at 72 Bank Street with her husband, Lingard Loud, in 1925 according to the New York State Census. She lived there until she was evicted in 1964; Patrick Dennis, whose real name was Edward Everett Tanner III, would deny that his aunt Marion was an inspiration for Auntie Mame. The two had a falling out in the late 1950s and never spoke again; Becky Morehouse to Allan Ellenberger, October 28, 2008.

23. "The Real Life Story of Fredric March," *Screenland*, July 1932.

24. *New York Telegram*, undated clipping; *New York Times*, March 10, 1925.

25. The Shubert Theater is located at 247 College Street, New Haven, Connecticut. The theater is still in operation.

26. *New Haven Journal-Courier*, June 2, 1925.

27. "Filial Devotion Takes the Day," *New Haven Register*, September 29, 1925.

28. Miriam played the role of Beth Calhoun, the same part that Peg Entwistle would later play on Broadway; "More About Miriam," unidentified clipping, January 1933; Paramount Studio biography, circa 1930s.

29. Liveright and Boni were the first to take an interest in the writings of Eugene O'Neill, Ben Hecht, and Ernest Hemingway. Liveright had a rule that any young author's first book should always be given an opportunity to succeed on the chance that the second book might be good.

30. Liveright wanted to cast actors who "absolutely looked the part," so based on photographs and Clines's advice, Liveright agreed that Miriam was right for the part. *Syracuse Herald*, August 15, 1926; "More About Miriam," unidentified clipping, January 1933.

31. Opening night competition included Jeanne Eagels in *Rain*, Helen Hayes at the Bijou in *What Every Woman Knows*, and the Anita Loos play *Gentlemen Prefer Blondes*, playing at the Times Square Theater. Also, the Theatre Guild was premiering Franz Werfel's *Juarez and Maximilian*.

32. Keith Newlin, ed., *A Theodore Dreiser Encyclopedia* (Westport, CT: Greenwood Publishing Group, 2003), 3–4.

33. "'American Tragedy' and New Guild Play Score," *New York Graphic*, October 12, 1926.

34. Before tapering off to $9,000 per week the following April. Newlin, *A Theodore Dreiser Encyclopedia*, 4; unidentified and undated clipping.

35. Eells, *Ginger, Loretta and Irene Who?* 89.

36. "Brandon Peters" obituary, *Evening Standard*, March 7, 1956.

37. Michael Hopkins to Allan Ellenberger, January 20, 2007.

38. Bennett Cerf: Notable New Yorkers, Columbia Center for Oral History.

39. Ibid. Even though the romance was fleeting, their friendship remained strong until Cerf's death in 1971.

40. "More About Miriam," unidentified clipping, January 1933.

41. "What a Gal!" *New Movie Magazine*, October 1932.

42. Eells, *Ginger, Loretta and Irene Who?* 89.

43. "'Thou Desperate Pilot' a Symbolic Tragedy," *New York Times*, March 8, 1927.

44. Gavin Lambert, *On Cukor* (Ann Arbor: University of Michigan Press, 2000), 25–30.

45. Other plays in the series included *Is Zat So?*, *The Patsy*, and *The Poor Nut*; "More About Miriam," unidentified clipping, January 1933.

46. The *New York Sun* newspaper's offices were at 280 Broadway, known as the Sun Building. The building was recognized as a New York City landmark in 1986.

47. "Get a Loan of Otto Kahn," unidentified and undated clipping; Ward Morehouse, *Just the Other Day* (New York: McGraw-Hill, 1953), 131.

48. "Robert Montgomery Tells His Life Story," *Silver Screen*, December 1931.

49. Michael Hopkins to Allan Ellenberger, January 20, 2007.

50. "The Garden of Eden," *New York Mirror*, September 28, 1927.

51. "Ruby Hopkins Welch" obituary. *The Bainbridge Post-Searchlight*, December 19, 1990.

52. Tom Hopkins to Allan Ellenberger, October 8, 2006; Becky Morehouse to Allan Ellenberger, October 12, 2008.

53. Michael Hopkins to Allan Ellenberger, January 20, 2007.

3. Billy

1. Phyllis Duganne wrote mostly short fiction for *Collier's*, the *Saturday Evening Post*, and other commercial magazines. Their only daughter, Jane, was born in 1920.

2. Austin Parker resigned and enlisted in the Lafayette Escadrille, composed of aviators from various nations. Parker trained at an army flying school and fought several air battles against the Germans before the United States entered the war. Once the Yanks arrived, he transferred, becoming one of the first American aviators to see battle.

3. Miriam appeared in *Excess Baggage* in the evenings and played double-duty for three matinee performances in a revival of *John Ferguson* at the Theatre Marque. One review said her Hannah Ferguson, the daughter of the title character, displayed "genuine emotional ability and she also possesses a winning personality." *Excess Baggage* premiered Christmas week along with nineteen other productions, including *White Eagle*, a musical version of *The Squaw Man; Alice Brady in *Bless You Sister*, at the Forrest Theatre; Judith Anderson in George Kelly's *Behold the Bridegroom*, at the Cort Theatre; and Florenz Ziegfeld's musical *Show Boat*, at the Lyric.

4. Doris Eaton Travis, *The Days We Danced: The Story of My Theatrical Family* (University of Oklahoma Press, 2003), 141.

5. Doris Eaton Travis to Allan Ellenberger, January 12, 2008.

6. "Excess Baggage," unidentified and undated clipping; "Excess Baggage Enjoyed," *New York Times*, December 27, 1927.

7. The Forrest Hotel was at 224 West Forty-Ninth Street and is now the Time Hotel.

8. The Fifth Avenue Hotel was located at 24 Fifth Avenue in Greenwich Village and today is a co-op.

9. "Trouble Looms for Stage Star in Marriage Mix-up," *Rochester Evening Journal* and the *Post Express*, June 28, 1928.

10. Eells, *Ginger, Loretta and Irene Who?* 91.

11. "Miriam Hopkins Begins a New Life," *Movie Classic*, December 1935.

12. "Miriam Hopkins Tells Me," *Los Angeles Examiner*, July 7, 1934.

13. "What Marriage Has Taught Me," unidentified and undated clipping.

14. "Miriam Hopkins' Unusual Love Affair," *Movie Classic*, March 1935.

15. Charlotte Chandler, *The Girl Who Walked Home Alone* (New York: Applause Theatre and Cinema Books, 2007), 51.

16. Emanuel Levy, *George Cukor, Master of Elegance* (Ann Arbor: University of Michigan Press, 1994), 37.

17. "Excess Baggage," unidentified clipping, October 16, 1928; *Rochester Times*, October 16, 1928.

18. Ed Sikov, *Dark Victory: The Life of Bette Davis* (New York: Henry Holt, 2007), 33.

19. James Spada, *More Than a Woman: An Intimate Biography of Bette Davis* (New York: Random House, 1994), 58.

20. *Playboy*, July 1982.

21. Barbara Leaming, *Bette Davis: A Biography* (New York: Simon & Schuster, 1992), 66.

22. Levy, *George Cukor, Master of Elegance*, 37.

23. Lambert, *On Cukor*, 27.

24. Eells, *Ginger, Loretta and Irene Who?* 91.

25. Built around 1826, 108 Waverly Place and three others are the only ones that remain of nine original row houses. In 1906, architect Charles C. Haight created the cut masonry and crenellated cornices, simulating a castle.

26. *The Home Girl* was the fourth episode in the "Great Stars and Authors" series of 2-reel talking shorts that Paramount was experimenting with.

27. "Cane Crop," *Hartford Courant*, January 11, 1929.

28. *Time*, March 29, 1929.

29. John Garfield, not yet an actor, was given a job as a sixteen-year-old assistant on the production. Helen Westley sat on the Theatre Guild's board of directors; "Theatre Guild Gives a Czech Comedy," *New York Times*, April 16, 1929.

30. "The Bachelor Father," *London Times*, October 1, 1929; *London Daily Mail*, October 1, 1929; American-born Peggy O'Neil, who later became a famous stage actress and singer in England, replaced her.

31. The apartment building was demolished and the site is now the home of the New York University School of Law.

32. *New York Times*, October 1930.

33. *New York Amusements*, "Interview Department," July 21, 1930.

34. Ibid.

35. "Miriam Hopkins at Home," *New York Times*, March 15, 1936.

36. "Lysistrata review," unidentified and undated clipping.

37. "Seldes Version of Ancient Greek Farce a Live Offering," unidentified and undated clipping.

4. Of Paramount Importance

1. "Giggle Her Way to Film Stardom," *Daily Boston Globe*, November 1, 1931.

2. Miriam's Paramount contract included a clause that allowed her to perform in plays if it didn't "interfere with or conflict with the proper rendition of the actresses' services." Paramount Pictures contract, June 25, 1930, Chamberlain and Lyman Brown Collection, New York Public Library.

3. Paramount's Astoria, Long Island Studios was a meeting place for Broadway and Hollywood actors. Built in 1918, the studio saw the production of countless notable silent films; Erskine Johnson column, *Daily News*, August 12, 1950.

4. "Pictures Taught Miriam Hopkins Her Versatility," *Los Angeles Times*, August 10, 1934.

5. *New York Amusements*, "Interview Department," July 21, 1930.

6. "Those Clever People," *New York Times*, December 1, 1930; "Excellent Talk Film Unreeled," *Los Angeles Times*, November 15, 1930.

7. Laurence Reid. *Motion Picture News*, undated clipping.

8. Nydia Westman replaced Miriam as Kolonokia in *Lysistrata;* "Miriam Hopkins' Unusual Love Affair," *Movie Classic*, March 1935.

9. Series of telegrams between Miriam and Lyman Brown, September 29, 1930, to October 2, 1930, Chamberlain and Lyman Brown Collection, New York Public Library.

10. "His Majesety's Car," unidentified and undated clipping.

11. José Limón, *José Limón: An Unfinished Memoir* (Middletown, Connecticut: Wesleyan University Press, 1998), 69.

12. Robert Littell, "Down in Front," *New York World*, undated clipping.

13. Becky Morehouse to Allan Ellenberger, October 28, 2008; Letter from Miriam Hopkins to Minnie Hopkins Keever, September 30, 1939.

14. "Miriam Hopkins Strange Love Affair," *Movie Classic*, March 1935.

15. In addition to the French version, a British version was made. "We refilmed the scene where I refuse to be laughed at by a mere 'leftenant,'" Miriam said; Unidentified and undated clipping.

16. John Kobal, *People Will Talk* (New York: Knopf, 1985), 256.

17. Renee Carroll, *In Your Hat* (New York: Macaulay, 1933), 90.

18. *The Smiling Lieutenant* (1931).

19. "Happy Hopkins," *Silver Screen*, December 1932; "Miriam Hopkins Spends Evening in Amarillo by Going to the Movies," *Amarillo Globe-Times*, October 7, 1931.

20. "Colbert, Hedy Feud Overdue," *Prescott Evening News*, April 12, 1940.

21. "Mary Astor's Film Chosen," *Los Angeles Times*, February 28, 1931.

22. "What Marriage Has Taught Me," unidentified and undated clipping.

23. Eells, *Ginger, Loretta and Irene Who?* 94–95.

24. Ibid., 95.

25. Ibid.; Lois Long divorced Peter Arno later that year. They had one daughter, Patricia, born in 1929.

26. Ibid., 95

27. "M. Chevalier, Considerably Assisted by Herr Lubitsch," *Dallas Morning News*, August 8, 1931.

28. "To Retain Astoria Studios," *New York Times*, June 27, 1931.

29. "Giggled Her Way to Film Stardom," *Daily Boston Globe*, November 1, 1931.

30. Kobal, *People Will Talk*, 358.

31. "Trade Winds," *Saturday Evening Post*, March 30, 1946; The Shelton Hotel was located at Lexington and Forty-Ninth Street and today is the New York Marriott East Side.

5. Hollywood

1. "Miriam Hopkins Arrives in Town," *Los Angeles Illustrated Daily News*, June 9, 1931.

2. Morehouse, *Forty-Five Minutes Past Eight*, 131.

3. Miriam's beach house was located at 9 Las Tunas Beach.

4. Lilyan Tashman was originally cast as Rosie but was still filming *The Road to Reno* with Charles "Buddy" Rogers.

5. Unidentified and undated clipping.

6. Eells, *Ginger, Loretta and Irene Who?* 97.

7. Joseph Yranski to Allan Ellenberger, May 20, 2007.

8. "Why Men Fall for Miriam Hopkins," *Modern Screen*, March 1934.

9. "On and Off Broadway," *New York Times*, October 11, 1931.

10. "Miriam Hopkins' Unusual Love Affair," *Modern Classic*, March 1935.

11. Susan Delson, *Dudley Murphy, Hollywood Wild Card* (Minneapolis: University of Minnesota Press, 2006), 106–107.

12. Michael Hopkins to Allan Ellenberger, January 20, 2007.

13. Tom Hopkins to Allan Ellenberger, October 8, 2006.

14. Dan Thomas column, *Los Angeles Record*, September 12, 1931.

15. *American Screen Classic*, November/December 1976. *Dr. Jekyll and Mr. Hyde* was budgeted at $557,000. Miriam was paid $3,750 during rehearsals, $600 for expenses, and $7,083.34 for principal photography.

16. Gregory William Mank, *Women in Horror Films, 1930s* (Jefferson, NC: McFarland, 1999).

17. Tom Weaver, *Double Feature Creature Attack* (Jefferson, NC: McFarland, 2003), 162.

18. Doris Eaton Travis to Allan Ellenberger, January 12, 2008.

19. Weaver, *Double Feature Creature Attack*, 162.

20. David DelValle, "Interview with Rouben Mamoulian," *Video Watchdog*, July/August 1993, 54.

21. Kobal, *People Will Talk*, 361.

22. "Righteously Indignant," *Los Angeles Evening Herald*, September 18, 1931.

23. Kobal, *People Will Talk*, 360.

24. "Righteously Indignant," *Los Angeles Evening Herald*, September 18, 1931.

25. "Miriam Hopkins Irked," *Los Angeles Evening Herald*, October 3, 1931.

26. Ibid.

27. "Are You Up to Date About Miriam Hopkins?" *Motion Picture*, February 1932.

28. "Miriam Wants a Rest," *Hollywood*, August 1932.

29. DelValle, "Interview with Rouben Mamoulian," *Video Watchdog*, July/August 1993, 54.

30. In Chicago, the censors cut all scenes of Ivy after she took off the first garter. In Saskatchewan and Japan, Ivy's strip was deleted. MPAA/PCA Collection, Margaret Herrick Library, AMPAS.

31. Memo to Albert Deane from Lillian Brind, February 12, 1932. Rouben Mamoulian Collection, Library of Congress; Letter from Dora Nirva to Rouben Mamoulian, February 14, 1932. Rouben Mamoulian Collection, Library of Congress.

32. Unidentified and undated clipping.

33. "Screen Gains Masterpiece," *Los Angeles Times*, December 26, 1931.

6. "An Expensive Leading Woman"

1. "Lost Love Creates a Great Friendship," unidentified and undated clipping.

2. Leatrice Gilbert Fountain to Allan Ellenberger, January 4, 2008.

3. Ibid.

4. "Lost Love Creates a Great Friendship," unidentified and undated clipping.

5. *Life*, January 1932.

6. Unidentified and undated clipping.

7. The huge public dance hall set was filmed on Paramount's Stage 8, which was used in most *Star Trek* productions, including the first seven feature films, *The Next Generation*, *Voyager*, *Enterprise*, and the 2009 *Star Trek* movie. Stages 10 and 11 were used for the speakeasy and other sets.

8. Becky Morehouse to Allan Ellenberger, October 28, 2008.

9. Margot Welch to Allan Ellenberger, February 19, 2010.

10. Unidentified and undated clipping.

11. "30 Girls in a Race for Stardom," *Photoplay*, April 1932.

12. "Stardom Is Miriam Hopkins' Dream," *Los Angeles Evening Herald Express*, March 12, 1932.

13. Four reels of scenes filmed during the revolution were used and Russian aristocrat exiles were hired as extras. To add authenticity, scenes were shot at San Pedro Harbor aboard the army transport *Playa De Ensenada*.

14. "Hollywood in Person," *Dallas Morning News*, June 8, 1933.

15. Mark A. Vieira, *Irving Thalberg: Boy Wonder to Producer Prince* (Berkeley: University of California Press, 2009), 227.

16. Jean Dalrymple, *September Child: The Story of Jean Dalrymple* (New York: Dodd, Mead, 1963).

17. "Miriam Hopkins Adopts Child," *Los Angeles Times*, May 5, 1932.

18. "Miriam Hopkins Adopts Orphanage Baby Boy," unidentified clipping, May 5, 1932.

19. Tom Hopkins to Allan Ellenberger, October 8, 2006.

20. Paramount records, AMPAS.

21. Chris Hopkins to Allan Ellenberger, January 20, 2007.

22. Michael Hopkins to Allan Ellenberger, January 20, 2007.

23. "Lost Love Creates a Great Friendship," unidentified and undated clipping.

24. Letter from Miriam Hopkins to Minnie Hopkins Keever, September 30, 1939.

25. Eells, *Ginger, Loretta and Irene Who?* 102.

26. "Miriam's Adopted Son," *Modern Screen Magazine*, August 1932.

27. The rights to *I Married an Angel* were later sold to MGM and not produced for another decade, with Jeanette MacDonald in the lead; The film adaptation of *The Honest Finder*, a play by Aladar Laszlo, wouldn't receive its final title *Trouble in Paradise* until nearly a month after it was completed.

28. Samson Raphaelson, *New Yorker*, May 11, 1981.

29. Scott Eyman, *Ernst Lubitsch: Laughter in Paradise* (New York: Simon & Schuster, 1993), 190.

30. "Ernst Lubitsch Triumphs Again," *Los Angeles Times*, November 13, 1932.

31. Christopher Lynch, *When Hollywood Landed at Chicago's Midway Airport: The Photos and Stories of Mike Rotunno* (Charleston, SC: History Press, 2012), 59.

32. Ibid., 60.

33. "Program of Ardmore Unit Is Enjoyable," *Oklahoman*, November 10, 1932.

34. Kobal, *People Will Talk*, 362–363.

35. "Art, Sex and Miriam Hopkins," *Screen Book*, June 1934.

36. "Strangers in Love," *Frederick Post*, October 29, 1935.

37. "Faulkner was Wrong about Sanctuary," *New York Times*, February 22, 1981.

38. "Dostoyefsky's Shadows in the Deep South," *New York Times*, February 15, 1931; "Books: Baudelaire with Loving Care," *Time*, February 16, 1931.

39. MPPDA file on *The Story of Temple Drake*, Margaret Herrick Library, AMPAS.

40. "Will His First Big Role Make or Break Jack La Rue," *Movie Classic*, May 1933.

41. Stone Wallace to Allan Ellenberger, October 10, 2006.

42. Memo from Will Hays to James Wingate, February 9, 1933; Memo from James Wingate to Will Hays, February 10, 1933. MPPDA file on *The Story of Temple Drake*, Margaret Herrick Library, AMPAS.

43. "Will His First Big Role Make or Break Jack La Rue," *Movie Classic*, May 1933.

44. Memo from Emanuel Cohen to Will Hays, March 4, 1933, AMPAS.

45. Jean Negulesco, *Things I Did and Things I Think I Did* (New York: Simon & Schuster, 1984), 91–92.

46. Kobal, *People Will Talk*, 356.

47. "A Rebel Against Life," *Photoplay*, July, 1933.

48. "Art, Sex and Miriam Hopkins," *Screen Book*, June 1934.

49. Becky Morehouse to Allan Ellenberger, October 28, 2008.

50. Ibid.

51. Letter from James Wingate to Adolf Zukor, March 16, 1933.

52. Becky Morehouse to Allan Ellenberger, October 28, 2008.

53. MPPDA, Margaret Herrick Library, AMPAS.

54. *Motion Picture Daily*, May 6, 1933; "The Screen," *New York Times*, May 6, 1933.

55. *Washington Times*, undated clipping; *New York American*, undated clipping.

56. "My Movie Moral Code," *Movie Classic*, October 1933.

57. "The Human Side of a Menace," *Modern Screen*, February 1940.

58. "The Story of Temple Drake," *Sydney Morning Herald*, February 12, 1934; "Temple Drake," *Dallas Morning News*, June 18, 1933.

59. *Nation*, May 15, 1933, 594–95; "Stage First with Miriam Hopkins, Hollywood Fine in Small Doses," *Pittsburgh Press*, October 10, 1934.

60. Stone Wallace to Allan Ellenberger, October 10, 2006.

61. "Nothing Frightens Miriam Hopkins," unidentified and undated clipping.

62. "The Screen," *New York Times*, July 28, 1933.

7. The Lubitsch Touch

1. Memo, January 26, 1933, MPAA/PCA Collection, Margaret Herrick Library, AMPAS.

2. *Design For Living*, AFI Catalogue notes.

3. Richard Dicks, *The Wit of Noël Coward* (London: Leslie Frewin, 1968), 85.

4. Eyman, *Ernst Lubitsch*, 208.

5. Ibid.

6. King Vidor, *A Tree Is a Tree* (New York: Harcourt, Brace, 1952), 277–78.

7. Eyman, *Ernst Lubitsch*, 209.

8. Becky Morehouse to Allan Ellenberger, October 28, 2008.

9. Berthold and Salka Viertel lived at 165 Mabery Road, Santa Monica. The Viertels and their three sons arrived in Hollywood from Germany in 1927.

10. Peter Viertel, "Miriam Hopkins," *Architectural Digest*, 211.

11. Nancy Dowd and David Shepard, *King Vidor* (Directors Guild of America, 1988), 143.

12. "Excellent Direction, Fine Performances," *Hollywood Reporter*, undated clipping.

13. Ibid.; unidentified and undated clipping.

14. "Stage First with Miriam Hopkins," *Pittsburgh Press*, October 10, 1934.

15. "Blonde Miriam Hopkins Hits Autocracy of Film Studios," *Daily Boston Globe*, February 26, 1934.

16. Lyman and Chamberlain Brown Collection, New York Public Library.

17. Myron Selznick, the brother of David O. Selznick, established himself as a powerful agent in the late 1920s. Producers had operated under a "gentlemen's agreement" whereby they wouldn't invade one another's studios for talent when their contracts came up for renewal.

18. "Stage First with Miriam Hopkins, Hollywood Fine in Small Doses," *Pittsburgh Press*, October 10, 1934.

19. Owen Davis, *My First Fifty Years* (Boston: Walter H. Baker Company, 1950), 127.

20. Tallulah Bankhead, *Tallulah: My Autobiography* (New York: Harper, 1952), 212.

21. Their professional affiliation survived for several years. They remained friends until Hayward's death in 1971.

22. *Variety*, December 15, 1933.

23. Miriam was not the only Hollywood actress returning to Broadway that season. Helen Hayes was in *Mary of Scotland* and Katharine Hepburn was in *The Lake*. Other plays competing with *Jezebel* include Eugene O'Neill's *Ah, Wilderness!*, *Roberta*, and *Tobacco Road*.

24. "The Play," John Mason Brown, *New York Post*, December 20, 1933.

25. Davis, *My First Fifty Years in the Theatre*, 127.

26. Robert Garland, "Jezebel, at Last . . . ," *New York World-Telegram*, December 20, 1933; "Miriam Hopkins in Owen Davis's Drama of the Pre-Civil War Southland," *New York Times*, December 20, 1933.

27. Adolph Zukor Collection, Margaret Herrick Library, AMPAS. Telegram, January 4, 1934.

28. Eells, *Ginger, Loretta and Irene Who?* 100–101.

29. Danton Walker, *Spooks Deluxe* (New York: Franklin Watts, 1956), 44; Bankhead, *Tallulah: My Autobiography*, 212.

30. "Stage First with Miriam Hopkins, Hollywood Fine in Small Doses," *Pittsburgh Press*, October 10, 1934.

31. Eells, *Ginger, Loretta and Irene Who?* 101.

8. Sutton Place

1. A renowned leader in theatrical, literary, political, and civic life, Elisabeth Marbury was George Bernard Shaw's agent. Crossing the Atlantic seventy times, she saw Paris in ruins after the Prussian victory of 1897, and she was decorated by several governments. In the 1922 governor's election, she campaigned for Al Smith and fought against prohibition.

2. Eells, *Ginger, Loretta and Irene Who?* 101–2.

3. "About Bing's New Co-Star, Miriam Hopkins," *Screenland*, September 1934.

4. "About Bing's New Co-Star, Miriam Hopkins," *Screenland*, September 1934; Miriam and Bing Crosby and their families were good friends. Michael and Cros-

by's oldest son, Gary, who was a year younger, would play together when Bing's wife, Dixie Lee, very pregnant at the time, visited the set. Dixie gave birth to twin boys the following July; Kobal, *People Will Talk*, 361.

5. Ibid.

6. Ibid.

7. Kitty Carlisle to Allan Ellenberger, September 16, 2006.

8. "Mr. Bing Crosby has Good Plot and Songs Here," *Chicago Daily Tribune*, August 4, 1934.

9. William Drew, *At the Center of the Frame: Leading Ladies of the Twenties and Thirties* (Vestal, NY: Vestal, 1999), 95.

10. Eells, *Ginger, Loretta and Irene Who?* 102–3. The drawing room walls were covered in a bird chintz and framed in pine from France. A piece of the same chintz hung in the Boston Art Museum.

11. Memo from Joseph Breen to B. B. Kahane, July 11, 1934, RKO Studio Records circa 1928–1958, UCLA.

12. "The Proper Things to Do," *Picture Play* magazine, undated clipping.

13. John Hay Whitney and Cornelius Vanderbilt Whitney owned a substantial portion of Technicolor stock. That year, they produced the first Technicolor short, "La Cucaracha." Whitney and his partner, Merian C. Cooper, formed Pioneer Pictures Inc. The studios had used color sequences in films but were fearful of the added cost and problems that went with it.

14. Miles Krueger to Allan Ellenberger, October 25, 2006.

15. Letter from F. Scott Fitzgerald to Bennett Cerf, November 20, 1934. Random House Archive, Columbia University Library.

16. Letter from Bennett Cerf to F. Scott Fitzgerald, November 23, 1934. Random House Archive, Columbia University Library. Three years later when MGM retained the rights for *Tender Is the Night* from Goldwyn, Fitzgerald still wanted Miriam and Fredric March for the leads, but Thalberg died before they could proceed.

17. Eells, *Ginger, Loretta and Irene Who?* 102.

18. Letter from Miriam Hopkins to Minnie Hopkins Keever, September 30, 1939.

19. Eells, *Ginger, Loretta and Irene Who?* 118.

20. Charlotte Cox Smith to Allan Ellenberger, January 9, 2011.

21. Letter from Miriam Hopkins to Minnie Hopkins Keever, September 30, 1939.

22. Ruby married Jack Welch on May 26, 1933; Letter from Miriam Hopkins to Minnie Hopkins Keever, September 30, 1939.

23. Margot Welch to Allan Ellenberger, February 19, 2010.

24. Michael Hopkins to Allan Ellenberger, January 20, 2007.

25. Letter from Miriam Hopkins to Minnie Hopkins Keever, September 30, 1939.

26. Ibid.

27. Miriam Hopkins-Pioneer Pictures contract, September 25, 1934, David O. Selznick Collection, HRC.

28. The *Lux Radio Theatre* series premiered on October 14, 1934, from New York on the NBC Blue Network with a production of *Seventh Heaven*, starring Miriam Hopkins and John Boles in a full-hour adaptation of the 1922–1924 Broadway production.

29. The dinner was held on Sunday, November 11, 1934, at Cerf's apartment. Bennett Cerf, Notable New Yorkers, Columbia Center for Oral History, session 6, 282.

30. Ibid.

31. Nancy Grove, *Isamu Noguchi Portrait Sculpture* (Washington, DC: Smithsonian Institution, 1989).

32. "The Screen," *New York Times*, June 14, 1935; *Los Angeles Times*, February 24, 1935.

33. "Becky Sharp and a Leading Lady," *New York Times*, April 7, 1935.

34. "Pioneer Film Director with a Colorful Past," *Los Angeles Herald-Examiner*, November 25, 1984.

35. *Lady with Red Hair file*, Warner Bros. Archives, USC.

36. "Grand Larceny in Films Wins Only Approval," *Dallas Morning News*, August 9, 1936.

37. Drama-Logue, Issue No. 47, November 22–28, 1984.

38. "Star Ill," *Los Angeles Illustrated Daily News*, January 19, 1935.

39. William Saroyan, "Rouben Mamoulian Directing Miriam Hopkins in Becky Sharp for Me," *Sons Come and Go, Mothers Hang in Forever* (New York: McGraw-Hill, 1976), 90–91.

40. Dickran Kouymjian to Allan Ellenberger, January 22, 2008.

41. Saroyan, *Sons Come and Go, Mothers Hang in Forever*, 91–92.

42. "Glamour with a Grin!" *Screenland*, November 1935.

43. "Miriam Hopkins Discusses Technicolor," *New York World-Telegram*, April 24, 1935.

44. Memo from Lowell Calvert to Kenneth MacGowan, December 26, 1934, Miriam Hopkins legal file, JWC, HRC, University of Texas at Austin; Emily Carman, *Independent Stardom* (Austin, TX: University of Texas Press, 2016), 55.

45. *New York Mirror*, June 14, 1935.

46. *Amarillo Globe*, October 24, 1935.

47. "Becky Sharp Gorgeous Pic," *Hollywood Reporter*, June 15, 1935.

48. *Time*, May 27, 1935; Ward Morehouse, unidentified and undated clipping.

9. Goldwyn

1. *Harrison's Reports;* Frances Marion, a two-time Academy Award winner, submitted a script that Goldwyn liked but changed his mind the following

day. Marion suggested that he find another writer. Letter from Samuel Goldwyn to Frances Marion, September 14, 1933. Samuel Goldwyn Collection, AMPAS.

2. During his screen test, Walter Brennan asked Howard Hawks if he wanted him "with or without?" Hawks asked what he was referring to. "Teeth," Brennan replied. He removed his dentures and so amused Hawks that he expanded his role; Alvin H. Marill, *Samuel Goldwyn Presents* (New York: A.S. Barnes, 1976), 153.

3. The *Barbary Coast* set was a huge, enclosed preproduction of a schooner and the San Francisco waterfront covering three acres on the Goldwyn lot.

4. Edward G. Robinson and Leonard Spigelgass, *All My Yesterdays: An Autobiography* (Portland, OR: Hawthorne, 1973), 156.

5. Ibid.

6. Ibid.

7. Unidentified and undated clipping.

8. Letter from Joel McCrea to Colleen Cross, June 23, 1984.

9. Joel McCrea was 6'3" and Miriam was 5'2."

10. Kobal, *People Will Talk*, 311–312.

11. Robinson and Spigelgass, *All My Yesterdays*, 160.

12. Alan L. Gansberg, *Little Caesar: A Biography of Edward G. Robinson* (Lanham, MD: Scarecrow, 2004), 57.

13. Robinson and Spigelgass, *All My Yesterdays*, 161.

14. Gansberg, *Little Caesar*, 58.

15. Robinson and Spigelgass, *All My Yesterdays*, 180.

16. *New York American*, undated clipping.

17. *New York Times*, October 14, 1935; *Hollywood Reporter*, undated clipping.

18. Scott Breivold and Howard Hawks. *Howard Hawks: Interviews* (Jackson: University Press of Mississippi, 2006), 22.

19. Eells, *Ginger, Loretta and Irene Who?* 105.

20. Delmar took *Hands Across the Table* to Paramount, where once again one of Miriam's castoffs was a success for Carole Lombard.

21. Goldwyn lured Crothers to Hollywood with her first original screenplay by offering a share of the films profits instead of a salary. Goldwyn felt that percentage deals would take the place of salaries; Eells, *Ginger, Loretta and Irene Who?* 105.

22. Grant Hayter-Menzies, *Mrs. Ziegfeld: The Public and Private Lives of Billie Burke* (Jefferson, NC: McFarland, 2009), 160–61.

23. "Flim Flam with Sidney Skolsky," *Hollywood Citizen-News*, November 22, 1935.

24. "Miriam Hopkins Likes Directors and Sometimes Directs Them," *Dallas Morning News*, March 27, 1937.

25. "Miriam Hopkins at Home," *New York Times*, March 15, 1936.

26. "Glamour with a Grin," *Screenland*, November 1935.

27. Arthur Marx, *Goldwyn: A Biography of the Man Behind the Myth* (New York: W. W. Norton, 1976), 271.

28. Memo from Joseph Breen to Will Hays, January 6, 1935. MPAA/PCA Collection. AMPAS.

29. "Merle Talks About Miriam and Herself," *Screenland*, February 1936.

30. Jan Herman, *A Talent for Trouble: The Life of Hollywood's Most Acclaimed Director, William Wyler* (New York: G. P. Putnam's Sons, 1995), 142.

31. Scott A. Berg, *Goldwyn: A Biography* (New York: Knopf, 1989), 270.

32. "Merle Talks About Miriam and Herself," *Screenland*, February 1936; Eells, *Ginger, Loretta and Irene Who?* 105.

33. Kobal, *People Will Talk*, 311.

34. Eells, *Ginger, Loretta and Irene Who?* 99.

35. Michael Hopkins to Allan Ellenberger, January 20, 2007.

36. "Glamour with a Grin," *Screenland*, November 1935.

37. "The Low-Down of a High-Up," *Modern Screen*, undated clipping.

38. Eells, *Ginger, Loretta and Irene Who?* 107; "If I Should Love Again," *Modern Screen*, August 1934.

39. Ibid.

40. Michael Gartside, "Marcia Mae Jones: Hollywood Child Star," *Classic Images*, February 2000.

41. "The Screen," *New York Times*, March 19, 1936.

42. Ibid.

43. Eells, *Ginger, Loretta and Irene Who?* 105–106.

44. Letter from Miriam Hopkins to Minnie Hopkins Keever, September 30, 1939.

45. "Miriam Hopkins at Home," *New York Times*, March 15, 1936.

46. Frank Capra, *The Name above the Title* (Boston: Da Capo, 1971), 163.

47. "Miriam Hopkins Is Dead at 69," *New York Times*, October 10, 1972.

48. "Miriam Hopkins at Home," *New York Times*, March 15, 1936.

49. "Is It Love at Last for Miriam Hopkins?" *Photoplay*, May 1937.

50. Eells, *Ginger, Loretta and Irene Who?* 106.

51. Teletype from Katherine Brown to David O. Selznick. David O. Selznick Collection, University of Texas-Austin.

52. Victor Saville and Roy Moseley, *Evergreen: Victor Saville in His Own Words* (Carbondale: Southern Illinois University Press, 2000), 92

53. "Miriam Hopkins Sings Praises of British Star," unidentified and undated clipping.

54. Sebastian Shaw's career was unspectacular, but he gained some international fame in 1983, when director George Lucas cast him as the dying Darth Vader in *Return of the Jedi*. In a small but crucial role, his son, Luke Skywalker, unmasks the dying Vader in the film's climax. He later appears as the disembodied spirit of Anakin Skywalker.

55. The theater interiors were filmed at the Alhambra, Leicester Square, which was scheduled to be demolished but was postponed so that *Men Are Not Gods* could be filmed there; Patrick McGilligan, *Backstory 2: Interviews with Screenwriters* (Berkeley: University of California Press, 1991), 220.

56. Rex Harrison, *A Damned Serious Business: My Life in Comedy* (New York: Bantam, 1991), 60; Rex Harrison, *Rex: An Autobiography* (London: Macmillan, 1974), 50.

57. "Mecca for Film Folk," *Los Angeles Examiner*, September 13, 1936.

58. "I'd Rather be Dead, Says Miriam Hopkins," *Modern Screen*, March 30, 1937.

59. "Men Are Not Gods," unidentified clipping, January 2, 1937; "Men Are Not Gods," *Variety*, November 27, 1936.

60. Michael Hopkins to Allan Ellenberger, January 7, 2007; Tom Hopkins to Allan Ellenberger, October 8, 2006.

10. Tola

1. Bennett Cerf: Notable New Yorkers, Columbia University Libraries Oral History Research Office, 1968.

2. Ibid.

3. Negulesco, *Things I Did and Things I Think I Did*, 183.

4. Letter from Miriam Hopkins to Minnie Hopkins Keever, September 30, 1939.

5. Ibid.

6. "Woman Chases Man," *Life*, May 17, 1937.

7. Jerome Lawrence, *Actor: The Life and Times of Paul Muni* (New York: Samuel French, 1982), 230–31. Miriam was not in fact under contract to RKO. She was a loan from Goldwyn.

8. Ibid.

9. "Anatole Litvak Give Orders to Best Girl," *Dallas Morning News*, February 11, 1937.

10. Lawrence, *Actor*, 231.

11. "Aristocrat of the Films," *Oakland Tribune*, December 6, 1936.

12. "She'd Rather Be Dead," *Modern Screen*, March 30, 1937.

13. Memo from Walter MacEwen to Roy Obringer, January 29, 1937, Warner Bros. Archives, USC.

14. Sikov, *Dark Victory*, 116.

15. *Hollywood Reporter*, undated clipping.

16. Becky Morehouse to Allan Ellenberger, October 28, 2008; "Miriam Hopkins and Gable Slated for Leads in 'Gone With the Wind,'" *New York Times*, March 19, 1937.

17. "Scarlett O'Hara Again," unidentified and undated clipping.

18. Eells, *Ginger, Loretta and Irene Who?* 88.

19. Darden Asbury Pyron, *Southern Daughter: The Life of Margaret Mitchell* (Harper Perennial, 1992), 364.

20. "Public Picks Miriam as Scarlett But Who Is the Public?" *Dallas Morning News*, May 23, 1937.

21. Becky Morehouse to Allan Ellenberger, October 16, 2008; Daniel Selznick believed that if Miriam were a lesser star, his father might have considered her for the Una Munson role. "But she was much too big a star to do a supporting role like Belle Wattling," Daniel Selznick to Allan Ellenberger, April 9, 2008.

22. Telegram from Samuel Goldwyn to Miriam Hopkins, April 23, 1937, Warner Bros. Archives-USC.

23. "Miriam Hopkins Has Fun Planning Home," *Los Angeles Examiner*, April 25, 1937.

24. *Hollywood Reporter*, undated clipping.

25. Ibid.; Letter from Miriam Hopkins to Minnie Hopkins Keever, September 30, 1939.

26. *Woman Chases Man* file, Samuel Goldwyn Collection, AMPAS; *Daily Variety*, April 27, 1937.

27. Becky Morehouse to Allan Ellenberger, October 28, 2008.

28. Harold Grieve was married to silent film actress, Jetta Goudal. Grieve was an art director but left the studios to begin his own interior design business. Grieve decorated the homes of Bing Crosby, Lily Pons, Norma Shearer, and the designer of Colleen Moore's famous doll house; "Miriam Hopkins," *Architectural Digest*, April 1998.

29. Leatrice Gilbert Fountain to Allan Ellenberger, January 3, 2008; Michael remembered: "My mother was interested in many things and read a lot. She accumulated many books that her visitors would also enjoy. I remember when Ronald Reagan would visit, instead of socializing with the other guests he would retreat to the library and read books."

30. Tino Balio, *Grand Design: Hollywood as a Modern Business Enterprise, 1930–1939* (Berkeley: University of California Press, 1993), 153.

31. Kenneth Schuyler Lynn, *Hemingway* (Cambridge, MA: Harvard University Press, 1995), 451; Miriam Hopkins FBI file. Source of letter not given.

32. Louella Parsons, *The Gay Illiterate* (New York: Doubleday, 1944), 156–57.

33. The Litvaks were not the only famous couple to wed that day in Yuma. Eight hours earlier, Alice Faye and Tony Martin were married in the law library of the Yuma courthouse.

34. Tom Hopkins to Allan Ellenberger, October 8, 2006; unidentified and undated clipping.

35. "Lightly Diverting Movie Seen in 'Wise Girl,'" unidentified and undated clipping.

36. Unidentified and undated clipping.

37. Lawrence Langner, *The Magic Curtain: The Story of a Life in Two Fields* (New York: Dutton, 1951), 266.

38. Ibid., 267.

39. "Miriam Hopkins in 'Wine of Choice,'" *Pittsburgh Press*, January 11, 1938.

40. Langner, *The Magic Curtain*, 267; The Guild replaced Miriam with Claudia Morgan, a veteran Broadway actress of nearly twenty plays.

41. "If I Should Love Again," *Modern Screen*, August 1934.

42. Austin Parker's written instructions and will left his estate, worth more than $11,000, to his daughter Jane Parker, seventeen at the time, providing her a trust fund of $100 per month.

43. "Friendly Talk: A Right Guy's Funeral," *Oklahoman*, March 23, 1938.

11. West Hollywood to Burbank

1. Emily Carmen, *Independent Stardom: Freelance Women in the Hollywood Studio System* (Austin: University of Texas Press), 179.

2. There are claims that Bette Davis tried to convince Jack Warner to purchase the rights to *Dark Victory* for her, but he refused because he didn't believe anyone wanted to see someone go blind. Press reports and the Warner Bros. legal file agree that the rights were bought for Miriam Hopkins on the advice of Anatole Litvak.

3. Letter from Miriam Hopkins to Minnie Hopkins Keever, September 30, 1939.

4. Letter from Miriam Hopkins to Jack L. Warner, June 20, 1938, Warner Bros. Archives-USC.

5. Letter from Jack L. Warner to Miriam Hopkins, June 22, 1938, Warner Bros. Archives-USC.

6. Carmen, *Independent Stardom*, 24.

7. Letter from Miriam Hopkins to Minnie Hopkins Keever, September 30, 1939.

8. Robinson and Spigelgass, *All My Yesterdays*, 159.

9. Larry Ceplair and Steven Englund, *The Inquisition in Hollywood: Politics in the Film Community, 1930–1960* (Berkeley: University of California Press, 1970), 91.

10. Allen Rivkin and Laura Kerr, *Hello Hollywood* (New York, NY: Doubleday, 1962), 425.

11. Motion Picture Democratic Committee brochure, circa 1938; *Studio Call*, June 30, 1938.

12. "Hedda Hopper's Hollywood," *Los Angeles Times*, August 6, 1938.

13. Miriam Hopkins's FBI File.

14. "Six Stars Listed as Aiding Reds," *Los Angeles Times*, August 23, 1938.

15. Letter from Reese Espry, attorney for Samuel Goldwyn, to Warner Brothers, July 6, 1938, Warner Bros. Archives-USC.

16. Becky Morehouse to Allan Ellenberger, October 28, 2008.

17. James Spada, *More Than a Woman: An Intimate Biography of Bette Davis* (New York: Random House Publishing Group, 1994), 158.

18. Letter to Jack Warner and Hal Wallis from Charles Feldman, July 18, 1938, Warner Bros. Archives-USC.

19. Ibid.

20. As part of the deal, Warner Bros. agreed to lend Pat O'Brien to Paramount for one picture, *The Night of Nights* (1939).

21. "Miriam Hopkins Named in Tax Lien," *Los Angeles Times*, March 23, 1939.

22. Delson, *Dudley Murphy, Hollywood Wild Card*, 164.

23. Letter from Miriam Hopkins to Minnie Hopkins Keever, September 30, 1939.

24. Bette Davis, *The Lonely Life* (London: MacDonald, 1962), 186.

25. *Good Morning America*, April 1981.

26. Michael Hopkins to Allan Ellenberger, January 20, 2007.

27. Erskine Johnson interview, *Daily News*, August 12, 1950.

28. "Tyrone Power Slated as Co-Star with Sonya," *Los Angeles Times*, February 7, 1939; Memo from Al Alleborn to Tenny Wright, February 7, 1939, Warner Bros. Archives-USC.

29. Memo from Roy Obringer to Hal Wallis, undated memo, Warner Bros. Archives-USC.

30. Memo from Henry Blanke to Al Alleborn, February 18, 1939, Warner Bros. Archives-USC.

12. "Perfect Little Bitches"

1. Edmund Goulding Q and A with biographer Matthew Kennedy, *Alternative Film Guide* (www.altfg.com), 2008.

2. Davis, *The Lonely Life*, 186.

3. Memo from Al Alleborn to Tenny Wright, March 16, 1939, Warner Bros. Archives-USC.

4. Davis, *The Lonely Life*, 186.

5. Ibid., 187.

6. Daniel Bubbeo, *The Women of Warner Brothers: The Lives and Careers of 15 Leading Ladies* (Jefferson, NC: McFarland, 2002), 39.

7. Matthew Kennedy, *Edmund Goulding's Dark Victory: Hollywood's Genius Bad Boy* (Madison: University of Wisconsin Press, 2004), 186–87.

8. Memo from Al Alleborn to Tenny Wright, March 28, 1939, Warner Bros. Archives-USC.

9. Kennedy, *Edmund Goulding's Dark Victory*, 185.

10. Memo from Al Alleborn to Tenny Wright, April 8, 1939, Warner Bros. Archives-USC.

11. Memo from Al Alleborn to Tenny Wright, April 19, 1939, Warner Bros. Archives-USC

12. "Film Stars Square Off for Camera," unidentified and undated clipping.

13. "Hedda Hopper's Hollywood," *Los Angeles Times*, May 9, 1939.

14. *Lady with Red Hair* file, Warner Bros. Archives-USC.

15. "Hollywood's Prince Hal," *Dallas Morning News*, October 18, 1975.

16. Letter from Miriam Hopkins to Jack L. Warner, May 18, 1939, Warner Bros. Archives-USC.

17. Letter from Carl Zuckmayer to Annemarie Seidel, April 6, 1940, trans. Peter Panholzer.

18. Kennedy, *Edmund Goulding's Dark Victory*, 192.

19. Letter from Miriam Hopkins to Jack L. Warner, September 22, 1939, Warner Bros. Archives-USC.

20. Ibid.

21. Memo from Roy J. Obringer to Charles Feldman, June 9, 1939, Warner Bros. Archives-USC.

22. Eells, *Ginger, Loretta and Irene Who?* 110.

23. Letter from Miriam Hopkins to Minnie Hopkins Keever, September 30, 1939.

24. Memo from Charles Feldman to Ralph Blum, June 20, 1939, Charles K. Feldman Papers, AFI Library.

25. Memo from Charles Feldman to Ralph Blum, June 21, 1939, Charles K. Feldman Papers, AFI Library.

26. Miriam Hopkins contract, June 21, 1939, Warner Bros. Archives-USC.

27. *Hollywood Citizen-News*, September 8, 1939; "Goulding, Hopkins, Davis, Bryan Excel," *Hollywood Reporter*, July 29, 1939.

28. "Misses Davis, Hopkins Triumph in 'Old Maid,'" *Los Angeles Times*, July 29, 1939; *Los Angeles Examiner*, September 8, 1939; "Hedda Hopper's Hollywood," *Los Angeles Times*, August 4, 1939.

29. Letter from Miriam Hopkins to Minnie Hopkins Keever, September 30, 1939.

30. Becky Morehouse to Allan Ellenberger, October 28, 2008.

31. "Star Takes Plane for Reno," *Los Angeles Examiner*, August 29, 1939.

32. "Hedda Hopper's Hollywood," *Los Angeles Times*, September 2, 1939.

33. "Actress Arrives Here to Secure Divorce," *Reno Evening Gazette*, August 29, 1939.

34. "Miriam Hopkins on Way to Reno to Sue Anatole Litvak," *Daily News*, August 29, 1939.

35. "Hedda Hopper's Hollywood," *Los Angeles Times*, October 24, 1939; "'Oomph Girl' Is Weary of Title," *St. Petersburg Times*, October 24, 1939.

36. Negulesco, *Things I Did and Things I Think I Did*, 188.

37. Letter from Miriam Hopkins to Minnie Hopkins Keever, September 30, 1939.

38. "The Human Side of Menace," *Modern Screen*, February 1940.

39. Letter from Miriam Hopkins to Minnie Hopkins Keever, September 30, 1939.

40. Richard F. Rheem was a cofounder, with his brother Donald, of Rheem Manufacturing Company, in California; Letter from Miriam Hopkins to Minnie Hopkins Keever, September 30, 1939.

41. Letter from Miriam Hopkins to Minnie Hopkins Keever, September 30, 1939.

42. Ibid.

13. All This, Jack Warner, and Bette Davis, Too

1. Letter from Miriam Hopkins to Minnie Hopkins Keever, September 30, 1939.

2. Barry Brannon was the attorney for the Screen Directors Guild before the National Labor Relations Board.

3. Letter from Miriam Hopkins to Minnie Hopkins Keever, September 30, 1939.

4. Ibid.

5. Letter from Carl Zuckmayer to Annemarie Seidel, April 6, 1940, trans. Peter Panholzer.

6. Telegram from Miriam Hopkins to Hal Wallis, October 16, 1939, Warner Bros. Archives-USC.

7. Letter from Carl Zuckmayer to Annemarie Seidel, April 6, 1940, trans. Peter Panholzer.

8. Becky Morehouse to Allan Ellenberger, October 28, 2008.

9. Eells, *Ginger, Loretta and Irene Who?* 111.

10. Letter from Carl Zuckmayer to Annemarie Seidel, April 6, 1940, trans. Peter Panholzer.

11. *Virginia City* file, Warner Bros. Archives-USC.

12. "Miriam Hopkins Wants to Play a Ghost," unidentified and undated clipping.

13. Ronald L. Davis, *Words into Images: Screenwriters on the Studio System* (Jackson: University Press of Mississippi, 2007), 141.

14. John Hilder, "On Location at Virginia City," *Hollywood*, April 1940.

15. "Sidney Skolsky Presents," *Hollywood Citizen-News*, November 13, 1939.

16. Dick Jones to Allan Ellenberger, November 12, 2006.

17. Letter from Carl Zuckmayer to Annemarie Seidel, April 6, 1940, trans. Peter Panholzer.

18. Sikov, *Dark Victory*, 55.

19. "The Life and Times of Miriam Hopkins," unidentified and undated clipping.

20. Memo from Frank Mattison to Tenny Wright, December 9, 1939, Warner Bros. Archives-USC.

21. Memo from Frank Mattison to Tenny Wright, December 16, 1939, Warner Bros. Archives-USC.

22. "I Want to Loudspeak," *Virginia City* file, Warner Bros. Archives-USC

23. Memo from Hal Wallis to Jack L. Warner, January 8, 1940, Warner Bros. Archives-USC; Sikov, *Dark Victory*, 157.

24. Memo from David Lewis to Hal Wallis, January 10, 1940, Warner Bros. Archives-USC.

25. "The Life and Times of Miriam Hopkins," unidentified and undated clipping.

26. Letter from Carl Zuckmayer to Albrecht Josef, February 1940, trans. Peter Panholzer.

27. "Miriam Hopkins Find N.Y. Too, Too Tiring," unidentified and undated clipping.

28. Morehouse, *Just the Other Day*, 131.

29. "Miriam Hopkins Sends Wire to Reno," *Nevada State Journal*, March 17, 1940.

30. "Mere Five Million Lost in Virginia City," *Dallas Morning News*, March 24, 1940.

31. "Miriam Hopkins and a Love," unidentified and undated clipping.

32. Ibid.

33. The following year, when American entered the war, Tullio Carminati's politics and pro-Fascist leanings led to his incarceration at Ellis Island. Carminati, however, denied that he was a Fascist. He would have been allowed to remain in the United States had he renounced his Italian citizenship, but he refused. Instead, he was deported to Italy, where he invested his American-made money.

34. "Miriam Hopkins and a Love," unidentified and undated clipping.

35. "Summer Theatre," unidentified and undated clipping.

36. Tennessee Williams, *The Selected Letters of Tennessee Williams: 1920–1945* (New York: New Directions, 2002), 255; A letter to Audrey Wood from T. Williams, July 5, 1940.

37. Ibid., 261.

38. Unidentified and undated clipping.

39. Memo from Jack L. Warner to Bryan Foy, August 1, 1940, Warner Bros. Archives-USC.

40. Stuart Jerome, *Those Crazy Wonderful Years When We Ran Warner Bros.* (Secaucus, NJ: Lyle Stuart, 1983), 10.

41. Ibid., 260, 257.

42. Ibid., 258.

43. "Lou Payne See His Famed Wife Brought to Life," *Dallas Morning News*, October 21, 1940.

44. Warner Bros. publicity, Warner Bros. Archives-USC.

45. Memo from Bryan Foy to Miriam Hopkins, August 29, 1940, Warner Bros. Archives-USC.

46. Memo from Jack L. Warner to Bryan Foy, September 5, 1940, Warner Bros. Archives-USC.

47. Memo from Eric Stacey, September 4, 1940, Warner Bros. Archives-USC.

48. Memo from Eric Stacey, September 16, 1940, Warner Bros. Archives-USC.

49. Charles Higham, *The Celluloid Muse: Hollywood Directors Speak* (Washington, DC: Regnery, 1971).

50. *Lady with Red Hair* file, Warner Bros. Archives-USC.

51. Higham, *The Celluloid Muse*, 211.

52. Jerome, *Those Crazy Wonderful Years When We Ran Warner Bros.*, 260.

53. Williams, *The Selected Letters: 1920–1945*.

54. Letter from Tennessee Williams to Theresa Helburn, October 11, 1940, Theatre Guild correspondence.

55. Julie Gilbert, *Opposites Attract: The Lives of Erich Maria Remarque and Paulette Goddard* (New York: Pantheon, 1995).

56. The rumors reportedly found their way to the White House, as President Franklin Roosevelt asked Helen Gahagan Douglas if they were true. As far as Douglas knew, they were, but she took the story further, saying the couple had had intercourse. "I love it, I love it," Roosevelt allegedly said; Doris Kearns Goodwin, *No Ordinary Time: Franklin and Eleanor Roosevelt*, (New York: Simon & Shuster), 39.

57. Jimmy Starr, *Barefoot on Barbed Wire: An Autobiography of a Forty-Year Hollywood Balancing Act* (Scarecrow Press: 2001), 255.

58. Negulesco, *Things I Did and Things I Think I Did*, 188–89.

59. Arthur Laurents to Allan Ellenberger, October 4, 2007.

60. Becky Morehouse to Allan Ellenberger, October 28, 2008.

61. *Los Angeles Times*; "Lady with Red Hair," *Variety*, November 12, 1940; *Hollywood Reporter*, November 12, 1940.

14. Angels Battle in Boston

1. "Miriam Hopkins Back from 7 Years in Movies," *Daily Boston Globe*, December 22, 1940.

2. Margaret Webster, *Don't Put Your Daughter on the Stage* (New York: Knopf, 1972), 66.

3. Milly S. Barranger, *Margaret Webster: A Life in the Theater* (Ann Arbor: University of Michigan Press, 2004), 110.

4. Letter from Tennessee Williams to his family, November 18, 1940.

5. Barranger, *Margaret Webster: A Life in the Theater*, 111.

6. Tennessee Williams, *Battle of Angels* (Dramatist Play Service, 1941).

7. Charlotte Cox Smith to Allan Ellenberger, January 9, 2011.

8. Lawrence Langner, *The Magic Curtain: The Story of a Life in Two Fields* (New York: Dutton, 1951), 332.

9. Ibid., 114; Williams, *The Selected Letters: 1920–1946*, 299.

10. Barranger, *Margaret Webster*, 114.

11. Ibid.

12. Lillian Ross, *The Fun of It: Stories from The Talk of the Town* (New York: Modern Library, 2001).

13. Tennessee Williams, *The History of a Play (With Parentheses): Plays 1937–1955* (New York: Library of America, 2000), 285.

14. "Plays Here," *Boston Globe*, December 31, 1940; "Second Thoughts on Hart, Williams Play," *Boston Herald*, January 5, 1941.

15. Langner, *The Magic Curtain*, 333.

16. Barranger, *Margaret Webster*, 116.

17. Ibid., 117.

18. "Miriam Hopkins Afoul of Boston Censorship," *Montreal Gazette*, January 8, 1941.

19. Charlotte Cox Smith to Allan Ellenberger, January 9, 2011.

20. "Miriam Hopkins at Home Discussing Any Subject," unidentified and undated clipping.

21. "Hedy Lamarr is on Strike and Off Again," *Dallas Morning News*, February 11, 1941.

22. Patrick McGilligan, *Fritz Lang: The Nature of the Beast* (New York: St. Martin's Press, 1997), 236.

23. Eells, *Ginger, Loretta and Irene Who?* 82.

24. Ibid., 107; Michael Hopkins to Allan Ellenberger, January 20, 2007.

25. "Miriam Hopkins Surprised at Harvard Pick of 'Worst,'" *Los Angeles Times*, January 28, 1941; Others on the list included Jane Withers and Mickey Rooney, as the "most objectionable movie children," and Joan Bennett in *The Son of Monte Cristo* and Henry Fonda in *The Return of Frank James*, as worst performances.

26. Sheilah Graham, "Judy Garland Back Beauty with Acting," *Dallas Morning News*, April 19, 1941.

27. Becky Morehouse to Allan Ellenberger, October 28, 2008.

28. Ward Morehouse, "Broadway After Dark," circa 1943.

29. The *Story of Heliotrope Harry* was filmed three times before, first in 1920 as *Heliotrope* and again in 1928 and 1936 as *Forgotten Faces* for Paramount.

30. Edward Small Collection, USC.

31. *Hollywood*, undated clipping.

32. "Star Denies She's Troublesome," *Toledo Blade*, November 26, 1941.

33. "Marin, Strong Cast Distingquish Prod'n," *Hollywood Reporter*, March 13, 1942; "*A Gentleman After Dark*, with Brian Donlevy and Miriam Hopkins," *New York Times*, April 17, 1942; "Heliotrope Harry Makes Another Screen Comeback," *Dallas Morning News*, April 4, 1942.

34. Telegram from Lyman Brown, April 20, 1942, Chamberlain and Lyman Brown Collection, New York Public Library.

35. Telegram from Lyman Brown, July 31, 1942, Chamberlain and Lyman Brown Collection, New York Public Library.

36. "Here's the Latest Gossip, Serious and Light About Hollywood," *Oklahoman*, December 14, 1942.

37. Letter from Henry Blanke to Edmund Goulding, July 14, 1942, Warner Bros. Archives-USC.

15. "This Is Pure Hopkins"

1. *Old Acquaintance* was a critical success on Broadway for seven months for Jane Cowl and Peggy Wood.

2. Letter from John Van Druten to Henry Blanke, August 17, 1942, Warner Bros. Archives-USC.

3. Letter from Henry Blanke to Edmund Goulding, July 14, 1942, Warner Bros. Archives-USC.

4. Memo from Henry Blanke to Jack L. Warner, August 21, 1942, Warner Bros. Archives-USC.

5. Letter from John Van Druten to Henry Blanke, August 17, 1942, Warner Bros. Archives-USC.

6. Kennedy, *Edmund Goulding's Dark Victory*, 209; Letter from Edmund Goulding to Heinz, July 23, 1942; memo from Henry Blanke to Jack L. Warner, August 21, 1942, Warner Bros. Archives-USC.

7. Memo from Henry Blanke to Jack L. Warner, August 21, 1942, Warner Bros. Archives-USC.

8. Eells, *Ginger, Loretta and Irene Who?* 113.

9. Telegram from Edmund Goulding to Jack L. Warner, September 3, 1942, Warner Bros. Archives-USC.

10. Kennedy, *Edmund Goulding's Dark Victory*, 210.

11. Spada, *More Than a Woman*, 197.

12. Kobal, *People Will Talk*, 559.

13. Sherman had worked with Dolores Moran in his recent film *The Hard Way* (1943); Vincent Sherman, *Studio Affairs: My Life as a Film Director* (Lexington: University Press of Kentucky, 1996), 120.

14. Ibid., 121.

15. Kobal, *People Will Talk*, 560.

16. Shaun Considine, *Bette & Joan: The Divine Feud* (New York: Dutton, 1989), 140.

17. Sherman, *Studio Affairs*, 122.

18. Ibid., 123.

19. Kobal, *People Will Talk*, 560.

20. *Time*, undated clipping.

21. Kobal, *People Will Talk*, 561.

22. Sherman, *Studio Affairs*, 124.

23. Kobal, *People Will Talk*, 560.

24. Ibid., 561.

25. *Pittsburgh-Post Gazette*, March 8, 1943.

26. Hedda Hopper, "Cinema Queens Convert Movie Set into a Fight Ring," *Oklahoman*, January 26, 1943.

27. "Miriam Hopkins Denies Feud with Bette Davis," *Miami News*, April 11, 1943.

28. *Nebraska State Journal*, August 8, 1943.

29. Telegram from Jack L. Warner to Vincent Sherman, January 8, 1943, Warner Bros. Archives-USC.

30. Letter from Miriam Hopkins to an unnamed friend, undated, Warner Bros. Archive-USC.

31. Memo from Jack L. Warner to Henry Blanke, January 29, 1943, Warner Bros. Archives-USC.

32. Sherman, *Studio Affairs*, 124.

33. Davis, *The Lonely Life*, 188; Sherman, *Studio Affairs*, 124.

34. Sherman, *Studio Affairs*, 125.

35. Davis, *The Lonely Life*, 188.

36. Sherman, *Studio Affairs*, 125.

37. Ibid.

38. Considine, *Bette & Joan*, 141.

39. Davis, *The Lonely Life*, 188.

40. Sherman, *Studio Affairs*, 125.

41. "Miriam Hopkins Denies Feud with Bette Davis," *Miami News*, April 11, 1943.

42. "Bette Davis in Fiery Mood over Miriam Hopkins' 'Feud' on Visit to Protégée Here," *Daily Boston Globe*, August 2, 1943.

43. Old Acquaintance memo, October 30, 1943, Warner Bros. Archives-USC.

44. *Time*, November 22, 1943; Louella Parsons, "Davis, Hopkins Team Hailed," *Los Angeles Examiner*, November 24, 1943; "Old Acquaintance, with Bette Davis and Miriam Hopkins," *New York Times*, November 3, 1943; *Hollywood Reporter*, November 3, 1943; *Los Angeles Times*, July 29, 1939.

45. Erskine Johnson, Hollywood, *Frederick Post*, May 17, 1943.

46. Erskine Johnson, *Daily News*, August 12, 1950.

16. To New York and Back

1. "The Human Side of Menace," *Modern Screen*, February 1940.

2. Unidentified and undated clipping.

3. The Plymouth Theatre, at 235 West Forty-Fifth Street, is now known as the Gerald Schoenfeld Theatre.

4. "Star Advises Others Not to Take Advice," *Hartford Courant*, August 9, 1934.

5. Lizabeth Scott to Allan Ellenberger, January 15, 2008.

6. Burton Rascoe, *New York World-Telegram*, May 17, 1943.

7. "Miriam Hopkins Tidy Carbon Copy of Tallulah Bankhead in Wilder's Play," unidentified and undated clipping.

8. Lizabeth Scott to Allan Ellenberger, January 15, 2008.

9. Unidentified and undated clipping.

10. "Miriam Denies the Talk About Her Feudin'," unidentified and undated clipping.

11. Joseph Yranski to Allan Ellenberger, May 20, 2007.

12. Michael Janeway, *The Fall of the House of Roosevelt* (New York: Columbia University Press, 2004), 105–6.

13. Unidentified and undated clipping.

14. "Miriam Hopkins Tidy Carbon Copy of Tallulah Bankhead in Wilder's Play," unidentified and undated clipping.

15. "Eddie's Giving Up Cigars—Is Liz Allergic to 'Em," *Pittsburgh Post Gazette*, March 4, 1959.

16. Unidentified and undated clipping.

17. Attending Miriam's birthday party was Dorothy Parker and her husband, Alan Campbell, dressed in uniform, as he was about to depart for Europe. Grace Moore, who had rented Miriam's Tower Grove house in Beverly Hills, argued with a Greek ex-minister about how she should wear her hair. Lord Stanley of Alderley was with Sylvia Fairbanks, and Eliot Janeway joined Miriam in telling the Wendell Willkie story.

18. Elsa Maxwell, *Toledo Blade*, October 27, 1943.

19. "My Turn," *Great Bend Daily Tribune*, May 23, 1963.

20. *New Yorker*, May 11, 1981.

21. Letter from Miriam Hopkins to Cheryl Crawford, September 7, 1944, The Cheryl Crawford Papers, New York Public Library.

22. "Miriam Hopkins is Heckled," *Miami News*, November 5, 1944.

23. *New Yorker*, May 11, 1981.

24. Joyce Van Patten to Allan Ellenberger, March 20, 2013.

25. Eells, *Ginger, Loretta and Irene Who?* 115–16.

26. "The Play," *New York Times*, October 27, 1944.

27. "Miriam Hopkins Delayed by Fog," *Boston Post*, May 6, 1946.

28. Eells, *Ginger, Loretta and Irene Who?* 115.

29. "Miriam Hopkins: Up to Star Status," *Los Angeles Times*, September 5, 1965.

30. "Miriam Hopkins Deserted 'Art' to Thrill Mystery-Mad Crowds," *Daily Boston Globe*, May 12, 1946.

31. Eells, *Ginger, Loretta and Irene Who?* 116; Fridolin's real name was Gratien Gelinas.

32. "St. Lazare's Opens Here," *Montreal Gazette*, December 7, 1945.

33. Eells, *Ginger, Loretta and Irene Who?* 116.

34. Ibid.

35. *Billboard*, January 5, 1946.

36. Williams, *The Selected Letters of Tennessee Williams*, 30; "Fridolin Returns from Chicago with Broadway, Screen Offers," *Montreal Gazette*, March 7, 1946.

37. "Miriam Hopkins Deserted 'Art' to Thrill Mystery-Mad Crowds," *Daily Boston Globe*, May 12, 1946.

38. *Variety*, undated clipping.

39. Miriam originally paid $42,000 in 1937 for the former John Gilbert estate. After Selznick's marriage to Jennifer Jones in 1949, Selznick lived there until his death, in 1965; "Miriam Hopkins Deserted 'Art' to Thrill Mystery-Mad Crowds," *Daily Boston Globe*, May 12, 1946.

40. *New York Times*, April 17, 1947.

41. To heal her wounded pride after the disappointment of *Message for Margaret*, Miriam and Ray Brock accepted an invitation from Tennessee Williams to visit him in Key West. They met at Ernest Hemingway's former house on Whitehead Street but checked into the "finest hotel in Key West," according to William's brother Dakin. Tennessee Williams, *The Selected Letters of Tennessee Williams: 1945–1957* (Sewanee, Mississippi: University Press of the South, 2004), 86.

42. "Weary of Wicked Roles, Miriam Hopkins Would be Chaste Maid," *Daily Boston Globe*, July 13, 1947.

43. Harold J. Kennedy, *No Pickle, No Performance: An Irreverent Theatrical Excursion from Tallulah to Travolta* (New York: Doubleday, 1978), 58–59.

44. Erskine Johnson, *Daily News*, August 12, 1950.

45. "Small Cast Features Spa Theater Play," *Schenectady Gazette*, July 30, 1947; "Miriam Hopkins Returns to Play 'Off-Center' Role," *Los Angeles Times*, July 25, 1948.

17. "A Little Off-Center"

1. Telegram from Rouben Mamoulian to Miriam Hopkins, November 3, 1947, The Rouben Mamoulian Collection, Library of Congress.

2. "Glow of 'Lubitsch Touch' Is Rekindled Here: Frothy '30's Films Shown in Tribute at Modern Art Director's Style Is Recalled by Aides and Friends," *New York Times*, November 15, 1968.

3. "Miriam Hopkins Returns to Play 'Off-Center' Role," *Los Angeles Times*, July 25, 1948.

4. Tony Oursler, a boyhood friend of Michael's and the son of writers Fulton Oursler and Grace Perkins, said Brock "was a drunk." Coincidently, Oursler's mother was one of the first women to get sober in Alcoholics Anonymous, so he was familiar with the disease. One evening, both families dined. "I think Ray Brock was one of the first persons that I saw to get high at a dinner," Tony Oursler to Allan Ellenberger, August 2, 2008; Michael Hopkins to Allan Ellenberger, January 20, 2007; Eells, *Ginger, Loretta and Irene Who?* 117.

5. Brock had worse problems with Theda Bara, because she wanted to return to the stage on her terms doing something different than her well-known "Vamp" routine; Joseph Yranski to Allan Ellenberger, May 20, 2007.

6. Olivia de Havilland to Allan Ellenberger, August 11, 2007.

7. "Miriam Hopkins Returns to Play 'Off-Center' Role," *Los Angeles Times*, July 25, 1948.

8. A. C. Lyles to Allan Ellenberger, November 30, 2006.

9. "Fashion Is a Joke," *Boston Globe*, May 14, 1967; Eells, *Ginger, Loretta and Irene Who?* 81.

10. Patricia Bosworth, *Montgomery Clift: A Biography* (New York: Harcourt Brace Jovanovich, 1978), 126–27.

11. Olivia de Havilland to Allan Ellenberger, August 11, 2007; Robert Osborne to André Soares, July 25, 2007.

12. Olivia de Havilland to Allan Ellenberger, August 11, 2007.

13. During the run of *Happy Birthday*, Miriam made peace with another old nemesis, George Raft. At one performance, Raft sat in the front row of the Biltmore applauding his former costar. During the making of *The Heiress*, there was a reunion wherein they both made amends.

14. Becky Morehouse to Allan Ellenberger, October 28, 2008.

15. Olivia de Havilland to Allan Ellenberger, August 11, 2007.

16. "Miriam Hopkins Stars at Norwich in 'The Heiress,'" *Hartford Courant*, August 19, 1949.

17. Miles Krueger knew Harvey Grossman since 1941. At the time of this interview, Grossman was living in Belgium; Miles Krueger to Allan Ellenberger, October 26, 2006.

18. "'The Heiress,' With Olivia de Havilland in Leading Role, Arrives at Music Hall," *New York Times*, October 7, 1949.

19. "'The Heiress' Distinguished Dramatic Event of Screen," *Los Angeles Times*, October 21, 1949; "Wyler Production is Rich in Atmosphere," *Hollywood Reporter*, September 8, 1949.

20. McGilligan, *Back Story 2*, 233.

21. David Chierichetti, *Mitchell Leisen: Hollywood Director* (Los Angeles: Photoventures Press, 1995), 270–71.

22. "'The Mating Season' Delightful Comedy," *Daily Box Office*, January 20,

1951; "'Mating Season' Cheery, Sentimental Comedy," *Los Angeles Times*, March 30, 1951.

23. "Miriam Hopkins Tells Many Good Stories—Off the Record," *Reading Eagle*, August 25, 1950.

24. Jay Jorgenson, *Edith Head: The Fifty-Year Career of Hollywood's Greatest Costume Designer* (Philadelphia: Running Press, 2010), 183.

25. "The New Film," *Pittsburgh Post-Gazette*, August 9, 1952.

18. "They Are Sure Reds"

1. Louis Budenz statement to the FBI, Miriam Hopkins's FBI file.

2. Miriam's association with so-called Communist fronts included memberships in the following organizations: League of Women Shoppers (1938); American Committee to Save Refugees and the United American Spanish Aid Committee (1941); Joint Anti-Fascist Refugee Committee (1942); Motion Picture Arts Committee and the Hollywood Democratic Committee (1944); Independent Citizens Committee of the Arts, Sciences and Professions (1944, 1945); Spanish Refugee Appeal of the Joint Anti-Fascist Refugee Committee (1945, 1946); Motion Picture Guild (1947).

3. The *C* was FBI coding for Communist, Miriam Hopkins FBI File.

4. An anonymous letter was received on September 5, 1939, while Miriam was staying in Reno, Nevada, awaiting her divorce from Anatole Litvak; Letter to J. Edgar Hoover, Miriam Hopkins FBI File.

5. Lloyd Gough and his wife, actress Karen Morley, were brought before HUAC and both invoked the Fifth Amendment. They were blacklisted in Hollywood and didn't work in films for years.

6. "Reagan's Hollywood Days Show True Self," *Redding Pilot*, March 12, 1987.

7. Michael Hopkins to Allan Ellenberger, July 28, 2007.

8. Eells, *Ginger, Loretta and Irene Who?* 117–18.

9. "At Corning Theater, Miriam Hopkins Shines, but Play Slow-Moving," unidentified and undated clipping.

10. Daryl F. Zanuck wanted Bette Davis or Marlene Dietrich for the role, but they turned it down, Matt Amato conference, USC; "On Downtown Screens," *Dallas Morning News*, August 8, 1952.

11. Michael and Chris Hopkins to Allan Ellenberger, January 20, 2007.

12. Paul Avila Mayer to Allan Ellenberger, March 3, 2008.

13. *Variety*, August 20, 1952; *New York Post*, August 20, 1952.

14. Stephen D. Youngkin, *The Lost One: A Life of Peter Lorre* (Lexington: University Press of Kentucky, 2012), 364.

15. Ibid.

16. Letter from Miriam Hopkins to Rouben Mamoulian, October 27, 1952, The Rouben Mamoulian Collection, Library of Congress.

17. Telegram from Miriam Hopkins to Rouben Mamoulian, November 6, 1952, The Rouben Mamoulian Collection, Library of Congress

18. Letter from Miriam Hopkins to Rouben Mamoulian, October 27, 1952, The Rouben Mamoulian Collection, Library of Congress.

19. Youngkin, *The Lost One*, 364.

20. Telegram from Miriam Hopkins to Rouben Mamoulian, November 6, 1952, The Rouben Mamoulian Collection, Library of Congress.

21. Telegrams from Miriam Hopkins to Rouben Mamoulian, December 3 and December 22, 1952, The Rouben Mamoulian Collection, Library of Congress.

22. Whether it was Miriam impersonating her maid on the telephone with Brock or the maid herself, the voice suggested that Brock send the script to former silent screen actress Nita Naldi, with the explanation, "She needs the work." Ironically, Brock sent the script to Naldi, but she wasn't interested in working. Joseph Yranski to Allan Ellenberger, May 20, 2007.

23. "Miriam Hopkins De-Englishes 'Hay Fever,' to Be Given on Cape," unidentified and undated clipping.

24. *Detroit News*, May 20, 1953; Judith E. Barlow, *Plays by American Women: 1930–1960* (New York, NY: Applause, 2001), 402.

25. Tennessee Williams, *The Selected Letters of Tennessee Williams*, vol. 2, *1945–1957* (Sewanee, TN: University of the South, 2004), 509.

26. Steve Siporin to Allan Ellenberger, September 14, 2014.

27. "Miriam Hopkins De-Englishes 'Hay Fever,' to Be Given on Cape," unidentified and undated clipping.

28. Williams, *The Selected Letters of Tennessee Williams*, 511.

29. The French invaded Morocco in 1912, and when the capital at the time, Fez, became unstable, it was moved to Rabat; Chris Hopkins to Allan Ellenberger, July 28, 2007.

30. Michael Hopkins to Allan Ellenberger, July 28, 2007.

31. Telegram from Miriam Hopkins to Rouben Mamoulian, May 1, 1954, The Rouben Mamoulian Collection, Library of Congress.

32. Charlotte 'Cissy' Cox Smith to Allan Ellenberger, January 9, 2011.

33. Becky Morehouse to Allan Ellenberger, October 28, 2008.

34. Charlotte 'Cissy' Cox Smith to Allan Ellenberger, January 9, 2011.

35. Michael Thomas Hopkins was born on April 18, 1955, and was called Tom or Tommy throughout his childhood. However, in adolescence and later in life, he preferred to be called Mike. So there is no confusion with his father, for this biography, he will be referred to as Tom or Tommy.

36. Chris Hopkins to Allan Ellenberger, July 28, 2007, and June 14, 2014.

37. Letter from Miriam Hopkins to Minnie Hopkins Keever, September 30, 1939; Michael Hopkins to Allan Ellenberger, July 28, 2007.

38. Chris Hopkins to Allan Ellenberger, July 28, 2007.

39. In addition to television, Miriam appeared in two more road plays: *The Matchmaker* and *Time of the Cuckoo*; unidentified and undated clipping.

40. "Miriam Hopkins De-Englishes 'Hay Fever,' to be Given on Cape," unidentified and undated clipping.

19. "How Many Times Can You Come Back?"

1. Hugh Griffith received a Best Supporting Actor Oscar for his role as Sheik Ilderim in Wyler's *Ben-Hur*.

2. "The Theatre: 'Look Homeward, Angel': Luminous Adaptation of Wolfe Novel Opens The Cast," *New York Times*, November 29, 1957.

3. "Newcomer Signs for Theatre Plum," *New York Times*, April 28, 1958.

4. Andrew Prine to Allan Ellenberger, October 4, 2007.

5. Eells, *Ginger, Loretta and Irene Who?* 119; Erskine Johnson, *Daily News*, August 12, 1950.

6. *New York Post*, undated clipping; Ward Morehouse, N.A.N.A., undated clipping.

7. "Miriam Hopkins Happy to Play Mother Role in Wolfe's 'Angel,'" *Milwaukee Journal*, August 23, 1958.

8. Andrew Prine to Allan Ellenberger, October 4, 2007.

9. Ibid.

10. Ibid.

11. *Pasadena Independent*, August 5, 1959.

12. "Phil Giriodi Behind the Scenes in the '50s," *Films of the Golden Age* 63 (Winter 2010–2011), 74.

13. *Pasadena Independent*, August 5, 1959.

14. Unidentified and undated clipping.

15. Eells, *Ginger, Loretta and Irene Who?* 119.

16. Ibid.

17. "'Acidy Cassidy, that Woman from Chicago," *Chicago Tribune*, October 11, 2013.

18. Eells, *Ginger, Loretta and Irene Who?* 119–20.

19. Ibid.

20. "'Look Homeward Angel' Stirring Stage Hit," *Los Angeles Times*, July 13, 1960.

21. Gabriel Miller, *William Wyler: The Life and Films of Hollywood's Most Celebrated Director* (Lexington: University Press of Kentucky, 2013), 327.

22. "Director Discusses 'Children's Hour,'" *Hollywood Citizen-News*, December 8, 1961.

23. "Wyler Discusses Changes in Movies," *New York Times*, April 20, 1961.

24. Paul Parla and Charles P. Mitchell, *Screen Sirens Scream!: Interviews with 20 Actresses from Science Fiction* (Jefferson, NC: McFarland, 2009), 112.

25. Veronica Cartwright to Allan Ellenberger, November 10, 2013.

26. Ibid.

27. "What a Gal!" *New Movie Magazine*, October 1932.

28. "Miriam Hopkins Now Plays Her Own Aunt," *Los Angeles Mirror*, August 24, 1961.

29. "'Children's Hour' Oscar Potential," *Los Angeles Times*, December 8, 1961; "'Children's Hour' Woeful Film Saga," *Los Angeles Times*, December 20, 1961.

30. "Shirley MacLaine: The Children's Hour Suffered Because Director Had 'Trepidations' about Lesbian Theme," GayStarNews.com, March 31, 2015.

31. Letter from Miriam Hopkins to Minnie Hopkins Keever; Becky Morehouse to Allan Ellenberger, October 12, 2008.

32. Eells, *Ginger, Loretta and Irene Who?* 118.

33. Paul Kwilecki to Allan Ellenberger, December 17, 2006.

34. "Thoroughly Modern Miriam," *Atlanta Constitution*, November 9, 1997.

35. Paul Kwilecki to Allan Ellenberger, December 17, 2006.

36. Stan Raiff to Allan Ellenberger, January 30, 2008.

37. David Frankham to Allan Ellenberger, February 1, 2008.

38. Stan Raiff to Allan Ellenberger, January 30, 2008.

39. The Theatre De Lys was at 121 Christopher Street, Greenwich Village. It is now the Lucille Lortel Theatre; Eells, *Ginger, Loretta and Irene Who?* 120.

40. Eells, *Ginger, Loretta and Irene Who?* 120–21.

41. Stan Raiff to Allan Ellenberger, January 30, 2008.

42. Eells, *Ginger, Loretta and Irene Who?* 121.

43. Stan Raiff to Allan Ellenberger, January 30, 2008.

44. Ibid.

45. Eells, *Ginger, Loretta and Irene Who?* 122.

46. Kobal, *People Will Talk*, 354.

47. *Fanny Hill*'s author John Cleland was arrested for "corrupting the King's subjects" a year after the book was published. The book was published by Putnam in the United States in 1963 but was banned for obscenity. Putnam challenged the ban in New York State and won; it was found not to be obscene; Kobal, *People Will Talk*, 354–55.

48. Miriam Hopkins's FBI File.

49. David DelValle, "She Loved and Trusted Him . . . Until He Cut Off Her Head!" *The DelValle Archives*, April 25, 2011.

50. Ibid.

51. "Fanny Hill, Bawdy Classic Heroine is Good Girl in Film," *Boston Globe*, March 18, 1965.

52. "Miriam Hopkins: Up to Star Status," *Los Angeles Times*, September 5, 1965.

53. "KKK Book to Be Horror Film Topic," *Los Angeles Times*, May 22, 1965; "Miriam Hopkins: Up to Star Status," *Los Angeles Times*, September 5, 1965.

54. "Miriam Hopkins: Up to Star Status," *Los Angeles Times*, September 5, 1965.

55. "The Chase," *Motion Picture Herald*, February 2, 1966; *Saturday Review*, February 19, 1966.

56. James Robert Parish, *Fiasco: A History of Hollywood's Iconic Flops* (Wiley: 2007); Richard Schickel, "Small Flop Grosses into a Disaster," *Life*, March 4, 1966.

20. The Final Years

1. Michael Hopkins to Allan Ellenberger, January 20, 2007.

2. Sheila MacRae, *Hollywood Mother of the Year: Sheila MacRae's Own Story* (Bethesda, MD: Carroll, 1992), 149–51.

3. Tom Hopkins to Allan Ellenberger, October 8, 2006.

4. Morehouse, *Just the Other Day*, 130.

5. Becky Morehouse to Allan Ellenberger, October 12, 2008; Ward Morehouse III to Allan Ellenberger, May 28, 2008.

6. Becky Morehouse to Allan Ellenberger, October 12, 2008.

7. Ibid.

8. Ibid.

9. Ibid.

10. Tom Hopkins to Allan Ellenberger, October 8, 2006.

11. Chris Hopkins to Allan Ellenberger, June 14, 2014.

12. Michael Hopkins to Allan Ellenberger, July 28, 2007.

13. Tom Hopkins to Allan Ellenberger, October 8, 2006.

14. Ibid.

15. Eells, *Ginger, Loretta and Irene Who?* 81; Peter Garey lived to be eighty-two years old and died at the Actors Home in Englewood, New Jersey, on December 20, 1999.

16. Becky Morehouse to Allan Ellenberger, October 12, 2008.

17. Weaver, *Double Feature Creature Attack*, 162.

18. "Lena Horne: Time Cooled Her Anger," *New York Times*, May 3, 1981.

19. Eells, *Ginger, Loretta and Irene Who?* 124.

20. Becky Morehouse to Allan Ellenberger, October 12, 2008.

21. Eells, *Ginger, Loretta and Irene Who?* 125.

22. Stan Raiff to Allan Ellenberger, January 30, 2008.

23. Ward Morehouse III to Allan Ellenberger, May 28, 2008.

24. MacRae, *Hollywood Mother of the Year*, 150.

25. Eells, *Ginger, Loretta and Irene Who?* 123.

26. "Miriam Hopkins Will Appear on 'Flying Nun,'" *Dallas Morning News*, May 27, 1969.

27. "Miriam Hopkins Doesn't Fit the 'Comeback' Pattern," *ABC Press Release*, November 6, 1969.

28. *Savage Intruder* (1970).

29. Fred Beldin, *AllMovie* (http://www.allmovie.com/movie/the-savage-intruder-v42988/review).

30. Eells, *Ginger, Loretta and Irene Who?* 124.

31. Becky Morehouse to Allan Ellenberger, October 12, 2008.

32. Margot Welch to Allan Ellenberger, February 19, 2010.

33. Becky Morehouse to Allan Ellenberger, October 12, 2008.

21. "If I Had to Do It Over Again"

1. Becky Morehouse to Allan Ellenberger, October 12, 2008.

2. Eells, *Ginger, Loretta and Irene Who?* 125.

3. Kobal, *People Will Talk*, 352.

4. Eells, *Ginger, Loretta and Irene Who?* 126.

5. "Follies of God by James Grissom," *Maureen Stapleton on Miriam Hopkins*, 1991, (jamesgrissom.blogspot.com).

6. "Paramount on Parade: 'Choke on Your Food!'" *Village Voice*, July 20, 1972.

7. Kobal, *People Will Talk*, 352.

8. Eells, *Ginger, Loretta and Irene Who?* 126.

9. Becky Morehouse to Allan Ellenberger, October 12, 2008.

10. Eells, *Ginger, Loretta and Irene Who?* 126.

11. Ibid., 123.

12. Eells, *Ginger, Loretta and Irene Who?* 126; "Hopkins Films of the 30's Amuse, Amaze her Now," *New York Post*, July 17, 1958.

13. Kobal, *People Will Talk*, 353.

14. Ibid.

15. Ibid.

16. Margot Welch to Allan Ellenberger, February 19, 2010.

17. Eells, *Ginger, Loretta and Irene Who?* 127.

18. Becky Morehouse to Allan Ellenberger, October 12, 2008.

19. Eells, *Ginger, Loretta and Irene Who?* 127.

20. Chris Hopkins to Allan Ellenberger, January 20, 2007.

21. Margot Welch to Allan Ellenberger, February 19, 2010.

22. Ibid.

23. Tom Hopkins to Allan Ellenberger, October 8, 2006.

24. Letter from Jean Negulesco to Michael Hopkins, October 11, 1972.

25. Letter from Rouben Mamoulian to Michael Hopkins, circa October 1972.

26. Roy Moseley, *Bette Davis: An Intimate Memoir* (London: Sidgwick and Jackson, 1989), 105; Bryan Forbes, *Ned's Girl: The Authorized Biography of Dame Edith Evans* (London: Elm Tree Books, 1977), 202; Andrew Prine to Allan Ellenberger, October 4, 2007.

27. Tennessee Williams, "In Memory of Miriam Hopkins," circa October 1972, courtesy of Michael Hopkins.

28. Letter from Seymour (Sy) Peck to Rebecca Morehouse, November 19, 1972. (Courtesy of Becky Morehouse).

29. Williams, "In Memory of Miriam Hopkins," circa October 1972, courtesy of Michael Hopkins.

30. H. C. Potter, *Miriam Hopkins Memorial*, eulogy, October 13, 1972, courtesy of Michael Hopkins.

31. Michael Hopkins to Allan Ellenberger, January 20, 2007.

32. "May Mann's Hollywood," *Movieland and TV Time*, circa October 1972.

Epilogue

1. Letter from Ruby Hopkins Welch to Miriam Hopkins Film Festival, Bainbridge, Georgia, September 1986.

2. Michael Hopkins to Allan Ellenberger, January 20, 2007.

3. Tom Hopkins to Allan Ellenberger, October 8, 2006.

4. Margot Welch to Allan Ellenberger, February 19, 2010.

5. Tennessee Williams, "In Memory of Miriam Hopkins," circa October 1972, courtesy of Michael Hopkins.

Bibliography

Antheil, George. *Bad Boy of Music*. Garden City, NY: Doubleday, Doran, 1945.

Balio, Tino. *Grand Design: Hollywood as a Modern Business Enterprise, 1930–1939*. Berkeley: University of California Press, 1993.

Bankhead, Tallulah. *Tallulah: My Autobiography*. New York: Harper, 1952.

Barlow, Judith E. *Plays by American Women: 1930–1960*. New York: Applause, 2001.

Barranger, Milly S. *Margaret Webster: A Life in the Theater*. Ann Arbor: University of Michigan Press, 2004.

Berg, Scott A. *Goldwyn: A Biography*. New York: Knopf, 1989.

Black, Gregory D. *Hollywood Censored*. New York: Cambridge University Press, 1996.

Bosworth, Patricia. *Montgomery Clift: A Biography*. New York: Harcourt Brace Jovanovich, 1978.

Bubbeo, Daniel. *The Women of Warner Brothers: The Lives and Careers of 15 Leading Ladies*. Jefferson, NC: McFarland, 2002.

Buckley, Gail Lumet. *The Hornes: An American Family*. New York: Knopf, 1986.

Capra, Frank. *The Name Above the Title*. Cambridge, MA: De Capo Press, 1971.

Carman, Emily. *Independent Stardom: Freelance Women in the Hollywood Studio System*. Austin: University of Texas Press, 2016.

Carroll, Renee. *In Your Hat*. New York: Macaulay, 1933.

Ceplair, Larry, and Steven Englund. *The Inquisition in Hollywood: Politics in the Film Community, 1930–1960*. Berkeley: University of California Press, 1970.

Cerf, Bennett. *At Random: The Reminisces of Bennett Cerf*. New York: Random House, 2012.

Chandler, Charlotte. *The Girl Who Walked Home Alone*. New York: Applause Theatre and Cinema, 2007.

Chierichetti, David. *Mitchell Leisen: Hollywood Director*. Los Angeles: Photoventures Press, 1995.

Considine, Shaun. *Bette & Joan: The Divine Feud*. New York: E. P. Dutton, 1989.

Dalrymple, Jean. *September Child: The story of Jean Dalrymple*. New York: Dodd, Mead, 1963.

Davis, Bette. *The Lonely Life*. London: MacDonald, 1962.

Davis, Owen. *My First Fifty Years*. Boston: Walter H. Baker Company, 1950.

Davis, Ronald L. *Words into Images: Screenwriters on the Studio System.* Jackson: University Press of Mississippi, 2007.

Delson, Susan. *Dudley Murphy: Hollywood Wild Card.* Minneapolis: University of Minnesota Press, 2006.

Dicks, Richard. *The Wit of Noël Coward.* London: Leslie Frewin, 1968.

Dowd, Nancy, and David Shepard. *King Vidor.* Metuchen, NJ: Scarecrow Press, 1988.

Drew, William M. *At the Center of the Frame: Leading Ladies of the Twenties and Thirties.* New York: Vestal, 1999.

Durgnat, Raymond, and Scott Simmon. *King Vidor American.* Berkeley: University of California Press, 1988.

Eells, George. *Ginger, Loretta and Irene Who?* New York: G. P. Putnam's Sons, 1976.

Eyman, Scott. *Five American Cinematographers.* Metuchen, NJ: Scarecrow Press, 1987.

———. *Ernst Lubitsch: Laughter in Paradise.* New York: Simon & Schuster, 1993.

Forbes, Bryan. *Ned's Girl: The Authorized Biography of Dame Edith Evans.* Kent: Mandarin, 1977.

Gansberg, Alan L. *Little Caesar: A Biography of Edward G. Robinson.* Metuchen, NJ: Scarecrow, 2004.

Gavin, James. *Stormy Weather: The Life of Lena Horne.* New York: Simon & Schuster, 2009.

Grove, Nancy. *Isamu Noguchi Portrait Sculpture.* Washington, DC: Smithsonian Institution, 1989.

Hayter-Menzies, Grant. *Mrs. Ziegfeld: The Public and Private Lives of Billie Burke.* Jefferson, NC: McFarland, 2009.

Herman, Jan. *A Talent for Trouble: The Life of Hollywood's Most Acclaimed Director.* New York: G. P. Putnam, 1995.

Higham, Charles. *The Life of Bette Davis.* New York: Macmillan, 1981.

Israel, Lee. *Miss Tallulah Bankhead.* New York: G. P. Putnam, 1972.

Janeway, Michael. *The Fall of the House of Roosevelt.* New York: Columbia University Press, 2004.

Jerome, Stuart. *Those Crazy Wonderful Years When We Ran Warner Bros.* Secaucus, NJ: Lyle Stuart, 1983.

Jorgensen, Jay. *Edith Head: The Fifty-Year Career of Hollywood's Greatest Costume Designer.* Philadelphia: Running, 2010.

Kanin, Garson. *Hollywood.* New York: Viking, 1967.

Kear, Lynn, and John Rossman. *Kay Francis: A Passionate Life and Career.* Jefferson, NC: McFarland, 2006.

Kennedy, Harold J. *No Pickle, No Performance: An Irreverent Theatrical Excursion from Tallulah to Travolta.* New York: Doubleday, 1978.

Kennedy, Matthew. *Edmund Goulding's Dark Victory: Hollywood's Genius Bad Boy.* Madison: University of Wisconsin Press, 2004.

Kobal, John. *People Will Talk*. New York: Knopf, 1985.

Lambert, Gavin. *On Cukor*. Ann Arbor: University of Michigan Press, 2000.

Langner, Lawrence. *The Magic Curtain: The Story of a Life in Two Fields*. Boston: Dutton, 1951.

Lawrence, Jerome. *Actor: The Life and Times of Paul Muni*. New York: Samuel French, 1982.

Leaming, Barbara. *Bette Davis: A Biography*. New York: Simon & Schuster, 1992.

Levy, Emanuel. *George Cukor: Master of Elegance*. Ann Arbor: University of Michigan Press, 1994.

Limon, Jose. *José Limón: An Unfinished Memoir*. Middletown, CT: Wesleyan University Press, 1998.

Lynch, Christopher. *When Hollywood Landed at Chicago's Midway Airport: The Photos and Stories of Mike Rotunno*. Charleston, SC: History, 2012.

Lynn, Kenneth Schuyler. *Hemingway*. Cambridge, MA: Harvard University Press, 1995.

MacRae, Sheila. *Hollywood Mother of the Year: Sheila MacRae's Own Story*. New York: Carroll, 1992.

Mank, Gregory William. *Women in Horror Films, 1930s*. Jefferson, NC: McFarland, 1999.

Martinson, Deborah. *Lillian Hellman: A Life of Little Foxes and Scoundrels*. Berkeley, CA: Counterpoint, 2005.

Marx, Arthur. *Goldwyn: A Biography of the Man Behind the Myth*. New York: W. W. Norton, 1976.

McCarthy, Todd. *Howard Hawks: The Grey Fox of Hollywood*. New York: Grove, 2000.

McGilligan, Patrick. *Backstory: Interviews with Screenwriters of Hollywood's Golden Age*. Berkeley: University of California Press, 1986.

———. *Backstory 2: Interviews with Screenwriters*. Berkeley: University of California Press, 1991.

———. *Fritz Lang: The Nature of the Beast*. New York: St. Martin's, 1997.

Miller, Gabriel. *William Wyler: The Life and Films of Hollywood's Most Celebrated Director*. Lexington: University Press of Kentucky, 2013.

Morehouse, Ward. *Forty-Five Minutes Past Eight*. New York: Dial, 1939.

———. *Just the Other Day*. New York: McGraw-Hill, 1953.

Mordden, Ethan. *All That Glittered: The Golden Age of Drama on Broadway*. New York: St. Martin's, 2007.

Moseley, Roy. *Bette Davis: An Intimate Memoir*. London: Sidgwick and Jackson, 1989.

Negulesco, Jean. *Things I Did and Things I Didn't Do*. New York: Simon & Schuster, 1984.

Newlin, Keith, ed. *A Theodore Dreiser Encyclopedia*. Westport, CT: Greenwood, 2003.

Parish, James Robert. *The Paramount Pretties*. New Rochelle, NY: Arlington House, 1972.

———. *Fiasco: A History of Hollywood's Iconic Flops*. Hoboken, NJ: Wiley, 2007.

Parla, Paul, and Charles P. Mitchell. *Screen Sirens Scream!: Interviews with 20 Actresses from Science Fiction*. Jefferson, NC: McFarland, 2009.

Parsons, Louella. *Tell it to Louella*. New York: G. P. Putnam's Sons, 1961.

———. *The Gay Illiterate*. New York: Doubleday, 1944.

Pyron, Darden Asbury. *Southern Daughter: The Life of Margaret Mitchell*. New York: Harper Perennial, 1992.

Quirk, Lawrence J. *Fasten Your Seat Belts*. New York: William Morrow, 1990.

Rivkin, Allen, and Laura Kerr. *Hello Hollywood*. New York: Doubleday, 1962.

Robinson, Edward G., and Leonard Spigelgass. *All My Yesterdays: An Autobiography*. Portland, OR: Hawthorne, 1973.

Ross, Lillian. *The Fun of It: Stories from The Talk of the Town*. New York: Modern Library, 2001.

Saroyan, William. *Sons Come and Go, Mothers Hang in Forever*. Franklin Center, PA: Franklin Library, 1976.

Saville, Victor, and Roy Moseley. *Evergreen: Victor Saville in His Own Words*. Carbondale: Southern Illinois University Press, 2000.

Sherman, Vincent. *Studio Affairs: My Life as a Film Director*. Lexington: University Press of Kentucky, 1996.

Sikov, Ed. *Dark Victory: The Life of Bette Davis*. New York: Henry Holt, 2007.

Spada, James. *More Than a Woman: An Intimate Biography of Bette Davis*. New York: Random House, 1994.

Travis, Doris Eaton. *The Days We Danced: The Story of My Theatrical Family*. Seattle: Marquand, 2003.

Vidor, King. *A Tree Is a Tree*. New York: Harcourt, Brace, 1952.

Vieira, Mark A. *Irving Thalberg: Boy Wonder to Producer Prince*. Berkeley: University of California Press, 2009.

Watson, Jay. *Faulkner and Whiteness*. Jackson: University Press of Mississippi, 2011.

Weaver, Tom. *Double Feature Creature Attack*. Jefferson, NC: McFarland, 2003.

Webster, Margaret. *Don't Put Your Daughter on the Stage*. New York: Knopf, 1972.

Williams, Tennessee. *The Selected Letters of Tennessee Williams: 1920–1945*. New York: New Directions, 2002.

———. *The Selected Letters of Tennessee Williams: 1945–1957*. Sewanee, TN: University of the South, 2004.

Wright, William. *Lillian Hellman: The Image, The Woman*. New York: Simon & Schuster, 1986.

Yablonsky, Lewis. *George Raft*. San Francisco: Mercury House, 1974.

Youngkin, Stephen D. *The Lost One: A Life of Peter Lorre*. Lexington: University Press of Kentucky, 2012.

Index

Index

Screen Classics

Screen Classics is a series of critical biographies, film histories, and analytical studies focusing on neglected filmmakers and important screen artists and subjects, from the era of silent cinema through the golden age of Hollywood to the international generation of today. Books in the Screen Classics series are intended for scholars and general readers alike. The contributing authors are established figures in their respective fields. This series also serves the purpose of advancing scholarship on film personalities and themes with ties to Kentucky.

Series Editor

Patrick McGilligan

Books in the Series

Mae Murray: The Girl with the Bee-Stung Lips
    Michael G. Ankerich
Hedy Lamarr: The Most Beautiful Woman in Film
    Ruth Barton
Rex Ingram: Visionary Director of the Silent Screen
    Ruth Barton
Conversations with Classic Film Stars: Interviews from Hollywood's Golden Era
    James Bawden and Ron Miller
You Ain't Heard Nothin' Yet: Interviews with Stars from Hollywood's Golden Era
    James Bawden and Ron Miller
Von Sternberg
    John Baxter
Hitchcock's Partner in Suspense: The Life of Screenwriter Charles Bennett
    Charles Bennett, edited by John Charles Bennett
My Life in Focus: A Photographer's Journey with Elizabeth Taylor and the Hollywood Jet Set
    Gianni Bozzacchi with Joey Tayler
Hollywood Divided: The 1950 Screen Directors Guild Meeting and the Impact of the Blacklist
    Kevin Brianton
He's Got Rhythm: The Life and Career of Gene Kelly
    Cynthia Brideson and Sara Brideson
Ziegfeld and His Follies: A Biography of Broadway's Greatest Producer
    Cynthia Brideson and Sara Brideson
The Marxist and the Movies: A Biography of Paul Jarrico
    Larry Ceplair
Dalton Trumbo: Blacklisted Hollywood Radical
    Larry Ceplair and Christopher Trumbo
Warren Oates: A Wild Life
    Susan Compo
Improvising Out Loud: My Life Teaching Hollywood How to Act
    Jeff Corey with Emily Corey
Crane: Sex, Celebrity, and My Father's Unsolved Murder
    Robert Crane and Christopher Fryer